America's Best Day Hiking Series

Hiking WISCONSIN

MARTIN HINTZ

Human Kinetics

Library of Congress Cataloging-in-Publication Data

Hintz, Martin.
    Hiking Wisconsin / Martin Hintz:
        p.   cm. -- (America's best day hiking series)
    ISBN 0-88011-567-X
    1. Hiking--Wisconsin--Guidebooks.   2. Trails--Wisconsin-
    -Guidebooks.   3. Wisconsin--Guidebooks.   I. Title.   II. Series.
    GV199.42.W6H55   1997
    796.51′09775--DC21   96-48419
                                                      CIP

ISBN-10: 0-88011-567-X
ISBN-13: 978-0-88011-567-4

Acquisitions Editor: Patricia Sammann
Developmental Editor: Julie A. Marx
Assistant Editors: Coree Schutter, Andrew Smith, and Jacqueline Eaton Blakley
Editorial Assistant: Jennifer Jeanne Hemphill
Copyeditor: Joyce Sexton
Graphic Designer: Robert Reuther
Graphic Artists: Sandra Meier and Francine Hamerski
Cover Designer: Jack Davis
Cover Photograph: Mississippi River, Crawford County, Wisconsin/© A.B. Sheldon
Interior Photographs: Martin Hintz
Illustrators: Gretchen Walters/Studio 2D; Jennifer Delmotte; M.R. Greenberg
Printer: Versa Press

The maps on the following pages were adapted from maps from the Wisconsin Department of Natural Resources: 4, 10, 14, 18, 30, 38, 42, 46, 54, 80, 88, 92, 98, 102, 106, 110, 112, 116, 130, 154, 162, 170, 172, 176, 178, 180, and 194.

Human Kinetics books are available at special discounts for bulk purchase. Special editions or book excerpts can also be created to specification. For details, contact the Special Sales Manager at Human Kinetics.

Printed in the United States of America   10   9   8

Human Kinetics
Web site: www.HumanKinetics.com

United States: Human Kinetics, P.O. Box 5076, Champaign, IL 61825-5076
800-747-4457
e-mail: humank@hkusa.com

Canada: Human Kinetics, 475 Devonshire Road, Unit 100, Windsor, ON N8Y 2L5
800-465-7301 (in Canada only)
e-mail: info@hkcanada.com

Europe: Human Kinetics, 107 Bradford Road, Stanningley
Leeds LS28 6AT, United Kingdom
+44 (0) 113 255 5665
e-mail: hk@hkeurope.com

Australia: Human Kinetics, 57A Price Avenue, Lower Mitcham, South Australia 5062
08 8372 0999
e-mail: info@hkaustralia.com

New Zealand: Human Kinetics, Division of Sports Distributors NZ Ltd.
P.O. Box 300 226 Albany, North Shore City, Auckland
0064 9 448 1207
e-mail: info@humankinetics.co.nz

To the Native Americans,
who were here first.
We are only following their footsteps.

Acknowledgments

A special nod of appreciation goes to Wisconsin Department of Natural Resources personnel and all the hardworking volunteers, naturalists, county and city employees, wildlife managers, and the others who maintain trails and recreational areas for our use. They keep the system alive and working.

For their help in the preparation of this book, thanks to hikers Steve Drake, Hans Wronka, Linda Gray, George Rogers, Beth Mittermaier, Maureen Klovers, Marty Wacker, Joe Jopek, Bob Rusch, Michael Malcore, Pam Alt, Michelle Zierhut, Joann Engel, Darlene Schubert, Connie Loden, Mary O'Connor, Derek Duan, Paul Regnier, and many, many more outdoors lovers. Without their insights and observations, I would have worn out three pairs of boots instead of two.

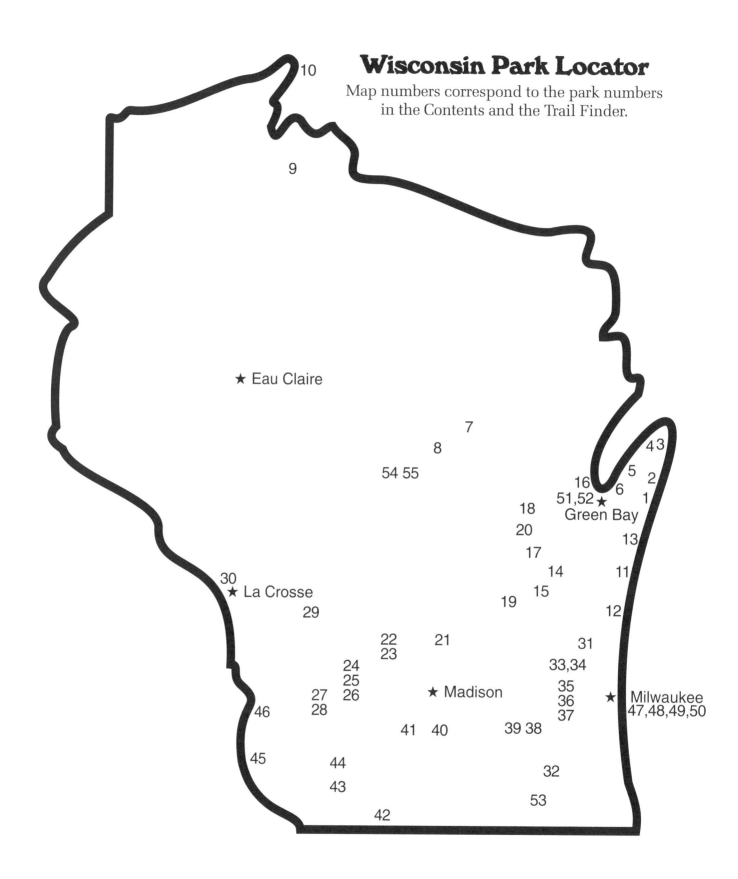

Wisconsin Park Locator

Map numbers correspond to the park numbers
in the Contents and the Trail Finder.

10

9

★ Eau Claire

7

8

54 55

4 3

5
2

16
6
1

51,52 ★
Green Bay

18

13

20

17

14

11

15

30
★ La Crosse

19

12

29

22
23

21

31

33,34

24

25

26

35

★ Madison

36

37

★ Milwaukee
47,48,49,50

27

28

46

41   40

39 38

45

44

32

43

53

42

iv

Contents

How to Use This Book

Hiking is an antidote to modern life. It gives the body some much-needed (and enjoyable) exercise, and it gives the mind both rest and stimulation. It even lifts the spirit to connect again with this earth that we're a part of but seldom have time to think about. With the America's Best Day Hiking Series, we hope to provide you with an incentive to start or continue hiking, for the pleasure and the challenge of it.

Each book in the series offers information on 100 or more of the most interesting and scenic trails in a particular state, as well as notes about recreational, historical, and sightseeing destinations located near the trails. The assortment of trails ranges from short, easy hikes for occasional hikers and families with young children to longer, more rugged ones for the experienced trailblazer. None of the trails takes more than a day to hike, although some trails may be linked together to create a hike of several days.

The trails are divided into four main areas—North, Central, South, and Urban. Within each area, trails are listed from east to west. Divider pages signal the beginning of each new area, and those pages include information on the local topography, major rivers and lakes, flora and fauna, weather, and best features of the area.

The innovative format is designed to make exploring new parks and trails easy. Information on each park or other nature area always appears on a right-hand page. It begins with the park's name and a small state map that shows the park's general location. Bulleted highlights then point out the trails' most interesting features. A description of the park's history and terrain comes next, with practical information on how to get to the park and the park's hours, available facilities, permits and rules, and the address and phone number of a contact who can give you more information. The section entitled "Other Points of Interest" briefly mentions nearby parks and recreational opportunities, with phone numbers to call for more information.

After the general information follows a selected list of trails in the park. The length and difficulty of hiking each is given, along with a brief description of its terrain. The difficulty rating, shown by boot icons, ranges from one (the easiest) to four (the most difficult).

On the other side of the page is a full-sized map of the park. Our book's larger format allows us to provide clear, readable maps that are easy to follow.

easiest **🥾 🥾 🥾 🥾** most difficult
      1   2   3   4

The next right- and left-hand pages are usually descriptions of the two best hikes in that park, along with a trail map at the bottom of each page (a few parks have only one hike, with just one map that primarily shows the trail). Each hike begins with information on the length and difficulty of the trail, and the estimated time to walk it, plus cautions to help you avoid possible annoyances or problems. The description of the trail provides more than directions; it's a guided tour of what you will see as you hike along. The scenery, wildlife, and history of the trail are all brought to life. Points of interest along the trail are numbered in brackets within the text, and those numbers are shown on the trail map to guide you. The approximate distance from the trailhead to each point of interest is given.

The park descriptions, maps, and trails are all kept as a unit within an even number of pages. Parks for which only one trail is highlighted take up only two pages; extended trails might take six or eight. We've perforated the book's pages so you can remove them if you like, or you can copy them for your personal use. If you carry the pages with you as you hike, you might want to use a plastic sleeve to protect them from the elements. You can also make notes on these pages to remind you of your favorite parts of the park or trail.

If you want to quickly find a park or trail to explore, use the trail finder that appears on the next pages. It gives essential information about each highlighted trail in the book, including the trail's length, difficulty, special features, and park facilities.

We hope the books in the America's Best Day Hiking Series inspire you to get out and enjoy a wide range of outdoor experiences. We've tried to find interesting trails from all parts of each state. Some are unexpected treasures—places you'd never dream exist in the state. Some may be favorites that you've already hiked and recommended to friends. But whether you live in a city or in the country, are away vacationing or are at home, some of these trails will be near you. Find one you like, strap on your hiking boots, and go!

Trail Finder

KEY

RV camping	tent camping	swimming	canoeing
fishing	boating	picnicking	biking

	Trail Sites and Trails	Park Facilities	Miles	Trail Difficulty Rating	Hills	Prairie/Grassland	Forest	Lake	Wetlands	Overlook	River/Stream	Page #
1	**Whitefish Dunes State Park**	swimming, tent camping, picnicking, biking										
	Red Trail		2.8	3 boots	✓		✓	✓	✓	✓		5
	Brachiopod Trail		1.5	1 boot	✓		✓	✓	✓			6
2	**The Ridges Sanctuary**	swimming	1.4	1 boot	✓		✓	✓		✓		8
3	**Newport State Park**	tent camping, swimming, biking, picnicking										
	Rowley Bay/Ridge Trail		3.5	3 boots	✓		✓	✓		✓		11
	Forest Heritage Trail		1	2 boots	✓		✓			✓		12
4	**Peninsula State Park**	RV camping, tent camping, swimming, boating, fishing, biking										
	Skyline Trail		3	3 boots	✓		✓	✓	✓	✓		15
	Eagle Trail		2	3 boots	✓		✓	✓		✓		16
5	**Potawatomi State Park**	biking, picnicking, RV camping, tent camping, fishing, boating										
	Tower Trail		3.5	2 boots	✓		✓	✓		✓		19
	Hemlock Trail		2.5	2 boots	✓		✓	✓		✓		20
6	**Bayshore County Park**	fishing, tent camping, RV camping, boating, picnicking										
	Loop A—Lime Kiln Trail		1.2	2 boots	✓		✓	✓		✓		23
	Loop B—Bluff Trail		.9	2 boots	✓		✓	✓		✓		24
7	**Ice Age Trail—Kettle Bowl Section**		14.5	4 boots	✓		✓	✓	✓	✓		26
8	**Dells of the Eau Claire County Park**	RV camping, tent camping, swimming, fishing, picnicking	2	2 boots			✓			✓	✓	28
9	**Copper Falls State Park**	tent camping, RV camping, biking, swimming, fishing, picnicking	1.5	2 boots	✓		✓			✓	✓	30
10	**Apostle Islands National Lakeshore**	tent camping, swimming, fishing, boating										
	Julian Bay/Anderson Point Trail		1.8	2 boots	✓		✓	✓	✓	✓		33
	Michigan Island Trail		2	2 boots	✓		✓	✓	✓			34

Continued ☞

	Trail Sites and Trails	Park Facilities	Miles	Trail Difficulty Rating	Hills	Prairie/Grassland	Forest	Lake	Wetlands	Overlook	River/Stream	Page #
11	**Kohler-Andrae State Parks**	(icons)										
	Kohler Dunes Cordwalk		2.5	●●	✓			✓		✓		39
	Woodland Dunes Nature Trail		1.5	●	✓		✓	✓		✓	✓	40
12	**Harrington Beach State Park**	(icons)										
	Nature Trail		1.4	●					✓	✓		43
	Quarry Lake Trail		2	●●			✓	✓		✓		44
13	**Point Beach State Forest**	(icons)										
	Ridges Trail		3	●●	✓		✓	✓	✓			47
	Red Pine Trail		3.1	●●	✓		✓	✓	✓			48
14	**Lower Cato Falls**	(icons)										
	Trail A		1.2	●●	✓					✓	✓	51
	Trail B		1	●●	✓					✓	✓	52
15	**Kettle Moraine State Forest, Northern Unit**											
	Greenbush Hiking and Ski Trails	(icons)										
	Red Trail		1.5	●●	✓		✓		✓			55
	Green Trail		3.6	●●●●	✓		✓					56
	Parnell Tower	(icons)										
	Ice Age Trail		2.6	●●●●	✓		✓			✓		57
	Parnell Tower Trail		2.9	●●●●	✓		✓			✓		58
	New Fane Trails	(icons)										
	Green Trail		2.5	●●●	✓		✓					59
	Yellow Trail		3.1	●●●●	✓		✓					60
	Zillmer Trails	(icons)										
	Brown Trail		1.2	●	✓		✓					61
	Red Trail		3	●●●●	✓		✓			✓	✓	62
16	**Barkhausen Waterfowl Preserve**	(icons)										
	Mosquito Creek Trail		2.3	●●			✓		✓	✓		65
	Shores Trail		5	●●		✓	✓	✓	✓	✓		66
17	**Brillion Nature Center**	(icons)										
	Sugar Maple Link		1.25	●●		✓	✓		✓	✓		69
	White Oak Trail		1.25	●●			✓			✓		70

Terrain/Landscape

Continued ☞

	Trail Sites and Trails	Park Facilities	Miles	Trail Difficulty Rating	Hills	Prairie/Grassland	Forest	Lake	Wetlands	Overlook	River/Stream	Page #
27	**Tower Hill State Park**	(facilities)	1.5/.5	2 boots	✓		✓		✓	✓	✓	110
28	**Governor Dodge State Park**	(facilities)										
	White Oak Trail		4.5	3 boots	✓		✓	✓	✓	✓		113
	Mill Creek Ski/Hiking/Bike Trail		3.3	3 boots	✓	✓			✓	✓		114
29	**Wildcat Mountain State Park**	(facilities)										
	Old Settler's Trail		2.5	2 boots	✓		✓			✓		117
	Hemlock Nature Trail/ Mt. Pisgah		1.4	4 boots	✓		✓			✓	✓	118
30	**Hixon Forest Nature Center**											
	Lookout Trail		3	4 boots	✓	✓	✓			✓		121
	Oak Trail		1.4	3 boots	✓		✓					122
31	**Riveredge Nature Center**	(facilities)										
	Loop A		3.4	2 boots	✓	✓	✓		✓		✓	127
	Loop B		1.6	1 boot					✓	✓	✓	128
32	**Bong State Recreation Area**	(facilities)										
	Blue Trail (South Loop)		4.2	1 boot	✓	✓	✓	✓	✓			131
	Gray Trail (North Loop)		1.7	1 boot	✓	✓	✓	✓				132
33	**Bugline Recreation Trail**											
	Bugline I		3.6	1 boot		✓	✓					135
	Bugline II		2.6	1 boot		✓	✓			✓		135
	Bugline III		6	1 boot			✓					136
34	**Menomonee Park**	(facilities)										
	Bridle/Hiking Trail		2.8	2 boots	✓		✓		✓			139
	Center Nature Trail		.7	1 boot	✓		✓		✓			140
35	**Muskego Park**	(facilities)										
	Hardwoods Trail		1.3	2 boots	✓		✓		✓			143
	Marsh Trail		1.5	2 boots			✓		✓			144
36	**Nashotah Park**	(facilities)										
	Red Trail		1	2 boots	✓	✓	✓		✓			147
	Green Trail		3	2 boots	✓	✓	✓		✓			148
37	**Minooka Park**	(facilities)										
	Red Trail		1.3	1 boot	✓	✓	✓					151
	Green Trail		3	2 boots	✓	✓	✓					152

Terrain/Landscape

	Trail Sites and Trails	Park Facilities	Miles	Trail Difficulty Rating	Hills	Prairie/Grassland	Forest	Lake	Wetlands	Overlook	River/Stream	Page #
49	**Wehr Nature Center**		1.7	👢👢		✓	✓	✓	✓		✓	192
50	**Havenwoods State Forest**	🏕️⛺ 🚲										
	Nature Trail—Orange Loop		1.4	👢		✓		✓	✓		✓	195
	Loop A		2.1	👢👢		✓		✓	✓		✓	196
51	**Cofrin Memorial Arboretum**	🚲										
	Wildflower Trail		1.5	👢👢				✓			✓	199
	White Cedar Trail		2	👢				✓		✓		200
52	**Bay Beach Wildlife Sanctuary**	🏕️⛺	5.8	👢			✓	✓	✓	✓		202
53	**Lake Geneva**	🐟🛶 🚐⛺										
	Trek I		3.5	👢👢				✓				205
	Trek II		2.1	👢👢👢👢	✓		✓	✓				206
54	**Schmeeckle Reserve**	🛶🐟 🚲	1.5	👢			✓	✓	✓			208
55	**Green Circle Tour**	🚐⛺ 🚲🐟	24	👢👢	✓		✓				✓	211

North

Topography

At one time, all of northern Wisconsin was covered by a vast inland sea. Hundreds of feet of sand covered the granite bedrock, eventually being turned to stone itself by the time and pressure. Then came the last ice age, a succession of towering sheets of ice grinding south out of Canada. It took hundreds of thousands of years to change the surface of the land. Where the land was high, the earth was flattened. Where it was flat, debris piled up to create high ridges. The landscape was battered and scraped by the ice and the rubble it picked up along the way as the glaciers charged and retreated.

This combined one-two punch acted as a rolling pin and a scouring pad. The sandstone cliffs were flattened and wide fertile plains resulted from glacial run-off. Yet some of the highlands escaped the last big crunch of 10,000 years ago. These escarpments, along with towering ridges of rubble dumped during the big melts, created rugged, rolling hills throughout northern Wisconsin. This northern highland covers some 15,000 square miles between the central plains of Wisconsin and Lake Superior. It contains the highest land features, carpeted by extensive forests and dotted with thousands of glacially born lakes.

Major Rivers and Lakes

Glacially formed Lake Superior is the most prominent feature of the north country. It is the largest body of fresh water in the world. The lake is 350 miles long and 160 miles wide; it covers 31,820 square miles, with an average depth of 475 feet. But it is only one of thousands of lakes dotting northern Wisconsin. Many were carved out by the ice sheets, while others are kettles. The latter were formed when ice left by the retreating glaciers was covered by earth. When the ice melted, the ground collapsed to form depressions that then filled with water. Green Bay, an arm of Lake Michigan, borders this part of the state on the east. The bay is 90 miles long and 20 miles wide at its mouth. The northeastern end of the bay merges with the mouths of Big Bay de Noc and Little Bay de Noc.

The Wisconsin River rises in the Lac Vieux Desert, on the boundary between Wisconsin and Michigan, beginning its 403-mile south-southwest run through the state. Adding muscle to its flow, the river picks up the overflow of lakes in Vilas and Oneida Counties in northern central Wisconsin. Other major rivers also course throughout this area. The winding, rugged St. Croix forms northern Wisconsin's western border with Minnesota. The Peshtigo, Wolf, Eau Claire, and Chippewa Rivers are part of the fanlike system of waterways that range from foaming whitewater to gentle, broad streams.

Common Plant Life

White pine, once the forest king of northern Wisconsin, blanketed the countryside before the arrival of Europeans. Towering more than 100 feet in height, with trunks three feet or more in diameter or greater, these monarchs fueled the state's timber industry. Now, only scattered white pine survivors can be found, and the northern third of the state is mostly second-growth forest land. Much of the harvested timber country has been replanted with plantations of fast-growing red pine. Oak, birch, tamarack, basswood, and maple are also plentiful. Door County, on the eastern rim of the state, is famous for its rank upon rank of apple and cherry orchards.

Throughout the north, prickly raspberry bushes with their luscious fruit and brilliantly flaming sumac creep into any open space where they can get the full benefit of sunlight. Ferns and lichens snuggle into the secretive, shadowed cliff faces. Wild flowers in season—from Jack-in-the-pulpits to goldenrod—provide carpeting of color from spring to autumn.

Common Birds and Mammals

Northern Wisconsin is a Noah's ark of wildlife. Even the rare wolf has made a comeback, but a hiker will be lucky to see even a footprint left by this elusive hunter. However, its nighttime cries can be unsettling yet are beautiful with their wild strain. More common are moose, black bears, porcupines, coyotes, white-tailed deer, beavers, rabbits, chipmunks, otters, and

© Leslie Noa

raccoons. An occasional rattlesnake can also be found in the rocky hill country.

The northern highlands are home to sharp-tailed grouse, bald eagles, loons, egrets, mallards, wild turkeys, finches, pileated woodpeckers, blue jays, cardinals, and hundreds of other species. Migrating birds pause on the lakes, which are regular homes for hooting loons and trilling shorebirds. A good set of binoculars is a viewing necessity.

Climate

Average temperatures in the north are moderate, despite images of snowbound residents. While early-spring temperatures can be in the low teens, they often reach the high 80s or 90s by May. Summer is a usually pleasant 50 to 80 degrees and autumn temperatures average in the 30s to 60s. Even winter can be "temperature friendly," hovering between 10 to 30 degrees. But the thermometer often cuts to well below zero, with wind chills of −60 degrees Fahrenheit. It is always advisable to dress for the weather. And, as Wisconsinites say, "If you don't like the weather now, wait a minute. It will change."

Rainfall ranges up to 30 inches a year, with snow sweeping down from the north off Lake Superior to coat the north with drifts up to seven to eight feet deep. The snow often remains in the deepest woods until late April or early May, making for a snowshoer and skier heaven despite the sometimes mushy conditions.

Best Features

Outdoors enthusiasts appreciate Wisconsin's north woods for its variety of landscapes and recreational opportunities. In addition to hiking challenges, there is canoeing, off-road biking, snowmobiling, cross-country skiing, fishing, hunting, waterfall-counting, sailing, bird-watching, berry picking, and picnicking. The wilderness setting is one of the premier draws to the area, giving space and time away from the grind of daily life. Hundreds of thousands of acres of national, state, and county forests are only a few hours away from the state's major urban areas, making the seemingly remote not quite so far away. A network of highways, as well as regional airports and lake marinas, make northern Wisconsin easy to visit by land, air, and water.

Superior is the largest city in the far northwest where Wisconsin snuggles up to Minnesota. Green Bay anchors the lower southeast, and Eau Claire hunkers down on the west. Regardless of their size, communities such as Rhinelander, Wausau, Marsh-field, Black River Falls, Chippewa Falls, and their smaller urban cousins cater to the lover of the outdoors. Outfitters, bait and tackle suppliers, and taxidermist and craft shops are plentiful. Even far out in the pine country, the fabled north-woods steak house offers its simple but hearty meat-and-potatoes menu. Such meals, topped by warm homemade pie and a generous dollop of Wisconsin ice cream, have been the favorite of American presidents, vacationing gangsters, and the ordinary traveling family for generations. After all, hiking does work up an appetite.

1. Whitefish Dunes State Park

- Walk along a boardwalk placed atop ancient dunes and study the effects of Lake Michigan on the shoreline.
- Climb to the top of an observation platform high atop one dune and look out on the countryside.
- Learn how to spell "brachiopod" and discover what it means.

Park Information

Whitefish Dunes State Park contains the most extensive dune system in Wisconsin, with one dune towering 93 feet. The 900-acre park was established in 1967 to protect and interpret the dunes, showing the various stages of progression from beach to forest. The dunes are atop a massive sand formation dating back 3,000 years, from a time when Lake Michigan was at least 28 feet higher than it is today. As the lake receded, it left rocks and other debris that were eventually buried by the ever shifting sand.

At least five different human occupations have been recorded at Whitefish Dunes. The first was a prehistoric fishing camp dating back to 300 A.D. The second and third took place some 1,000 years ago when Woodland Native Americans, drawn to the region by the excellent fishing, had a village here. The Oneota, who lived here between 1200 and 1300, made up the fourth occupational group. The last occupation occurred during the mid-19th century when whites and Native Americans had extensive commercial fishing operations along the shore. Extensive archaeological excavations have been conducted throughout parklands. The park has prepared a descriptive booklet about all these civilizations entitled "The People of the Dunes," which is available in the Nature Center.

Directions: The park is 8 miles north of Sturgeon Bay on State Highway 57, then 4 miles east on Clark Lake Road.

Hours Open: 8 A.M. to 8 P.M. daily, year round. The Greeting Center is open from 8 A.M. to 4:30 P.M. daily.

Facilities: 11 miles of hiking trails plus 12 miles of ungroomed cross-country ski links, as well as interpretive programs, swimming, picnic sites, toilets, water, and bike trails.

Permits and Rules: Wisconsin state park vehicle stickers are required. Vehicle rates for state residents are $18 per year and $9 per year for seniors (65 and older). You can also get day rates for $3 per day. Out of state rates are $25 per year and $7.50 per day. No camping or climbing on protected dunes. Cooking fires allowed only in the picnic area. Observe "No Swimming" signs in the first 225 yards of the beach because of the rip currents during peak-wave days. No off-road vehicles allowed.

Further Information: Contact Superintendent, Whitefish Dunes State Park, 3701 Clark Lake Road, Sturgeon Bay, WI 54235; 414-823-2400.

Other Points of Interest

The **Ahnapee State Trail** is a 15-mile-long former rail bed, linking Algoma and Sturgeon Bay. Hikers, mountain bikers, and cross-country skiers are taken along the crushed-gravel pathway past farm fields and through woods. A bridge spans the Ahnapee River where observers can spot herons, Canada geese, and other waterfowl. Call 414-743-8869 for more information.

Whitefish Dunes State Park is among the many attractions of **Door County,** one of Wisconsin's most popular vacation areas. There are four other state parks in the county: Peninsula (see park #4), Potawatomi (see park #5), Newport (see park #3), and Rock Island. For more information, call the Door County Chamber of Commerce, 414-743-4456.

Park Trails

Yellow Trail —4.2 miles—This trail is a continuation of the Green Trail, passing through a desertlike area of sand dunes before moving into a red pine plantation.

Green Trail —1.8 miles—The path goes along the base of an ancient dune. This is a good trail for studying summer flowerings, like fireweed, catnip, ground cherry, butter-and-eggs, black-eyed Susans, and bedstraw. A .7-mile spur trail off the Green takes hikers to the shore of Clark Lake inland from Lake Michigan.

White Trail —2.5 miles—Walk through a forest of mixed hardwoods, with a predominance of maple. The soil is shallow here, with many exposed rocks battered during the last ice age. The trail cuts through the eastern edge of Cave Point County Park. To see the caves on the shoreline, hikers need to leave the White Trail and walk over to the lake edge.

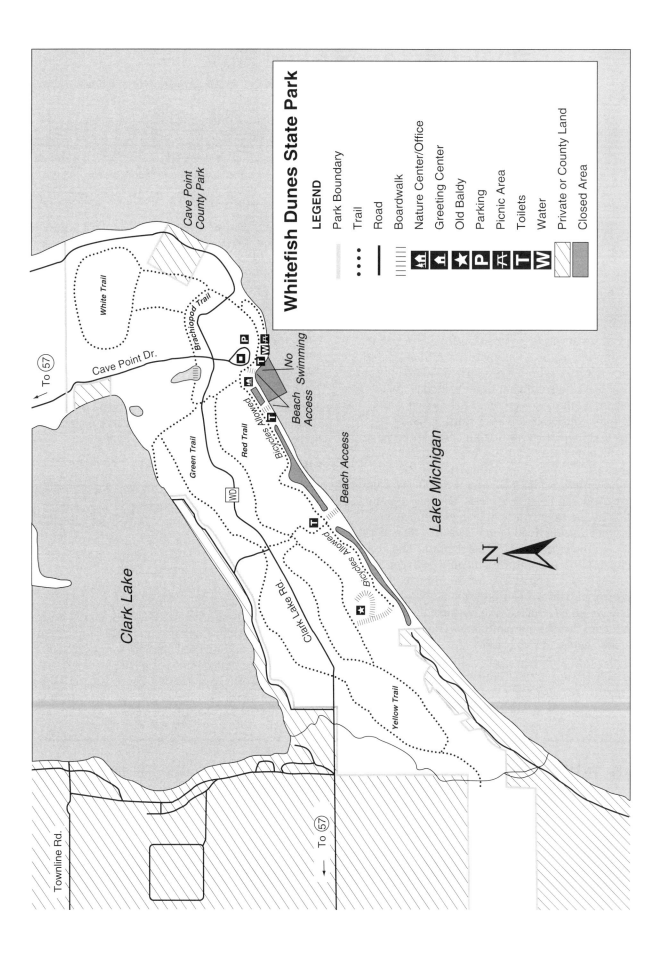

Whitefish Dunes State Park

LEGEND

Park Boundary

Trail

Road

Boardwalk

Nature Center/Office

Greeting Center

Old Baldy

Parking

Picnic Area

Toilets

Water

Private or County Land

Closed Area

Red Trail

Distance Round-Trip: 2.8 miles

Estimated Hiking Time: 1.2 hours

Cautions: Hikers should carry water or juice because of the heat reflecting up from the dunes. There is often tough walking through sand.

Trail Directions: Start at the marked trailhead to the right of the Nature Center front door. The Green, Yellow, and Red Trails leave from the same point.

From the Nature Center, walk down the slope on the right side of the building into a grove of cedar trees **[1]**. Two major archaeological digs were undertaken here in 1986 and 1992, and artifacts from the various human habitations over the centuries were found (.1-.2 mi.) **[2]**. On both sides of the trail, the examples of camps used by the ancient people have been erected. First is a fishing camp dating from 1,000 years ago; then you can see a Woodland Indian hunting camp and an Oneota bark house dating from 1300 A.D.

The trail becomes sandy at .2 mi. as you begin climbing a slope. At .3 mi., you'll see an overlook across the dunes to the left **[3]**. Barricades along the left side of the trail have prevented the drifting sand from covering the pathway. Beach access to the left is allowed at .4 mi. **[4]**, and swimmers are encouraged to use the boardwalk steps that go up and over the dunes to protect the remainder of the dune system. Toilets are on the beach level.

The trail becomes dirt packed here, and you pass a depression that can be muddy after a rain. But it is back to sand almost immediately, making for slow walking. There are several angles in the trail, but stay focused on the path even where some drifting has occurred. At .9 mi., you move up another hill **[5]** with a profusion of asters, black-eyed Susans, fleabane, and mustard. Red pine are arranged along the trail, their bases buried in the sand.

Another beach access point is at 1.1 mi. **[6]**, where steps again take hikers over the dunes. Toilets are located on the right side of the main trail. You now enter a state natural area, indicated by a large sign on the right (1.3 mi.) **[7]**. The trail here is harder, often shared by cyclists pedaling through the spruce and birch forest. A deep valley is to the left; more dunes are to the right.

Go down a slope before turning right and hooking up the path to the park's tallest dune, nicknamed Old Baldy, which rises 93 feet above the lake (1.4 mi.) **[8]**.

You get to the platform atop the dune by climbing along an uneven boardwalk that could be difficult for a hiker with balance problems. After the boardwalk, climb up two levels of stairs to the observation deck. From here you can see for miles, with the dunes to the left and meadow and forests to the right.

Retrace your steps down the boardwalk and pick up the trail again (1.6 mi.) **[9]**. Walk to the right (north) along the trail to the intersection with the Yellow Trail (1.7 mi.) **[10]**. Turn right at the junction and proceed through the open ground that is mostly dunes. There is a bench here (1.8 mi.) **[11]** where you can pause for a drink from your flask.

Keep going along the path; a large dune appears to the right and open meadow to the left. There is another bench at 2 mi. **[12]** facing to the left, overlooking the open area as it changes from dune to undergrowth and eventually to forest. Edge into a cedar grove where there are exposed roots on the trail. Five large boulders stand to the left of the path (2.2 mi.) **[13]**. Next is welcome shade from a clump of pines and maples. There is a bench at the tree line.

Continue walking through the woods, following the trail that has become a dirt pathway. It becomes gradually steeper as you approach the end of the trek, with cars driving along County Highway WD occasionally seen through the trees on the left (2.5 mi.) **[14]**. Pick up the junction with the Green and Brachiopod Trails (2.6 mi.) **[15]** and head back to the Nature Center.

1. Cedars
2. Encampment displays
3. Overlook
4. Beach access
5. Hill
6. Beach access
7. State natural area
8. Old Baldy
9. Trail
10. Trail intersection
11. Bench
12. Bench
13. Boulders
14. County Highway WD
15. Trail intersection

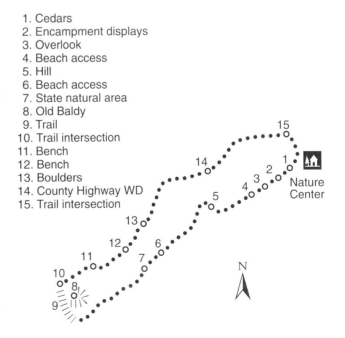

Brachiopod Trail 🥾

Distance Round-Trip: 1.5 miles

Estimated Hiking Time: 1 hour

Cautions: There is some walking along sand that might be difficult for those with physical challenges.

Trail Directions: The trail begins at a fossil-rock wall near the shore in the picnic area. Look for the limestone boulders with the numbered metal plates that lead you along the route.

The rock wall **[1]** shows off the geologic history of the limestone bedrock of Door County. Study the numerous fossils embedded in the stone, a reminder that this land was all under a vast sea 425 million years ago. You can climb out on the rocks along the shoreline (.1 mi.) **[2]** to see the lake. Look to the south to the sand beach, with Cave Point to the north.

Leave the shore and walk inland through the pine and hemlock grove. The trail joins the White Trail (.3 mi.) **[3]** where it goes north along a crushed-rock path. A bench is along the trail near several large hunks of granite. These are "erratics," carried to Door County by the glaciers. Schauer Road, which leads to Cave Point County Park, is on the right. This is very dusty during a dry spell, so avoid walking along the shoulder unless you don't mind becoming coated with limestone. However, you need to cross the road to pick up the Brachiopod Trail where it continues through a hardwood climax forest of sugar maple and beech trees (.5 mi.) **[4]**. In this stretch of the path there are some sugar maple trees **[5]** that are tapped for sap. The trees are from 75 to 100 years old and remain healthy and productive.

The White Trail splits off to the right at .7 mi. **[6]**. But keep walking to the left on the Brachiopod Trail, passing several large beech trees identifiable by their smooth gray bark. Sometimes you can see wild turkeys eating the beechnuts that have fallen to the ground. Since the earth is so shallow here, many trees have toppled over (1 mi.) **[7]** and are decomposing on the forest floor. Subsequently there are a number of open spaces in the foliage, allowing plenty of sunlight in to regenerate growth. Go across Cave Point Drive **[8]** where there is an ancient beach line, one hard to see in the undergrowth.

Several log benches are along this stretch, made by the Wisconsin Conservation Corps **[9]**. Come to a cool swampy area to the left and cross the boggy ground via a boardwalk (1.2 mi.) **[10]**. There are many water-loving white cedar trees in the vicinity. About midway along the boardwalk on the left is a small pontoon platform where you can get closer to the marsh. Cattails, reeds, and rushes poke above the shallow water. On the side where the land is firmer you'll see starflowers and goldthread.

Take a left turn and cross County Highway WD (1.3 mi.) **[11]**, where you'll soon join the Yellow, Green, and Red Trails. Pass along the ridge to the right and look at the wood ferns and other plants that like the shade here. There are taller plants, as well, such as wild raspberry, thimbleberry, and cow parsnip. Some of the leaves are waist high. You then arrive back at the Visitor Center.

1. Rock wall
2. Shoreline
3. Trail intersection
4. Sugar maples/beeches
5. Sugar maples
6. Split in trail
7. Fallen trees
8. Cave Point Drive
9. Benches
10. Bog
11. County Highway WD

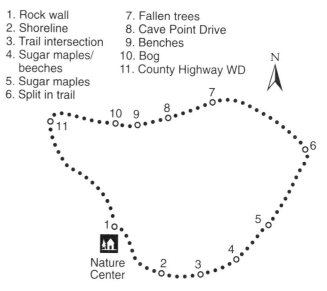

2. The Ridges Sanctuary

- Study 25 varieties of native orchids.
- Hike around a remnant boreal (northern) forest.
- Take an interpretive tour.

Park Information

If you'd like to get an idea what ancient Wisconsin looked like, The Ridges Sanctuary provides a hint. Two thousand years ago, Lake Michigan covered the area where the sanctuary is now located. But over the ages, sand built up from wave action, and each new ridge became overgrown and sturdier. Now hikers can see how various lake shorelines developed over the centuries. The action is continuing, and a sharp eye can spot underwater ridges being built up in the bay of Bailey's Harbor.

The U.S. Lighthouse Service once managed 40 acres of land where the sanctuary now stands, building two range lights at the mouth of Baileys Harbor shallow waters in 1869. In 1937, a group of citizens took over the property, enlarged it, and formed the nonprofit Ridges Sanctuary to protect the site. The sanctuary now covers 1,200 acres. It was named Wisconsin's first state natural area in 1967 and has been designated a national natural landmark. Some 13 endangered or threatened plant species are in the refuge.

Directions: Take Wisconsin Highway 57 north from Baileys Harbor. Turn right on County Highway Q and enter the first driveway on the right.

Hours Open: The Nature Center is open from 9 A.M. to 4 P.M. daily from May through October. The sanctuary grounds are open at all times.

Facilities: Rest rooms, nature center, hiking trails, observation decks, bathing beach.

Permits and Rules: The picking or disturbing of any plant is prohibited. Stay on the trails and bridges. No pets are allowed. No bikes, snowmobiles, motor-cycles, baby strollers, or all-terrain vehicles allowed. No smoking. Donations are welcome.

Further Information: Contact The Ridges Sanctuary, Highway Q, Baileys Harbor, WI 54202; 414-839-2802.

Other Points of Interest

Peninsula State Park (see park #4) is north of Fish Creek in Door County. The park has high cliffs that make great overlooks for vistas of Lake Michigan. The park also has extensive beaches and an array of beech and maple forests. Herring gulls, terns, and other shorebirds are a bird-watcher's dream. Call 414-868-3258 for more information.

The back roads of **Door County** are popular with cyclists who cruise past apple and cherry orchards, art galleries, and trendy little restaurants that seem tucked into every corner of the peninsula. The American Folklore Theater, Birch Creek Music Theater, and Peninsula Players are among the creative companies performing throughout the summer tourist season. For details call 414-743-4456.

Park Trails

Red Loop 🥾—1.2 miles—Enter the trailhead at the rear of the Nature Center and make an oval to the east along the ridge top. An observation platform is at the far end of the trail where it turns north and then back west to the Center. The platform looks out over the sanctuary toward the lake. With binoculars, hikers can spot warblers, sparrows, chickadees, catbirds, gulls, and dozens of other bird species.

Green Loop 🥾—.8 mile—The trail angles along the same walkway as the Blue Loop, turning north (back to the Center) about .6 mi. It crosses several board-walks over the sandy soil and leads up a hill past cranberry bushes and red maple. It covers about half the length of the Blue Loop.

Wintergreen, Deerlick, and Pine Trails 🥾—1.2 miles—These are small offshoots of the main nature trails, cutting through the woodlots between loops of the major pathways. They are not marked and cover much the same landscape as the others.

Blue Loop 👢

Distance Round-Trip: 1.4 miles

Estimated Hiking Time: 1.5 hours

Trail Directions: From the parking lot, take the Kinnikinick walkway to the Nature Center. Start with a visit to the Nature Center building **[1]** and learn the history of the sand ridges and Lake Michigan shoreline. Walk out the back door onto the walkway. Here you can see the first ridges of sand built up by the wind and lake. When the lake ice melted thousands of years ago, huge chunks of ice broke off from the main pack and were pushed up to the shore by the waves. On the way, they shoved rocks up with them to form a steep, angled slope.

A 120-year-old spruce on the lake side of the walkway has two trunks (.3 mi.) **[2]**. This could have been caused when a limb was broken off years ago and a side bud developed, eventually forming a new trunk. Walk straight ahead to see one of the Lighthouse Service's range lights **[3]**, built to alert sailing ships to the dangers of the shallow harbor mouth. Turn left on the boardwalk (.4 mi.) **[4]** and walk past an old dune that local hunters used to call Deerlick Ridge. They set out a salt block there as a lure to attract deer.

Follow the boardwalk down to the beach (.6 mi.) and look out over the water to spot several underwater ridges of sand and stone **[5]**. The bands of brownish water parallel to the shore mark the spot. A modern range light **[6]** and the bathing beach **[7]** are on the south side of Ridges Drive. Also at the end of the boardwalk is the second of the Lighthouse Service's lights **[8]**. Come back up the boardwalk to the path (.7 mi.) **[9]** that runs north of Ridges Drive. Along the way are red pine and tamaracks buffeted by the wind and lake spray. A few tall white pines reach high above the other trees.

Just behind the trail marker at .8 mi. **[10]** is evidence of dwarf mistletoe, a parasite that attaches itself to spruce trees and causes abnormal growth. Oblivious to the mistletoe are some northern white cedar, which grow well throughout Door County.

Fifty years ago, a garden was planted along the sandy ridge (.9 mi.) **[11]**. Pine and spruce are slowly reclaiming the old vegetable plot. Turn left. Walk along on a boardwalk section of low-lying trail (1 mi.) **[12]**. This is called a swale, which is a wet depression between two ridges. Lichens are growing on many of the trees along the path. The flaky blotches on tree limbs and trunks grow only where the air quality is good.

Turn right on the boardwalk where there are several black spruce and more tamarack. Look for a "mother" tree behind a circle of new spruce. Branches of these trees can touch the ground and become rooted, forming new trees. Eventually the mother tree dies off as the younger ones flourish.

Cross another boardwalk area (1.1 mi.) **[13]** and walk through a grove of balsam fir and red pine. Next is a small open area with a spread of reindeer moss covering the ground. About 500 feet farther is a sprawl of ground juniper. At 1.2 mi., turn right on the boardwalk and walk uphill past a clump of highbush cranberry and some red maple trees **[14]**. Then follow the trail back to the Nature Center.

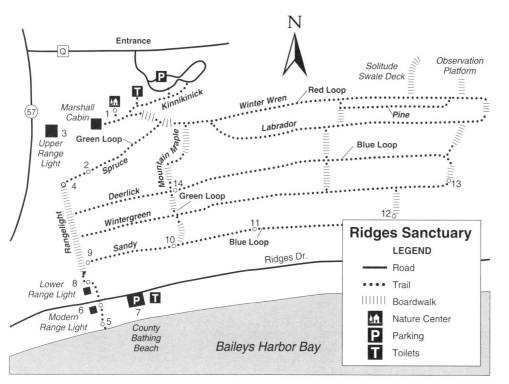

1. Nature Center
2. Spruce
3. Range light
4. Boardwalk
5. Underwater ridges
6. Modern range light
7. Beach
8. Range light
9. Path
10. Trail marker
11. Old garden
12. Swale
13. Boardwalk
14. Cranberry bushes

3. Newport State Park

- Backpack from 1 to 3 miles to your secluded camping spot.
- Trek the rolling backwoods of the upper Door County Peninsula.
- Enjoy the pristine, sandy beach along Lake Michigan as the sun rises.

Park Information

This park is a semi-wilderness area with a minimum amount of development. A century ago, the logging village of Newport stood where the park is now located. Newport once had 20 buildings, with a long pier leading out into the lake. Both sailing ships and steamers called on the community, but the village eventually died out and was abandoned in the early part of the century. Hikers can find remains of a few cabins far into the thick woods. Foundations of the town store and post office are in the park's picnic area. A kiosk at parking lot #3 marks the location of one home and describes the village.

Today, the park offers 11 miles of shoreline along Lake Michigan, including a 3,000-foot-long beach. This makes sunbathing and swimming popular pastimes for visitors.

Newport State Park allows only backpacking camping to its sites, located from 1 to 3.5 miles from the parking lot. Since the park has maintained its rustic feel, many varieties of wildlife inhabit it. More than 175 species of birds have been counted.

Directions: The park is located 5 miles northeast of Ellison Bay on State Highway 42, then east on County Highway NP.

Hours Open: Open daily, year round, from dawn to dusk.

Facilities: The park offers changing stalls at the beach, 16 secluded campsites, and a picnic area for people with physical disabilities. There are also 28 miles of hiking trails, as well as 2.3 miles of ungroomed cross-country trails. Biking is allowed in some areas.

Permits and Rules: Winter camping is allowed, but campers have to check in with the park office first. No snowmobiles are allowed in the park. Note that water must be carried in and all garbage must be carried out.

Further Information: Contact Superintendent, Newport State Park, 415 South County Highway NP, Ellison Bay, WI 54210; 414-854-2500.

Other Points of Interest

Door County is one of the state's most popular tourist destinations. In addition to Newport State Park and several county parks, there are four other state parks in the area: Peninsula at Fish Creek (see park #4), Whitefish Dunes near Sturgeon Bay (see park #1), Potawatomi at Sturgeon Bay (see park #5), and Rock Island. Door County has 250 miles of shoreline, both on Lake Michigan and on Green Bay, which means there are plenty of fishing, boating, and swimming opportunities. The county also offers music festivals, outdoor theater, and shops. Call the Door County Chamber of Commerce at 414-743-4456 for details.

Shipping and boating have long been mainstays of the Door County economy. Along the coastline, hikers can see several **lighthouses,** built to protect vessels from the reefs and sandbars that rim the land. One of the favorites with photographers is the Cana Island lighthouse on County Highway Q north of Baileys Harbor. The structure was built in 1851.

Park Trails

Newport Village/History Tour 👢—1.5 miles—The trek traces the outlines of old buildings and locates sites where Newport once stood. Start at the historical kiosk at the beach area off parking lot #3 and walk through the picnic area and along the shoreline. There are several loops that can be added to this casual trek. Take the Lynd Point history tour on Europe Bay Trail and return on the Lynd Point Trail to see the remains of loggers' homesites. At the far end of Lynd Point is a path leading to the ruins of a cabin. At the lake, hikers can see the Pilot Island lighthouse.

Duck Bay History Loop 👢👢—2 miles—Follow the Newport Trail to campsite #5 and return by the Sand Cove Trail. The path undulates through the thick cedar and pine forest along the shore of Duck Bay. Near the campsite at the far south end of the trail was once a cluster of cabins called Bohemian Town. Several families from that part of Europe settled and cleared land. Hikers can see the remains of a pier that served the tiny community just offshore.

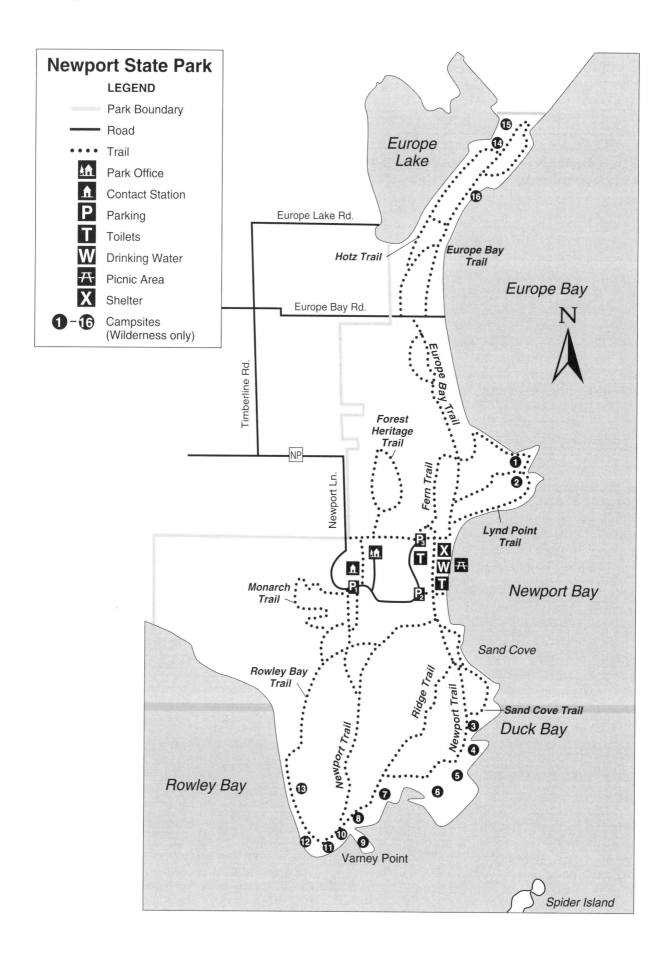

Newport State Park

LEGEND

- Park Boundary
- Road
- Trail
- Park Office
- Contact Station
- **P** Parking
- **T** Toilets
- **W** Drinking Water
- Picnic Area
- **X** Shelter
- ❶ – ⓰ Campsites (Wilderness only)

Europe Lake

Europe Lake Rd.

Hotz Trail

Europe Bay Trail

Europe Bay

N

Europe Bay Rd.

Timberline Rd.

Europe Bay Trail

Forest Heritage Trail

Fern Trail

❶

❷

Lynd Point Trail

NP

Newport Ln.

P3

T

X W 🛆

T

Monarch Trail

P

P2

Newport Bay

Sand Cove

Rowley Bay Trail

Ridge Trail

Newport Trail

Sand Cove Trail

❸

Duck Bay

❹

❺

Rowley Bay

Newport Trail

❻

❼

❶3

❽

❿

❻

❾

⓬

⓫

Varney Point

Spider Island

Rowley Bay/Ridge Trail 👢👢👢

Distance Round-Trip: 3.5 miles

Estimated Hiking Time: 2.6 hours

Cautions: The trail proceeds over generally level ground but is rough in spots, with exposed roots and rocks.

Trail Directions: Park in lot #1 near the contact station at the park entrance. The marker post is at the edge of the woods.

Proceed into the thick timber [1], made up mostly of maples, beech, and birch. There are numerous toppled trees because of the shallow soil that doesn't allow extensive root support. Walk past the boulders dumped here by the last ice age [2]. Such erratics are scattered throughout the entire forest. The intersection with the Monarch Trail is at .4 mi. [3]. On the right is a wide meadow filled with wildflowers in the spring and summer. Bluestem, milkweed, asters, side oats, black-eyed Susans, and numerous other colorful species flow from the forest edge to the park service road to the east. The trail name is appropriate in midsummer because of the numerous monarch butterflies that flit across the field.

The Rowley Bay Trail moves left, back into the forest. In any scattered open spaces along the way there are ferns, spruce saplings from three to four feet high, and other vegetation taking advantage of the sun (.4 to .9 mi.) [4]. Go through a red pine grove at .7 mi. [5] and come to a Y-intersection that leads to campsite #13. The path is thick with pine needles, making for a comfortable, quiet walk. At the mile marker, more and more stones [6] are cropping up through the path surface, so watch your step. At 1.4 mi., you are walking along the edge of Rowley Bay [7], with the waves lapping against the rocks on the right.

At 1.8 mi. is a pebble beach, fronted by a cedar grove [8]. The gnarled roots find their way through any crevasse in the rocks. The water's edge is about a five-foot drop below the pathway. Several large trees have been blown down; their damaged trunks lean away from the bay, attesting to the force of the wind that sometimes whips through here. Cormorants, gulls, and terns can be seen dipping and flying high over the blue-green water.

Pass under an old cedar whose trunk lies across the trail about head high (1.9 mi.) [9]. Many wild raspberry bushes can be found along the next stretch. They can be in season anytime from early July to mid-August, depending on the spring rainfall.

In quick succession, the trail passes campsites #12 to #10, with a short path leading to the right out to #9 on Varney Point (2.1 to 2.3 mi.) [10], with its picturesque view of Spider Island off to the southeast. Continue back along the path to the right and move past a bike trail. At 2.5 mi. [11], you can continue north on the Ridge Trail or angle east to the Newport Trail. The latter goes eastward to Duck Bay and runs up the shore to Sand Cove.

Take the Ridge Trail, which leads back into the forest away from the bay. You ascend a slight slope and continue on a straight line to the north. While there aren't a lot of curves on this section, it undulates for the next mile or so in a constant up-and-down motion. At 2.8 mi., the path widens and passes the intersection with a path leading to Sand Cove [12]. Link with the Newport Trail and come out at the picnic area by the beach near parking lot #2. You need to turn left and walk another .5 mi. back along the shoulder of the park road to lot #1 where you left your vehicle.

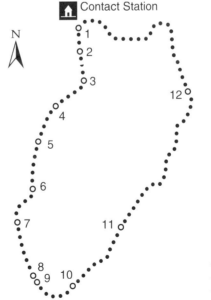

1. Thick timber
2. Boulders
3. Trail intersection
4. Open spaces
5. Red pine grove
6. Stony path
7. Rowley Bay
8. Beach
9. Cedar
10. Campsites
11. Trail intersection
12. Trail intersection

Forest Heritage Trail 👢👢

Distance Round-Trip: 1 mile

Estimated Hiking Time: 1 hour

Cautions: The trail is uneven in spots.

Trail Directions: Pick up the trail on the service road behind the central park office.

Start in a meadow that was once forest **[1]**, walking along a path that in the past was a road from Newport to Ellison Bay. The early settlers thought that the soil would support crops since the timber was so thick. Subsequently they cleared hundreds of acres and sold the wood. After the trees were gone, however, the thin earth was not even very suitable for hay. Historical reports tell of settlers going hungry because the crops did not do well. The land here was part of a farm, so there are apple trees, lilac bushes, and other "exotic" species still growing. An air-monitoring station stands where there was once a cabin.

Walk past several sugar maples (.2 mi.) **[2]**, the remnants of much larger stands cut for cordwood years ago and shipped to Milwaukee, where the wood was used to fuel brickyard kilns. This open area is slowly being taken over by aspen saplings. The park has both the trembling and bigtooth species, another cash source for the pioneers who cut the trees for the manufacture of paper pulp as early as 1885. The trees are making a comeback and are slowly reclaiming the pastures and farm fields.

The next upper meadow is also being reclaimed by field junipers and white pine, with their small blue berries in season making for colorful display. A clump of spruce trees to the side marks where a cabin once stood (.3 mi.) **[3]**. A stone wall remains, visible even from County Highway NP to the left. A gravel pit nearby was quarried from the 1920s until the opening of the park. The shallow depression is now carpeted with saplings and underbrush.

Enter a young forest of birch trees (.5 mi.) **[4]** and move on to a clump of balsam fir. Sailors from lake vessels used to cut down the balsams for holiday resale in the larger cities to the south. The local newspapers told how crews not used to landlubbers' work had a difficult time in the woods. One ship, the *South Side,* hauled a load of Christmas trees out of Newport in 1893. But it sprang a leak offshore and had to winter in Baileys Harbor, its cargo a loss.

Another cash timber crop around Newport was hemlock, used for railroad ties and for tanning leather. Several hemlocks can be seen in this vicinity (.7 mi.) **[5]** just before the end of the trail. By the 1920s, logging had ended in the Newport area, and the land that is now the state park was acquired by Ferdinand Hotz, who let it return to its natural state.

Stick to the trail as it leads back to the parking lot. You'll pass through another grove of fir trees as you stroll along the way. If it is late afternoon, there is a chance the deer might peek out from the undergrowth.

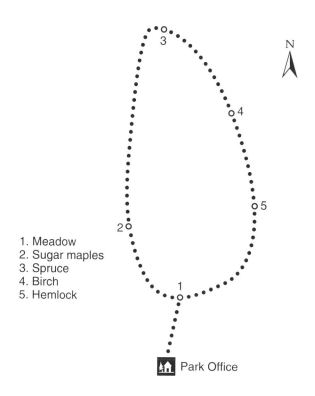

1. Meadow
2. Sugar maples
3. Spruce
4. Birch
5. Hemlock

Park Office

4. Peninsula State Park

- Tour the hiking trails of Wisconsin's second-oldest state park.
- Climb the 75-foot-high Eagle Tower and look out over the surrounding countryside and bay.
- Walk along towering limestone bluffs and miles of rock and cobblestone beaches.

Park Information

Peninsula State Park covers 3,763 acres on the shores of Green Bay. It is one of the most popular parks in Wisconsin, attracting more than one million visitors each year. The park's backbone is made up of miles of bedrock called Niagara dolomite, formed millions of years ago by an ancient sea. There are cliffs and caves to see along several of the park trails.

As early as 7000 B.C., Paleo-Indians lived here. Waves of other native people called this their home for generations before the whites arrived. Prior to park acquisition in 1910, there were farms, orchards, and logging operations throughout the vicinity. Now all that has slowly crumbled back into a more natural setting, yet hikers can still see old stone walls, foundations, and other signs of pioneer passing.

There is more to Peninsula State Park today than walking in the woods. The University of Wisconsin Extension's Heritage Ensemble gives musical performances with an historical flavor in the park amphitheater in July and August. The Door County Historical Society offers guided tours of the Eagle lighthouse from mid-June to Labor Day.

Directions: The park is located on State Highway 42 at the northern edge of Fish Creek.

Hours Open: Open year round. Campground visitors need to leave by 11 P.M.

Facilities: The park has 472 campsites, 100 with electricity. There is also a group campground. Some winter sites with electricity are available. Flush toilets, showers, and handicapped facilities are on-site. Other amenities are a beach, boat landings, nature programs, bike and boat rental, fishing pier, tennis court, 18-hole golf course, nature center, 19 miles of hiking trails, 17 miles of snowmobile trails, plus a snowshoe trail and a sledding hill.

Permits and Rules: Reservations for campsites are encouraged. Reservations during the summer months are necessary to ensure a site. Pets are not allowed in mowed picnic areas and must be on a leash. Fires only allowed in designated areas. Quiet hours in the campgrounds are from 11 P.M. to 6 A.M. A state park vehicle admission sticker is required.

Further Information: Contact Park Manager, Peninsula State Park, P.O. Box 218, Fish Creek, WI 54212; 414-868-3258.

Other Points of Interest

America's oldest professional summer theater program performs Broadway shows at the **Peninsula Players Summer Theater** on Peninsula Players Road. The playhouse is open from late June to mid-October. Call the theater at 414-868-3287 for details.

Rock Island State Park is off the coast of Washington Island on Lake Michigan at the far end of Door County. The 905-acre island is reached by ferryboat. The park has a 1-mile self-guided nature trail. Several other trails crisscross the island. For more information, call 414-847-2235.

Park Trails

Hemlock Trail—1.8 miles—This trail takes hikers over a rock-and-rolling countryside. There are views of the dolomite base rock on the swales as it passes through thick hemlock patches.

Lone Pine Trail—.6 mile—This is a challenging stretch of pathway that leads into some of the more remote areas of the park. Hikers can pick up the trail as a continuation of the Minnehaha Trail.

Minnehaha Trail—.7 mile—The best access for this straight link is from Nicolet Beach. Gentle terrain makes it easy for youngsters to walk through the mixed hardwood timber.

Nicolet Bay Trail—2.2 miles—This is a relatively easy path through red and silver maple for experienced hikers, but be aware that there is gently rolling terrain that has some climbing to it.

Sentinel Trail—2-mile loop—This pathway rolls over gentle terrain through a pine and hardwood forest.

Sunset Trail—5.1 miles—This is a bike path, but it is open to hikers. The wide, graveled surface makes the entire length accessible to persons in wheelchairs, although there are some low hills to traverse.

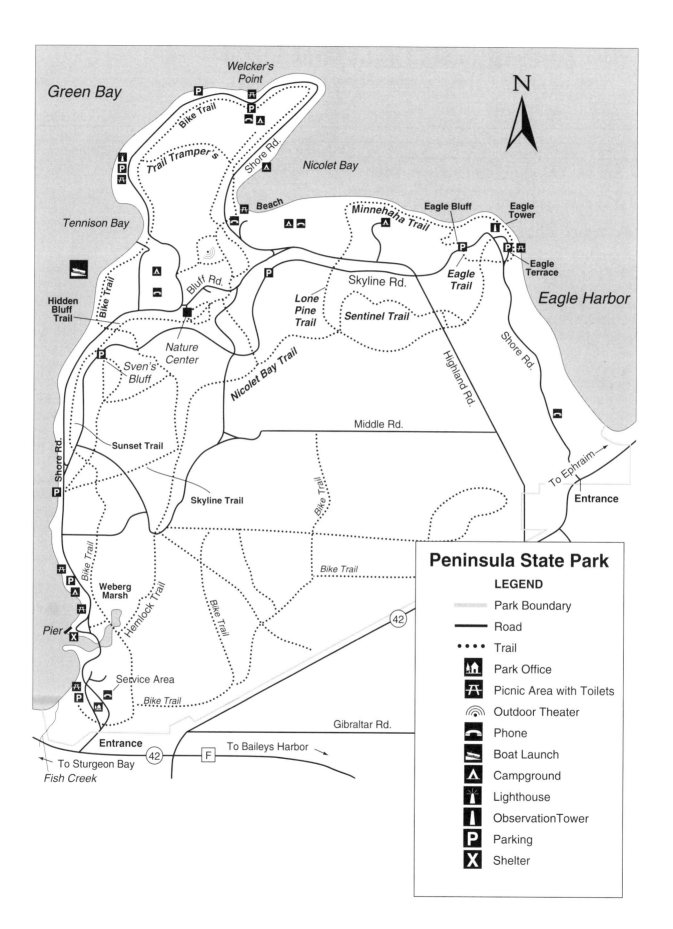

Green Bay

Welcker's Point

Nicolet Bay

Tennison Bay

Bike Trail

Trail Tramper's

Shore Rd.

Beach

Minnehaha Trail

Eagle Bluff

Eagle Tower

Hidden Bluff Trail

Bluff Rd.

Skyline Rd.

Eagle Trail

Eagle Terrace

Eagle Harbor

Nature Center

Lone Pine Trail

Sentinel Trail

Sven's Bluff

Nicolet Bay Trail

Highland Rd.

Shore Rd.

Sunset Trail

Middle Rd.

To Ephraim

Shore Rd.

Skyline Trail

Bike Trail

Entrance

Bike Trail

Weberg Marsh

Hemlock Trail

Bike Trail

42

Pier

Service Area

Bike Trail

Gibraltar Rd.

Entrance

42

F

To Baileys Harbor

To Sturgeon Bay
Fish Creek

Peninsula State Park

LEGEND

- Park Boundary
- Road
- Trail
- Park Office
- Picnic Area with Toilets
- Outdoor Theater
- Phone
- Boat Launch
- Campground
- Lighthouse
- ObservationTower
- Parking
- Shelter

Skyline Trail 👢👢👢

Distance Round-Trip: 3 miles

Estimated Hiking Time: 2.5 hours

Cautions: Portions of the trail become boggy after a rain.

Trail Directions: Leave from the parking lot on the bay side of Shore Road. Cross the road and pick up the trail by the tennis courts.

Walk up the gravel slope from the road **[1]**, move past the tennis courts **[2]**, and head into the woods where the path goes into a downhill run. You then immediately begin walking over a series of swales (.1 mi.) **[3]** that give a roller-coaster effect to the hike. Be aware that in rainstorms, torrents of water rush down these pathways because they are clear of vegetation. Subsequently there are often gullies in the path where the water has dug deeply into the surface. The trail runs to the north, parallel to Shore Road **[4]**, on the bluffs overlooking Green Bay to the west. An add-on loop takes hikers to Sven's Bluff, on a hummock overlooking the lake. To reach the bluff, get off the Skyline Trail where it makes the first major right turn (1.2 mi.) **[5]**. Cross Shore Road on the left to get to the parking lot **[6]**, where you can get an uninterrupted sight of the blue-green waters. The bay is several hundred feet below the parkway drive. Retrace your steps across the road and head back into the tree line by coming down a slight slope and picking up the Skyline Trail again as it drifts eastward. You connect briefly with the Hemlock Trail (1.8 mi.) **[7]**, which presents more of the same rolling effect that you had when starting out. Thick stands of red maple line both sides of the trail, making for a blast of crimson on an autumn hike. There are also some red pine scattered along the way.

Angle left and go up a small hill (2.1 mi.) **[8]**, and walk down again as the ground rolls unevenly ahead. The next small pine-framed clearing (2.2 mi.) **[9]** is a great place to come across deer grazing in the late afternoon. A careful hiker can often get within several hundred feet of the shy animals before they bound away. Fawns, does, and bucks scatter in all directions if you approach loudly.

An old fence line (2.4 mi.) **[10]** is broken by the path. Its length of stone piles is crumbling now, and is only thigh high. A century ago, the piles were probably waist high or more. Continue along the up-and-down path past more deer yards ripe with thick ground cover such as goldenrod, Queen Anne's lace, and black-eyed Susans. There is some thistle scattered about as well. The latter is ignored by the deer as they browse on low-hanging branches.

Turn right when the trail makes a swing to the west. You'll cross Middle Road (2.8 mi.) **[11]** on the way back to the trailhead. You will soon see the tennis courts on the right. Cross Shore Road again to your vehicle in the lot along the bluff.

1. Gravel slope
2. Tennis courts
3. Swales
4. Shore Road
5. Bluff path
6. Parking lot
7. Trail intersection
8. Small hill
9. Clearing
10. Fence line
11. Middle Road

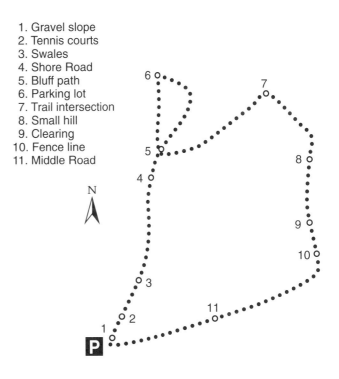

Eagle Trail 👢👢👢

Distance Round-Trip: 2 miles

Estimated Hiking Time: 1.7 hours

Cautions: There is a steep, rocky descent to Eagle Harbor.

Trail Directions: Park in the lot at Eagle Tower. The trailhead starts there; just look for the marker. You can also start from Eagle Terrace near the Information Center or from the parking lot at Eagle Bluff.

This is an expandable trail, one that can be lengthened by going along interconnecting links with the Minnehaha, Lone Pine, and Sentinel systems. But at first, stick to the Eagle Trail as it goes into the maple forest across from the tower **[1]**. A fenced-in deer-study area is the first stop **[2]**; here you can see the effects that too many browsing deer can have on a section of forest. This first leg is actually the conclusion of the Sentinel Trail, so walk along until you come to the major intersection with the actual Eagle Trail (.5 mi.) **[3]**.

You can go either right or left, so take the right turn and angle past the thick maple stands (.6 mi.) **[4]** while heading to the northwest. The trail dips and dives across the topography carpeted with lady's slippers, trillium, butter-and-eggs, ferns, and other forest plants. Watch out for the poison ivy. Cross Shore Road again **[5]** and head along the steep, rocky bluff where the trail follows Eagle Harbor **[6]** for the next mile. If seabirds are your game, there are terns, gulls, and white cormorants to watch soaring high overhead.

Your walk now runs adjacent to Shore Road, which you cross again at 1.7 mi. **[7]**. On the other side of the road to your left (south) is a state natural area that is thickly timbered. The Sentinel Trail runs through this portion of the park with its hawthorn, white pine, and quaking aspen. Open spaces along here allow goldenrod and cow vetch to blossom and grow well. Turn right at the trail intersection and come back to the trailhead, where your vehicle is parked.

1. Tower
2. Deer-study area
3. Trail intersection
4. Maple
5. Shore Road
6. Eagle Harbor
7. Shore Road

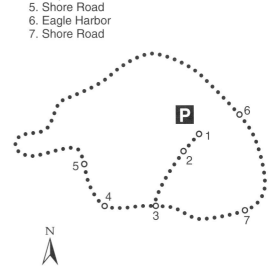

N

5. Potawatomi State Park

- Climb a 75-foot-high observation tower on top of a 150-foot-high bluff overlooking Sturgeon Bay and Green Bay.
- Camp in wooded sites near hiking trails that meander through the woods.
- Take in a park interpretive program that tells of the glacial formation of the region.

Park Information

In the 1920s, the federal government owned the land that is now the state park. It was originally intended for use as a military base but was made a park in 1928. The facility is at the entrance to Sturgeon Bay, its cliffs and rugged landscape overlooking the rolling green waters far below.

The park is named after the Potawatomi nation; the name means "keeper of the fire" ("bo-de-wad-me"). The nation once occupied 30 million acres of land in the Great Lakes area and were the dominant Native American group throughout the 1600s and the early 1700s. They became an important link in the fur trade when whites arrived on the scene.

In 1815, the Potawatomi signed a treaty with the U.S. government and ceded their land. They subsequently dispersed as the frontier disappeared; bands now live in Canada, Oklahoma, Kansas, and Michigan, as well as throughout Wisconsin.

Directions: The park is located 4 miles southwest of Sturgeon Bay off State Highway 42/57. Follow the signs to Park Drive.

Hours Open: The park is open year round from 6 A.M. to 11 P.M. daily.

Facilities: Dump and recycling station, fish-cleaning station, hiking and cross-country ski trails, firewood purchase, 125 wooded campsites (of which 23 have electrical hookups), boat ramp, interpretive programs, downhill ski slope, picnicking, and biking.

Permits and Rules: State park vehicle admission sticker required. Vehicle rates for state residents are $18 per year and $9 per year for seniors (65 and older). You can also get day rates for $3 per day. Out of state rates are $25 per year and $7.50 per day. Only two motor vehicles allowed per camping site. Garbage is on a carry-in and carry-out system for day-use areas. Fishing licenses are required for anyone over 16. Fires are allowed only in fire pits, charcoal grills, or fireplaces in shelters. No chain saws allowed.

Further Information: Contact Superintendent, Potawatomi State Park, 3740 Park Drive, Sturgeon Bay, WI 54235; 414-746-2890.

Other Points of Interest

The park is south of the shipbuilding city of Sturgeon Bay, county seat of Door County. Because of its location between Green Bay and Lake Michigan, **fishing** opportunities abound for charter and for onshore anglers. There is easy access to fishing locales, as well as guide services that take fishing fans out on the bay and lake. Call the Sturgeon Bay Area information center for details, 414-743-3924.

The **Door County Maritime Museum** is located at the foot of Florida Street, next to Sunset Park. The two-story facility has a variety of artifacts dealing with shipbuilding and the county history. The museum is open daily from Memorial Day to mid-October. For more information, call 414-743-8139.

The **Door County Historical Museum,** at 4th and Michigan Streets, includes a complete fire company unit with bell tower, pole, and antique trucks. A street scene presents several storefronts, with windows opening to the inside displays. Call 414-743-5809 for details.

Park Trails

Ice Age Trail —23.5 miles—The Door-Kewaunee County trail starts at the observation tower in Potawatomi State Park and runs south. Along several stretches it parallels the Ahnapee River and the state hiking/biking trail there. The distance makes it a challenging walk through bogland and woods and along farm fields. Hikers will pass the Forestville Millpond, a wayside stop maintained by the Door County Parks Department. In Algoma, the state's self-proclaimed coho salmon fishing capital, hikers can take a quick detour to the Von Stiel Winery to stock up on Montmorency cherry wine.

Ancient Shores Natural Trail —.5 mile—This is a quick trek that even kids can enjoy, especially since it tracks the ice age coastline. At one time, Door County was an island cut off from the mainland, and this trail moves along the ancient shore high above today's beaches.

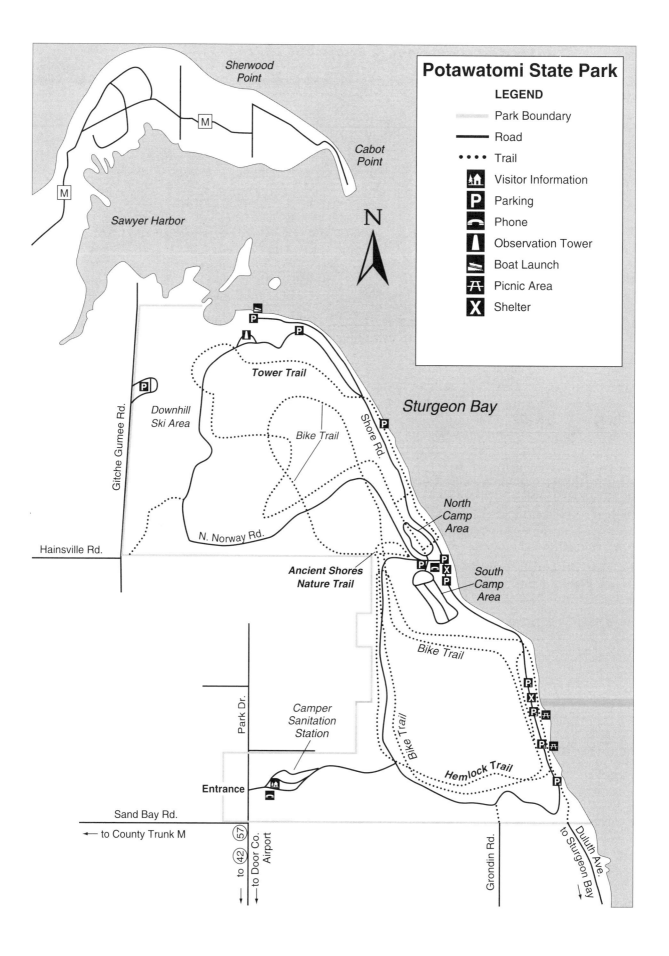

Potawatomi State Park

LEGEND

- Park Boundary
- Road
- •••• Trail
- Visitor Information
- **P** Parking
- Phone
- Observation Tower
- Boat Launch
- Picnic Area
- **X** Shelter

Sherwood Point

Cabot Point

Sawyer Harbor

N

Sturgeon Bay

Tower Trail

Downhill Ski Area

Bike Trail

Gitche Gumee Rd.

Shore Rd.

North Camp Area

N. Norway Rd.

Ancient Shores Nature Trail

South Camp Area

Hainsville Rd.

Bike Trail

Park Dr.

Camper Sanitation Station

Bike Trail

Hemlock Trail

Grondin Rd.

Entrance

Sand Bay Rd.

← to County Trunk M

to (42) (57)

to Door Co. Airport

to Sturgeon Bay

Duluth Ave.

Tower Trail 👢👢

Distance Round-Trip: 3.5 miles

Estimated Hiking Time: 2.7 hours

Cautions: The trail can be rough at times, with exposed roots and rocks to trip the unwary hiker.

Trail Directions: Start in the north campground, which is bisected by the Tower Trail. The trail can also be picked up at the observation tower or at other entry points along Shore Road.

Head out of the campground **[1]** and walk north along the trail, turning to the left where you see the path extend up a steep slope (.1 mi.) **[2]**. Leaves from the thick stands of maple, beech, and basswood litter the trail, covering up some of the exposed roots. There are uneven flagstones of granite that also make it awkward walking once you get to the top of the slope. But keep going to more level ground where there are ferns growing in profusion (.5 mi.) **[3]**. Early-morning cobwebs often have to be brushed out of your face when you proceed along this link. Cross a bike path and walk parallel to North Norway Road; you'll occasionally see a car to the left through the trees.

At .9 mi., cross the intersection with the return loop of the wide off-road bike/cross-country trail **[4]**. At 1.1 mi., edge around an extensive mud patch **[5]**, an obstacle that does not bother deer, whose tracks can be seen throughout this area. At 1.2 mi., there is an off-road bike/cross-country trail **[6]** marked out through the woods. Keep to the left. The trail makes several curves through the woods and runs along a field (1.4 mi.) **[7]** where you can sometimes see wild turkeys amid the wildflowers. A high-power line runs overhead above this section of trail. Follow the path when it jogs to the left.

The trail again crosses North Norway Road and you enter the downhill ski area (2 mi.) **[8]**. The site is owned by the Department of Natural Resources but managed by volunteers from the Potawatomi Ski Club. Snow-grooming equipment, warming chalet, and a chairlift serve guests. Walk along the path that

is on the left (northwest) side of the road and emerge from the woods at the observation tower (2.4 mi.) **[9]**. Take a minute to climb to the top and admire the view. At the base of the cliff is a landing for small boats in Sawyer Harbor. Toilets are available near the tower parking lot.

Walk back across the road and reenter the woods. The trail now moves up and down along the ridgeline through thick stands of maple and beech. Occasionally you can spot a deer bounding off into the distance through the foliage. Cross Shore Road (2.6 mi.) **[10]** and walk along the hill overlooking the water's edge. You pass a government navigational aid (2.8 mi.) **[11]**; the brightly colored marker on its steel tower helps direct ships through Sturgeon Bay on their way to the city docks. You are now probably walking along on a thick carpet of cedar needles.

You can either cut across the road again when you pass a trail intersection at 3.2 mi. **[12]** that leads inland, or continue to the Daisy Field campground and pick up the trailhead there. To know the spot, it helps if you have been camping here.

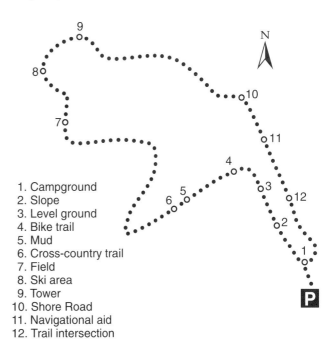

1. Campground
2. Slope
3. Level ground
4. Bike trail
5. Mud
6. Cross-country trail
7. Field
8. Ski area
9. Tower
10. Shore Road
11. Navigational aid
12. Trail intersection

Hemlock Trail 👢👢

Distance Round-Trip: 2.5 miles

Estimated Hiking Time: 1.8 hours

Cautions: There are some steep hills and rocky portions of the trail.

Trail Directions: Start at parking lot #2 in the picnic area. Rest rooms and drinking water are available.

The trail meanders along the service road in the picnic area **[1]** adjacent to Sturgeon Bay. You are close enough to the water to hear it lapping up on shore. There are several open places along here where you can fish for brown trout and bass while your picnic grill is being fired up. Track the path north along the shore and then follow it across Shore Road (.3 mi.) **[2]**

and into the mixed hardwoods on the other side. Here you are along the upper side of the south campground, tracing the ancient shoreline of what geologists call Glacial Lake Algonquin, the predecessor of Lake Michigan.

Beyond the campground, the trail angles right (northwest) where there is bare rock with smatterings of lichens (.5 mi.) **[3]**. The park lies on the Niagara Escarpment, the backbone of Door County. The escarpment consists of Niagara dolomite that runs 900 miles east to Niagara Falls. The rock was exposed when the last glaciers ground their way southward from Canada during the final ice age. The lichens, as dainty-appearing as they are, will eventually, over the course of thousands of years, break down this hard rock with their acid.

Coming down off the ancient shoreline cliff, cross Norway Road (.8 mi.) **[4]** and enter a field of black-eyed Susans, goldenrod, Queen Anne's lace, and coneflowers. This is a transition area slowly being reclaimed by the forest, as evidenced by the saplings and bushes creeping in around the edges of the opening. You cross Norway Road again (1.5 mi.) **[5]** and enter an area with a mixed tree growth that includes beech, red maple, and even pine. The ground slowly rises until you are atop a bluff (1.8 mi.) **[6]** overlooking the lake. Continue on the path as it descends through the trees and crosses Shore Drive. Pick up the service road in the picnic area and walk along it back to your starting point (2.5 mi.).

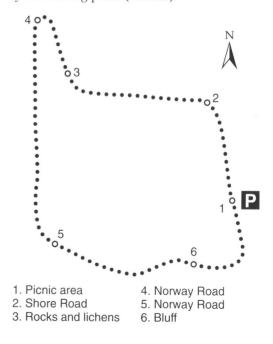

1. Picnic area
2. Shore Road
3. Rocks and lichens
4. Norway Road
5. Norway Road
6. Bluff

6. Bayshore County Park

- Walk the ledges overlooking Green Bay.
- Use the park's boat launch to set out on a quest for lake trout and salmon.
- Explore an old lime kiln by scrambling down a rough and rugged path.

Park Information

The park is atop the bluffs overlooking Green Bay and is a favorite spot of local picnickers. The facility has an abandoned lime kiln, dating from pioneer days. There is no longer a resident manager so reservations to camp are on the honor system, but are checked regularly by visiting park staff.

A sign honoring Cecil J. Depeau, the late director of the Brown County parks, is inside the park entrance.

Directions: The park is 15 miles north of the city of Green Bay on State Highway 57, overlooking the waters of Green Bay.

Hours Open: The park is open from 7 A.M. to sunset. The campground closes at 10 P.M.

Facilities: The park has an 80-site campground with electricity, wood, and water, as well as a play area, volleyball nets, picnic shelter, softball diamond, hiking trails, shower, toilets, and a boat ramp with six launching lanes. A modern shelter house can be rented with its refrigerator, stove, and stone fireplace.

Permits and Rules: Fires are permitted only in designated areas. No firearms or alcohol are allowed.

Overnight mooring of boats is not permitted. Snowmobiles are restricted to marked trails. Pets must be leashed. Camping cost is $14 with electrical hookup and $11 without.

Further Information: Contact Brown County Park Department, 305 East Walnut Street, Room 616, Green Bay, WI 54301; 414-448-4466.

Other Points of Interest

The **Barkhausen Waterfowl Preserve** (see park #16) and **Fort Howard Paper Foundation Wildlife Area** offer more than 8 miles of hiking and groomed cross-country ski trails along the west shore of Green Bay. The topography ranges from wetlands to meadows and forests. The facility is a prime locale for watching waterfowl during the migration season, with Canada geese and numerous species of ducks flying through the area. The preserve has a resident naturalist who offers interpretive programs and leads tours. For additional information, call 414-448-4466.

Lily Lake Park in western Brown County was formed during the last ice age. It is well stocked with bass and crappie, and a dock and boat ramp are provided for motorized and nonmotorized craft. The park also offers picnic tables, grills, and playground equipment, as well as a log shelter, for guests. The park has a short nature trail. Call 414-448-4466 for more information.

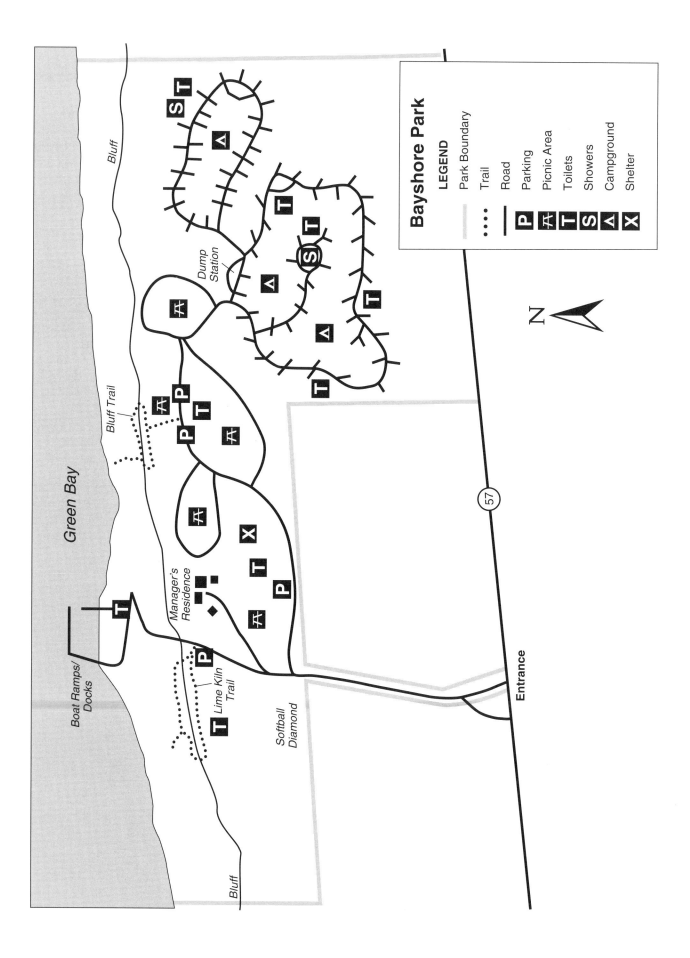

Loop A—Lime Kiln Trail

Distance Round-Trip: 1.2 miles

Estimated Hiking Time: 45 minutes

Cautions: The stairs leading down the slope are crumbling in some sections, so watch your step. The trail can also be slippery when wet.

Trail Directions: Park in the lot overlooking the bay near the ball diamond. The trailhead is marked by an iron railing leading down some steps.

Take the steps **[1]** and move down the slope to a gravel path. At .1 mi. is another set of steps, followed by a flat area and then more steps **[2]**. Continue down the bluff face, using handrails if necessary. The trail forks at .2 mi. **[3]**, with the left going up the bluff again through a break in a rock formation. The right leg continues its descent.

Take the trail to the right and follow it down the slope, through a grove of birches and maples. There is an overlook at .3 mi. **[4]**, where you get a good view of Green Bay to the north and west. Cedar trees overhang the trail all along this stretch. There are four more sets of stairs leading down to the old lime kiln (.4 mi.) **[5]** that is tucked into the bluff face. The shaded, cool area is moist enough to support a large colony of ferns of several types **[6]**. This is the end of this trail section, so you need to retrace your steps to the fork in the path.

Take that right link upward as it goes through several narrow passages in the limestone (.5 mi.) **[7]**,

rocks created millions of years ago by the ancient seas that once covered this entire region. There are several ledges where you can stand to look out over the bay. But be aware that there are no protective barricades here. A fall would have an unpleasant conclusion.

After a scramble up the slope, you emerge at the top of the bluff to pick up a loop trail to the right. This is a wide grassy path that makes for easy walking. The trail then loops to the left and aims back toward the parking lot. Red maples, birches, and beech predominate along this stretch of trail, with raspberry bushes as ground cover. You come out of the tree line at a picnic area near the park's softball diamond. It is then a quick stroll back to your vehicle.

1. Steps
2. Steps
3. Fork in trail
4. Overlook
5. Lime kiln
6. Ferns
7. Narrow passages

Loop B—Bluff Trail 🥾🥾

Distance Round-Trip: .9 mile

Estimated Hiking Time: 30 minutes

Cautions: The bluff is steep, with steps in need of repair.

Trail Directions: Park in the lot next to the rest rooms at the east end of the park. Cross the parking lot toward the bay, walk through the shaded picnic area, and look for the railings. The stairs here take you to the beach.

While descending the stairs **[1]**, be sure to hang on to the railings because some of the steps are in bad shape. The concrete steps evolve into wooden stairs on the second leg of the downhill trek as it moves onto a dirt and gravel path under a huge limestone overhang (.2 mi.) **[2]**. There is a steep drop-off on the right, so stick close to the cliff face on the left. The next section of this trail loop now continues ahead, while the turn to the right goes down the bluff **[3]**. There are 15 steps in the next descent stage, moving to a flat surface. Angle right around a large outcropping of limestone and continue down more steps to the pebble beach (.3 mi.) **[4]**. You can walk up and down along the surf line. To the left are the boat launch and a parking lot. Retrace your route to the trail fork and turn right on the new path. This section is only shoulder width as you clamber up a crevasse (.7 mi.) **[5]** and emerge at the top of the bluff. Shaded by maples and cedar, the picnic area here is pleasant and cool even on the warmest days.

Walk along the bluff top and ease into one of several swinging benches (.8 mi.) **[6]** that are spotted along the trail. Dangle your feet and look out over the bay. After resting, stroll back to your vehicle in the nearby lot.

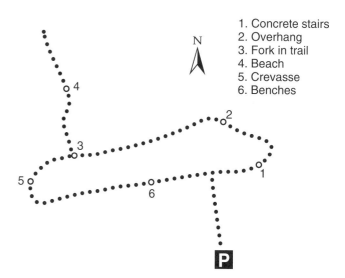

1. Concrete stairs
2. Overhang
3. Fork in trail
4. Beach
5. Crevasse
6. Benches

7. Ice Age Trail—Kettle Bowl Section

- Study the topographical formation of glacially-created kettle lakes.
- Trek an area where nomadic Ice Age hunters might have walked.
- Look for wildlife living amid the pines and hardwoods of the forest.

Trail Information

The Ice Age Trail follows a 1,000-mile route that marks the rim of the last glaciers to crunch across Wisconsin's landscape. The trail winds through 23 counties. In 1981, the United States Department of the Interior designated the Ice Age Trail as a "national scenic trail," one of nine in the country.

The Kettle Bowl section of the Ice Age Trail starts at Polar at an elevation of 1,550 feet and gradually rises to more than 1,700 feet. The trail earned its name for the kettles, or depressions, caused when glacial ice covered by earth eventually melted and collapsed inward. The trail passes through rough country dotted with large granite boulders dumped here by the glaciers. Deer, grouse, red squirrels, and porcupines are plentiful. The best time to hike this leg of the trail is in spring or autumn. Heat and insects make summer trekking a much less enjoyable experience.

Directions: Drive out of Antigo and head northeast on State Highway 52 for 19 miles until you reach the Kettle Bowl Ski Area. Turn right (south) onto the Kettle Bowl access road. Park along this road. You may wish to leave a second vehicle or arrange a pickup in Polar at the south end of your hike, somewhere along Mueller Lake or on Polar Road. This crossroads village is 10 miles west of Antigo on State Highway 64.

Hours Open: Dawn to dusk, year round.

Facilities: None.

Permits and Rules: No firearms. No camping. No fires.

Further Information: Contact the Langlade Chapter of the Ice Age Trail, Box 460, Antigo, WI 54409.

Other Points of Interest

The **Wolf River** offers a variety of canoe, kayak, and rafting challenges, varying from calm stretches to rough whitewater. Area outfitters can provide canoe and raft rentals, with road access available at crossings. Most takeouts are at Markton, along County Highway M, just before entering the Menominee Reservation. For more information, contact the Langlade County Forest & Parks Department, 800-288-6236 or 715-627-6236.

Try a farm vacation at **Mother Earth Lodge** in Elton, 13 miles east of Antigo and 8 miles west of Langlade. Guests can stay in an octagon-shaped home or cabin after helping with chores, picking vegetables, and working in the garden. The lodge also offers cross-country skiing, hiking, canoeing, rafting, fishing, and hunting in the area. Call 715-882-4911 for details.

Kettle Bowl Trail 👢👢👢👢

Distance One-Way: 14.5 miles

Estimated Hiking Time: 8 to 10 hours

Cautions: This is rugged country. Hike with a partner or let someone know where you are and when you should return. Follow the yellow trail blazes. Watch for stones and exposed roots.

Trail Directions: The trail begins near the bottom of the south ski run at the Kettle Bowl ski area. Walk past the chalet (.3 mi.) **[1]** and head into the forest where the trail begins its up-and-down trek southward. You'll walk along a narrow, rocky path with valleys and kettle bowls on the left side.

Continue walking south as the pathway climbs the north face of the Summit Lake moraine. Mature oak, maple, birch, and hemlock make up the forest. The ensuing 3 mi. or so present much of the same topography as you pass a continual litter of large stones and boulders dumped along the trail by glaciers.

At 3.8 mi., meet the intersection to an unmarked logging road **[2]** that takes you to the Kent Lookout Tower to the left (east) of the main pathway. The structure is 1,903 feet above sea level. The tower is closed to the public, but it is manned regularly by fire watchers during any dry season.

Returning to the main trail, pass the former Jackson Deer Camp (3.9 mi.) **[3]** and keep walking until

you reach a clearing (4.6 mi.) **[4]**. At 4.8 mi. you'll meet Burma Road **[5]**, a logging road that doubles as part of the county's snowmobile system and the Ice Age Trail. Look for the orange blazes indicating the snowmobile route as well as the occasional logging truck along the roadway. Swing to the right (west) as the trail loops past thick stands of aspen and maple. The trail now swings down into several gullies and back out again (4.9 mi.) **[6]**, zig-zagging along the hills until it reaches what is locally called the Frost Pocket turnoff (5.7 mi.) **[7]**. Pass another logging road (6 mi.) **[8]** and continue following the trail where it makes a sharp left (south) turn at 6.1 mi. **[9]**.

The trail now runs in a fairly straight, but just as hilly, route through more Georgia Pacific lumber lands (7.3 mi.) **[10]**. Now go west along the path, then turn left (south) at another logging road (7.8 mi.) **[11]** and plunge back into the woods. There is soon a clear-cut vista (8.1 mi.) **[12]** where you can look around the rough and tumble landscape while catching your breath.

Pass the next intersection (8.2 mi.) **[13]** and walk until you come to the Dodge Lake turnoff to the left (east) (9 mi.) **[14]**. Dodge Lake is a typical kettle depression in Wisconsin's north country. Return to the main trail and keep walking southwest. Just before reaching Oak Road turn sharply southeast, where the route was redirected to the rear of an old pioneer cemetery (9.7 mi.) **[15]** in 1996.

On the other side of the cemetery, the trail goes almost due west except for minor meanderings. At 10.5 mi., meet Price-Polar Road **[16]** and turn left (south) to walk along the ditch to reach Groth Road (11.8 mi.) **[17]**. Groth Road runs into Polar Road (12.9 mi.) **[18]**, which takes you into the village of Polar (14.5 mi.) **[19]**.

—*Joe Jopek*

Ice Age Trail—Kettle Bowl
LEGEND

——	Road
••••	Trail
P	Parking
★	Radio Tower
Ⅰ	Kent Lookout Tower

1. Chalet
2. Trail to tower
3. Jackson Deer Camp
4. Clearing
5. Burma Road
6. Gullies
7. Frost Pocket turnoff
8. Logging road
9. Sharp left
10. Lumber company land
11. Logging road
12. Vista
13. Intersection
14. Dodge Lake
15. Cemetery
16. Price-Polar Road
17. Groth Road
18. Polar Road
19. Polar

8. Dells of the Eau Claire County Park

- View ancient rock strata.
- Camp and picnic in a pristine setting.
- Hike through pine, oak, and birch forests.

Park Information

The Dells along the Eau Claire River are now a Marathon County park. Volunteers began laying the trail system here in the mid-1970s, linking the park with the village of Ringle, which is 13 miles to the south on Highway 29. The Dells parkland provides a perfect couple of hours for casual strollers interested in the story of the riverway and its amazing rock formations.

Ten thousand years ago, two lobes of the last ice age glaciers collided at Antigo (in Langlade County to the northeast). They melted to form a vast lake that was drained by the Eau Claire River. Its ancient streambed was eventually plugged by glacial debris and forced into its current course. At the Dells, the rampaging water smashed into the ancient rocky volcanic refuse that ages of underground stress had vertically split and pushed upward. The relentless Eau Claire had thousands of years in which to erode a drop of 65 feet over a 1.5-mile stretch of this rock shelving in what is now the Marathon County park.

Directions: Drive 15 miles east from Wausau on State Highway 29 and turn north on County Y at the village of Hatley. Go 7 miles to the first park entrance. An alternative route is via County Z east from Wausau's north side to Y, where the park entrance is only about a mile to the left. The second entrance is about .25 mile farther on Y. Cross the Eau Claire River and look for the signs on the right indicating the campgrounds. The entrance to the group picnic shelter is another several hundred feet up a hill on Y. Turn left into the marked entrance.

Hours Open: The Dells of the Eau Claire County Park is open only between May 1 and October 31. Except for registered campers, the park closes at 11 P.M.

Facilities: Tent and RV camping, fishing, picnicking, and swimming. An overlook of the Dells on the northwest side of Highway Y is accessible to persons with disabilities, but stairs and handholds must be used in some sections.

Permits and Rules: Hunting and trapping are not allowed. Dogs must be on a leash not exceeding eight feet, and pets are not allowed on the bathing beach, in picnic areas, or on children's playgrounds. A closed shelter is available for a fee; reservations must be made with the park department's permit station. Camping is permitted only in the 25 sites of the East Unit or in the North Unit campgrounds, both of which have electric hookups. Camping fees are $6 a day. Reservations for the group campground may be made through the county park department.

Further Information: Contact Marathon County Park Department, Courthouse, Wausau, WI 54401-5568; 715-847-5235.

Other Marathon County Trails

Nine-Mile Recreation Area —19 miles— The heavily forested area is excellent for extended hiking, biking, and skiing. Loops range from .5 to 9.6 miles. The recreational area is 1.25 miles off County Highway N along Red Bud Road, south of Wausau (3.5 miles west of U.S. Highway 51). None of the trails are specifically marked for hikers, bikers, or horseback riders, and they either double for cross-country skiing or are marked for snowmobiles in the winter. Bring a trail map and compass. It is easy to get turned around on the less-traveled loops. Complete trail maps can be obtained from the Marathon County Forestry Department, Courthouse, 500 Forest Street, Wausau, WI 54401; 715-847-5267

Big Eau Pleine Park —13.4 miles—This is one of the more remote trail systems in Marathon County, traversing the banks of the Big Eau Pleine River. The terrain was molded by glaciers, forming a rough landscape perfect for hikers needing a challenge. There are three major trails: The outer loop is an intensive 6.9-mile round-trip walk, with an A Loop at 2.8 miles and a B Loop at 3.6 miles. In the winter, each leg is groomed for cross-country skiing. To get to the park, take U.S. Highway 51 south from Wausau 6 miles to State Highway 153. Turn west and go through the old timber town of Mosinee. Drive another 2.5 miles to Eau Pleine Park Road and turn south again to the park entrance.

River Trail 🥾🥾

Distance Round-Trip: 2 miles

Estimated Hiking Time: 1 hour

Trail Directions: Park in the small lot on the south end of the park just before County Y crosses the Eau Claire River near the stone bridge. Two trails depart from this site, which has a large picnic shelter. The River Trail goes straight before jogging to the right, and the Forest Preserve Story of the Soil Trail goes to the left. They intersect again in the pine woods (.2 mi.) **[1]**. Stay on the marked River Trail and follow it until it reaches the Eau Claire River (.4 mi.) **[2]**.

The trail now runs along the south bank. The trail rises as the ground gets progressively higher. You can see the Eau Claire River moving more swiftly here. Peer over the riverbank to see huge stone outcroppings **[3]** surrounded by brown-black eddies. The Dells themselves appear from around a bend in the trail (.5 mi.) **[4]**. Potholes pock the surface of the stone; the depressions were cut out over time by the swirl of smaller rocks caught up by the water.

The River Trail leads to the stone bridge over County Y where hikers can either cross the road (.8 mi.) **[5]** or return to the parking lot. By returning to the lot, you pass the picnic shelter again.

But by crossing the highway, you'll soon find a footbridge over a dam that slows the Eau Claire flow

(.9 mi.) **[6]** just before it hits the Dells. The path leads through the pines to a large, grassy picnic area (1 mi.) **[7]**. Just beyond the grass are the park's second major parking lot, rest rooms, and a beach (1.1 mi.) **[8]**. The Beach Trail runs for 800 feet along the north side of the river, making for an easy walk.

While taking this leg back toward the highway, remain on the path near the redwood-stained fence. If you walk through the picnic area, notice that benches face the river for anyone wanting to perch and watch the canoers and fisherfolk. A buoy stretches across the river to block boaters from going over the dam and encountering the rough water of the Dells.

You have three options on returning. First, either walk west along the Beach Trail to County Highway Y or go back via the bridge across the dam. Second, instead of retaking the River Trail here, take the Forest Preserve Trail, which also goes back toward the highway. Third, meander along the Beach Trail to the highway, cross the road, and pick up the Bluff Trail for a view of the Dells from the north side of the river. You can continue walking along this bank to a footbridge back to the south where you again pick up both the River Trail and the Forest Preserve Trail. From there it is a pleasant stroll through the pines back to your car. The mileage and estimated hiking time were based on the third option, the most scenic route.

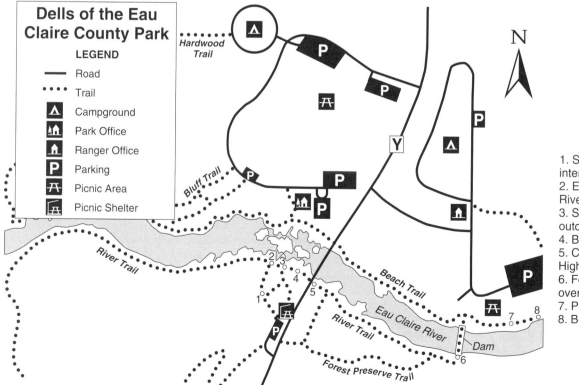

Dells of the Eau Claire County Park

LEGEND

— Road

···· Trail

△ Campground

🏛 Park Office

🏠 Ranger Office

P Parking

🏕 Picnic Area

🏕 Picnic Shelter

1. Soil Trail intersection
2. Eau Claire River
3. Stone outcroppings
4. Bend in trail
5. County Highway Y
6. Footbridge over dam
7. Picnic area
8. Beach

9. Copper Falls State Park

- Discover ancient lava flows.
- Enjoy the sight of roaring water tumbling over some of Wisconsin's most picturesque falls.
- Take in a natural history interpretive program.

Park Information

Copper Falls State Park is part of the Penokee-Gogebic Range. More than a billion years ago, this region was covered by a vast shallow sea. Then volcanic action created a line of mountains taller than the Rockies. Over the eons, the mountains eroded. The area is rich in mineral deposits, especially copper—hence the name.

There are several major waterfalls in the park, among them the 30-foot-high Bad River Falls. Tyler's Fork River cascades over a line of ancient rocks before pouring down Brownstone Falls. There are several self-guided walks around the waterfalls, with numerous overlooks.

Directions: Copper Falls State Park is 2 miles northeast of Mellen on State Highway 169.

Hours Open: Daily, year round.

Facilities: 56 campsites, 13 with electricity; group camping, beach with lifeguard, fishing, playgrounds, toilets, water, picnic area.

Permits and Rules: State vehicle admission sticker required. Rates for state residents are $18 per year and $9 per year for senior citizens (65 and older). The day rate is $3. For out-of-state visitors, the rates are $25 per year and $7.50 per day. No firearms. Fires only in designated areas.

Further Information: Contact Superintendent, Copper Falls State Park, Box 438, Mellen, WI 54546; 715-274-5123.

Other Points of Interest

Fishing is the big sport in the Mellen vicinity, with Lake Galilee and English and Day Lakes among the many bodies of nearby water. Muskie, bass, and walleye are the popular catches. Guides are available, as well as boat and canoe rentals in communities around the lakes. For more information, call the Mellen Area Chamber of Commerce, 715-274-2330.

South of Mellen is the **Chequamegon National Forest,** a sprawling 850,000 acres with camping, hiking, fishing, skiing, and hunting opportunities. Trails wend through the maple and pine carpeting the national forest's rugged hills and valleys. Forest headquarters is in Park Falls. Call 715-762-2461 for more information.

Several **mountain bike trails** are located just southeast of the park registration office at Copper Falls State Park. In addition, the 2-mile-long **North Country National Scenic Trail** leads south to the Red Granite Falls area—a popular site among hikers for wading in the gentler downstream waters of the Bad River. For details, call the state park at 715-274-5123.

Park Trails

Red Granite Trail —2.5 miles—This easy-to-walk section takes hikers past stands of mature hardwoods and into thick pine and hemlock groves along the east side of the river. There are five small waterfalls to see, ranging in height from 8 to 12 feet. This stretch of trail is among the most scenic, and secret, places in the park. Most hikers stay close to the upper canyon and its rougher water, but the Red Granite offers a quieter look at nature. This is a good trail for spotting white tail deer.

North Country National Scenic Trail — 6 miles—The trail runs from the north through the park's heavy hardwood mix of maple and basswood. The north section of the trail is easier than the lower end. Two popular backpacking camp sites are accessible from here, located within sight of the river. They are several hundred feet from the water. Hikers need to walk into the forest about 2 miles to find the campground area. Across the river are spectacular sandstone ledges.

Nature Trail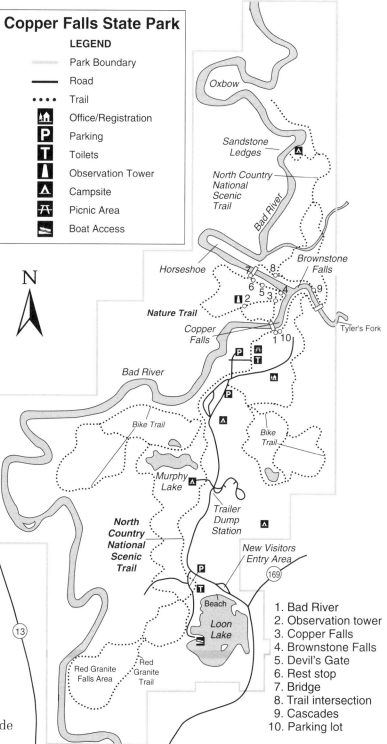

Distance Round-Trip: 1.5 miles

Estimated Hiking Time: 1 hour

Cautions: Stay on the trail because of the rugged surroundings. Do not cross under timber rail partitions.

Trail Directions: Take Highway 169 north from Mellen and the Chequamegon National Forest. Near the north end of Loon Lake, turn left at the Copper Falls State Park entry sign. Follow the road to a bridge .1 mi. northeast of the park registration office.

Proceed across the Bad River **[1]** and pick up the trail on the west bank. Follow the trail as it loops along the riverbank to the left in heading toward a 60-foot-high observation tower (.1 mi.) **[2].** After climbing the tower and looking over the countryside, return to the base. The right-hand path loops around several S-curves before coming back to the Bad River. Go left and proceed along the riverbank to a view of Copper Falls (.2 mi.) **[3].** The falls get their name from the copperlike color of the water, the result of tannin released by decomposing pine needles. The trail now follows a deep gorge cut into the jointed and fractured basalt bedrock.

At .3 mi., hikers can see Brownstone Falls **[4]** tumbling over a 30-foot drop on the north side of the river. Hardwoods and pines decorate the landscape in all directions. Turn along the path as it bends to conform to the river. At .7 mi., you will see Devil's Gate **[5],** where the contact between the basalt downstream and folded, metamorphosed sediment is apparent. Just past Devil's Gate is a covered rest stop with a bench **[6].**

Follow the trail across a second bridge (.8 mi.) **[7]** to get a view from the opposite side of the river. An offshoot path **[8]** leads north .8 mi. to several backpack campsites at the river's edge.

Get a glimpse of Brownstone Falls from the north side of the river and keep walking along the bluff to reach the overlook above the cascades (1.1 mi.) **[9],** where the river rushes through a narrow channel. After crossing one final bridge, enjoy a quieter stretch of river. A backwoods parking lot (1.3 mi.) **[10]** with

toilets is located a short distance past the bridge on the south side of the trail. A short trail, accessible to persons with physical disabilities, leads from the parking lot to the main trail along the river. The trail then ascends gradually back to the trailhead (1.5 mi.).

—Hans Wronka

Copper Falls State Park

LEGEND
- Park Boundary
- Road
- Trail
- Office/Registration
- Parking
- Toilets
- Observation Tower
- Campsite
- Picnic Area
- Boat Access

1. Bad River
2. Observation tower
3. Copper Falls
4. Brownstone Falls
5. Devil's Gate
6. Rest stop
7. Bridge
8. Trail intersection
9. Cascades
10. Parking lot

10. Apostle Islands National Lakeshore

- View the breathtaking Lake Superior scenery.
- Enjoy recreational boating, diving, fishing.
- Visit historic harbors, lighthouses, and fishing camps.

Park Information

The Apostle Islands National Lakeshore is one of the youngest parks in the national system, having celebrated its 25th anniversary in 1995. The naming of the string of 22 islands off Wisconsin's Lake Superior shore as a national park was important, however. It demonstrated that there were significant areas of natural beauty needing to be protected in America's heartland.

For generations, the Ojibwa nation used the islands as campsites and provisioning points for their journeys across the lake. Following their lead, French voyageurs traveled in their 36-foot-long trading canoes to outposts they built on the islands. With the demise of the fur trade, logging, fishing, and sandstone quarrying became important. Tourists flocked here as early as the 1850s.

Directions: Drive north along the east coast of the Bayfield Peninsula along State Highway 13. The historic community of Bayfield is the jumping-off point for cruise-ship tours, sea kayaking, sailing, and motorboating around the islands. Bayfield is 10 miles north of Washburn and 20 miles north of Ashland, where U.S. 2 joins Highway 13.

Hours Open: The Bayfield Visitor Center is open from 8 A.M. to 6 P.M., Memorial Day through Labor Day; from 8 A.M. to 5 P.M., Labor Day to October 20; and from 8 A.M. to 4:30 P.M., October 20 to Memorial Day. The Little Sand Bay Visitor Center is open from 9 A.M. to 5 P.M. daily, June 8 through Labor Day; and from 9 A.M. to 5 P.M. on Fridays, Saturdays, and Sundays through September. The Stockton, Raspberry, and Manitou Visitor Centers are open from 8 A.M. to 4:30 P.M. from mid-June through Labor Day. Volunteers man the lighthouses on Sand, Outer, Devils, Raspberry, and Michigan Islands from mid-June to Labor Day. A ranger is based on Raspberry Island in the summer.

Facilities: Outfitters in Bayfield and other Lake Superior shoreline communities can supply camping and sailing gear. Many ranger-led activities are available at the lakeshore Visitor Centers, including fishing camp and lighthouse tours, bird walks, and bog and beach walks. Audiovisual presentations can be seen at the lakeshore Visitor Center in Bayfield. Books, charts, maps, and other materials can also be purchased there. The Little Sand Bay Visitor Center also has displays highlighting the shoreline and lake.

Permits and Rules: Island camping is allowed only at designated campsites. Free permits are available at the Visitor Centers and ranger stations. Fires can be built only in grills, pits, or rings at the campsites. All trash must be packed out and not buried. All natural features of the landscape are protected and are not to be disturbed. Winter campers must register at park headquarters. Pets must be leashed.

Cautions: Since the Lake Superior waters seldom rise above 65 degrees, swimming is best in protected bays near shore where the water is warmer. When camping, use bear-proof food-storage lockers or hang food out of bears' reach. Filter or boil lake water for two minutes or more before drinking. Be on the lookout for ticks, especially in the summer.

Further Information: Contact Superintendent, Apostle Islands National Lakeshore, Route 1, Box 4, Bayfield, WI 54814; 715-779-3397.

Park Trails

Sand Island 👢👢—2 miles one-way—The trail connects the campground at East Bay with the island's lighthouse. The trail passes through an overgrown hayfield and an orchard. There are also several sea caves, and the trail leads through a grove of virgin white pine.

Basswood Island 👢👢—5.5-mile loop—The trail begins and concludes in a clearing up a small hill from the 70-foot-long dock midway up the west side of this island. The trail passes through an old farm site, follows an old logging road, and leads to overlooks of an abandoned quarry. The Apostle Islands Water Taxi provides a daily run from Bayfield to Basswood Island from May to October. Call 715-779-3397 for a schedule.

Overlook Trail (Oak Island) 👢—1.8 miles—The trail can be picked up on the interior of the island, about 2 miles from the dock on the southwest side of the 5,078-acre rock. This trail leads to an overlook 200 feet above the lake. This walk is one of five good trails (total of 11.5 miles of paths) on the island.

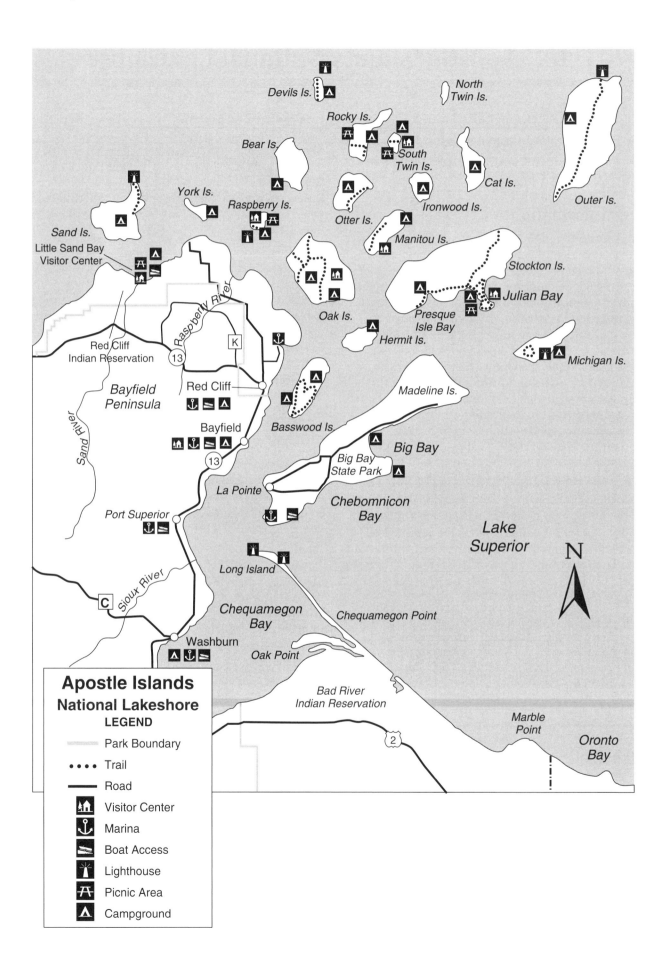

Apostle Islands
National Lakeshore
LEGEND

Park Boundary	
••••	Trail
──	Road
Visitor Center	
Marina	
Boat Access	
Lighthouse	
Picnic Area	
Campground	

Julian Bay/Anderson Point Trail 🥾🥾

Distance Round-Trip: 1.8 miles

Estimated Hiking Time: 1.5 hours

Cautions: Stockton Island has one of the largest concentrations of black bears in the world. Report all bear sightings to the rangers, who date and mark the animals' presence on a large map in the Visitor Center. Don't feed or harrass the animals.

Trail Directions: From the dock at Presque Isle Bay, stop at the Visitor Center to get maps and look over the displays. This is also a snug place to visit during the frequent spring and summer rains. The trailhead is behind the park office building to the right **[1]**. The island was shaped in the last ice age, about 10,000 years ago. The glaciers removed everything down to the sandstone bedrock, with resulting erosion carving exotic arches and stacks of rock along the coast. The island consists of 10,054 acres and is one of the largest in the Apostles. With its size and diversity of plant life—more than 430 species at last count—the island supports abundant wildlife. Foxes, beavers, and otters can sometimes be spotted. Deer love the Canada yew that grows on Stockton. Stands of this tree are scattered through the island, guaranteeing the presence of deer.

The Julian Bay Trail (.4 mi. one-way) cuts directly across the south tip of the island to the bay. The Anderson Point Trail (1.4 mi.) is a more leisurely loop, following the shoreline on the south side of the island. Hikers can see many rock formations **[2]** when edging along the cliffside as they first start out on the Julian. The path then moves through a stand of 200-year-old yellow birch (.1 mi.) **[3]**, survivors both of loggers and of extensive fires that swept the island after the timber cutting. Scars from a 1934 fire can still be seen on several trees. The thick tree canopy causes heavy shade, with resulting fern growth on the forest floor (.2 mi.) **[4]**. Several species of maple trees have taken over where once white pine grew in abundance. The leaves of the sugar, red, and mountain maple coat the trail, making it slippery walking after a rain. Collecting maple sugar on Stockton was once a big income-producer for early Bayfield County residents. The path now edges into a low-lying marshy area (.4 mi.) **[5]**. Balsam fir, eastern hemlock, and cedar trees cover the mushy ground.

The exposed woods are now hit with the stormy northeast wind off the lake, so the tree variety changes to the hardy white pine and spruce. The rocky soil is slippery, making for an uneven surface as the path descends to more marshland (.5 mi.) **[6]**. The bog is undergoing a transition as rosemary, laurel, blueberry, and huckleberry bushes creep in around the edges of the shallow water. A sandy dune to the right supports a thick stand of red pine.

The trail comes out at Julian Bay (.5 mi.) **[7]** where the results of heavy wave action can be seen. Only 5,000 years ago, Stockton Island and Presque Isle were two separate land masses. Over the ensuing centuries, sand whipped up by the lake linked the two islands. The sandbars were eventually exposed to form beaches. Such a sand bridge is known by the Italian word *tombolo*. Bogs, lagoons, and the ancient shoreline can be seen from the trail.

The Anderson Point Trail turns to the right and rims the lakeshore **[8]** along the water. You can see rock formations **[9]** through the pines **[10]** while you walk along back to the Presque Isle dock.

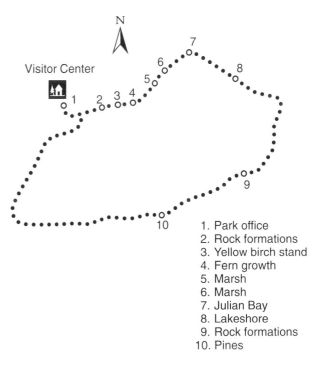

1. Park office
2. Rock formations
3. Yellow birch stand
4. Fern growth
5. Marsh
6. Marsh
7. Julian Bay
8. Lakeshore
9. Rock formations
10. Pines

Michigan Island Trail 👢👢

Distance Round-Trip: 2 miles

Estimated Hiking Time: 1.5 hours

Cautions: Mosquitoes are plentiful in summer, so use insect repellent when going through the woods. Also be alert for Lake Superior storms, which can strand campers on the island for up to two or three days. Monitor the marine radio Channel 16 for the latest weather details.

Trail Directions: The trail can be picked up from the rear of the lighthouse keeper's home **[1]**, atop the 123-foot-high bluff overlooking the dock where supplies are unloaded. Goods have to be either carried up the 142 steps to the bluff top or wenched up on a small cable car. This lighthouse is an important marker on this stretch of Lake Superior. Between 1886 and 1940, ore boats from Ashland used the 600-foot-deep south channel of Chequamegon Bay to run past Michigan Island on their way to Chicago and Cleveland. During that era, a keeper and two assistants were on duty during the season. In 1941, the light was automated and the keeper's house was empty. But volunteer Park Service staff are now on duty in the summer, in contact via radio to the mainland.

After entering the second-growth woods, the unsigned path heads down a slope of glacial till, cutting across several meandering streams and low-lying spots. The island was heavily logged at the turn of the century. Today's maples and birch have replaced the once magnificent stands of white pine. After about .25 mi., the path reaches the beach **[2]** on the north side of the island. From there, turn left and walk toward the western tip of the island. Shells, driftwood, and gull feathers abound. A large marsh covers much of this end of the island (.5 mi.), but one needs to push thick brush out of the way to see it **[3]**. It is worth the sweating and

grunting, though, to see the blue herons and other birdlife there.

Just around the western tip is a primitive campsite (.8 mi.) **[4]** where fires are allowed. Access it by anchoring offshore and wading in or grounding a flat-bottom boat on the wide beach. Piles of driftwood mark the wave line, so be sure to soundly anchor a boat or tie it down so it does not drift off. Continue along the beach and look carefully to the left for the ruins of an old fishing camp (1.2) **[5]**. Often the brush is so thick that even a large stove-in boat at the site is hidden in the foliage. A huge pile of storm-tossed trees blocks off the beach (1.5 mi.) **[6]**, but a careful climb along the trunks can get a hiker across the rolling lake water surging below. Then it is the climb back up those stairs from the dock for a great view of the lake.

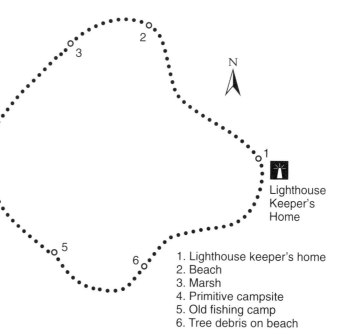

1. Lighthouse keeper's home
2. Beach
3. Marsh
4. Primitive campsite
5. Old fishing camp
6. Tree debris on beach

Central

Topography

Central Wisconsin is nature's masterful blend of farmland, forest, marsh, hills, and prairie. In the east is a glacially created moraine and kettle landscape, a living reminder of the last ice age a mere 10,000 years ago. The northern Kettle Moraine topography is shrouded with a thick blanket of oak and maple. But the hiker knows that a completed trek over this countryside is a real leg-stretcher. The spinelike moraine ridges and steep slopes rival any walking experience elsewhere in the country.

In the center of the state are the glacially created, relatively flat, sandy outwash fields and pasturelands that are perfect for potato farms, long-distance biking, and marathon hiking. Out here, the stroller can see Big Sky forever. Toward the west are still more rolling hills and soaring limestone cliffs spared by the ancient glacial rolling pin. These upland bluffs and steep valleys usually feature a river snaking through the landscape far below the crest.

Major Rivers and Lakes

Water has made the face of central Wisconsin what it is. The Wisconsin River is finally getting up a head of steam as it rolls southward and then west, its tannin-colored waters surging through the craggy Wisconsin Dells on the 430-mile route to the Mississippi River. The La Crosse, Black, Pecatonica, and Baraboo Rivers provide leisurely boating opportunities, except when spring rains kick them up over their banks. The Kickapoo River is considered the most crooked river in the world by canoeists who know about such things.

The state's largest lakes are here. Again, Lake Michigan makes its presence known on the eastern border. Lake Winnebago, Wisconsin's largest inland body of water, is a runner-up in size, temperament, and recreational potential. This lake is 30 miles long and 5 to 10 miles wide, covering 215 square miles. Green Lake and Devil's Lake are two others appreciated by outdoor-recreation enthusiasts who boat, fish, water ski, and canoe. Horicon Marsh's damp acreages are another watery reminder of the glaciers.

Common Plant Life

Bur oak, silver and red maple, ironwood, black walnut, birch, and poplar are a few of the major tree varieties that carpet the hills and string along the fencerows. As the topography changes, so do the flora. In the cool, dim glens of the Wisconsin Dells are forests of ferns. But don't be surprised to see cactus on the dry, hot bluffs above the Wisconsin River. Around the edges of old fields are staghorn sumac and other transitional plants. Without the burning process that limits encroachment of sapling and trees, many former pastures and clearings are being reclaimed by hardier forest species.

There is a profusion of wildflowers because central Wisconsin was the transition grounds between the northern pine forests and vast prairies. However, few undisturbed, original prairie sites remain after more than one hundred years of plowing. Yet goldenrod, asters, side oats, bluestem, prairie smoke, and their wind-tickled cousins are making a strong comeback. Environmentally minded communities, civic groups, and individuals are encouraging replantings along roadsides, in parks, and near private dwellings.

Common Birds and Mammals

White-tailed deer, raccoons, coyotes, badgers, woodchucks, beavers, and muskrats populate the forests and parklands throughout the center of the state. The Department of Natural Resources encourages farmers who lease land from the state to make several plantings geared only to animals. This way, every living thing benefits.

Hundreds of bird species are tallied by enthusiastic counters every year, especially during migration season when Canada geese, tundra swans, mallards, teal, wood ducks, and dozens of other species flock through the region on their north-south journeys. It helps to have cornfields butting up against the marshland and wet zones where the birds can augment their diet. Yet Wisconsin is not just a pit stop on the flyways. During the year, swallows, owls, starlings, hawks, orioles, woodpeckers, and humming-birds flock, flutter, and fly around the countryside.

Climate

The growing season reaches from 130 to 150 days in the heart of the state, with precipitation averaging 30 inches. Without high hills to block them, winter winds make the central plain a wild-and-woolly place in winter. Temperatures can drop well below the freezing point, with an added wind-chill factor that can decrease the temperature to −50 degrees Fahrenheit or lower. Generally, however, the temperatures are temperate, with summers hovering between 50 and 90 degrees. The rim seasons of spring and autumn are always hit with frost and cold, but also can be unseasonably warm. The adage for hikers is "Dress for the weather" and "Do it in layers." Any given day might start cool and damp and become hot and sunny with an hour. Or vice versa.

Best Features

On a grade of one to ten, central Wisconsin's outdoor fun potential hovers in the 9.5 range. There are rivers to canoe and peaks to climb, berries to pick, and birds to watch. The hiker can't go wrong with the Kettle Moraine State Forest and the Mississippi River coulee country framing the gentle central landscape. Several of the state's major conservation education centers are located here: the MacKenzie, Hixon, Brillion, Marsh View, and Gordon Bubolz environmental facilities give visitors a not-to-be-missed, behind-the-scenes peek at the outside world.

But other worlds are just as fun and relaxing. Major cities and tourist attractions lie within this central belt. Sit on the deck behind the University of Wisconsin Memorial Union and watch the summer sun dancing on Madison's Lake Mendota. Take a Wisconsin Dells cruise and nibble chocolate fudge in Lake Delton. Enjoy a bed and breakfast in Stevens Point, visit the Amish quilt auction in Amherst, and watch the potato harvesters outracing hungry sandhill cranes in Plover. For a touch of history, tune in to the "talking houses" tour in Fond du Lac and visit the Old Wade stagecoach stop in Greenbush. Exercise your mind in a seminar at the rustic Baptist conference center in Green Lake. And above all, hike, hike, hike.

11. Kohler-Andrae State Parks

- Experience the unique sand dunes of the park.
- Enjoy Lake Michigan's multifaceted personality.
- Stroll along the long stretches of open, clean beach.

Park Information

These adjoining parks brag that they have the best air-conditioning in the Wisconsin system. Because of their location on wind-tossed Lake Michigan, the claim is not challenged. The topography is a mix of marsh, pine, and hardwood forests and beaches. The lake and land are the product of ancient Wisconsin's constant battle with ice and water. The area was affected by at least four ice age glaciers, with the last one gouging out today's lake basin. However, 9,000 years ago parts of Kohler-Andrae were under what was then prehistoric Lake Algonquin. Even at this early date, Paleo-Indian nomadic hunters were already living on the edge of the cold water.

The lake level dropped about 6,000 years ago when the retreating glaciers farther north opened new drainage around the current Lake Huron. The new lake was called Lake Nipissing, which existed here about 3,500 years ago. The beachline frrom this ancient waterway can still be seen in the northeast corner of Kohler-Andrae, about 14 feet above the current level. Over these centuries, Native Americans lived in the region, including effigy mound builders whose work can still be seen in Indian Mound Park to the north of Kohler-Andrae.

French trappers and traders explored the region in the late 1600s and early 1700s, with white settlement taking place in 1840. In 1927, one of the property owners donated 122 acres of dunes to the state, to be called the Terry Andrae State Park. In 1966, a 280-acre parcel was added to the original park as a memorial to John Michael Kohler, a Wisconsin industrialist who lived in nearby Sheboygan. The state has subsequently purchased another 600 acres, making the combined property about 1,000 acres. The park is divided into two units, both managed by the Department of Natural Resources.

Directions: Exit I-43 east onto County Highway V. Take V to KK, which leads to the park entrance on Old Park Road. The two parks are 4 miles south of Sheboygan.

Hours Open: Open year round from 6 A.M. to 11 P.M.

Facilities: A concession stand and bathhouse is located at the beach area. Telephones are available at the concession stand. There are 28 camping sites. One of the sites accommodates persons with physical disabilities. An enclosed picnic shelter with fireplace is across from the showers. There is also a nature center.

Permits and Rules: A state vehicle park sticker is required. The vehicle rates for state residents are $18 per year ($9 per year seniors, 65 or older). Day rates are $3. Out-of-state rates are $25 per year and $7.50 per day. A camping fee is additional. Quiet hours are 11 P.M. to 6 A.M. Camping and cooking in the park shelter are not permitted. Stay on the cordwalk when walking on the dune path.

Further Information: Contact Superintendent, Kohler-Andrae State Parks, 1520 Old Park Road, Sheboygan, WI 53081; 414-451-4080.

Other Points of Interest

The **Black River Trail** lies north of Kohler-Andrae about 1.5 miles. On the trail's eastern rim is the Black River, separating the reserve from the private Kohler Company Wildlife Refuge. The 2.5-mile trail system is on County Highway V, winding its way through a pine plantation and across a meadow. The trail is open for horses, mountain bikers, and hikers, as well as cross-country skiers in the winter. For details, call 414-451-4080.

The **Plank Road Trail** extends for 17 miles west from Sheboygan to near Greenbush, at the junction of State Highway 23 and Plank Road. The biking/hiking trail follows a pioneer plank road that led from the lake port to the interior. Call the Sheboygan County Convention and Visitors Bureau, 800-957-9497.

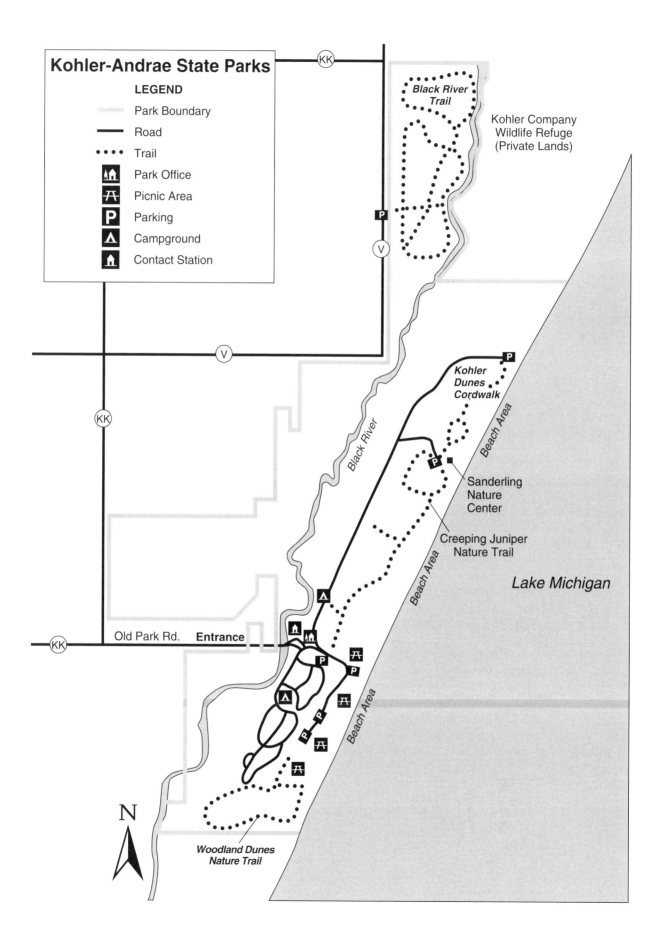

Kohler-Andrae State Parks

LEGEND

Park Boundary
Road
Trail
Park Office
Picnic Area
Parking
Campground
Contact Station

Black River Trail

Kohler Company Wildlife Refuge (Private Lands)

Black River

Kohler Dunes Cordwalk

Beach Area

Sanderling Nature Center

Creeping Juniper Nature Trail

Lake Michigan

Old Park Rd.   Entrance

Beach Area

Beach Area

Woodland Dunes Nature Trail

N

Kohler Dunes Cordwalk 👢👢

Distance One-Way: 2.5 miles

Estimated Hiking Time: 2 hours

Cautions: The park is located next to the lake; therefore there can be strong westerly winds that stir up the sand of the dunes. Eye protection is recommended. As you walk, note the boardwalk planks that make up the trail, protecting the dunes. It can be easy to lose your footing on the planks. In midsummer, the sand can get very hot since it soaks up much of the sun's heat. Be aware there is no shading foliage around the trail to provide protection.

Trail Directions: Park at the main parking lot directly after the entrance near the Visitor Information Center. The trail begins just north of the parking lot adjoining the trailhead to the beach. Or you can start behind the park office or from the group campsite to the south. Either way, the trail takes hikers through a fairly easy walk over the vast dunes. There are two lookout points and several benches overlooking Lake Michigan.

From the campsite **[1]**, move to the east up the wooden staircase to the top of the first dunes. Pick up the cordwalk (.1 mi.) **[2]** and begin the trek up and down above the lakeshore. Deer and skunk tracks can be seen cutting across the sand. At .5 mi., a bench **[3]** provides a wide view of the lake. A grove of wind-swept birches rears up to the left **[4]** as you approach a state natural area (.6 mi.). Sedge grass and small bushes tenaciously hang on along the way.

At 1 mi., an auxiliary trail **[5]** to the left carries walkers deeper into the dune system for a few hundred feet, to experience the expanse of shifting sand. Return to the main cordwalk and continue walking toward the Creeping Juniper Nature Trail Loop (1.3 mi.) **[6]**. Glacial ice had carried this sand southward. When the glacier melted, it deposited the sand, rocks, silt, and clay along this whole area. The mix was then covered by a high glacial lake.

As the water levels dropped, the wave actions carried the sand in and out of the lake. That, along with the wind, created the dunes. The wind sometimes creates deep depressions in the sand, exposing the lower levels of pebbles and small stones. At 1.5 mi., there is an open-field community of hardy meadow that has taken root in the thin soil. A clump

of Scotch pine (1.8 mi.) **[7]** was planted here years ago as a windbreak.

A few rare plant species are scattered around the vicinity. The endangered dune thistle can be found only in three other Wisconsin counties. Several white pines remain standing (1.9 mi.) **[8]** in a ragged cluster, survivors of the logging boom of the late 1800s and early 1900s. Goldenrod and thick spikes of wheatgrass dapple the area, and monarch butterflies flutter around the milkweed.

The Nature Trail Loop concludes at the front of the Sanderling Nature Center (2.1 mi.) **[9]**. The building is staffed by volunteers and park employees who present exhibits and environmental programs. Outside the center is the keel beam of the 90-foot schooner *Challenge,* which was built in Manitowoc in 1852. This "belle of Lake Michigan" burned and sank in 1918.

After touring the center, cross the parking lot and continue on the cordwalk up on higher dunes to the north. Along the way to the overlook at the end of the cordwalk are several benches. From the observation deck (2 mi.) **[10]**, you can watch the sailboats and fishing vessels far offshore. Return to the camping area by walking along the beach. Look for colorful rocks and shells and observe the gulls and other shorebirds.

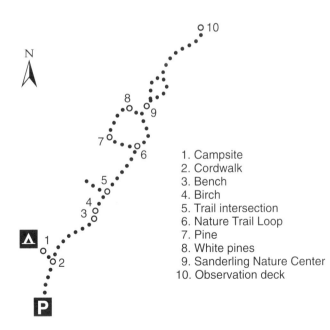

1. Campsite
2. Cordwalk
3. Bench
4. Birch
5. Trail intersection
6. Nature Trail Loop
7. Pine
8. White pines
9. Sanderling Nature Center
10. Observation deck

Woodland Dunes Nature Trail

Distance Round-Trip: 1.5 miles

Estimated Hiking Time: 45 minutes

Cautions: This trail goes through heavily wooded areas, so the insects tend to be thick. Watch out for mountain bikers.

Trail Directions: This trail begins just south of the campground area. After entering the park, take a right turn down by the campsites and look within the actual campground area for the signs for the trail.

The wood-chip trail runs through a heavily wooded section of the park **[1].** Walk east toward the lake past the picnic area (.1 mi.) **[2].** The path rolls along ridges and depressions of sand, earth, and rock where the whispering of the pines is a counterpoint to the lake's wave sounds. Turn right as the trail angles to the south (.2. mi.) **[3]** and walk along the rim of the woods and the beach.

You can see the lake from a slight rise while walking parallel to the shore. Off this area, Native Americans used to wade out waist-deep into the lake to net and spear giant whitefish. It is not uncommon to find their fishhooks, stone weights, and harpoon tips. As the wind blows the sand around, these artifacts are sometimes exposed after being hidden for centuries.

The path turns right (west) **[4]** at .4 mi. and makes its way along the south border of the park. There are several S-curves along the way (.7 mi.) **[5]** as the path flows between the stately trees. Even as you walk away from the shoreline, there is always the presence of the lake nearby, both with scents and with sounds.

Angle right (north) (.9 mi.) **[6]** as the trail sweeps around past the rocks and ridges that compose this far end of the park. To the left through the grove is the meandering Black River, mostly hidden by the undergrowth. Follow the path back to the park area or the picnic site.

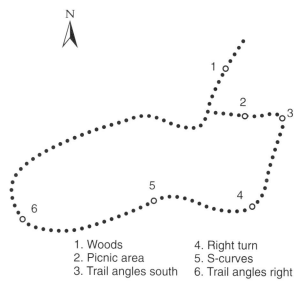

1. Woods
2. Picnic area
3. Trail angles south
4. Right turn
5. S-curves
6. Trail angles right

12. Harrington Beach State Park

- Walk around the rim of an old quarry lake.
- Take a nature tour into the woods fronting Lake Michigan.
- Count the deer feeding at sunset.

Park Information

During the first 20 years of the 20th century, the park was a limestone quarry. Now it has a 50-foot-deep, 26-acre lake with great views of Lake Michigan. Around the park, hikers can also see exposed limestone scraped by glaciers from the last ice age. In the 1880s, ownership of the land that now composes Harrington Beach changed hands many times. In the early 1890s, limestone was discovered, and quarrying operations started. A company town was built for the workers, most of whom were Italians supervised by Luxembourgers. Hikers can still see foundations of old structures around the park.

The Lake Shore Stone Company sold its land in 1925, and the buildings were razed or moved. The quarry gradually filled with water once the pumps were closed. Forest growth returned, running down to the lake where lawns and streets had once been. In 1958, the National Park Service identified the site as having potential for a park, since it was one of the few remaining undeveloped areas along this stretch of Lake Michigan shore. In 1968 the park was established and named after the late E.L. Harrington, a former superintendent of the Wisconsin Conservation Commission.

The current 637-acre park is also a wildlife refuge, with white-tailed deer and other animals regularly seen in the woods, lowlands, and meadows and along the lakefront.

Directions: The park is 10 miles north of Port Washington on I-43 to County Highway D, then 1 mile east.

Hours Open: 6 A.M. to 11 P.M. daily, year round.

Facilities: Picnic sites, playground, beach house, swimming area, hiking, and cross-country ski trails. There are no lifeguards on the beach. A free shuttle bus runs to the beach from an upper parking lot near Puckett's Pond and picnic area near the park entrance. There are several stops around the park where visitors can board or get off.

Permits and Rules: A state vehicle admission sticker is required. Rates for state residents are $18 per year and $9 per year for seniors (65 and older). Day passes are $3. Out-of-state rates are $25 per year and $7.50 per day. Observe speed limits on park roads. No off-road vehicles. Keep pets leashed. No swimming, boating, or diving allowed in Quarry Lake. Neither bikes nor pets are allowed on the trails.

Further Information: Contact Superintendent, Harrington Beach State Park, 531 County Highway D, Belgium, WI 53004; 414-285-3015.

Other Points of Interest

Wisconsin's **Ethnic Settlement Trail,** a state heritage tourism project, runs along Lake Michigan on state and county highways from the Illinois to the Michigan border. It passes settlements that still have a strong overseas flavor, including the village of Belgium near Harrington Beach State Park. The concentration of immigrants along this section of Wisconsin was one of the highest in the United States by the turn of the last century. Visitors along the trail can look at pioneer homesteads, take in festivals, and look through museums. The trail system is also part of the Lake Michigan Circle Tour, which runs entirely around the lake. For more information, call the tourism offices or chambers of commerce of towns along the way.

Cedarburg Bog, covering 1,000 acres, is one of the state's few remaining fens, or low, flat marshy areas. The University of Wisconsin Extension maintains a field office on the site and offers tours. There are several short hiking paths into the bog area, a prime bird-watching and plant-study area. The bog is about 20 miles southwest of Harrington Beach State Park. For more information, call the field station at 414-675-6844.

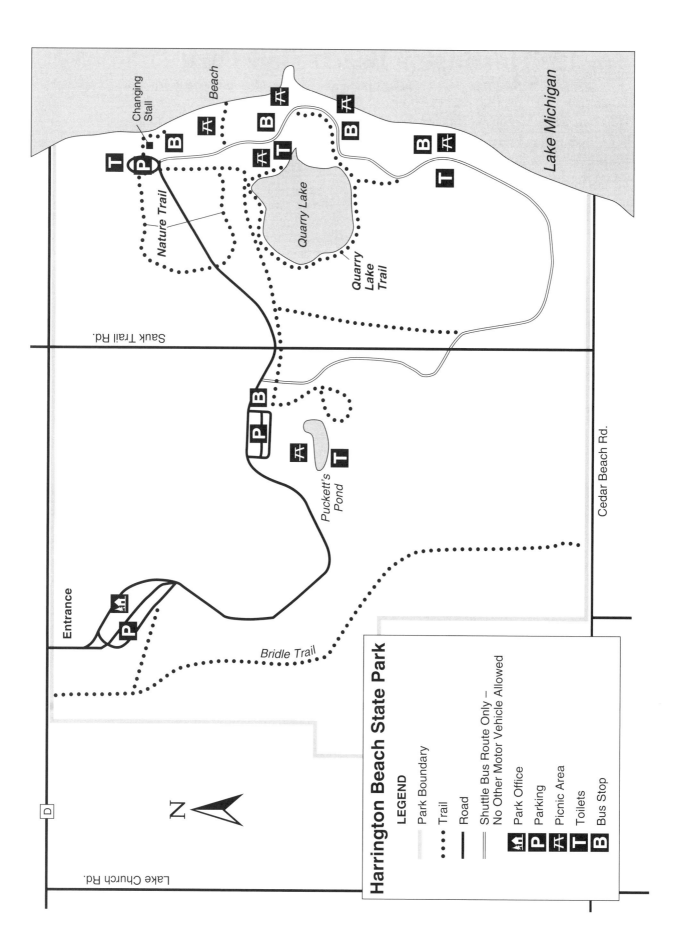

Lake Church Rd.

Sauk Trail Rd.

Cedar Beach Rd.

Entrance

Bridle Trail

Puckett's Pond

Nature Trail

Quarry Lake

Quarry Lake Trail

Beach

Changing Stall

Lake Michigan

N

Harrington Beach State Park

LEGEND

Park Boundary

· · · · Trail

Road

Shuttle Bus Route Only –
No Other Motor Vehicle Allowed

Park Office

P Parking

Picnic Area

T Toilets

B Bus Stop

Nature Trail 🥾

Distance Round-Trip: 1.4 miles

Estimated Hiking Time: 45 minutes

Cautions: Bring insect repellent during the spring and summer. Some sections of the path through the bottomlands can be wet and boggy after a rain.

Trail Directions: Leave your vehicle in the park's lot, walk across the picnic/play area to the west, and pick up the trailhead, which is marked by a sign.

The trail is initially covered with wood chips but eventually becomes a plank boardwalk (.1 mi.) **[1]** across a marshy section. There were once 35 million acres of such wetlands in Wisconsin, yet now most have been drained or developed. The boardwalk zigzags through the white cedar growth. At .2 mi., the trail again is back on firmer ground **[2]** with wood chips making a pungent, soft walk.

Along the path are several large boulders, called "erratics," left behind by retreating glaciers 10,000 years ago (.3 mi.) **[3]**. The path is level through this area, curving around rotting stumps and downed trees. Deer perform natural pruning operations on the cedar, birch, and beech in the area, so the hiker can see deep into the forest without the cover-up of low-hanging branches. Cedar thrives in such moist ground, as do the park's dogwood, basswood, and black ash.

Cross the park service road at .4 mi. **[4]** after passing through a plot of ferns. Leopard frogs live in the muddy ponds in the surrounding backwoods, with brown bats flitting overhead in the evening. Pass by or sit on a bench on the left side of the path. There is a lot of groundwater on the surface here because the dolomite rock underground does not allow seepage. In dry months, little ponds in the marshland dry up. To the left and right are several such depressions that fill with water in the rainy season (.5 mi.) **[5]**. In the spring, this stretch of pathway is ringed by Jack-in-the-pulpits and wild leeks.

The water here is nutrient rich because of the cedar, unlike more acidic spruce swamps. Pass the trail intersection (.6 mi.) **[6]** to the right (south) that links up with the Quarry Lake Trail. Cross a small culvert used for run-off from one low-lying wet spot

to another on the two sides of the trail. Pass a section of the trail near a stand of cedar about 100 years old (.8 mi.) **[7]**. The trees sprang up from saplings left when settlers cut back more mature trees a century ago to make shingles and fence posts. The French called the white cedar the *l'arbre de vie,* or "tree of life," because of its many uses.

At 1.4 mi., you pass what was called Little Quarry **[8]**. The first quarrying operations were conducted here in the late 1890s. Look for the six-foot-deep depression rimmed with trees. When more extensive quarrying began where the large lake now is, this small site was made into a wading pool for the stoneworkers' children. Leave the woods and aim straight ahead toward the lot where you parked.

But first turn right and look at the old lime kiln by the tree line. The beehive-shaped structure was used to change the raw limestone into lime that could be used for mortar and as fertilizer. The furnace was stoked with burning wood, creating a blaze as hot as 1,800 degrees Fahrenheit. Carbon dioxide was burned off, leaving the lime after a cooldown period of 48 hours. There is still some lime left at the bottom of the kiln from the last burning almost a century ago.

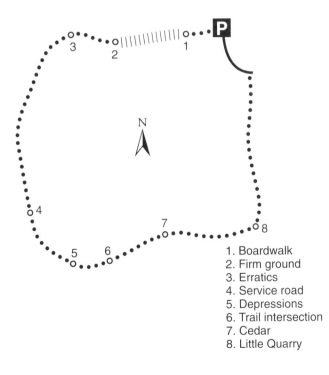

1. Boardwalk
2. Firm ground
3. Erratics
4. Service road
5. Depressions
6. Trail intersection
7. Cedar
8. Little Quarry

Quarry Lake Trail 👢👢

Distance Round-Trip: 2 miles

Estimated Hiking Time: 1.5 hours

Cautions: Stay away from the lake edge because there are steep drop-offs. However, split-rail fences along portions of the path provide some protection. Remember that swimming and diving are prohibited. There are no lifeguards.

Trail Directions: Start at the intersection of the Nature Trail and the Quarry Lake Trail in the white cedar bog. Enter the woods where you see the old lime kiln **[1]** south of the parking lot. The trail, however, can be joined at numerous spots around the lake, accessed from picnic areas and a roadway.

After leaving the Nature Trail, walk about 100 feet toward the lake to pick up the Quarry Lake Trail. Turn left at the junction. A picnic area can be seen through the trees (.1 mi.) **[2]**. The path rims the lake, leading to an inlet where the quarry's stone crusher once operated (.2 mi.) **[3]**. All that remain today are the machinery foundations seen in the clear water.

You now need to walk out on the park road to the left by proceeding through a brushy area. Across the street is Picnic Point (.3 mi.) **[4]**, an open area that was a ball field for the quarry company employees from 1900 to 1909. To the left are the foundations of a company foreman's home, moved several times as quarrying operations crept close to the front door. The house was eventually moved to the town of Belgium.

Walk along the lakeshore, past the beach, and enter a grove of trees. But first look at the anchor (.4 mi.) **[5]** on the shoreline. The 3,000-pound artifact was brought ashore by divers in 1964 as they explored the wreck of the *Niagara,* a ship that burned and sank just 60 feet offshore of this site in 1852. It is estimated that 169 persons died in the catastrophe.

The path goes through the trees and out to a spit of sandy land where there was once a 700-foot-long pier (.6 mi.) **[6]** from which stone was loaded onto ships. All that remain of the 50-foot-high structure are some pilings and foundations. Goldenrod softens the edges of the sand around the base of the few trees here. You can sit on a bench and look out over the lake.

Walk back toward the road and cross when you see the trail leading into the woods again (.7 mi.) **[7]**. After a few hundred feet, the path reemerges from the woods and runs along the road once more. Nearby was once a cabin where in the early 1900s a stone-cutter killed another in a fight. The murderer was convicted on the basis of evidence gleaned from the pattern of shotgun pellets found in the dead man and in the wall of the house. This marked one of the first instances in the nation's history of a court's finding someone guilty based on such forensic detail.

Pass a shuttle-bus stop where there are two sets of benches, and enter the woods. Pick up the trail (.8 mi.) **[8]**, crossing a small plank bridge on the way to the lake rim. You can see fossils embedded in the limestone along the route. The path now goes up and down the rolling landscape around Quarry Lake. At 1 mi. is a hole **[9]** bored through the rock; dynamite used to be dropped through the hole to shave off chunks of limestone. There are several bridges over gullies (1.1-1.4 mi.) **[10]** along this stretch on the lake's west side. Just stick to the trail by keeping the lake on the right side. The path then reconnects with the Nature Trail (1.9 mi) **[11]** and leads back out toward the parking lot.

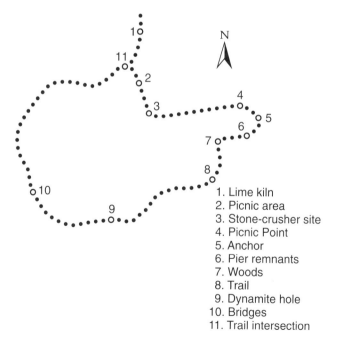

N

1. Lime kiln
2. Picnic area
3. Stone-crusher site
4. Picnic Point
5. Anchor
6. Pier remnants
7. Woods
8. Trail
9. Dynamite hole
10. Bridges
11. Trail intersection

13. Point Beach State Forest

- Tour the nearby Point Beach Nuclear Plant, a facility that produces one-sixth of all the electricity used in Wisconsin.
- Search for artifacts from old shipwrecks.
- Loaf on sandy beaches along Lake Michigan.

Park Information

The Point Beach State Forest includes 2,900 acres of forest bordered by Lake Michigan on the east, with 6 miles of prime beach frontage. There are several demonstration plantings of various types of trees, red pine being the hardiest. Pine plantings were begun 40 years ago, with Scotch pine not taking well to the soil. Dead trees are being thinned out, but some have been retained as a buffer and wild-animal shelter. Red oak, red pine, and maple seedlings are taking root, with saplings seen throughout the forest.

Frontiersman Peter Rawley operated an Indian trading post on this point of land that bears his name. But Rawley Point is better known as a graveyard of ships. During the days of wooden sailing vessels, more than 30 schooners and brigs sank in the treacherous rocky waters just off the point. Even today, pieces of these old shipwrecks sometimes wash ashore.

The Coast Guard has operated and maintained lighthouses along here since 1853. The steel lighthouse seen by today's hikers was built in 1894. It is one of the brightest on the Great Lakes, being visible 19 miles out on the lake; it operates from 30 minutes before sunset to 30 minutes after sunrise.

Directions: The forest is located 5 miles northeast of Two Rivers on County Highway O.

Hours Open: Open year round. Day-use areas are closed from 11 P.M. to 6 A.M. The concession stand is open from 11 A.M. to 4:30 P.M., Monday; 10 A.M. to 6:30 P.M., Tuesday through Thursday; 10 A.M. to 8:30 P.M., Friday; 9 A.M. to 7:30 P.M., Saturday; and 9 A.M. to 5 P.M., Sunday. The Nature Center is open from 11 A.M. to 4 P.M., Monday through Friday.

Facilities: The park has 127 campsites, 59 of which have electricity. Reservations are accepted. There is an indoor group camp for 18 and an outdoor group camp for 50; reservations are required. Six campsites with electricity are maintained in winter. Camping and picnic facilities for persons with physical disabilities are available. There are 10 miles of hiking trails, a nature center, a concession stand, and picnic areas.

Permits and Rules: Fires are allowed only in fire pits or grills. Pets must be leashed. A state park vehicle admission sticker is required. Visitors to the campsites must leave by 11 P.M.

Further Information: Contact Forest Manager, Point Beach State Forest, 9400 County Highway O, Two Rivers, WI 54241; 414-794-7480.

Other Points of Interest

The **Point Beach Nuclear Plant Energy Information Center** gives free tours daily, year round. The Center also has a .5-mile nature trail relating the role that plants and animals play in the environment. An observation tower outside the building allows good views of the lake and surrounding forestland. For details, call 414-794-7771.

The **Manitowoc Maritime Museum** is the largest such museum on the Great Lakes. Open daily year round, the facility has displays on shipbuilding, wrecks, and commercial fishing. There is even a facade of the city's 19th-century waterfront. The submarine USS *Cobia,* a national historic landmark, is moored behind the museum. During World War II, Manitowoc plants produced dozens of such subs for the military. Call at 414-684-0218 for more information.

Park Trails

Blue Loop 🥾🥾—5.5 miles—The trail is a continuation of the Red Loop, extending farther to the south along the marshland making up the heart of the Point Beach Forest. The trail is an up-and-down route over small hummocks, framed by pine and cedar. Scattered poplar and birch are among the primary trees.

Yellow Loop 🥾🥾—7.2 miles—This trail is an extension of the Blue and Red Loops, moving across similar terrain. It makes a turnaround at Molash Creek in the southern portion of the forest and comes back north. The entire route also doubles as a cross-country ski trail, with routes marked for one-way travel.

Swales Nature Trail 🥾—.5 mile—Located at the north end of the playground and picnic area of the state forest, the trail is a self-guided look at the region's flora and fauna. The wood-chip path weaves in and around stands of maple, beech, cedar, and pine trees, with signs telling hikers what they are viewing.

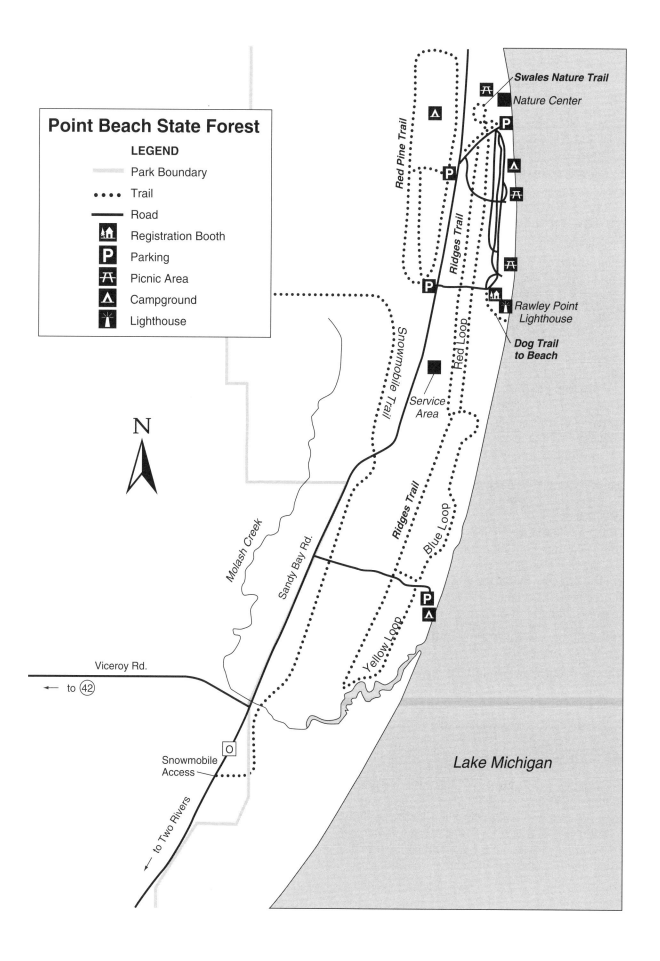

Point Beach State Forest

LEGEND

- ▦ Park Boundary
- •••• Trail
- —— Road
- 🏠 Registration Booth
- P Parking
- ⛱ Picnic Area
- ⛺ Campground
- 🗼 Lighthouse

Swales Nature Trail

Nature Center

Red Pine Trail

Ridges Trail

Red Loop

Service Area

Rawley Point Lighthouse

Dog Trail to Beach

Snowmobile Trail

Ridges Trail

Blue Loop

Molash Creek

Sandy Bay Rd.

Yellow Loop

N

Viceroy Rd.

← to 42

O

Snowmobile Access

to Two Rivers

Lake Michigan

Ridges Trail 👢👢

Distance Round-Trip: 3 miles

Estimated Hiking Time: 2 hours

Cautions: Bring insect repellent because the trail runs along marshland almost its entire length.

Trail Directions: Begin at the Nature Center parking lot and look for the marker at the entrance to the forest.

Leaving the parking lot **[1]**, head west into the maple forest and proceed down a slope to the playground and picnic area (.1 mi.) **[2]**. Turn left and walk along the tree line to the service road (.2 mi.) **[3]**. Cross the road; you will see a marshy pond about 500 feet to the right and the forest campground to the left. The southbound track closely parallels the northbound trail, with the former on a lower level than the latter. Cross a second forest road (.5 mi.) **[4]**

and aim for the picnic shelter, with the trail continuing around the structure and splitting as it hits the tree line again.

The trail is on a hummock running along swamp areas on both the right and the left. Cattails and marsh reeds are thick along both sides of the trail, just beyond the line of pines, spruce, and cedar. There are many fallen trees because of the shallowness of the soil. The trail is relatively straight, but undulating. There are some raspberry bushes along the pathway (.7 mi.) **[5]**, with ferns tucked into the shaded areas where it is cool and damp. Cross the park entrance road (1 mi.) **[6]**, where there is a bench overlooking the marsh. A pause there is not suggested during mosquito and mayfly season in midsummer.

After crossing the road, you'll see more red pine and cedar trees separating the trail from the marsh (1.2 mi.) **[7]**. At 1.5 mi., you can see the forest service area to the right **[8]**, with a wood yard and repair facilities. Angle left as the trail goes among the trees, with the turnaround back north at 1.6 mi. **[9]**. Proceed past several low-lying areas that can become muddy when it rains.

As you walk this trail, the southbound route is not visible to the left. But the terrain of this trail is also up-and-down. Keep walking straight through the trees and cross the same service roads you met on the southbound route to return to the trailhead.

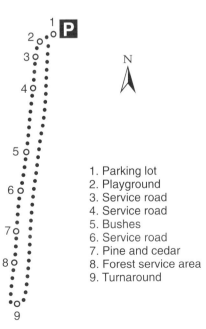

1. Parking lot
2. Playground
3. Service road
4. Service road
5. Bushes
6. Service road
7. Pine and cedar
8. Forest service area
9. Turnaround

Red Pine Trail 👢👢

Distance Round-Trip: 3.1 miles

Estimated Hiking Time: 2.6 hours

Cautions: This is a hilly section of trail, with long stretches of undulating landscape. Liberal use of insect repellent is recommended.

Trail Directions: The trail begins in the parking lot located west of County Highway O, directly across from the forest entrance road.

Walk straight ahead into the pine plantation **[1]** from the parking lot and proceed down a long sandy slope (.1 mi.). This is a narrow track through patches of goldenrod and other surface plants that range along the edges of the trail. The path immediately progresses into an up-and-down topography (.2 mi.) **[2]** that the hiker confronts for the remainder of the jaunt.

By moving straight ahead, you cut across the midsection of the Red Pine system. Pine cones cover the ground, with thick stands of ferns on the shaded north slopes. There are several steep gullies and ridges in quick succession. (.4 mi.) **[3]**. Arriving at the intersection of the trails on the far side of the loop (.5 mi.) **[4]**, turn a hard right and plunge into the thick maple woods. This is easy walking at first because the wide path doubles as a lumber road. It goes through several S-curves, with loads of fresh gravel dumped and spread at strategic but often muddy sections (.7 mi.) **[5]**.

There are logged areas on both sides of the route (.8-.9 mi.) **[6]**. Several deer paths cross the main hiking trail, and careful watchers can often see the white-tails browsing in the morning and late afternoon.

Turn right as the trail meets the northern end of the forest (1.2 mi.) **[7]**; angle down a slope, turn still more to the right, then left, then right again before finally straightening a bit. Blue jays flit through the trees and hawks wheel overhead, visible whenever the tree canopy clears.

Pass through the group camp area (1.5 mi.) **[8]** with its pump, shelters, and open space for tents. You need to walk along the left rim of the grounds and find the trail on the opposite side of the camp. The trail picks up past a large dumpster with its sign warning that fish entrails should be put in the freezer back at the main station. Continue going south along the path that parallels County Highway O. You can hear the vehicles better than you can see them through the thick brush.

There are many damp areas (1.6 mi.) **[9]** in the woods along here, with small frogs hopping across the trail wherever there is mud. Keep going until you leave the forest at the parking lot again. If you wish, you can keep going on the southern section of the Red Pine Trail, which mirrors the north loop.

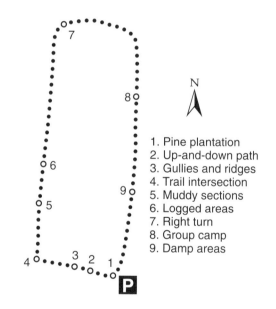

1. Pine plantation
2. Up-and-down path
3. Gullies and ridges
4. Trail intersection
5. Muddy sections
6. Logged areas
7. Right turn
8. Group camp
9. Damp areas

14. Lower Cato Falls

- View a rustic waterfall tumbling over rocks.
- Sit on a bench and watch deer come to a river to drink in the evening.
- Climb down a steep set of stairs in order to walk along a riverbank.

Park Information

Lower Cato Falls encompasses 84 acres of open space, wood, and river. The upland area of the park has been developed into a picnic and ball-playing site, while the lower area has been kept in its natural state.

The Manitowoc River forms the park's northern boundaries, flowing through a gorge that has interesting rock formations and a waterfall. The demolition of a dam along the Manitowoc at Manitowoc Rapids has encouraged trout spawning, with good angling results for fishing fans. The park has about 2,000 feet of river frontage. Two wooden staircases lead from the bluff top to the river.

Directions: Lower Cato Falls is 8 miles west of the city of Manitowoc on County Highway JJ.

Hours Open: Dawn to dusk, daily, year round.

Facilities: Picnic site, toilets, water, playground, hiking trails, scenic overlooks.

Permits and Rules: No fires. Keep pets leashed. No camping.

Further Information: Contact Manitowoc County Planning and Park Commission, 1701 Michigan Avenue, Manitowoc, WI 54220; 414-683-4185.

Other Points of Interest

Point Beach State Forest includes more than 2,900 acres of forest land, bounded by six miles of sandy beach along Lake Michigan. The Coast Guard has operated a lighthouse at the site since 1853. A steel tower replaced an old brick structure in 1894. Rising 113 feet above the water, it is one of the tallest such guard structures on the lake. The forest is located at 9400 County Trunk Highway O near Two Rivers. Call 414-794-7480 for more information.

Ed Beners, a local druggist, is credited with inventing the ice cream sundae in Two Rivers in 1881. A replica of his ice cream parlor is found in the **Two Rivers Historical Society,** 1622 W. Jefferson Street, Two Rivers, WI 54241; 888-857-3529 or 414-793-2490.

Don't miss the boat! Take the **Lake Michigan car ferry** from Manitowoc to Ludington, Michigan from May through October. Crossing time is four hours, which beats a two-day trip driving around the lake to get to the opposite side. For reservations and other information, call 800-841-4243.

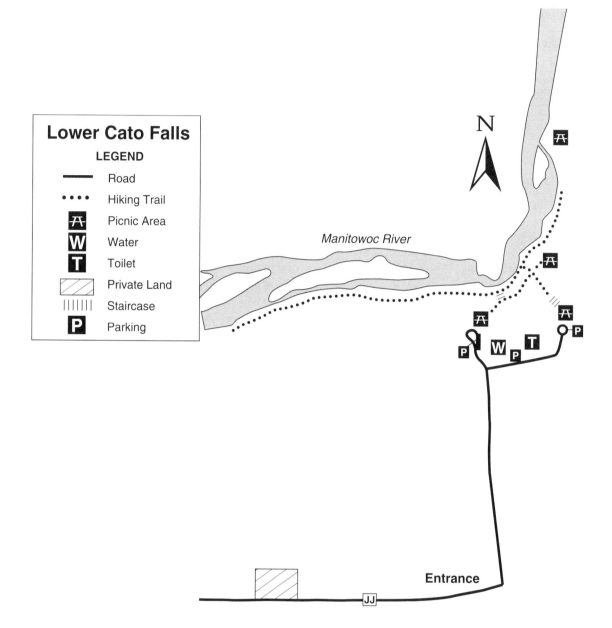

Trail A 👢👢

Distance Round-Trip: 1.2 miles

Estimated Hiking Time: 45 minutes

Cautions: There is a steep staircase down the slope. In addition, the trail runs along the riverbank and is not always level.

Trail Directions: Park in the playground parking lot at the east end of the park. Walk across the grass toward the sign that says "Watch Your Step." A bench is by the trailhead here.

Go down the stairs after passing the sign **[1].** There are some 80 steps to the bottom, but stepping is better than rolling through the brush down the hill to reach the riverbank. At the bottom of the stairs, walk straight ahead to the river, about 100 feet (.1 mi.) **[2].** Turn left amid the cedar trees and follow the path around a corner to the left. Sit on a bench there and look through the foliage at the waterfall upriver from this point. The branches make for a fine frame.

Now walk about 25 feet to the right and stand on the rock overhang, about 50 feet above the cascade. A split-rail barricade keeps you away from the drop-off; however, it is obvious that many people crawl through the railing and stand close to the edge to take photos. Continue to the right and pick up the dirt path that leads along the top of the bank through the thick forest. You pass through the park's lower picnic area on the right (.3 mi.) **[3].** Keep walking on the trail as it sweeps along above the water.

The path winds in and out of the trees, with a high slope to the right. The trail is often uneven, with exposed roots and some rocks, so be careful. Several outcroppings of limestone above the river can be seen through the foliage on the left. Climb higher on the path as it makes its way along. From here you get a better view of the mud-brown flow below the lip of

the bluff (.4 mi.) **[4].** The trail continues into a brushy area through which you can scramble to reach the river bottom (.5 mi.) **[5].**

Sandbars, reeds, and rushes come into view along the way. Note the numerous animal tracks. Deer, raccoons, muskrats, and other creatures use this part of the bank for their water source. Some quiet pools across the river provide a haven for ducks. Walk along the shore for another 50 feet or so before the water blocks the route. Retrace your steps and walk back along the river for a few hundred feet.

Downed trees and muck prevent any more walking here, so climb back up the steep slope and find the trail. Follow the path back to the scenic overlook and the stairway. You can either return to your vehicle or continue walking to the west.

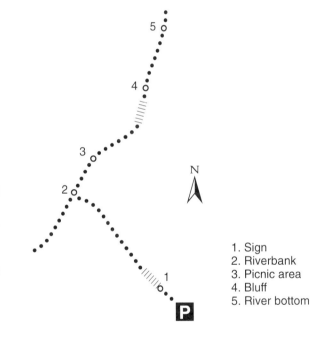

1. Sign
2. Riverbank
3. Picnic area
4. Bluff
5. River bottom

Trail B 🥾🥾

Distance Round-Trip: 1 mile

Estimated Hiking Time: 45 minutes

Cautions: There are many muddy patches along the way, with water flowing down the hill into the river. Be prepared for your walking shoes or boots to get wet and muddy.

Trail Directions: You can pick up this trail from the bottom of the stairwell leading to Trail A or from a second stairwell further to the west.

Leave from the waterfall observation area **[1]** at the foot of the first set of stairs. Approach the falls by walking along the bluff until you come to a cleared space (.2 mi.) **[2]**. You can now stand on the edge of the bluff and have a better look at the small waterfall. Keep walking along the river, keeping the bluff on your right side. You pass the second stairwell leading to the top of the hill. You can either climb back up or keep walking.

Beyond the stairs, the trail degenerates because of the water run-off. Park officials indicate, however, that this leg will be expanded and improved over the next few years. There are many burned logs littering the slope here, the result of vandalism. Cross a narrow bridge over one gully (.3 mi.) **[3]**, under which there is a stream flowing into the river. Beyond the bridge is a muddy, boggy area (.4 mi.) **[4]**; you either slog through or you can toss some of those logs into the muck to make your own plank walkway.

Cross another boardwalk laid down by park staff and proceed as far as you can until the trail ends in a brushy area. You now need to retrace your steps to the stairs and return to your vehicle.

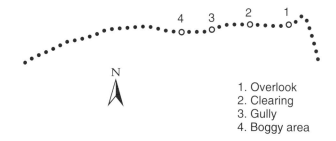

N

1. Overlook
2. Clearing
3. Gully
4. Boggy area

15. Kettle Moraine State Forest, Northern Unit

Forest Information

The northern unit of the Kettle Moraine Forest is a 29,000-acre spread of mixed hardwoods, marsh, and prairie in southeastern Wisconsin. The rugged landscape is the result of glacial action over hundreds of thousands of years. The last glacier retreated from the state only 10,000 years ago, leaving behind pothole lakes called kettles and depositing piles of rubble wherever the land had not been scraped flat when the sheets finally melted. Long ridges called moraines, conical hills called kames, and meandering ancient glacial riverbeds called eskers make for interesting hiking opportunities.

The Kettle Moraine Forest is a mixed bag of hardwoods, prairie, and marsh spreading through both Fond du Lac and Sheboygan Counties where there were once sheets of ice a mile (or more) high. The Kettle Moraine State Forest is popular with outdoors lovers who enjoy the hunting, fishing, camping, boating, hiking, snowmobiling, and cross-country skiing opportunities. Only about 1.5 hours north of Milwaukee, its trails are within easy access of the state's major urban areas. It offers plenty of challenge for the most avid hiker because of the numerous hills and ravines.

The northern unit of the Kettle Moraine State Forest is rich in history. The Northwest Fur Company and American Fur Company operated trading posts throughout the area in the 18th and 19th centuries. The fur-rich region had many other advantages as well. Early settlers eyed the timber and the potential of water power for their mills.

Directions: The forest headquarters is on Highway G, midway into the forest, on the east side of the road adjacent to Mauthe Lake. The borders of the northern unit cut generally along county highways. On the far north is County Highway C, with County Highway H on the far south. Along the west are county highways S, DD and State Highway 67, and on the east side of the park are Highways S, W, V, U, D and A. It is best to look at a state forest map to determine the exact boundaries.

Hours Open: The forest headquarters office is open from 7:45 A.M. until 4:30 P.M. weekdays. Offices at campgrounds are open from 9:15 A.M. to 10:30 P.M., Monday through Saturday, and from 9:15 A.M. to 7 P.M., Sunday, between Memorial Day and Labor Day. The recreation areas are open until 11 P.M. daily. The Ice Age Visitor Center is open from 8:30 A.M. to 4 P.M. weekdays, and from 9:30 A.M. to 5 P.M. weekends, year round.

Facilities: Facilities differ throughout various areas of the park.

Permits and Rules: A state park vehicle pass is required. Vehicle rates for state residents are $18 per year and $9 for senior citizens (65 and older). Day passes are $3. Out-of-state rates are $25 per year and $7.50 per day. Rules vary from area to area throughout the park.

Further Information: Contact Forest Supervisor, Kettle Moraine State Forest, Northern Unit, N1765 Highway G, Campbellsport, WI 53010; 414-626-2116.

Other Points of Interest

The **Wade House Stagecoach Inn** and the **Wesley June Carriage Museum** in Greenbush are popular visitor attractions in the Kettle Moraine. The facilities, operated by the State Historical Society of Wisconsin, are open daily from May through October. The inn was built before the Civil War to serve travelers making the long runs between northern and southern Wisconsin. Call 414-526-3271 for more information.

The **Henry S. Reuss Ice Age Interpretive Center** near Campbellsport offers detailed exhibits on how the land was formed by the glaciers. From the deck in back of the building, visitors can see many landmarks such as Dundee Mountain and other features made by the ice sheets. For details, call 414-533-8322.

There are many **camping** opportunities in the northern Kettle Moraine. Long and Mauthe Lakes have family campgrounds. There are also backpacking shelters and group camps in various sections of the forest. Campers can fish, hike, hunt, ride horses, ski, and bird-watch. They can also take advantage of nature hikes and free evening programs during the camping season from April through October. Call the forest headquarters at 414-626-2116 for more details.

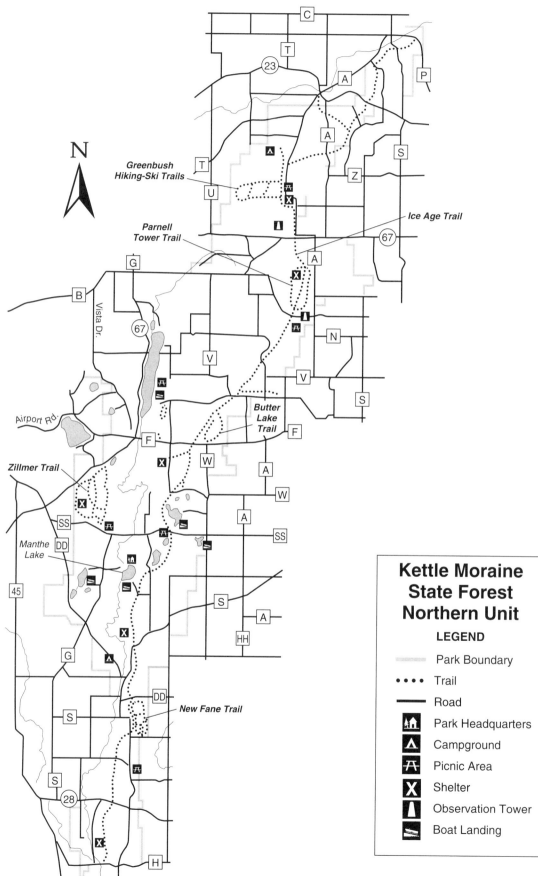

N

Greenbush
Hiking-Ski Trails

Parnell
Tower Trail

Ice Age Trail

Vista Dr.

Airport Rd.

Butter
Lake
Trail

Zillmer Trail

Manthe
Lake

New Fane Trail

**Kettle Moraine
State Forest
Northern Unit**

LEGEND

Park Boundary

•••• Trail

—— Road

Park Headquarters

Campground

Picnic Area

Shelter

Observation Tower

Boat Landing

Greenbush Hiking and Ski Trails

- Hike over interesting geological formations in Sheboygan County.
- Visit the Old Wade House, a nearby historic site.
- Look for white-tailed deer, turkeys, and other wildlife.

Directions: The trail system is 2.5 miles south of Greenbush and 1.5 miles north of State Highway 67 on Kettle Moraine Drive.

Facilities: Rest rooms, shelter, scenic views, bridle path, cross-country ski trails.

Permits and Rules: The 5.1-mile Yellow Trail is closed to biking each year through the small-game-hunting season.

Trails

Yellow Trail 👢👢👢👢—5.1 miles—This is the most difficult trail in the Greenbush system. Its length, as well as its up-and-down quality, is sure to test any devoted hiker. The paths run along high moraines and deep into valleys. Most of the trek is through mixed hardwood forests, with maple, basswood, and oak the predominant species. The trail also crisscrosses several pine plantations. Wildlife in large numbers hide amid the trees, rushes, and grasses.

Pink Trail 👢👢👢👢—.7 mile—This is another tough test for the hiker; the trail seems twice as long as it actually is because of the rough terrain it traverses. The trail is picked up near the overflow parking lot and concludes at the Greenbush Kettle. A kettle is a depression in the land caused when ice was covered with earth and eventually melted, causing the ground to collapse to form a bowl-shaped dip.

Red Trail 👢👢

Distance Round-Trip: 1.5 miles

Estimated Hiking Time: 1 hour

Cautions: The trail is not surfaced, so watch out for stones and loose gravel.

Trail Directions: Leave from the overflow parking lot on Kettle Moraine Drive. Look for the trail marker posts with bands of the appropriate colors around the top.

The trail heads down a wide pathway shared by the Yellow, Green, Pink, and Ice Age trails for the first .3 mi. The Red Trail then swings into the maples and oaks while the Green Trail moves north and the other two head south **[1].** Proceed ahead on the rolling pathway that extends through clouds of mosquitoes on hot summer days. The bugs find the thick vegetation a haven, so insect repellent can make life a trifle easier. Woodpeckers, ruffed grouse, ravens, and other birds rummage around in the trees.

The trail runs parallel to the Green Trail for the next .5 mi. This terrain is similar to that of the Green stretch, with a series of sharp hills and deep valleys (.6 mi.) **[2].** There is a kettle to the left, with a marshy area at the bottom (.7 mi.) **[3].** Cross the bridle path and loop to the south and then to the east through the forest. The trees are thicker here; maples, ash, birch, shagbark hickory, and oak jockey for position, their canopy being 50 to 60 feet overhead. The trail is littered with leaves, making for a quiet walk. Yet this can be slippery when wet.

Pass the intersection with the tough Pink Trail (1.3 mi.) **[4]** on a high point of the ridge and then move along downhill to the overflow lot and trailhead. There are picnic tables here on which to rest or just collapse in the grass under an oak.

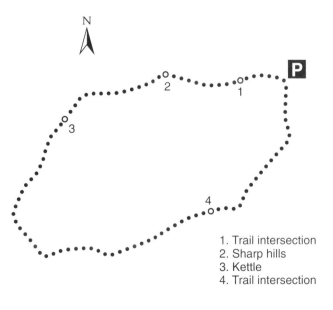

1. Trail intersection
2. Sharp hills
3. Kettle
4. Trail intersection

Green Trail 👢👢👢👢

Distance Round-Trip: 3.6 miles

Estimated Hiking Time: 3.1 hours

Cautions: There are many slopes and narrow ridges. Stay away from cliffsides. The trail is not surfaced, so be aware of rocks, roots, and loose gravel. Insects are pesty in the spring and summer.

Trail Directions: Park at the lot near the Greenbush Kettle, walk south to the Ice Age Trail marker, and pick up the Green Trail where it intersects with the Ice Age pathway.

Ascend the slight grassy slope running under the east-west power lines [1]. Turn right (west) when leaving the Ice Age Trail and walk through the tall grass. At .2 mi., there is a pine plantation on the left [2]. The clearing under the power line to the right is overgrown with brush and thus difficult to see over. For the next .25 mi., you will be going along a narrow path between the lines and red pine trees. At .3 mi. is an intersection with a snowmobile track [3]. Take that to the right (north) and cross a bridle path. The Green Trail then loops to the west, going under the power lines again, and continues on into a mixed hardwood forest.

The Green and Yellow Trails coincide, running over the same track for .25 mi. when the path swings south. Follow the yellow and green blazes on the trees alongside the trail. This is very hilly, a challenge for the mountain bikers who also use this trail. At the top of one hill (1 mi.) [4] is a bench available for a well-deserved rest. Summer mosquitoes shorten any pause, however. Cross under the power lines again; from here, the trail goes up another hill. The Yellow Trail splits off to the left (1.2 mi.) [5]. The woods thicken, with heavy stands of old maple, shagbark hickory, and oak jostling for space.

At 1.5 mi. is another bench [6] on the left of the trail. The path now slip-slides along loose gravel and half-hidden stones to make an angle to the west. Stick to the trail and look down at the deep kettle on the

left side. At 1.9 mi., the trail turns sharply to the right (north) [7] and you run parallel to the Yellow Trail, which can be seen occasionally through the undergrowth about 50 feet lower on the bluff.

The trail narrows to a rough track (2.1 mi.) [8] as it runs along the top of a moraine and plunges into a valley. It is almost a gallop down the path to prevent slipping. The trail then levels out, but ascends again quickly with a right turn at the peak. Go through the thick underbrush, with its raspberry branches sticking out to scratch unprotected skin as you pass. At 2.7 mi., cross the bridle path again while keeping an eye open for horses, which have the right-of-way [9]. The Green, Red, Ice Age, and Yellow Trails now join (3 mi.) [10] and run along the same track to the overflow parking lot where there is a picnic area. Many bikers and hikers set up small umbrella tents in a glade here, although it is not an official campground.

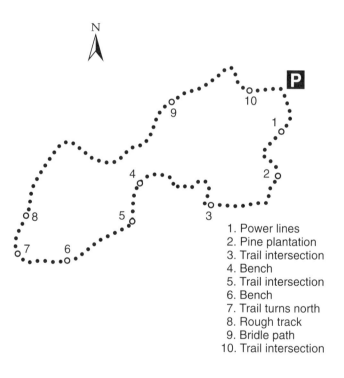

1. Power lines
2. Pine plantation
3. Trail intersection
4. Bench
5. Trail intersection
6. Bench
7. Trail turns north
8. Rough track
9. Bridle path
10. Trail intersection

Parnell Tower

- Climb to top of an observation tower for a vista of Sheboygan County.
- Connect with the Ice Age Trail.
- Find wild turkeys and white-tailed deer.

Directions: The Parnell Tower Trail entrance is 2 miles north of State Highway 67 on County High-way A. Turn left (west) on County Highway U and drive .25 mile to the forest entrance.

Facilities: Hiking trails, bridle paths, snowmobiling, trail shelter, Ice Age Trail connection, observation tower, rest rooms, water, phone, picnic tables.

Permits and Rules: No camping. No food or beverages are allowed at the top of the tower.

Ice Age Trail 👢👢👢👢

Distance One-Way: 2.6 miles

Estimated Hiking Time: 1.7 hours

Cautions: The trail is narrow, meandering over rough terrain. Since it is not a loop, hikers must either retrace their steps to return to their vehicle or have a pickup arranged for the conclusion of the walk.

Trail Directions: There are two entrances to the trail. The first is on the south side, along County Highway U (Kettle Moraine Scenic Drive). However, hikers have to park along the side of the road—a dangerous situation because of the close quarters. The best parking is on State Highway 67, about 1.5 mi. west of County Highway A. Pull up a small rise to the south of the highway where there is a gravel patch at the edge of a prairie ecosystem. Across the highway to the north is the Greenbush link of the Ice Age Trail.

Leave your vehicle and cut eastward through the grass for about 200 feet to pick up the trail where it crosses Highway 67. The meadow **[1]** is an easy passage through an Eden of goldenrod, milkweed, blazing star, prairie smoke, big bluestem, asters, and other prairie flowers. Turn south (right) and proceed through the meadow toward a spruce plantation. The tree line is about .3 mi. from the road and back up a gentle rise. This is a good place to spot turkeys in the summer, since they enjoy the tree shade on hot afternoons.

Continue down the trail, which runs between two sets of plantings. The trail connects after .5 mi. with a bridle path **[2]**. The trail makes a sharp left (east) (.7 mi.) **[3]** and goes straight for .12 mi. before making another turn to the right (south) **[4]**. From here the trail narrows as it floats up and down over more hilly terrain and crosses the bridle path again. It passes under a power line at 1.2 mi. **[5]**.

The path then angles through thick tree cover and along a fence line. After this it swings back to the east, and hikers proceed through a marsh area. In the spring, small frogs called peepers perform an aria. Bullfrogs boom their basso profundo in the summer and autumn. Move back into the tree line again on the south side of the marsh where you cross the bridle path once more **[6]**. At 2.5 mi., you intersect with the Parnell Tower Trail **[7]** at the backpackers' shelter just off the trail to the left. The two trails coincide for .25 mi. before the Parnell Tower Trail spins off to the left.

Continue on through more forest cover to exit on County Highway U **[8]**. Either keep moving ahead on the Ice Age Trail or turn around and trek back to your vehicle the way you came. An alternative is to walk east along the highway and enter the Parnell Tower Trail entrance to the state forest. You can then return over a different route, picking up the Ice Age Trail where the Parnell Tower Trail bypasses the bridle path at its north end near the power lines.

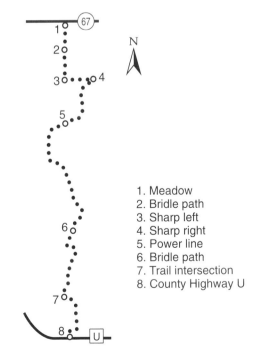

1. Meadow
2. Bridle path
3. Sharp left
4. Sharp right
5. Power line
6. Bridle path
7. Trail intersection
8. County Highway U

Parnell Tower Trail 👢👢👢👢

Distance Round-Trip: 2.9 miles

Estimated Hiking Time: 2.5 hours

Cautions: The trail involves steep slopes and rough segments with partially hidden roots and rocks. Be sure to have plenty of insect repellent.

Trail Directions: Park in the lot on County Highway U and walk due north to the trailhead. The women's rest room is on the left and the men's is on the right.

The trail immediately begins an ascent up a gravel path **[1]** and leads to a series of log steps that go about halfway up the hill. At .2 mi. is a bench **[2]** for resting and looking out over the maple forest. However, summertime bugs will probably prevent much of a pause. At .3 mi. are 63 additional steps **[3]** that lead to the base of the observation tower at the top of the hill.

There are 96 steps to the top of the tower, where hikers can get a panorama of the entire Kettle Moraine northern region. From this vantage point it is easy to identify the various types of glacial landscape. Up to 45 mi. in each direction can be seen on clear days. Descend the tower and pick up the trail to the left (east). The path descends down a rough, rocky hillside into the maple forest. At .4 mi., hikers encounter a series of S-curves **[4]** as the trail meanders around boulders and stumps and up and down ridges. Several downed trees (.5 mi.) **[5]** lie across the path. But step over or around them and continue walking. At .7 mi. there is a large pile of rocks on the left, the remains of a fence line that was there long ago **[6].** The rocks continue along the right side of the trail for about .12 mi. The path cuts through the pile and then runs along the right side. The rocks run out at the edge of a deep gully (.9 mi.) **[7].**

From the hills, one can often hear the snuffing of startled white-tailed deer hiding in the undergrowth near a stand of birch (1.1 mi.) **[8].** The Kettle Moraine State Forest is home of hundreds of the deer, plus foxes, skunks, chipmunks, and numerous other animals. A sun-filled glade is next (1.2 mi.) **[9],** rimmed by oaks, with a kettle bog off to the right. Go down the slope to the bottom of the next ravine **[10],** over a rocky section of trail.

Then next leg of the path is a roller coaster of hills, valleys, and turns over the rough-and-tumble glacial landscape. A thick birch grove stands out starkly against the rest of the forest at 1.6 mi. **[11].** Pass under a high-tension line that runs along the far north end of the trail (1.8 mi.) **[12].** Here you swing to the left and head back south again through thickets of raspberry bushes scattered around a glade.

The run to the south is mostly more of the glaciated landscape; it is as if you are walking across a mini-Rockies. To the right is a bridle path, but it is too far out of sight in the summer to see any horse-folk. At 2.5 mi., you pass a backpackers' shelter **[13]** that can sleep up to 10 persons. A permit is needed to stay there; the paperwork can be completed at the forest service headquarters. Near the shelter is the intersection with one link of the Ice Age Trail, part of the 1,000-mi. system that traces the Wisconsin rim of those old glaciers of eons ago. The two trails coincide for the next .25 mi. When they split again, the Ice Age connection continues straight south and the Parnell Tower Trail aims left (east). Go up a steep hill on this path. You come out about 100 feet south of the observation tower. Take the steps to the right and descend to the parking lot.

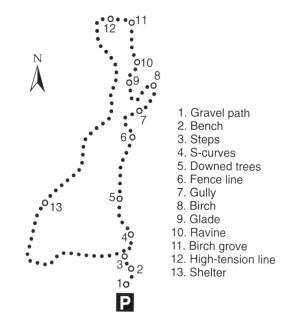

1. Gravel path
2. Bench
3. Steps
4. S-curves
5. Downed trees
6. Fence line
7. Gully
8. Birch
9. Glade
10. Ravine
11. Birch grove
12. High-tension line
13. Shelter

New Fane Trails

- Hike or mountain bike along challenging trails in Fond du Lac County.
- Look for dozens of songbird species.
- Keep an eye open for white-tailed deer along the paths.

Directions: Take County Highway S off State Highway 28 in Kewaskum, and drive north 2 miles to County Line Road. Turn right and drive 1 mile, looking for the sign that points to the New Fane Trail parking lot. Or motorists can take Highway 28 west to County Highway G, turning left and driving north 2 miles. Look for the signs to the trail parking site. Forest headquarters offices are located on County Highway G, 6 miles north of Kewaskum.

Facilities: Rest rooms and several picnic tables are located near the parking lot.

Permits and Rules: For camping, pay for vehicle sticker and camping fees (state resident, $7 per night; nonresident, $9 per night; electrical, $3; add $2 for weekends and holidays). No hiking is allowed on the nearby Crooked Lake and Forest Lake bridle paths, which double as snowmobile trails in the winter.

Green Trail 👢👢👢

Distance Round-Trip: 2.5 miles

Estimated Hiking Time: 2 hours

Cautions: Be wary of grass when it is wet and slippery.

Trail Directions: From the parking lot, walk east across the grass to the sign indicating the start of the trail. Follow the line of white posts to the top of the slope. Proceed left to where the Green and Brown Trails split. Keep going straight ahead for the Green.

From the marker post (.2 mi.) **[1]**, the Green Trail moves across the rolling glacial landscape. At .3 mi., a deep gully is on the right side, followed by a series of S-curves in the trail for the next .5 mi. **[2]**. After a field (.4 mi.) **[3]**, the trail descends into a kettle, a depression formed when glacial ice covered with earth finally melted. The ground covering eventually collapsed to form a "kettle" or bowl that filled with run-off or spring water. Hundreds of butterflies can usually be spotted in this area during the spring.

At .5 mi., hikers walk parallel with the Red and Yellow Trails, which are separated from the Green Trail by about 50 feet of brush. To continue on the Green Trail, turn to the left on a rocky hillside and proceed across a meadow.

The trail continues across the rolling countryside and through stands of savanna oak (.9 mi.) **[4]**. Keep going past the trees that crown the moraines along the route (1.2-1.7 mi.) **[5]**. At this point, the trail is about six feet wide, its surface varying between grass, dirt, and gravel. Next will be a plantation of red pine (2 mi.) **[6]**, planted in long neat rows. Hikers now meet the Red and Yellow trail link again **[7]** for the .5 mi. walk back to the trailhead.

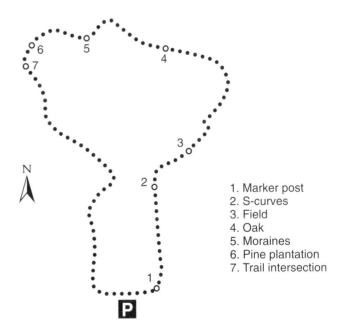

1. Marker post
2. S-curves
3. Field
4. Oak
5. Moraines
6. Pine plantation
7. Trail intersection

Yellow Trail 👢👢👢👢

Distance Round-Trip: 3.1 miles

Estimated Hiking Time: 2 hours

Cautions: There are several hills to climb with long, extended slopes, making it difficult for people with disabilities.

Trail Directions: All the loops on the New Fane Trail depart from the east side of the parking lot **[1]**. Hikers move up a slight slope carpeted with grass before heading into an oak forest (.2 mi.) **[2]**. At the top of the slope, the trails divide. To take the Yellow Trail, turn right and follow the white painted posts. For most of the trail, hikers will also be following the Red Trail, which proceeds over the same countryside.

The grassy path moves uphill past a cluster of sumac (.3 mi.) **[3]**, which makes for a brilliant crimson explosion in the autumn. Proceed through a heavy stand of oak (.5 mi.) **[4]** and cross a meadow on the far side. The remains of an old stone fence (.6 mi.) **[5]** are along both sides of the trail, a reminder that farms dotted this area up to the turn of the century. The trail makes several right and left turns as it goes along a clump of maples (.8 mi.) **[6]**. The trail now straightens out as it runs down a slope slippery with loose rocks, with a deep kettle on the right side (.9 mi.) **[7]**. The woods again open up, with the heaviest concentration of trees on the right as hikers move forward (1 mi.) **[8]**.

The path is well marked and maintained here as it edges through a scattering of pines with their thick, rich summer scent (1.4 mi.) **[9]**. Another kettle is on the left, followed by a trail curve to the left and then back to the right. You now have to go up and down several hills (1.5 mi.) **[10]**. The trail becomes more sandy along this stretch, but the ground is now fairly level (1.8 mi.) **[11]** and again encounters pines.

The Yellow link now turns left and makes a .5-mi.-deep loop through the trees while the Red section continues. The Yellow extension is also along sandy

soil, with a rolling feel to the landscape, before coming back out of the trees to rejoin the Red Trail (2.4 mi.) **[12]**. There are many deer throughout this section of the Kettle Moraine Forest, so you may be lucky to see one browsing along this stretch of pathway. The white-tails come out of hiding when it's early in the morning or late in the afternoon.

From here is a long straightaway (2.7 mi.) **[13]** that passes a field on the right. A section of the less-developed Ice Age Trail (2.8 mi.) **[14]** can be seen nearby as it moves southward along the rim of the ancient glacial front. Go down the next hill through thick undergrowth, pass a field, and climb back up the next slope (2.9 mi.) **[15]**. Now the Red/Yellow path links again with the Green Trail in a pine plantation. Watch out for the loose stones along the way. Another 200 feet down the trail, you link with the Brown Trail. They all move south to the trailhead. Down a long straightaway, hikers can spot the trail rest rooms.

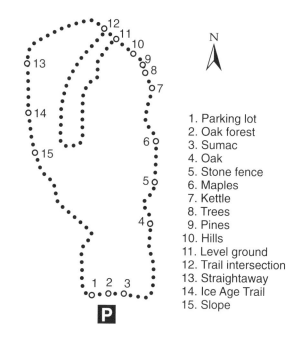

1. Parking lot
2. Oak forest
3. Sumac
4. Oak
5. Stone fence
6. Maples
7. Kettle
8. Trees
9. Pines
10. Hills
11. Level ground
12. Trail intersection
13. Straightaway
14. Ice Age Trail
15. Slope

Zillmer Trails

- Trek across scenic countryside created by glacial deposits.
- Stretch your legs climbing to high moraines.
- Plunge into cool, deep pine forests.

Trail Information

This Fond du Lac County trail system is named for the late Ray Zillmer, an attorney and an avid hiker who started the Ice Age Park and Trail Foundation. He was instrumental in promoting the Kettle Moraine as a major outdoor recreational destination. He lobbied governors and the legislature to provide land acquisition money for many of the trail segments in the Kettle Moraine.

Directions: Zillmer Trail is 2 miles east of State Highway 67 on County Highway SS, which is 10 miles north of Kewaskum.

Facilities: Rest rooms, shelter, picnic area, drinking water.

Permits and Rules: Fires are allowed only in the warming huts off the Red and Green Trails in the center of the system. Pets need to be leashed. A trail pass is necessary for mountain biking over designated pathways. For camping, pay for vehicle sticker and camping fees (state resident, $7 per night; nonresident, $9 per night; add $2 for weekends and holidays).

Trails

Yellow Trail—5.4 miles—The loop runs through a rich variety of glacial landscape, from upland forests to swamp. It is one of the longest developed trails within the Kettle Moraine State Forest, making it a challenge for any serious hiker. There is a great deal of up-and-down trekking along the moraines, the deposits of rock left behind by the glaciers 10,000 years ago. At its northeastern tip, the trail passes near the Ice Age Interpretive Center. Make time for a quick pit stop to look over the exhibits there.

Green Trail—1.8 miles—The Green Trail covers some of the same ground as the Yellow and Red Trail but is a more concentrated hike. It meanders through plantation pines, across swampland, and past brushy areas, just as do the other trail links. But the shorter distance is an important factor for hikers on a deadline.

Moraine Ridge Trail—.7 mile—This short trail, departing from the parking lot of the Henry S. Reuss Ice Age Interpretive Center, is great for families and folks who just want a sample of Kettle Moraine hiking. It loops around to the south, through mostly brushy areas and plantation pines. The scenery demonstrates the power of the glaciers that formed this region thousands of years ago. At its western rim, the trail skirts the Yellow Trail of the Zillmer Trail.

Brown Trail

Distance Round-Trip: 1.2 miles

Estimated Hiking Time: 45 minutes

Cautions: This is an unpaved trail, with many loose stones, uncovered roots, and grassy areas that can be difficult to traverse.

Trail Directions: From the marker **[1]**, the Brown Trail goes straight and heads into a pine plantation. By marker pole #5, hikers pass along an open area in the trees (.3 mi.) **[2]**; this is the remains of an old pasture now being taken over by second-growth vegetation. The branches of baby pines grow from three to five inches a year, and their fresh yellow tips tell of the spurt. A short series of left and right turns (.6 mi.) **[3]** is encountered now, so stick to the well-trod path.

The next .5 mi. or so proceeds along the rim of more open field, with trees along the right side. The path has been mowed through the tall grass, alive with butterflies. A hiker might spot a harmless garter

or black-and-yellow bull snake slithering across the walkway along here. From the meadow, hikers ascend the north slope of a small rise (.9 mi.) **[4]** and head back into the trees at marker pole #13. Then comes another timber stand and the western edge of the pine plantation. At the 1 mi. point **[5]**, the Brown Trail links with the Yellow, Red, and Green Trail for a combined path back to the trailhead.

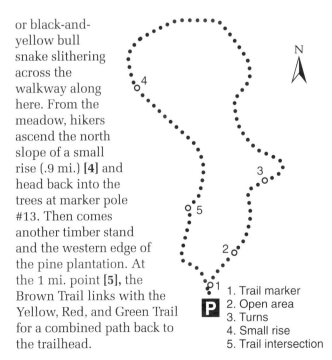

1. Trail marker
2. Open area
3. Turns
4. Small rise
5. Trail intersection

Red Trail 👢👢👢👢

Distance Round-Trip: 3 miles

Estimated Hiking Time: 2.5 hours

Cautions: The trail is not surfaced, so be alert for loose gravel and stones. The distance may be a factor for persons not used to hiking, especially with the rolling countryside.

Trail Directions: All trails leave from the parking area off County Highway SS. Follow the signs through a picnic area to a large boulder monument, from which a plaque has been removed. Unevenly spaced white marker poles along the entire route are numbered, an aid to determining where one is on a route.

Make an immediate right turn (east) when entering the picnic area trailhead to get on the Red Trail **[1]**. The trail is combined with the Yellow and Green Trails for the next .5 mi. through a pine plantation. At .2 mi., the trail makes a sharp left (north) **[2]** as it runs through the plantation, which is bordered on the right by posted private property. The well-packed trail is from 12 to 15 feet wide and is covered with a dense pine-needle carpet, muting the sound of a hiker's passage. However, a keen ear can still pick up highway sounds from County Highway SS on the south or Kettle Moraine Scenic Drive about 1 mi. to the east.

After .5 mi., an opening in the plantation leads to a series of hummocks and hills (.5 mi.) **[3]**. There is a low-lying area at marker pole #28 that gets muddy after rains (.7 mi.) **[4]**. However, the boggy patch is easy to step around. At .9 mi., hikers can see a meadow **[5]** to the left through which the Brown Loop runs. Near there, the Yellow Trail continues straight ahead and the Red and Green Trails turn to the left (west). Numerous sumac bushes are spotted through this stretch of path, making for an explosion of color in the autumn.

Rocks are peering up through the trail's thin soil cover, making it necessary to watch your step to avoid tripping (1.2 mi.) **[6]**. A plank bridge crosses a narrow, shallow stream (1.4 mi.) **[7]** where the Green Trail angles to the left and the Red continues forward. Move ahead, cross a culvert, and pick your way through a muddy patch. On both sides of the trail are tall oaks and maples (1.6 mi.) **[8]**. Hikers emerge from the grove and walk through another field, with a bench under a single maple on the left side of the trail. Then it is back into the forest, with a long moraine on the left side. The ground on both sides of the trail then slopes into deep, water-filled kettles. Thick underbrush obscures the terrain, but it is obvious this is an up-and-down walk. At 2 mi., the trail makes a sharp left turn and picks up the Yellow branch for about 100 feet before the latter turns to the right and disappears into the upland brush **[9]**.

There are several wind-shattered oaks here, and someone has been along to clear the trail with a chain saw. On both sides are the remains of the cleared timber (2.4 mi.) **[10]**. The next .25 mi. is a roller-coaster walk until you reach a second small bridge across the same stream you traversed before. A side trail to the right meanders through the woods to a log backpackers' shelter with a fire ring. Up to 10 persons can utilize the camping space here (2.5 mi.) **[11]**.

After the bridge, immediately turn right at the green trail marker instead of proceeding straight ahead, because that would take you back along the same Red and Green trail system. You proceed through a marsh and move back into a maple grove and the pine plantation where there is a link with the Yellow Trail. It is then a quick walk back to the original starting point.

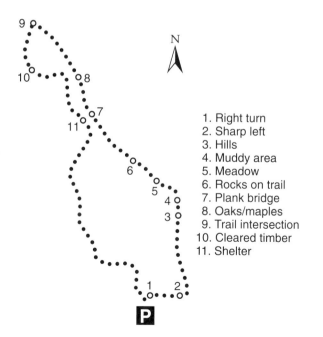

1. Right turn
2. Sharp left
3. Hills
4. Muddy area
5. Meadow
6. Rocks on trail
7. Plank bridge
8. Oaks/maples
9. Trail intersection
10. Cleared timber
11. Shelter

16. Barkhausen Waterfowl Preserve

- Bring the bird book to identify dozens of bird species.
- Take a naturalist-led hike into a marsh environment.
- Participate in educational programs focusing on waterfowl.

Park Information

The preserve offers 8 miles of trails that wind through 474 acres at Barkhausen and 446 acres at the adjacent Fort Howard Paper Foundation Wildlife Area. There are a total of 920 acres of forest, meadows, and wetlands supporting a wide variety of birds, plants, and animals. During autumn and spring migrations, thousands of ducks and geese use the area to rest and feed. Several hundred Canada geese stay year round. The preserve has extensive education programs.

The preserve, located on the west shore of Green Bay, is part of the Brown County Park Department. In 1926 the land was purchased by L.H. Barkhausen, who constructed several large water impoundments there as a waterfowl refuge. He donated the land to the park department in 1955. Fort Howard Paper Foundation added its land in 1976. But with Green Bay's suburbs creeping closer, the preserve will probably be an island of nature within an urban setting by the end of the decade. However, deer hunting by permit is still allowed on the property during the nine-day season in November.

Directions: Take U.S. Highway 41 north from Green Bay. Turn right on the Lineville Road exit (County Highway M). At the top of the ramp, turn right (east) to Lakeview Drive (County J). Then go north for .25 mile on County Highway J. The Barkhausen Waterfowl Preserve is on the right.

Hours Open: Open year round from 9 A.M. to 4 P.M. weekdays, and from noon to 4 P.M. weekends. Closed on holidays.

Facilities: 8 miles of hiking trails, interpretive center with educational displays, bathrooms, picnic grounds.

Permits and Rules: All pets, bicycles, motorized vehicles, and horses are prohibited. Do not collect plants or animals. Remain on marked trails and do not litter. There is no fee for hiking but a minimal fee for guided tours. Fee for cross-country skiing is $3 per day, and a seasonal pass is available. School programs are conducted by appointment.

Further Information: Contact Brown County Park Department, 305 East Walnut Street, Green Bay, WI 54301; 414-448-4466.

Other Points of Interest

Adventure fans enjoy riding the rapids on the Wolf River, about 30 miles west of Green Bay. **Shotgun Eddie Rafts** is one of the largest outfitters on this white water that loggers feared and kayakers appreciate. Shuttle service is available. Put-in is along State Highway 55 in White Lake. There are also tamer flowages for paddling on the upper Fox and Embarrass Rivers, if roaring water isn't your game. For more information, call 715-882-4461.

Providing a look into Green Bay's history, costumed interpreters at **Heritage Hill State Park** tell the frontier story. The 40-acre park has 25 buildings dating from the settler era. The site also has a Nature Center and a lookout tower from which to observe the surrounding countryside. Call 414-448-5150 for details.

Park Trails

Woodcock Trail 👢—.8 mile—This gravel/wood-chip trail is easily walked by youngsters and seniors. It bypasses a pond and a marsh, making two study areas for outdoors enthusiasts who want to learn more about aquatic life. The path is on the north side of the Interpretive Center. The path moves through a low wooded area of aspen and ash. As it returns to the Nature Center, the trail goes along the edge of one of Barkhausen's two 30-acre water impoundments. Hikers can view herons, egrets, and other waterfowl there.

Pot Hole Trail 👢👢—4.2 miles—This mowed, grassy path is at the far southern end of the Fort Howard Paper Foundation wildlife area, accessible from the Shores Trail, which starts at the Barkhausen Interpretive Center. The trail goes along several pools of water where invertebrates, insects, and amphibians can be studied in some detail. Hikers need to follow the Shores Trail markers south across Lineville Road and look for the connecting point. The trail moves over flat terrain.

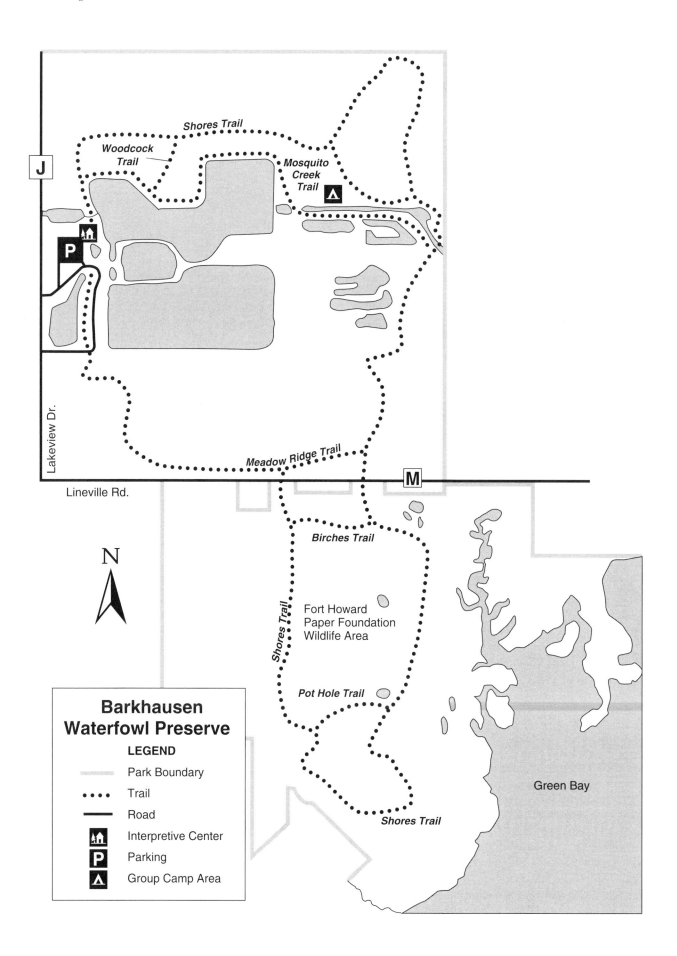

N

Barkhausen Waterfowl Preserve

LEGEND

- Park Boundary
- Trail
- Road
- Interpretive Center
- P Parking
- Group Camp Area

Shores Trail

Woodcock Trail

Mosquito Creek Trail

J

P

Lakeview Dr.

Lineville Rd.

Meadow Ridge Trail

M

Birches Trail

Shores Trail

Fort Howard Paper Foundation Wildlife Area

Pot Hole Trail

Green Bay

Shores Trail

Mosquito Creek Trail 👢👢

Distance Round-Trip: 2.3 miles

Estimated Hiking Time: 1.8 hours

Cautions: Wear proper footgear, because some areas can be damp or wet.

Trail Directions: Depart from the Interpretive Center on the marked pathway.

Go north past the Interpretive Center [1] and look for the trailhead with trail maps. A north trail (.1 mi.) [2] leads away from an impoundment, one of two man-made holding areas for water. This is lined with cattails, lily pads, and rushes, making for favored hiding and nesting places for water birds. Hikers have the option of turning left to explore the area around a picturesque pond with a short boardwalk crossing a small brook on the pond trail. After the bridge, turn left, following the lower trail. Part of the .8-mi. Woodcock Trail moves off to the right past a prairie restoration area.

Proceed along the main trail through a section of aspen and ash woods and the prairie restoration area. Then move back into the woods along Mosquito Creek. There are a few red maples and red oaks on the higher ground. The main trail has a four-foot-high observation stand (.2 mi.) [3] where hikers can take a breather and look out over a wetland restoration area. After the stand, continue east until the trail forks (.5 mi.) [4]. The left trail loops in a northeasterly direction, taking you into an ash/aspen/red maple woods. This is part of the Shores Trail and intersects with the Mosquito Creek Trail. If you want to keep going and skip the short northeast loop through the trees, take the right leg, which is the Mosquito Creek Trail.

The Shores and Mosquito Creek trails soon merge and continue together until you cross the creek. Make a sharp right turn to continue along the Mosquito Creek Trail where the Shores Trail veers left. You'll pass two ponds on the left (1.5 mi.) [5]. These also have cattails and reeds; the shallow waters are used by the University of Wisconsin Center for Great Lakes Studies for fish research. Mosquito Creek then loops to take you along the 30-acre impoundment, which has six- to eight-foot-high phragmites grass and wild grapevines growing along its banks. The last section of this trail is closed off and rerouted from the middle of September to the middle of May so that waterfowl are not disturbed. Continue to follow the trail to its conclusion at the Interpretive Center.

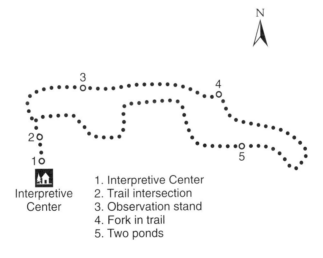

N

Interpretive
Center

1. Interpretive Center
2. Trail intersection
3. Observation stand
4. Fork in trail
5. Two ponds

Shores Trail 👢👢

Distance Round-Trip: 5 miles

Estimated Hiking Time: 2.7 hours

Cautions: Distance might be a factor here for in-experienced hikers, although the trek is not difficult.

Trail Directions: Begin at the Interpretive Center. All other trails divert off the Shores Trail, which loops back to the Center.

Walk north from the Interpretive Center, following the trail left as it skirts Otter Road **[1]**, leading to the study pond and marsh. There is a sandy stretch of track as the pathway moves east and proceeds past the observation platform (.2 mi.) **[2]** and wetland restoration. Look for ducks, egrets, deer, and hawks such as the northern harrier. The path can be damp here after a rain, but the frog chorus is spectacular in spring.

The trail makes an S-curve at the intersection with the path leading to the group camp area (.5 mi.) **[3]**. Take the left curve and continue walking into the forest of aspen, ash, and birch. Virginia creeper, poison ivy, red raspberries, and stinging nettle are predominant ground-cover plants, so stay on the trail. Swing south again from the top of the loop (1 mi.) **[4]**. Pick up the intersection with the Mosquito Creek Trail where there are several benches (1.5 mi.) **[5]**. Cross the shallow creek over a grass-banked culvert (1.7 mi.) **[6]**. It is still wooded as you move south, yet you cross an occasional meadow with its goldenrod, sumac, grasses, sunflowers, and asters. Three ponds are to the right with one featuring an observation blind (2 mi.) **[7]**.

Continue heading south to the marker post (2.5 mi.) **[8]** where the Meadow Ridge Trail heads right (west). However, to stay on the Shores Trail, go straight ahead and cross Lineville Road into the thickly wooded Fort Howard Paper Foundation Wildlife Area. Just past the road is the Birches Trail (2.9 mi.) **[9]**; the path plunges into a grove of birch trees to connect again with the Shores Trail on the west. There are more woods and clumps of shrubs as you approach Green Bay to the south. However, you can't see the water from here.

Toward the southern end of the Shores Trail, the Pot Hole Trail moves to the right (west) (3.1 mi.) **[10]**,

past several ponds. The Shores Trail continues to move south. There is a panoramic view of Green Bay (3.5 mi.) **[11]** as the shrub land opens up.

Follow the trail as it winds along the flat country-side before turning back north in a sweeping glide. Building foundations and a silo from an old home-stead can be seen on both sides of the trail (3.6 mi.) **[12]**. Curve east and south and go through a natural opening in the trees (3.8 mi.) **[13]**. Then continue walking north along the trail through a red maple woods (4 mi.) **[14]**. Pass the intersection with the western end of the Pot Hole Trail and keep walking north to the intersection with the Birches route.

The woods move from red maple back to birch, aspen, and ash. According to geologists, this small sandy ridge (4.1 mi.) **[15]** indicates the shoreline of ancient Lake Michigan. Cross Lineville Road, leaving the Fort Howard Paper Foundation Wildlife Area. Pass along a 30-acre block of cottonwood (4.5 mi.) **[16]**. Some traffic along Lineville can be seen through the heavy brush.

Take a right and then turn left (west) and proceed to the forest-study area (4.7 mi.) **[17]** where there are several benches used by pupils when teachers or naturalists make a presentation. Next make several sharp turns and cross a service drive on the way back to the Center.

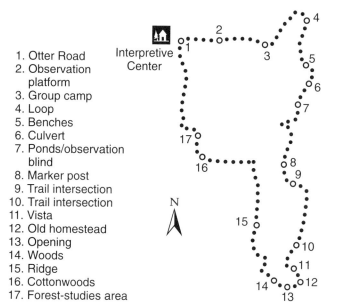

1. Otter Road
2. Observation platform
3. Group camp
4. Loop
5. Benches
6. Culvert
7. Ponds/observation blind
8. Marker post
9. Trail intersection
10. Trail intersection
11. Vista
12. Old homestead
13. Opening
14. Woods
15. Ridge
16. Cottonwoods
17. Forest-studies area

17. Brillion Nature Center

- Wander the nature trails and see a wide range of wildlife.
- Visit the Nature Center building and observe the displays.
- Get out the binoculars and look for dozens of bird species.

Park Information

The Brillion Nature Center is part of the Brillion Marsh Wildlife Area, a 5,700-acre wildlife project in Calumet County. The land is owned by the Department of Natural Resources, with the center being privately funded. The state began leasing land within the project in 1947, and a formal acquisition program began in 1963. The state owns 4,487 acres and leases 505 acres.

The ground is primarily swamp and wetland, although 8 miles of nature trails lead along the edge of the marsh, over prairie, and through the mixed hardwood forest. The marsh itself is surrounded by 800 acres of hardwoods, ringed in turn by 2,400 acres of fields and woodlots over which the hiker can stroll. Nesting areas for birds, consisting of old alfalfa fields, are out of the way and undisturbed.

Directions: The center is on Deerview Road, off County Highway PP, 10 miles east of the northeast corner of Lake Winnebago. The city of Brillion borders the northeast corner of the wildlife area, and the village of Hilbert is 2 miles west. The village of Potter lies along the southern boundary. The wildlife area is bounded by PP on the east, Hilbert and Reimer Roads on the south, Irish Road on the west, and Center and Conservation Roads on the north. It is only 7 miles east of High Cliff State Park.

Hours Open: Dawn to dusk, daily, year round. The Nature Center is open from 7 A.M. to sunset.

Facilities: Exhibits, observation platform, hiking trails that are used for cross-country skiing in the winter, picnic area, rest rooms.

Permits and Rules: Since the area is not completely owned by the state, hikers should check with the Department of Natural Resources to avoid trespassing on private land. Most private property is posted, but some might not be.

Further Information: Contact Department of Natural Resources, 101 West College Avenue, Appleton, WI 54914; 414-832-2746.

Other Points of Interest

The Nature Center is within 45 miles of **Appleton, Green Bay, Fond du Lac,** and **Manitowoc.** This makes it the hub of a major tourist area with a mix of indoor and outdoor recreational opportunities: museums, shopping, theater, canoeing, hiking, fishing, and hunting.

Football fans enjoy summer training sessions for the **Green Bay Packers** on the Oneida Street practice field. The site is east of Lambeau Field in Green Bay. Scrimmages and practice sessions are open to the public. The team begins training in mid-July. Call 800-236-EXPO or the Packer hotline at 414-496-7722 for more information.

Park Trails

Red Oak Trail —.5 mile—This short, easily walked link takes guests east into the forest toward an aspen clear-cut, where a path circles a special forestry-practice area. Stick to the trail, because land on the right side is private. Depart from the public parking lot east of the prairie restoration and walk into the woods for a quick overview of Brillion's topography and vegetation.

Cottonwood Trail —.7 mile—The trail departs from the west side of the Brillion Nature Center building and moves north along a thick stand of hardwoods. The trail angles to the east through a leased area and links up with a trail that takes walkers to a marsh overlook. The path also links with the White Oak Trail, continuing through the forest-land to the east.

Spring Trail —.2 mile—This 20-minute walk takes hikers past the foundations of long-gone farm buildings. There is an active spring. This trek goes through lowland forest and along a limestone ridge.

Marsh Platform Trail —.1 mile—An easy 10-minute walk extends from the Cottonwood Trail to a 12-foot-high observation platform overlooking the marsh. From this vantage point one can see sandhill cranes, great blue herons, red-tailed hawks, osprey, and many types of ducks and songbirds.

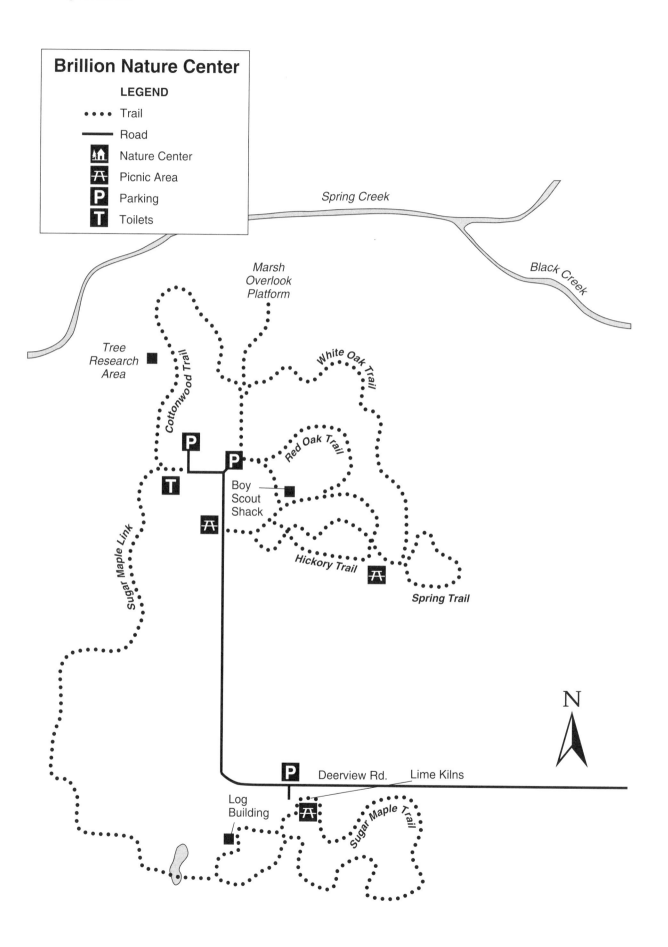

Brillion Nature Center

LEGEND

• • • • Trail

——— Road

🏕 Nature Center

🅰 Picnic Area

P Parking

T Toilets

Spring Creek

Black Creek

Marsh Overlook Platform

Tree Research Area

Cottonwood Trail

White Oak Trail

Red Oak Trail

P

P

T

🅰

Boy Scout Shack

Sugar Maple Link

Hickory Trail

🅰

Spring Trail

N

P Deerview Rd. Lime Kilns

Log Building

🅰

Sugar Maple Trail

Sugar Maple Link 👢👢

Distance One-Way: 1.25 miles

Estimated Hiking Time: 45 minutes

Cautions: The trail can become slippery when wet. Be aware that bugs are a natural nuisance in early summer. So load up on insect spray.

Trail Directions: The trail departs from the parking lot at the barnlike Brillion Nature Center. Walk west from the Nature Center about 100 feet to the marked area near the two outdoor toilets.

Leaving the parking lot **[1],** you quickly encounter a slight rise over uneven ground—a tallgrass prairie. Grasses such as big and little bluestem, Indian grass, side oats, and needlegrass are abundant. By September the grass is more than eight feet tall. Some forbs are also planted in the fields, such as compass plant, prairie dock, pale purple cornflower, and others. Look for some to bloom in late May. The color peaks in late July and early August.

A huge red oak stands alone (.5 mi.) **[2],** with the prairie on one side and a farm field on the other. There is more restored prairie at .6 mi. **[3]** with wild quinine, wild lupine, and butterfly weed.

There is now a great view of a marsh (.8 mi.) **[4]** on the right, with many dead trees as a result of a sweeping fire there in 1976. The fire opened up the marsh where succession had closed it in. This allowed more water in and caused some trees to die. It is an excellent area for viewing wildlife such as deer, sandhill cranes, and songbirds. The area is mostly cattails, rushes, fallen trees, and bracken.

Follow the trail left and go through a corner of a lowland forest (1 mi.) **[5]** for a few hundred yards. This is just long enough to get out of the sun for a few minutes. Look for wild ginger, mayapples, and violets. As you turn right again, the trail heads back into the sunlight and a grass-filled field. This is not restored prairie, so you'll see many domesticated and exotic plants.

The lowland forest, with ferns as thick ground cover, runs alongside the trail (1.1 mi.) **[6].** In late July, hikers can forage for blackberries here. The trail goes uphill (1.2 mi.) **[7]** onto a dike creating a man-made pond directly in front of you. Rain run-off collects in the pool, which is in a naturally low-lying area. Frogs and snapping turtles can often be spotted. Deer, raccoon, goose, and sandhill crane tracks attest to the importance of the pool for the region's wildlife.

Continue along the trail to a side trail leading to a log house built in the 1800s. The old place has wooden shingles. Later, a larger house was built here and the building was turned into a machine shed. A pulley system for lifting equipment can be seen.

At 1.2 mi., the Sugar Maple Link connects to the Sugar Maple Trail **[8].** A hiker can either take that trail, which is another 1.2 mi. long, or head back to the Nature Center. Either return by the link or walk down the road, which is framed by restored prairies and farm fields.

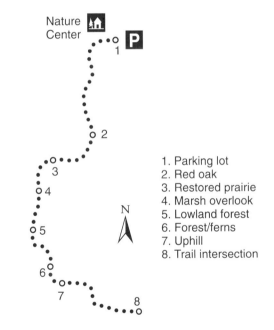

1. Parking lot
2. Red oak
3. Restored prairie
4. Marsh overlook
5. Lowland forest
6. Forest/ferns
7. Uphill
8. Trail intersection

White Oak Trail

Distance Round-Trip: 1.25 miles

Estimated Hiking Time: 1 hour

Cautions: There are several stretches of land along this section that are privately owned, so look for posted signs. The best idea is simply to follow the trail. Watch out for poison ivy.

Trail Directions: Leave your vehicle in the parking lot and walk back up the entrance road about 200 yards. The Hickory and White Oak trails begin off to the left. At the fork, the White Oak goes to the right.

The trail takes hikers through upland forest. Be careful of poison ivy (.1 mi.) **[1]**, especially along this first stretch of pathway. There are also bitternut, or yellow bud, hickories before you pass white and yellow birch trees on both sides of the trail. Look for the large hole along the trail ahead of you where limestone was quarried. The limestone formations making up this section of Wisconsin can easily be examined from the trail. At .2 mi., a ledge of the Niagara Escarpment **[2]** rises above the ground. This rock runs from Door County in northeast Wisconsin to south of Lake Winnebago. Most of the escarpment is underground, but it does surface in a few places such as here.

The trail heads into a large open area (.5 mi.) **[3]** that is suitable for picnicking. Just watch out for poison ivy. The path now doubles back into the woods (.6 mi.) **[4]**, where there are thick stands of birch, beech, white ash, and shagbark hickory. Large

granite boulders dumped by glaciers are strewn around the next leg of the trail (.7 mi.) **[5]**. These are called erratics.

When you reach the 1 mi. mark **[6]**, you finally see a magnificent stand of white oak, from which the trail received its name. The trail then connects with the Cottonwood and Marsh Platform Trails (1.2 mi.) **[7]**. Turn south (left) and head back to the parking lot.

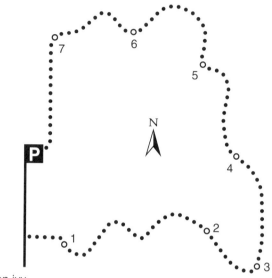

1. Poison ivy
2. Niagara Escarpment
3. Open area
4. Woods
5. Erratics
6. White oak
7. Trail intersection

18. Gordon Bubolz Nature Preserve

- Hike the winding trails through the heart of a white cedar forest.
- Marvel over the summer beauty of reestablished native prairies.
- Feed the trout at Albert's Foot Pond.

Park Information

The Gordon Bubolz Nature Preserve is a 782-acre wildlife wetland sanctuary that is a private, nonprofit preserve and environmental education facility. Support comes from corporate and individual donations, memberships, and programs. The landscape is a blend of white cedar forest and hardwood swamp, bordered by restored prairies, a sedge meadow, fields, deciduous forests, and pine plantations.

Six wildlife ponds are dispersed throughout the preserve. Albert's Foot Pond is stocked with rainbow and brook trout by Trout Unlimited-Fox Valley Chapter. The site is accessible to wheelchairs. No other fishing is allowed on the preserve.

The preserve has 8 miles of trail, 2 miles of which are wheelchair accessible. The forest lends itself to hiking, bird-watching, cross-country skiing, and nature study.

Directions: Traveling north to Appleton, take U.S. 41 north to County Highway OO East. Turn north on County Highway A. Travel north for 1.5 miles. The preserve is on the west side of County Highway A. If you are traveling south to Appleton, take U.S. Highway 41 south to Highway 47 North. Turn west on County Highway JJ, then turn south on County Highway A. Look for the preserve on the west side of County Highway A.

Hours Open: Dawn to dusk. The Nature Center building is open from 8 A.M. to 4:30 P.M., Tuesday through Saturday, and from 12:30 P.M. to 4:30 P.M. Sunday. The facility is closed Mondays and holidays. The building may also be closed during some regularly scheduled hours when staff are in the field. Call ahead to tour the building.

Facilities: There is an earth-sheltered nature center with natural history exhibits, nature store, rest rooms, auditorium, and offices. The preserve also has one cabin for overnight rental. There is also an outdoor amphitheater and picnic area.

Permits and Rules: Stay on the trails. No littering. No smoking on preserve property. No pets, alcoholic beverages, swimming, bicycling, or fishing. Collecting of natural materials is also prohibited.

Further Information: Contact Gordon Bubolz Nature Preserve, 4815 North Lynndale Drive, Appleton, WI 54915; 414-731-6041.

Other Points of Interest

Plamann Park is less than 5 miles northwest of the preserve. The park totals 257 acres, with two playground areas, a children's farm, picnic areas and shelters, a toboggan and sledding area, and swimming in the lake. The park is along County Road EE north of Appleton. For details, call 414-733-3019.

Park Trails

Four Seasons —.5 mile—This trail begins at the Nature Center building and is graveled and compacted for wheelchair accessibility. The trail runs directly west of the building and loops around the South Sugar Bush and then back to the Nature Center building. The trail is designated by signs numbered 1 to 16. These numbers correspond to information in a trail booklet, available in the Center, that describes what is along the pathway.

Esker Trail —.4 mile—This trail, accessible to people with physical disabilities, is indicated by signs numbered 17 to 27. It begins and ends at the Nature Center building and encompasses Albert's Foot Pond.

Wilderness Trail —4.5 miles—The Wilderness trek continues north off Deer Run Trail and ends on the southern side of Four Seasons. It skirts the northern and western boundaries of the preserve and shows the least amount of human impact. This is a seasonal trail, usually open from November through March. It meanders through a lowland hardwood forest, then continues through a drained wetland and back into another lowland hardwood forest.

North Bush Trail —.1 mile—This trail is used primarily during March for maple syrup collecting. It leads off from White Cedar Trail, just north of the separation of North Level Ditch and South Level Ditch. The path then makes a short loop through a northern hardwood forested area and back to the White Cedar Trail.

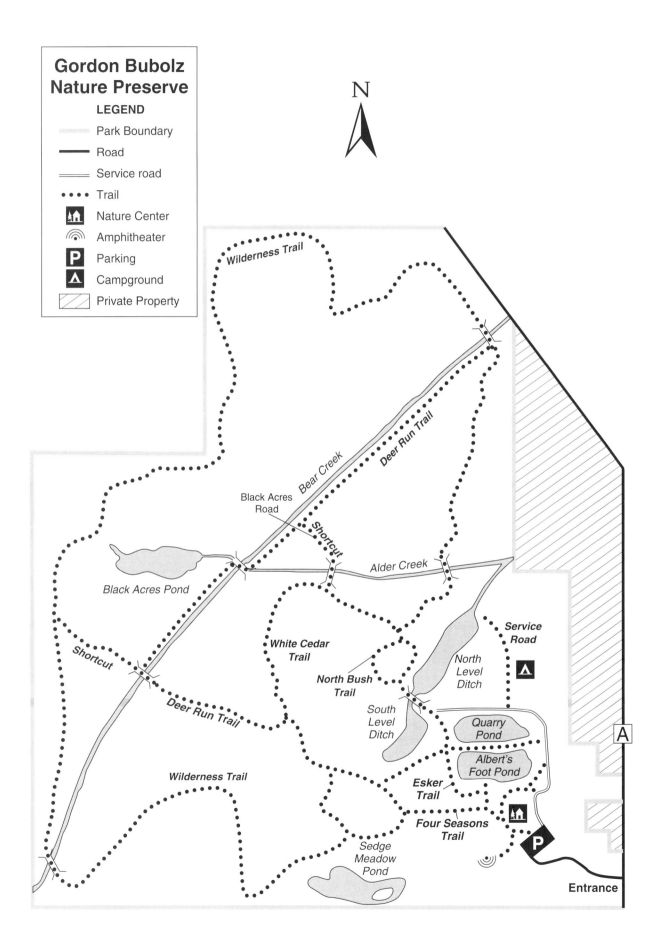

N

White Cedar Trail 🥾

Distance Round-Trip: 1.5 miles

Estimated Hiking Time: 45 minutes

Cautions: Watch for poison ivy and stinging nettle along the trail. It is advisable to wear mosquito repellent during the summer.

Trail Directions: Start at the Nature Center building and take Esker Trail past Albert's Foot Pond to the three Colorado blue spruce by station 28 **[1].** White Cedar Trail starts and ends here.

Head north for approximately .3 mi., at which point you will cross a bridge separating North and South Level Ditches **[2].** These "ponds" were constructed in 1972 to provide surface water for wildlife. Deer trails leading to the water's edge, ducks nesting in the pond weeds at the far end of North Level Ditch, and beaver dams and otter homes in the banks are evidence of a successful project.

Farther up the trail, you notice scattered red and silver maple trees (.5 mi.) **[3].** These soft maples are tapped annually in March to make maple syrup. Just a few yards farther, the trail to Deer Run begins.

Continue on White Cedar for about .5 mi., passing the Deer Run shortcut. You notice a change in habitat from upland hardwoods to lowland hardwoods **[4].** The white cedar forest is populated by myriad moisture-loving plants. Ferns and mosses are easy to spot. Being among the oldest plants on earth, they are nonflowering and reproduce through spores, not seeds. The spores are so thick in some ferns that when the plant is touched, a heavy cloud is released.

You will also notice numerous milkweed **[5]** and skunk cabbage along the trail (.7 mi.) that give off an array of odors to tempt your sense of smell. You will also notice on your hike through the woods that several trees are tipped over on their sides (.8 mi.) **[6].** White cedar trees have a very shallow root system because of the high water table. So when high winds come along, it does not take much to push them over.

On leaving the trail, notice a solitary white cedar (1.4 mi.) **[7]** out in front of you. There is a striking difference between the full body of this cedar growing in the open and the tall thin ones growing in the crowded swamp.

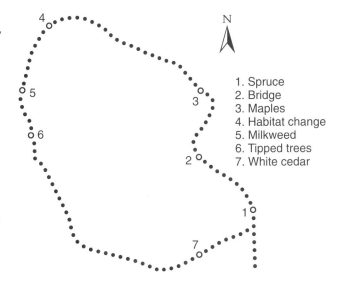

N

1. Spruce
2. Bridge
3. Maples
4. Habitat change
5. Milkweed
6. Tipped trees
7. White cedar

Deer Run Trail 🥾

Distance Round-Trip: 2.5 miles

Estimated Hiking Time: 2 hours

Cautions: Watch for poison ivy and stinging nettle. Wear mosquito repellent when warranted.

Trail Directions: The trail branches off the White Cedar Trail. Leave the Nature Center and walk past the small Albert's Foot Pond. Continue on to the three blue spruces. At the station marker there, numbered 28, you pick up the White Cedar Trail. Go to the right and take the trail where it passes the South Level Ditch on the left and the North Level Ditch on the right. Proceed through the woods and continue straight on the White Cedar Trail past the first junction of the White Cedar and Deer Run Trails. When you come to the second trail intersection, turn right onto Deer Run to begin the loop described below.

Hike for about .2 mi. to a small, dilapidated shack to the left **[1]**. Years ago, a logger spent his winters here while working in the woods. Continue farther north for another few hundred feet to a footbridge crossing the shallow Adler Creek **[2]**. The brush pile by the bridge is an excellent cover for rabbits, ground squirrels, and mice. It also provides a place of escape from the hawks that circle overhead. During late spring and early summer, bittersweet nightshade is in bloom here. Look for the small purple-and-yellow flowers attached to the nightshade stems growing throughout the brush.

Continue on the pathway called Black Acres Road and cross the second bridge you encounter, the one crossing Bear Creek **[3]**. Turn left on the trail. The area to the right is called Black Acres because during the 1940s and 1950s it was cleared of trees and drained by ditches, exposing the dark peat. Because the peat soil holds frost much longer than other soils, crops planted here failed and farming ceased. One ditch was dammed to create Black Acres Pond. This area supports abundant wildlife populations, including nesting blue-winged teal, sandhill cranes, Canada geese, otters, and beavers. A wide variety of reptiles and amphibians also live in the vicinity.

Walk about .1 mi. to the wildlife-viewing blind **[4]** on the right. You'll be glad if you have binoculars for a better look at the birds.

At .9 mi., turn left and cross the next bridge **[5]** over Bear Creek. Reenter the forest and walk back toward the White Cedar Trail **[6]** to return to the Nature Center.

—Joann Engel

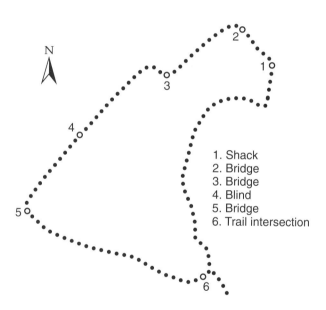

1. Shack
2. Bridge
3. Bridge
4. Blind
5. Bridge
6. Trail intersection

19. Horicon Marsh National Wildlife Refuge

- View thousands of waterfowl during the autumn migration.
- Spend hours bird-watching in marshland and prairies.
- Hike, cross-country ski, or bike over an ancient glacial lake bed.

Park Information

Horicon Marsh consists of 31,653 acres of bogland created by retreating glaciers 10,000 years ago. While the marsh may seem inhospitable, Indian mounds dating back hundreds of years have been found throughout the vicinity. Settlers hoped to drain the bog and use it for farmland. A dam was built on the river in 1846, creating a 51-mile-long lake. However, farming efforts were unsuccessful, as were several attempts to install canals through the region for ease in hauling commercial goods. The dam was removed in 1869. After a 20-year struggle on the part of the state's environmental community, the preserve was established in 1941.

The state administers 10,587 acres of the marsh on the south side of Highway 49, and the federal government takes care of 20,796 acres on the north side. The Wisconsin Department of Natural Resources office on Highway 28 will be made into an international education center by the turn of the century.

Directions: Horicon Marsh is located in east central Wisconsin, bordered on the south by State Highway 33, on the west by State Highway 26, on the north by State Highway 49, and on the east by State Highway 28 and County Highways TW and Z. It is 13 miles west of U.S. Highway 41. Nearby communities are Waupun on the northwest, Horicon on the south, and Maryville and Kekoskee on the east.

Hours Open: The marsh is accessible year round; however, the Visitor Center on County Highway P, just off Highway Z, is closed on weekends and holidays. The building is open from 8 A.M. to 4:30 P.M. weekdays.

Facilities: Visitors can hike, canoe, fish, and tour within the marsh.

Permits and Rules: No pets on the trails.

Further Information: Contact Supervisor, Horicon Marsh National Wildlife Refuge, Horicon, WI 53032; 414-387-2658. You can also use 1610 on your AM radio dial for general information.

Information can also be secured from the Horicon Chamber of Commerce, Barstow Street, Horicon, WI 53032; 414-485-3200. Its tourism office is open from 10 A.M. to 4 P.M. , Monday through Friday and on Sunday, and from 9 A.M. to 5 P.M. on Saturday, from May until October. The Department of Natural Resources office at the marsh is 414-387-7860.

Other Points of Interest

For tours of the marsh, try the **Blue Heron Landing,** which offers one-hour lecture visits to the inner marsh and two-hour rookery tours to the state's largest egret rookery. Be sure to bring your own binoculars. The Landing also hosts guided canoe tours, with optional shuttles. Rentals and tours can be arranged at the State Highway 33 bridge in downtown Horicon. Tours run from April through October. For details, call 414-485-4663.

The **Honey of a Museum,** located at Honey Acres outside Ashippun, offers the sweetest tour of any in the Horicon Marsh vicinity. Samples of various types of honey can be tried at the apiary, about 10 miles south of the city of Horicon on State Highway 67. Call the facility at 414-474-4411 for more information.

The easy 34-mile **Wild Goose Trail** proceeds over a flat, crushed limestone-rock surface from State Highway 60 in the center of Dodge County to the south side of the city of Fond du Lac. This is more of a bike trail than a hiker's delight because of the long stretches of straightaway over an old railroad bed. However, the path does go through several small towns with their restaurants, accommodations, and festivals. You can pick up the Wild Goose Trail where the path crosses State Highway 49 on the north side of Horicon Marsh, near the hiking trailhead in the marsh. The Wild Goose Trail runs along the marsh's western perimeter. However, there is a break in the trail where a leg is unfinished as one travels north from the marsh. This results in a detour to the west .3 miles on Church Road to Oak Center Road. You then rejoin the bike/hike path about 1.5 miles to the north again. No trail fees are required, but donation boxes are posted along the route.

Wild Goose Parkway is a marked 50-mile auto/bike tour around the Marsh along various state and county highways. There are numerous stops for scenic views, bird-watching, eating, and resting. Given the popularity of watching the fall migration of Canada geese, be alert for weekend traffic congestion. For details, call the Horicon Chamber of Commerce, 414-485-3200.

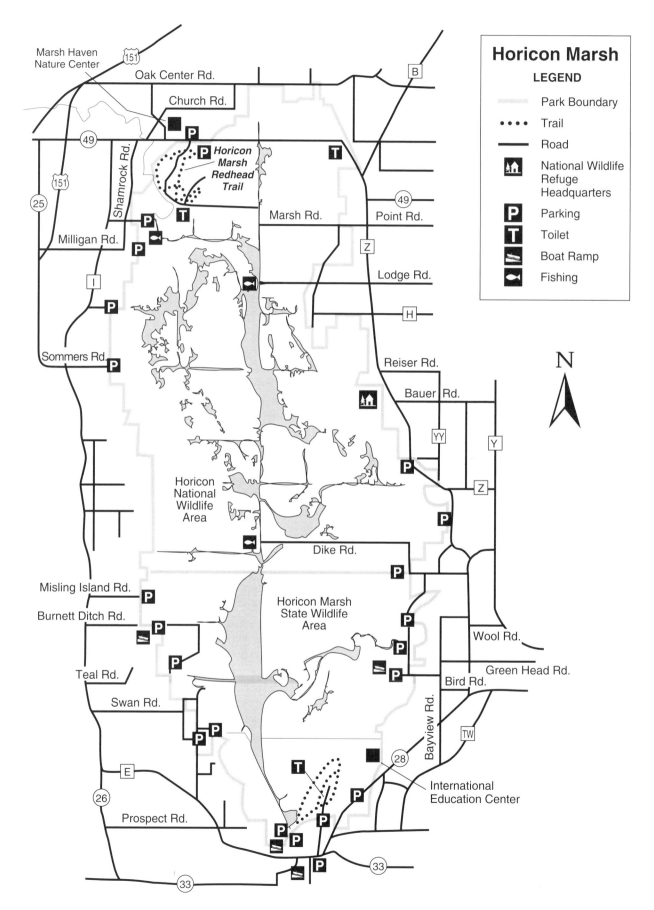

Horicon Marsh

LEGEND

	Park Boundary
••••	Trail
——	Road
🏛	National Wildlife Refuge Headquarters
P	Parking
T	Toilet
⛴	Boat Ramp
🐟	Fishing

Marsh Haven Nature Center

Oak Center Rd.

Church Rd.

Horicon Marsh Redhead Trail

Marsh Rd.

Point Rd.

Milligan Rd.

Lodge Rd.

Sommers Rd.

Reiser Rd.

Bauer Rd.

Horicon National Wildlife Area

Dike Rd.

Misling Island Rd.

Burnett Ditch Rd.

Horicon Marsh State Wildlife Area

Wool Rd.

Teal Rd.

Green Head Rd.

Bird Rd.

Swan Rd.

Bayview Rd.

International Education Center

E

26

Prospect Rd.

33

33

N

Horicon Marsh Redhead Trail

Distance Round-Trip: 2.5 miles

Estimated Hiking Time: 2 hours

Cautions: In wet seasons, sections of the trail can become boggy, so wear the appropriate footwear to prevent getting your feet wet. Mosquitoes can also be a problem in the early summer.

Trail Directions: The parking area for the Redhead Trail is on the north side of Horicon Marsh along State Highway 49. There is a .3-mi. service drive to the lot. The main trail leaves the lot in a southerly direction. There is also a short hike from a bird-watching vantage point 2 mi. east of the trailhead. The entrance to the parking lot is not well marked, but you see the site from the highway. Hikers stroll along the edge of the marsh from an information kiosk and blind to rest rooms adjacent to the parking site. Around the Redhead Trail is an auto drive, open from 8 A.M. to 3 P.M. weekdays from April 15 to September 15. However, vehicles are prohibited there on weekends and holidays.

Leaving the parking lot, walk up a small slope past an information kiosk **[1]**. At the top of the rise is a bench (.1 mi.) **[2]** overlooking the hiking area. Continue walking straight ahead through the high grasses (.3 mi.) **[3]**. At .4 mi., you walk across a plank walkway to the other end of a wet area **[4]**. The trail curves to the left (.4 mi.) and you walk along the marsh on the right through a patch of berry bushes **[5]**, You will be parallel with the auto-tour road for the next .25 mi., coming to an overlook at .5 mi. **[6]** with a sign that describes Scarp Pool.

As with many Wisconsin wetlands, the tenacious purple loosestrife has taken root and grows everywhere. The state and federal site managers are attempting to control the noxious weed, which started out as a decorative plant around pioneer homes. Some loosestrife may be seen in some areas of the marsh (.6 mi.) **[7]**.

Remains of a rock fence line (.7 mi.) **[8]**, a memory of an old farm field, can be spotted amid the second-growth brush now springing up on both sides of the trail. By now, you have edged around one large marsh/pond area where there is a bench on a small rise. Keep walking to the east and arrive at the intersection of the .5-mi. Red Fox Nature Trail (.8 mi.) **[9]**, which loops to the east and connects with the .4-mi. Egret Nature Trail

[10] extending through the boglands on the other side of the road.

To get to the Red Fox Nature Trail, follow the arrow on a green trail sign that is prominently posted at the intersection of the Red Fox and the main Redhead Trail. Take this nature trail for a short jaunt around the grassy path. The Egret Nature Trail is picked up by crossing the service road and following the directional arrows. Walk up a short hill on the path, and sit on a bench at the crest or cross over the ridge and descend to a pond. There you can observe the waterfowl. The Red Fox Nature Trail is not marked once you are on it, but it cuts across the south side of a bogland, so be alert for mallards, cranes, egrets, and green-winged teal. The marsh is the resting place for thousands of birds during the spring and autumn migration period, with thousands of others using the bogs for their nesting.

Returning from the nature loop, link again with the Redhead Trail and proceed across the sight-seeing road (1.2 mi.) **[11]** and into thick underbrush. A moraine (1.4 mi.) **[12]** is on the left side of the trail, a towering, overgrown pile of rubble. On the left, the Rock River slowly glides through the trees and into the marsh as you move south. Glaciers dumped numerous "erratic" stones, which were the bane of the farmers who tried to till the drier portions of the marsh. Edging the abandoned fields are the remains of fences they made from these rocks.

A boardwalk crosses a wet area before the path climbs a hill and moves around a marsh lake on the right (1.7 mi.) **[13]**. Then walk along the northwestern rim of the preserve (2 mi.) **[14]** and to the driveway entering the park. Walk east about 1,500 feet to the parking lot.

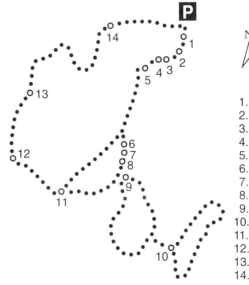

1. Information kiosk
2. Bench
3. High grass
4. Plank walkway
5. Marsh
6. Overlook
7. Purple loosestrife
8. Fence line
9. Red Fox Nature Trail
10. Egret Nature Trail
11. Sight-seeing road
12. Moraine
13. Lake
14. Preserve western rim

Marsh Haven Nature Center 🥾

Distance Round-Trip: 1.5 miles (prairie/woods); .75 mile (wetlands)

Estimated Hiking Time: 1.5 hours

Cautions: Mosquitoes are horrendous in the woods during the wet season. Part of the marsh link is also under water in the spring.

Trail Directions: The Nature Center is on State Highway 49 on the north side of Horicon Marsh, fronted by a large parking lot. To walk in the woods, follow the east trail leading to the trees from the parking lot. To walk along the marsh, follow the trail to the west from behind the main center building. The Wild Goose Trail for biking is on the property's western border.

Marsh Haven is a 47-acre nonprofit education center on the north side of the marsh, run by volunteers; admission is $1. There are two trail links, a bunkhouse for visiting schoolkids or Scouts, an amphitheater, and a picnic shelter. The facility has won numerous awards for its community-based service and programs. Inside the building is the Respect Our Earth theater. The center was the brainchild of Lawrence Vine, a Wisconsin Department of Natural Resources researcher who lives in nearby Juneau.

Start your trek at the center office **[1],** which consists of a walk-through wildlife exhibit with lifelike displays made by Beaver Dam taxidermist Greg Spencer. Ground-level windows allow visitors to look out eye-to-eye at chipmunks and birds around several feeders. Often, wildlife artists work on their canvases in the building and are happy to talk about their paintings. The building is open from 9:30 A.M. to 5 P.M. on Saturdays and Sundays, and from 10 A.M. to 4 P.M. weekdays, from May to December.

The prairie trail is a cut-grass pathway leading to the woods about .5 mi. to the east. Prairie bluestem and black sampson are among the plant varieties that can be identified. Numerous bird species, from the rare yellow-headed blackbird to the wren, flit in and out of the grassy stretch leading to the woods. Overhead, Canada geese, cranes, blue-winged teal, coots, and other wildfowl can usually be seen.

After traversing the prairie in a short, quick walk, hikers cross a small boardwalk bridge and enter the woods (.5 mi.) **[2].** While a four-foot pathway is fairly evident among the trees, there are many more small trails crisscrossing and zigzagging in no set fashion, making it easy to lose track of mileage. Twelve years of visits by youngsters to the center grounds has resulted in many shortcuts through the trees, up the hills, and around downed logs. But a hiker can get a good sense of second-growth timber, with plenty of oak and new maple springing from the rich soil. The Lee Gould Observation Tower (.9 mi.) **[3]** is about 50 feet high, allowing a look to the north over the fencerows and brush. From the tower, continue meandering through the dense timber. You cross several gullies that can be wet in the rain (1 mi.) **[4]** as you return to the opening in the woods. Then head back across the prairie to the parking lot. Animals that may be spotted in the area include raccoons, mink, skunks, white-tailed deer, possums, and muskrats. The well-walked grass and dirt path is easy to follow on the way back to the graveled parking lot, which can be seen in front of the main building. The low grass, reeds, and bushes are not enough to obstruct the hiker's sightline on the way back to the lot.

The path to the Vander Woude wetlands can be reached behind the main building or from the parking lot in front. The trail encircles Lake LaPresto with its cattails. Visiting terns and ruddy ducks splash about happily in the shallow water. High water in the spring often closes portions of the path (.2 and .5 mi.) **[5].** When this happens, hikers with binoculars can watch the waterfowl from the drier comfort of the center's picnic shelter **[6].** The wetland trail is graveled, making a distinguishable loop around the lake and through its surrounding wetland. If you stray off the pathway, you risk getting wet feet during wet weather. By taking the easy loop around the lake, hikers quickly find themselves strolling back to the parking lot and main building. Both can be seen straight ahead.

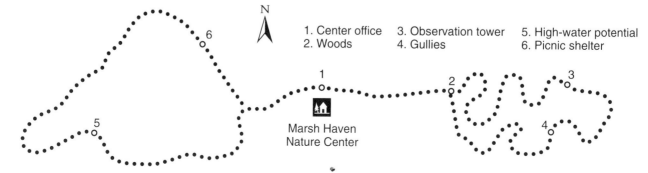

N

1. Center office   3. Observation tower   5. High-water potential
2. Woods   4. Gullies   6. Picnic shelter

Marsh Haven
Nature Center

20. High Cliff State Park

- View the state's largest lake from overlooks in the park.
- Scramble over limestone cliffs.
- Study effigy mounds built by early Native Americans hundreds of years ago.

Park Information

The name High Cliff State Park refers to the limestone cliffs of the Niagara Escarpment, which parallels the eastern shore of Lake Winnebago. The escarpment runs northeasterly toward the Door County Peninsula. The lake covers 215 square miles, a depression carved out by the Green Bay lobe of a glacier that covered this area 25,000 years ago.

The park was originally owned by the Western Lime and Cement Company, which started quarrying in the area in 1870. The limestone blocks and crushed limestone taken from the quarry were used in building construction. Remains of the quarry and adjoining lime kilns can still be seen.

In 1956 the area was sold to the state for development of a park, which opened in 1957. One of the prime features of the park is its Lake Winnebago marina with four boat-launching ramps. From the cliffs, hikers can see more than 30 miles to the north, west, and south. Maple, hickory, and oak make up the thick forest cover.

Directions: The park is 10 miles east of Appleton on the northeast shore of Lake Winnebago.

Hours Open: The trails are open daily, year round. Visitors must leave the campgrounds by 11 P.M. The park office is open from 8 A.M. to 4:30 P.M. daily.

Facilities: The park has 112 individual campsites (32 with electricity) and 8 group sites. It also has toilet facilities, showers, campground and trail accessible to persons with physical disabilities, picnic area, and shelters. There are 7.2 miles of hiking trails.

Permits and Rules: Fishing licenses are required.

Further Information: Contact Superintendent, High Cliff State Park, N7475 High Cliff Road, Menasha, WI 54952; 414-989-1106.

Other Points of Interest

The **Mack Wildlife and Observation Area** is 2.5 miles west of Black Creek on State Highway 54 and Bishkoff Road. The wildlife observation grounds cover 500 acres of the 1,829-acre Mack State Wildlife Area, one of several such sites in northwest Outagamie County. This is one of the few areas in Wisconsin where hikers can see migrating swans, as well as Canada geese, ducks, and other waterfowl.

For bird-watching, this area of Wisconsin is paradise. The 47-acre **Marsh Haven Nature Center** is on State Highway 49 east of Waupun. The parcel is on the north edge of Horicon Marsh, with an observation tower, visitor center with exhibits, and a trail system. For more information, call 414-386-2182. The 300-acre **1000 Islands Environmental Center** is a conservancy zone along the Fox River in Kaukauna. It hosts nesting eagles plus owls, bitterns, songbirds, and other wildlife. A naturalist is on duty at the center from 8 A.M. to 4 P.M. daily.

Park Trails

Red Bird Trail 🥾🥾—3.7 miles—This is the park's longest trail. It is gentle except for several steep slopes in the quarry. The pathway moves around the family campground. The 12-foot-high statue of Red Bird is one of the main features of the trail. The Ho-Chunk tribal leader, whose people lived in this area, is depicted standing on a huge granite rock. Red Bird died a self-imposed death of starvation in a Fort Winnebago prison at Portage in 1828. He was protesting the ongoing violence on the frontier between the Native Americans and the white settlers.

Forest Management Trail 🥾—1.3 miles—The trail starts behind the park pavilion, with 15 interpretive stops through the mixed hardwood forest. Various exhibits depict how trees are cared for from an outdoors management point of view.

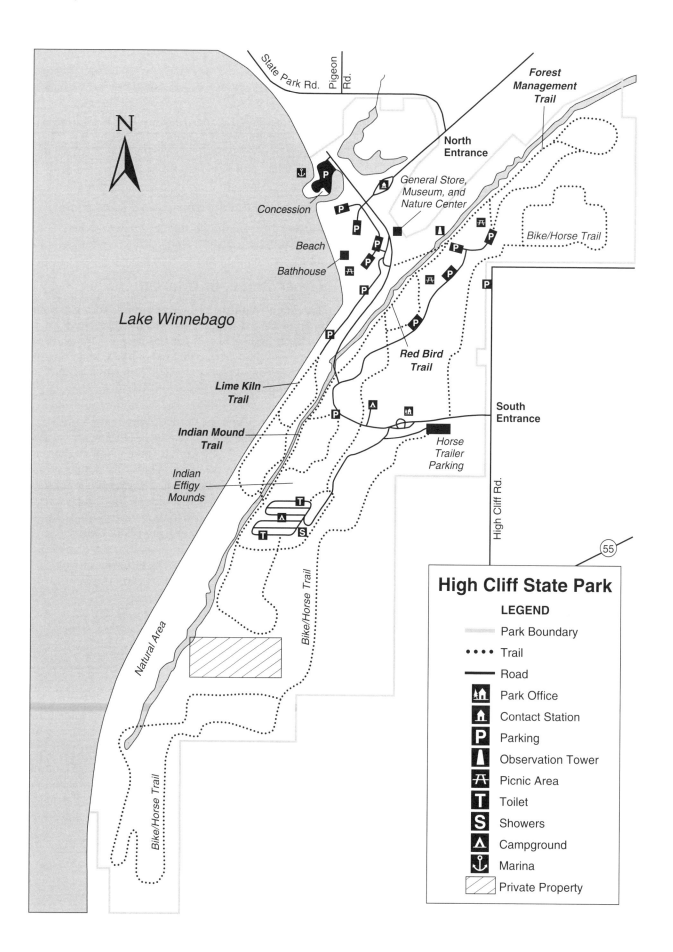

State Park Rd.

Pigeon Rd.

Forest Management Trail

North Entrance

General Store, Museum, and Nature Center

Concession

Beach

Bathhouse

Bike/Horse Trail

Lake Winnebago

Lime Kiln Trail

Red Bird Trail

Indian Mound Trail

South Entrance

Indian Effigy Mounds

Horse Trailer Parking

High Cliff Rd.

Natural Area

55

Bike/Horse Trail

Bike/Horse Trail

High Cliff State Park

LEGEND

~~	Park Boundary
••••	Trail
———	Road
🏠	Park Office
⌂	Contact Station
P	Parking
▯	Observation Tower
⩐	Picnic Area
T	Toilet
S	Showers
Δ	Campground
⚓	Marina
▨	Private Property

Lime Kiln Trail 👢👢

Distance Round-Trip: 2.3 miles

Estimated Hiking Time: 2 hours

Cautions: There are a few areas along the trail with steep ascents and descents.

Trail Directions: Follow the signs from either park entrance.

The parking lot overlooks ruins of old lime kilns **[1]**. The wide gravel trail begins at the south end of the lot. The lime industry was important to the surrounding area's economy from 1895 to 1956. The kilns are ovens that were used to make various types of lime from the stone.

Notice both the purple and white violets along the trail's edge. Pass through concrete remains of the old kilns (.2 mi.) **[2]** and cross a small stream. Continue going straight past the return loop of the trail as it appears on the left. Spotted wintergreen can now be seen decorating the trail, just before a cluster of Jack-in-the-pulpits and wild ginger. At .3 mi., the trail narrows slightly **[3]** and the land looks less disturbed. Maple trees predominate in the surrounding area.

Trout-lilies can sometimes be found along the next stretch of path in the spring. Sit on the bench here (.4 mi.) **[4]** and take in the view of Lake Winnebago. After enjoying the vista, keep going straight. At .6 mi., a cutoff trail intersects on the left. From here for the next .2 mi., you use narrow bridges to cross several small streams (.8 mi.) **[5]**. The water is trickling downhill toward the lake.

Virginia creeper makes its appearance among the trees (.9 mi.) **[6]**, with grosbeaks and cedar waxwings flying in and out of the undergrowth. You can see a towering cottonwood tree at 1 mi., with a bench **[7]** allowing for a rest before the steep climb up the trail from the lake. Stairs are built into the hillside to make it easier climbing. Another bench is strategically placed at 1.1 mi. **[8]** for a welcome respite.

The trail now turns left and ascends not as sharply as previously. Boulders are embedded in the trail. The trail straightens at 2.2 mi. **[9]**, where spur trails on the right lead to limestone cliffs. The trail descends slightly near a lush growth of ferns in the cool shade. Shelf fungi cling to nearby trees, with another bench placed above the wooden stairway (1.5 mi.) **[10]**. Reach the bottom of the stairs and cross a series of bridges (1.6 mi.) **[11]** that span the same streams you crossed on the lower elevation.

The wet hillside is rich in plant life, including elderberries. The birds love the berries, and many species can be spotted darting around to feed. Continue straight (1.7 mi.) **[12]**; you'll see another cutoff trail on the left. There is a steep descent at 2 mi., followed by another short climb **[13]**. At the T-intersection, turn right and return to the parking lot.

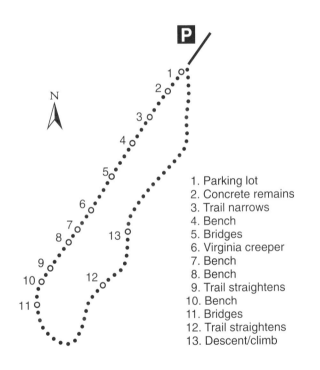

1. Parking lot
2. Concrete remains
3. Trail narrows
4. Bench
5. Bridges
6. Virginia creeper
7. Bench
8. Bench
9. Trail straightens
10. Bench
11. Bridges
12. Trail straightens
13. Descent/climb

Indian Mound Trail 🥾

Distance Round-Trip: .32 mile

Estimated Hiking Time: 30 minutes

Cautions: Trail is shared with bicyclists.

Trail Directions: Follow the signs from either the north or south entrance to the park. This is accessible to people with physical disabilities.

Leave the Indian Mound Trail at the parking lot **[1]**. Follow the spur from the west end of the lot. The first interpretive sign tells of the 1,000- to 1,500-year-old mounds found throughout the vicinity. Hidden in maple forest are the vestiges of a dozen effigy mounds made by nomadic Woodland Native Americans. These are burial sites, so do not disturb them. To see the mounds, hike through the maples, basswood, and hickories that line the six-foot-wide gravel path.

The bodies were laid on the ground, and dirt was piled on top of the deceased. The mounds either are shaped like animals or have geometric configurations. There are stands of mayapples, as well as trout-lilies and other forest plants that can be studied from the trail. The second interpretive marker tells of the importance of water to ancient civilizations. The drawing depicts a wild ricing operation. At the T-intersection **[2],** take the trail to the left. A scenic overlook (.1 mi.) **[3]** is on the right where columbine clings to the edge of the limestone cliff overlooking Lake Winnebago.

Retrace your steps to the T-intersection and past the violets and wild strawberries growing here. Go straight ahead toward some limestone pillars balancing on the right. Back at the T, turn right. A sign explains the burial mounds and their features. A lineal mound is on the right and a panther mound is

on the left. They are covered with a mixture of wildflowers.

The next sign speculates on the origins and significance of the mounds. There are conical mounds on the right. Walk past the spur trail to the campground on the right **[4]** and trek on the trail through the trillium on the left. As the trail turns left, go past the path to the family campground on the right. Another sign explains mound construction. A spur trail to the left leads to twin buffalo mounds. Retrace your steps to the main trail and turn left. At .2 mi., a sign explains the importance of oak trees to early cultures **[5].** Another panther mound is then on the left. The next sign demonstrates wigwam construction.

Walk past the spur trail on the right. There is a sign here that says "Thanks for visiting Indian Mound Trail." At .3 mi., return to the parking lot.

—Steve Drake

1. Parking lot
2. T-intersection
3. Overlook
4. Trail intersection
5. Sign

21. MacKenzie Environmental Education Center

- View numerous animals native to Wisconsin.
- Tour nature trails and study the vegetation and animal life.
- Visit the Conservation Museum, Logging History Museum, and Alien and Oddities Museum.

Park Information

The MacKenzie Environmental Education Center has been a major force in educating the state's citizens on conservation and environmental issues since 1934. The facility started as a breeding site for pheasants, attracting to the game farm many visitors who wanted to learn more about the birds. Over the years, the mission of the center has gradually been expanded to include educational programs far beyond the initial tours and lectures.

In many cases, animals came to the wildlife exhibit after being injured, orphaned, or taken from people who had possessed them illegally. Others were born in captivity. These animals could not be returned to the wild and consequently were kept here for study. There is a deer enclosure, plus compounds for wolves, coyotes, bison, foxes, bears, bobcats, hawks, owls, vultures, eagles, badgers, and other species native to Wisconsin. The area is accessible to persons with physical disabilities.

Directions: Take U.S. Highway 51 to Poynette. The Education Center is on County Highway CS to the northeast of the city. Go about 2 miles to the entrance on the right. The center is also 2 miles west of U.S. Highway 22.

Hours Open: The Center is open daily from 8 A.M. to 4 P.M., May 1 through mid-October, and from 8 A.M. to 4 P.M. Monday through Friday from mid-October through April 30. It is closed on winter holidays.

Facilities: There are wildlife exhibits, a picnic area, sawmill, pond, arboretum, nursery, fire tower, and seven nature trails. Two main bunkhouses sleep up to 80 with a main lodge offering kitchen, dining room, classroom, workshop, and library.

Permits and Rules: Do not feed, touch, or bother the animals. No smoking.

Further Information: Contact Supervisor, MacKenzie Environmental Education Center, W7303 County Highway CS, Poynette, WI 53955; 608-635-4498.

Other Points of Interest

Canoeing along the Wisconsin River is one of the more popular outdoor recreational activities in central Wisconsin near Poynette. The river is 7 miles northwest of the MacKenzie Center. Numerous outfitters can supply canoes, paddles, life jackets, and other pieces of gear. They can also assist with put-in and egress points.

Access to the 1,200-acre **Mud Lake Wildlife Area** is mostly by boat, with ramps off Tollefson Road along the west side of the flowage. Bird-watching is possible from State Highway 22. The area is 4 miles east of Poynette and 3 miles south of Rio in Columbia County, about 3 miles east of the MacKenzie Environmental Education Center. This is a diverse wildlife habitat with a fertile wetland loved by migratory birds. Tundra swans are among the waterfowl visiting the marsh. Ash, aspen, oak, and cherry make up the timber cover.

Park Trails

Ecology Trail —.5 mile—This heavily forested portion of the center is designed to demonstrate the interdependence of a complex community of plants and animals. The area has been left to grow in its natural state, so stick to the trail. The oak woodland is typical of what you will see within the rest of Wisconsin's southern hardwood forests, providing good ground cover, shrub layer, understory of young plants, and canopy of major trees. There is a large planting of conifers dating from the 1940s.

Wildlife Trail —.5 mile—The shorter portion of this trail is hard surfaced and accessible to those with physical disabilities, as well as to families using strollers. The blacktop mix includes recycled shredded tires. The trail is designed to show how a wildlife population can be maintained and diversified. Numerous birds may be seen along the route, depending on the season, including wrens, bluebirds, sparrows, larks, robins, turkeys, waxwings, catbirds, red-headed woodpeckers, and mourning doves among others. Along the way, you'll see various types of bird feeders that are easy to make.

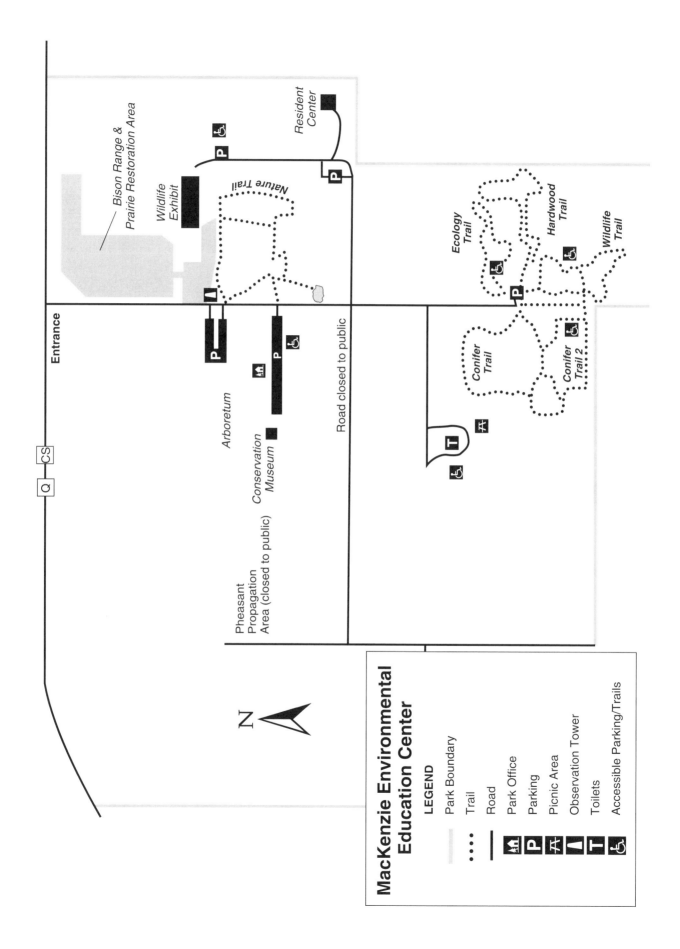

N

Entrance

Bison Range &
Prairie Restoration Area

Wildlife
Exhibit

Nature Trail

Resident
Center

Arboretum

Conservation
Museum

Pheasant
Propagation
Area (closed to public)

Road closed to public

Ecology
Trail

Hardwood
Trail

Wildlife
Trail

Conifer
Trail

Conifer
Trail 2

CS

Q

MacKenzie Environmental Education Center

LEGEND

- Park Boundary
- Trail
- Road
- Park Office
- P Parking
- Picnic Area
- Observation Tower
- T Toilets
- Accessible Parking/Trails

Conifer Trail/Conifer Trail 2 👢👢

Distance Round-Trip: 1 mile

Estimated Hiking Time: 1 hour

Cautions: Watch out for poison ivy and mosquitoes.

Trail Directions: Take the entrance service road from County Highway Q/CS and drive to the end. The trail parking lot is about .5 mi. down the road on the left. All trails depart from here. Look for the signs. Conifer Trail is dirt and bark covered, with white marker posts. Conifer Trail 2 is asphalt surfaced for accessibility, with yellow marker posts.

Cross the service road to the west to pick up the trailhead to the Conifer Trail. You bypass a gully with a giant white oak **[1]**, a survivor of timber cutting a century ago. A control plot (.1 mi.) **[2]** shows the difference in the growth rate between the managed and unmanaged forest. Trees with orange paint would have been trimmed out under a management plan.

The Conifer Trail and Conifer Trail 2 meet and cross. To stay on the Conifer Trail, follow the left route. The trails meet again within a few hundred feet, so just follow the appropriate markers to the next left turn. Take that to a firebreak demonstration that shows how plowing an 8- to 16-foot-wide area of soil between tree plots clears out flammable materials.

A cluster of white spruce is nearby (.2 mi.) **[3]**. This fast-growing tree can reach a height of 120 feet, making it valuable for the timber industry. At .3 mi. is a cord of pulpwood **[4]** with a picture showing how much paper can be made from a cord, a stack of wood 4 feet by 4 feet by 8 feet.

A gully (.4 mi.) **[5]** on the right side was caused years ago by poor farming techniques, resulting in water erosion. Trees have been planted around it to halt the run-off, although the valuable topsoil is gone.

A pruning plot and access lanes that double as fire lanes are marked to show more forest management techniques. A rule of thumb is that after every 20 rows of trees (about 300 feet) one row needs to be thinned out as an access lane. Some of the next pines have double trunks (.5 mi.) **[6]**. When these were first planted years ago, thousands of crows nested here in the winter. The weight of the birds sometimes broke the topmost branches, and other tips grew to replace them.

Now swing back to the right along the Conifer Trail to the intersection with Conifer Trail 2 **[7]**. The second trail goes along some of the same sections as the first trail, but at the intersection, continue on to the right. Look at the hole in the large oak (.7 mi.) **[8]** on the right side of the pathway. It is a raccoon home.

Pass the cordwood demonstration and turn left on the trail. You pass a stand of white spruce (.8 mi.) **[9]** with lots of "duff," or natural organic litter, around the base of the trees. As with the first trail, Conifer Trail 2 also shows a firebreak, a wildlife-cover plot, and an overgrown field (.9 mi.) **[10]** slowly being reclaimed by the forest. Go back to the Conifer Trail and turn right. The trail exits with a pathway to the parking lot.

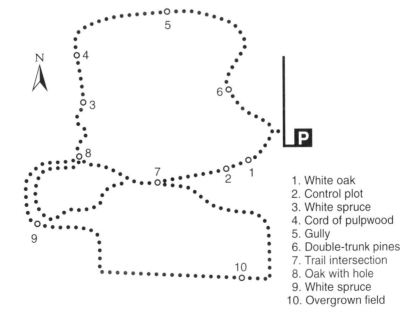

1. White oak
2. Control plot
3. White spruce
4. Cord of pulpwood
5. Gully
6. Double-trunk pines
7. Trail intersection
8. Oak with hole
9. White spruce
10. Overgrown field

Hardwood Trail 👢👢

Distance Round-Trip: .75 miles

Estimated Hiking Time: 35 minutes

Cautions: Stay on the trail. Poison ivy is abundant.

Trail Directions: The trail is in the center of the Mackenzie facility, near the middle parking lot, as part of the south trails system. Look for the marked trailhead on the east side of the parking lot.

This trail goes past several prairie plantings **[1]** as well as through the managed forest. On the left is a section planted in 1986, with a 1991 planting on the right. These are typical of Wisconsin's original prairies in pre-settler days. Hikers are asked to stay on the trail and not collect any seeds.

Oak, maple, and other trees are found along this section. Some are labeled for easy identification. Continue straight ahead when the trail branches (.1 mi.) **[2]** and follow it along past some older trees. They are kept to show how decay affects the trunk, diminishing its value as a timber resource. The next woodlot (.2 mi.) **[3]** shows various sizes, varieties, and density of trees to demonstrate how a mixed forest functions. Walk down into a shallow valley that was clear-cut in the last century. The trees here are of the same age because they started growing at the same time after the loggers left. A few oaks are scattered among the poplar.

Notice the different-colored paint markers on the next plot (.3 mi.) **[4].** Blue marks a property line; red shows the boundary for trees to be cut and sold to a sawmill. Orange or yellow paint indicates trees to be cut. The higher mark makes it simpler for the logger to find the correct timber. The lower mark on the trunk shows that the proper tree was cut. Green paint indicates that a tree is to be left alone. White marks an inventory tree.

Following the trail as it makes several turns, you encounter a cross-section planting of oak at .4 mi. **[5].** This shows how trees grow well when planted in the best spots, allowing for light, soil, and growing space. In the winter of 1966, the next area was logged **[6].** Mature and diseased trees were removed. Saplings have started to fill in the open spaces. Cross a service road that doubles as a fire lane and turn right along the trail. There are series of panels here that show how valuable various wood products are (.5 mi.) **[7].** The young trees in the next area (.9 mi.) **[8]** began growing when this area was clear-cut in 1920. The plot has subsequently been thinned to show proper management. But several isolated dead trees are left to show the effect of oak wilt.

Walk past an area that was once a planted field (.6 mi.) **[9].** The trees here are poplar or aspen, the first trees to begin growing after a fire or harvesting. They grow where there is a lot of light and can be harvested for pulpwood. A demonstration pile of logs (.7 mi.) **[10]** shows how allowing a tree to mature increases its value. The older trees provide more lumber, wider boards, and longer lengths. Meet the first part of the trail at the fork and proceed back to the parking lot.

1. Prairie plantings
2. Trail branch
3. Woodlot
4. Paint markers
5. Oak planting
6. Logged area
7. Signs
8. Young trees
9. Old field
10. Log pile

22. Mirror Lake State Park

- Look for white-tailed deer in the pine plantations.
- Have the kids join the Junior Ranger Wisconsin Explorer Program to learn about the area's plants and animals.
- Listen to the pileated woodpecker at work.

Park Information

It is easy to tell how Mirror Lake got its name. Protected by surrounding hills and trees, there is seldom a wind-stirred ripple on the water's calm surface. The park is a favorite of visitors who use it as a jumping-off point for exploring the tourism wonders of the Wisconsin Dells.

Early pioneer Horace LaBar built a dam in the creek to generate power to grind flour in his mill. Thus was Mirror Lake born. The old wooden dam was replaced by a concrete structure in 1925. The park was opened in 1966, consisting of more than 2,000 acres. Oak and pine surround the lake, with prairie and reclaimed farm fields beyond that.

Directions: Mirror Lake State Park is .5 mile south of I-90/94 on U.S. Highway 12. On Highway 12, drive west 1.5 miles on Fern Dell Road to the park entrance.

Hours Open: 6 A.M. to 11 P.M. daily, year round. The concession in the boat launch area is open from 10 A.M. to dusk daily from Memorial Day to Labor Day. After Labor Day, the stand is open on weekends until mid-October, weather permitting.

Facilities: Playground, 20 miles of hiking and cross-country ski trails (the only surfaced trail is one leading to a fishing pier for people with physical disabilities), picnic areas, beach, interpretive programs, boat launch, and canoe, pontoon, and rowboat rentals. There are three camping areas at the park,

with 146 sites (27 have electricity). Group camping is available. Cliffwood and Bluewater Bay campgrounds have showers. Reservations are necessary for summer weekends. Some sites are geared toward persons with disabilities.

Permits and Rules: In the winter, stay off the ice. Currents may weaken it, causing it to be thin. Marathon or skate skiing is permitted only on marked loops. Skate skiers should use only the left side of these trails. Hikers are warned to stay behind barricades and barriers near cliff edges and to keep away from areas without such protection. Maintaining a clean camp is recommended. Skunks and raccoons can raid food boxes.

Further Information: Contact Superintendent, Mirror Lake State Park, E10320 Fern Dell Road, Baraboo, WI 53912; 608-254-2333.

Other Points of Interest

The **Wisconsin Dells** is one of central Wisconsin's major tourist meccas. There are boat tours of the Upper and Lower Dells, as well as water slides, petting zoos, resorts, water ski presentations, country music shows, wax museums, fudge shops, and other attractions. Call the Dells Visitor and Convention Bureau for details, 800-22-DELLS or 608-254-8088.

Baraboo is home of the original Ringling Brothers Circus. Hikers can stroll through the historic town on a house tour, looking at the homes of long-ago circus performers and show directors. The **Al Ringling Theater** downtown features a range of music, drama, dance, and film. The barns and outbuildings of the old circus now make up the **Circus World Museum,** which houses one of North America's largest collections of circus wagons and other artifacts. For further information, call 608-356-8341.

Park Trails

Southwest Loop Trail—1.5 miles—This site for biking, hiking, and cross-country skiing is located southwest of the main park office, on the south side of Fern Dell Road. The trail crosses prairie land and loops through stands of jack pine. It is reached by crossing the road after trekking around the Time Warp Trail, a marked nature trail on the west side of the park.

Bluewater Bay Trail—.5 mile—Depart from the tent-only campsites on the east side of the park. The

sandy trail meanders through the campground area in the center of the park and emerges near the 200-foot-long beach at Mirror Lake. Extend this jaunt by linking with the hiking and ski trail that runs around the campground to the south. Look for the intersections.

Echo Rock Hiking Trail—.6 mile—The trailhead is at the parking site for Cliffwood Campground on the north end of Mirror Lake State Park. It is an easy loop to the northwest, moving through trees and along the shoreline of the upper lake before waltzing back to the camping area. You return near the flush toilet and showers adjacent to the parking lot.

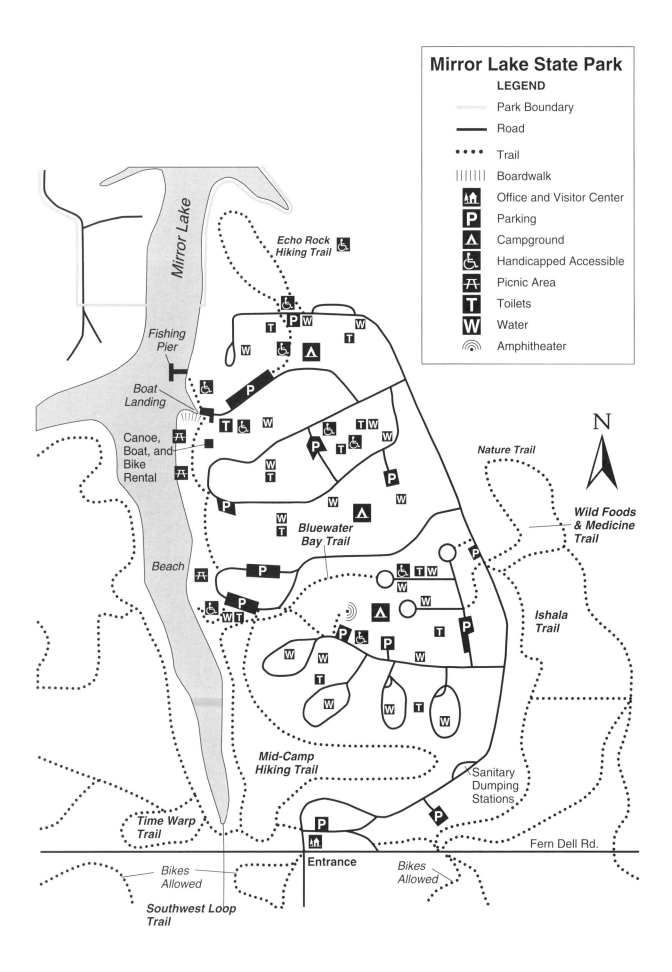

Mirror Lake State Park
LEGEND

Park Boundary
Road
Trail
Boardwalk
Office and Visitor Center
P	Parking
Campground
Handicapped Accessible
Picnic Area
T	Toilets
W	Water
Amphitheater

Mirror Lake

Echo Rock Hiking Trail

Fishing Pier

Boat Landing

Canoe, Boat, and Bike Rental

Beach

Nature Trail

Wild Foods & Medicine Trail

Bluewater Bay Trail

Ishala Trail

Mid-Camp Hiking Trail

Sanitary Dumping Stations

Time Warp Trail

Fern Dell Rd.

Bikes Allowed

Bikes Allowed

Entrance

Southwest Loop Trail

N

Wild Foods and Medicine/ Ishala Trails 👢👢

Distance Round-Trip: 2.1 miles

Estimated Hiking Time: 2 hours

Cautions: There are several steep hills with sandy pathways, making it slow going on hot days. Watch out for poison ivy.

Trail Directions: Both trails leave from the same trailhead across the camp service drive on the east side of the park. There is a parking space for 8 to 12 vehicles on the west side of the road.

Carefully cross the road and look for the trailhead signs **[1]**. Maps and trail guides for the .7-mi. Wild Foods and Medicine Trail can be secured at a covered box there for 25 cents. After 100 feet into the pine woods, the trail splits, with the Ishala Trail going to the right and the Wild Foods and Medicine Trail continuing ahead (.1 mi.) **[2]**. Go forward along the path down the hill, which doubles as a service road. This can be wet and muddy during rainy weather. Along this stretch of pathway are numerous maple trees from which maple sugar can be harvested (.2 mi.) **[3]**. Off in the forest are oaks, with their caps and leaves coating the pathway. There are some boggy wet spaces along the way where low-lying areas catch rain run-off and water the joe-pye weed and blue-flag iris.

Follow the S-curves around the right and left and right at the top of the next rise (.4 mi.) **[4]** just before connecting again with the return leg of the Ishala Loop. Look around for the raspberry bushes, which fruit out from early to mid-July. You can bypass the rest of the nature trail here by turning right and going along the main hiking leg. But if you continue left you will pass along a field backed by pine trees (.5 mi.) **[5]** and white oak. From here, keep following the trail back to the entrance area where you can pick up the Ishala Loop again for a full trek on that leg.

On the Ishala, walk south along the path that parallels the camp service road on the right. Cars can be seen through the trees before you plunge deeper into the oaks and maples about .2 mi. down the path **[6]**. Next is a field on the left, with the pine forest still on the right. At .3 mi., there are piles of wood chips

collected from ground-up trees. The chips are used for covering paths. Cross the service road leading to this storage area and proceed along the tree line to the right. You pass an intersection with a ski trail at .4 mi. **[7]**. Continue straight ahead for another .2 mi. and see some of the traffic along Fern Dell Road through the trees. On this stretch, you pass behind the park shops and service area.

Do not cross Fern Dell, but turn east and walk along the path that runs on the side of the road. After about 200 feet, the trail again enters the woods after ascending a rise. The peak is short because you immediately start going back down again on the far side of the hill and move on to a flat but curvy stretch of path heading back north (.8 mi.) **[8]**. There are several wide sandy stretches of open ground amid a pine planting, where it can be furiously hot during a midsummer trek. Pause for a drink after seeking some shade under a nearby tree.

At 1.1 mi., cross the ski trail intersection **[9]** and keep walking north. You will soon see those piles of wood chips again, over to the west. Continue along the trail through an open field dotted with a few wildflowers, such as blazing star, peeking up from the sandy soil. At 1.2 mi. is the intersection with the Wild Foods and Medicine Trail you traversed earlier **[10]**.

Turn left (west) here and continue back toward the trailhead and the parking lot.

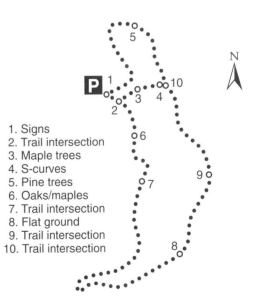

1. Signs
2. Trail intersection
3. Maple trees
4. S-curves
5. Pine trees
6. Oaks/maples
7. Trail intersection
8. Flat ground
9. Trail intersection
10. Trail intersection

Time Warp Nature / Mid-Camp Hiking Trails 👢👢

Distance Round-Trip: 1.5 miles

Estimated Hiking Time: 1.5 hours

Cautions: The trail can be slippery with pine needles.

Trail Directions: Cross the service road from the parking lot to the west of the park office. The Time Warp Nature Trail is officially .4 mi. long. The hiking trail is about 1.1 mi., skirting the edge of the central campground and its connecting leg to the Bluewater Bay group campground trail.

Enter the pine woods and walk .1 mi. into the trees to the intersection of the Time Warp Nature Trail to the west and the main hiking trail to the north **[1].** Turn right and take the hiking trail, saving the nature link for later in your stroll. Proceed up the hill, keeping an eye open for exposed roots that could trip you. After the hill, the trail is relatively flat, but it makes a series of S-curves (.2 mi.) **[2].** So simply follow the sandy track and see where it leads. You pass the campground on the right as you move along the wide path.

Move down the slope and angle to the right (north) (.3 mi.) **[3]** just before reaching the parking lot for the beach. Turn left at the intersection with the Bluewater Bay campsite trail and head toward the beach (.5 mi.) **[4].** Cross a mowed grassy area about 400 feet from the water and turn to the south (left) where the trail reenters the underbrush and oak woods. Often the "rat-a-tat-tat" sound of the large pileated woodpecker can be heard in the distance.

You have to clamber up a sandy hill (.6 mi.) **[5]** reminiscent of a scene from a Bob Hope-Bing Crosby film. Supposedly bikes are not allowed on this stretch, but kids often take their trail cycles and cut along this area. You will see their tracks cutting into the loose soil. You are walking along the southeast shore of the lake, which is partially hidden by the trees. The track is now a roller-coaster walk over the small dunes and rises in the forest. Connect with the Time Warp Nature Trail at .9 mi. **[6]** and turn right.

Cross a narrow plank bridge near a stand of red oaks that grow well in the sandy soil. The wetland here supports a variety of plants different from what you will see elsewhere as you walk in the park. Alder, boneset, and great angelica can be found. Angle to the right past an area that beavers cleaned out several years ago. Aspens and willows have regrown here. Turn left at the intersection. Move along the trail to an open prairie (1.1 mi.) **[7],** with its few scattered oak trees. Under the glare of the hot sun, hikers can identify rough blazing star, Indian grass, bluestem, gray goldenrod, prairie smoke, and other meadow plants. Cowbirds, swallows, and sparrows flit back and forth over the field.

After traversing a loop around the west end of the restoration area, spot a bench under a massive oak tree (1.3 mi.) **[8].** Years back there was an old homestead here. All that remain are a couple of lilacs growing off to the south of the prairie. A rest in the shade is welcome, much as it probably was for that farm family who lived here then. Now turn back east through the meadow and hit the red oak stand again. Follow the trail back to the access road (1.5 mi.) **[9].** On the way, you might be lucky and spot a white-tailed deer browsing amid the lady's slippers and wild columbine.

1. Trail intersection
2. S-curves
3. Right angle
4. Beach
5. Sandy hill
6. Trail intersection
7. Prairie
8. Bench
9. Access road

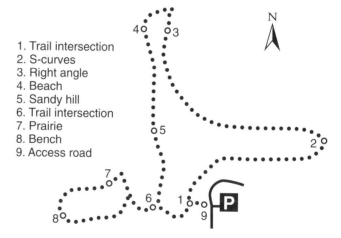

23. Devil's Lake State Park

- Climb the awesome cliffs surrounding the lake.
- Observe rock formations that are among the earth's oldest visible physical features.
- Swim in the warm waters of Devil's Lake.

Park Information

An ancient river was dammed by glacial debris to form what is today's Devil's Lake.

Landmark formations caused by nature's muscle include Balanced Rock, Devil's Doorway, Tomahawk Rock, and Elephant Rock. Prehistoric Native American people lived around the lake for centuries, building mounds that can be seen near the park's north shore entrance.

A million guests annually visit Devil's Lake State Park. Despite the crowds, there is plenty of room, although lines to the toilets on hot summer days can sometimes be daunting. The 8,500-acre park was created in 1911, although vacationers had been visiting since the 1850s.

Directions: The park is 20 miles north of Madison via U.S. Highway 12. Exit east on State Highway 159. Go east 1 mile to the intersection with State Highway 123. Turn south on 123 and follow it to the park entrances. Other access points to campgrounds in the park are along Sauk County Highway DL, South Shore Rd., and on South Lake Drive.

Facilities: A nature center with children's activities and lectures and extensive biking/hiking trails make Devil's Lake a popular getaway. Today's campgrounds quickly fill with lovers of the outdoors. There are plenty of motels in the vicinity as well.

Hours Open: The park is open year round, but trails are not maintained for winter use. The Nature Center is staffed from 9 A.M. to 4:45 P.M. during the peak summer months (June through early September) and from 9 A.M. to 3 P.M. Saturdays and Sundays from mid-September through October. Other times are by appointment. The park closes nightly at 11 P.M.

Permits and Rules: A $5 resident daily state park sticker is required for taking advantage of the park's opportunities. Nonresident stickers are $7. A resident annual fee is $18, with nonresident stickers at $25. An annual sticker for a second family vehicle is available at half price. The appropriate windshield tag can be purchased at the park office. Pets must be on a leash.

Further Information: Contact Superintendent, Devil's Lake State Park, S595 Park Road, Baraboo, WI 53913-9299; 608-356-8301.

Other Points of Interest

The **Pine Island Wildlife Area** covers 5,043 acres in Columbia and Sauk Counties, west of Portage along Levee Road off State Highway 78. Canoeing and boating on the Wisconsin River are fun. While there are no marked trails, hikers can simply bushwhack around the area. For more information, call the Poynette Department of Natural Resources station, 608-275-3242.

Park Trails

Johnson Farm/Glacial Moraine Loop (White Loop) —2.9 miles—This easy trail is accessible from the park's Ice Age Campground; simply follow the white blazes. The trail takes hikers on a walk through shagbark hickory groves, past a shallow frog-filled pond, around several marshes, and along a grassy meadow. Parking is available on Sauk County Highway DL, at the Steinke Basin parking lot.

Steinke Basin Loop (Green Loop) —2.5 miles— This is a gentle level trek over grassland and through oak woods covering the floor of what was once an ancient glacial lake. The easy walking makes it a good introduction to the outdoors for young hikers with very short legs. The best place to find the trail is at the marked parking site on County Highway DL.

CCC (Purple Loop) —.6 mile—This is one of the more difficult treks; you should count on taking at least an hour to climb the stone steps on the south face of the east bluff. This is not a surfaced trail and the rocks can be slippery with morning dew or after a rain, so stay away from the cliff edge. From the top, hikers can get a view of the entire lake.

Balanced Rock Trail —.3 mile— Although a short leg, this is one of the most difficult treks at Devil's Lake. It is a steep trail that involves crawling over stone steps along the south face of the east bluff. Yet the views are worth the climb.

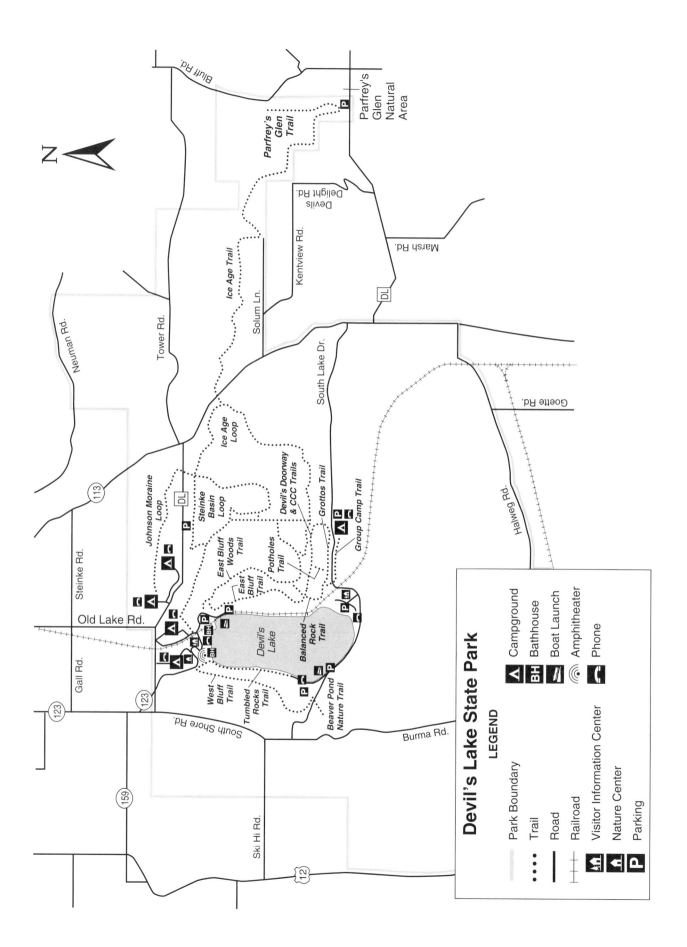

N

Devil's Lake State Park

LEGEND

Park Boundary

Trail

Road

Railroad

Visitor Information Center

Nature Center

Parking

Campground

Bathhouse

Boat Launch

Amphitheater

Phone

Bluff Rd.

Parfrey's Glen Trail

Parfrey's Glen Natural Area

Devils Delight Rd.

Kentview Rd.

Marsh Rd.

Ice Age Trail

Solum Ln.

DL

South Lake Dr.

Goette Rd.

Neuman Rd.

Tower Rd.

113

Steinke Rd.

Johnson Moraine Loop

Ice Age Loop

Steinke Basin Loop

DL

East Bluff Woods Trail

East Bluff Trail

Devil's Doorway & CCC Trails

Potholes Trail

Grottos Trail

Group Camp Trail

Halweg Rd.

Old Lake Rd.

Gall Rd.

123

123

West Bluff Trail

Tumbled Rocks Trail

Devil's Lake

Balanced Rock Trail

Beaver Pond Nature Trail

South Shore Rd.

Burma Rd.

159

Ski Hi Rd.

12

Devil's Doorway 👢

Distance Round-Trip: 1 mile

Estimated Hiking Time: 45 minutes

Cautions: Be aware of loose-gravel footing. Keep your eyes on the path. There are timber rattlesnakes in the park; sometimes they can be seen sunning on rocks along the trail. Just leave the snakes alone.

Trail Directions: This trail branches off from the East Bluff Trail (after about .2 mi.), which is at the top of the east cliff. The quickest way to the trail is from the south end of the park near the Visitor Information Center. Drive along South Lake Drive to the trail and look for the purple markers.

This is an easy, level .5-mi. trail along the edge of the top of the east bluff **[1]** overlooking the clear, cool lake 500 feet below the rim.

The lake is spring fed, varying in depth from 40 to 50 feet. There are a variety of wildflowers and grasses along here, especially where it is sunny and dry. Goldenrod, asters, and other plants have gained toeholds in the shallow soil and in the cracks (.1 mi.)

[2]. There are also scattered mountain maples and red elders, but the area is mostly a clearing and not heavily wooded.

All along the way is a panorama of the lake with drop-offs on the trail edge. Don't get too close to the rim, because there are no handrails. Looking out from over the cliff, you can see hawks that fly parallel to eye level.

There is a spur trail (.3 mi.) **[3]** with large stone steps leading to the Devil's Doorway rock formation **[4]**. The rocks here are precariously balanced on each other but are not in any danger of falling—yet. This is a good place for photographing the landscape. This is a beautiful, rewarding side jaunt. However, be cautious. At one point, it looks as though the trail has disappeared in a field of boulders. Just be persistent and continue picking your way along while looking for the markers.

Returning to the main trail, you will have only a short walk to the end of the pathway. But on this steep section you pass several potholes (.5 mi.) **[5]** created by spinning rocks twirled about by glacial run-off. Retrace your steps to arrive at the end of the trail.

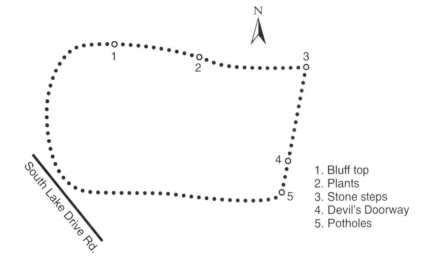

1. Bluff top
2. Plants
3. Stone steps
4. Devil's Doorway
5. Potholes

East Bluff Trail 👢👢👢

Distance Round-Trip: 2.6 miles

Estimated Hiking Time: 2.25 hours

Cautions: Watch for loose or wet, slippery rocks. Good hiking shoes should be worn.

Trail Directions: Enter the park from the north face area where the park headquarters is located. The entrance is off State Highway 123 East. Look for the yellow markers. The first half of the trek is along the bluff, with orange markers. A walk through the woods follows. So look for the yellow markers.

Follow the initial asphalt steps up the footway of the eastern cliff **[1]**. Here it is relatively cool, with ferns and other plants that revel in such comfortable temperatures even on the hottest days. The air gradually warms as you climb, with resulting changes in plant species. Continue on the climb as the uniform asphalt steps give way to large boulders moonlighting as a crude stairway (.2 mi.) **[2]**.

While pausing to catch your breath and take stock of the footpath's condition, note the scenic vantage points along the trail. You catch glimpses of the lake and surrounding countryside between the patches of forest and thick shrubbery.

Be careful of the steep drop-offs along this trail once it reaches the crest of the cliff (.4 mi.) **[3]**. Continue over the uneven pathway to a level area where you can stop and admire Elephant Cave and Elephant Rock (.6 mi.) **[4]**. These formations earned their names because of their size. Leaving the massive boulders behind, keep picking your way along the path. However, don't get close to the cliff rim. The path is relatively straight except for zigs and zags around the rocks. But the trail angles left at 1.1 mi. **[5]** where it connects with the East Bluff Woods Trail. This is an easy-to-moderate pathway, alternately grassy and rocky. It rolls over an undulating landscape of mixed hardwoods and clearings. Sumac and other transitional plants hover around the edges of the trees.

But you don't need to turn onto the woods trail immediately. You have the option of taking several other paths, including the CCC Trail (1.2 mi.) **[6]**. You also have the option of taking the Devil's Doorway Trail located near the CCC Trail. Follow the purple signposts along the rolling path from the East Bluff Trail to where it links with the other trails. Keep the signposts in sight and you can't go wrong.

Back on the woods loop, keep following the narrow path as it makes its way through the maple and oak trees. There are other varieties scattered along the way, such as a few birch. At 2.1 mi., the trail swings a bit to the left **[7]** and then straightens out again as it goes along a steep slope. This loop now takes you back to the parking lot.

—Michelle Zierhut

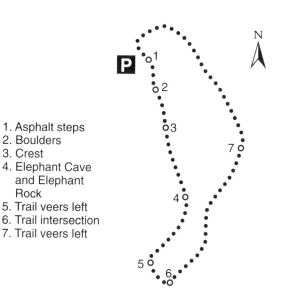

1. Asphalt steps
2. Boulders
3. Crest
4. Elephant Cave and Elephant Rock
5. Trail veers left
6. Trail intersection
7. Trail veers left

Ice Age Trail 👢👢

Distance Round-Trip: 3.6 miles

Estimated Hiking Time: 2 hours

Cautions: Lyme disease is spread through the bite of deer ticks, which are active from spring into fall in the Devil's Lake vicinity. Check yourself and pets for the ticks after hiking in the park, especially if you have gone through an unmowed portion of a trail. Remove the ticks with tweezers. Look at the tick exhibit in the park's Nature Center to learn the difference between the deer tick and the common wood tick, which does not carry the disease.

Trail Directions: Pick up this portion of the 1,000-mi.-long Ice Age Trail at the end of Solum Lane, a paved road exiting from State Highway 113. Solum Lane is on the east side of Devil's Lake State Park. You'll find trail markers indicating only the route heading back toward the park. To avoid becoming lost, follow the 1.5-mi. segment of the Ice Age Trail within the park to its connection with the 4-mi. Ice Age Loop (Red).

Both a private home on the south side of Solum Lane **[1]** and an access road to nearby electrical towers are heavily posted with "No Trespassing" signs, so stay on the north side of the road. The Solum Lane leg of the Ice Age Trail is seldom used by hikers. This provides a getaway feel that is missing in more heavily used locations closer to Devil's Lake itself. A shallow ditch hidden in the weeds just off the parking lot at the end of the lane could be an ankle-turner, so exercise caution.

After parking, you will immediately traverse a rich spread of wildflowers carpeting a meadow. A path to the tree line across the field is mowed irregularly. Thus by late summer it may be hard to track, so keep watching for signs on trailside posts. But the view of bloodroot, Dutchman's breeches, mayapple, black-eyed Susans, wild geraniums, evening primrose, and hundreds of other species is magnificent during the various seasons.

You'll hit the woods almost immediately (.2 mi.) **[2]**. The trail between your entry on Solum Lane and Highway 113 affords some stunning views of Devil's Lake to the far left as you move northwest. A decent, hard-earth path meanders through the trees, ascending and descending several small hills. About .5 mi. into the trek **[3]**, you can look to the southeast and on clear days see the state capitol building in Madison. In the summer, however, trees and underbrush usually hide that view. Aspen, birch, oaks, shagbark hickory, and a stray wild apple compose the principal foliage. On the bluffs, you will find more oaks. In the autumn, the fallen acorn crowns look like pixie caps strewn on the trail after an elfin party.

Keep following the posted blazes, which will lead you through the woods to the crossing of State Highway 113 (1.3 mi.) **[4]**.

Immediately to the other side of the road is the intersection with the park's Ice Age Loop (Red) **[5]**. Continue straight ahead and stroll across the grassy hills. You'll end this portion of the Ice Age trail where it intersects with the Steinke Basin Loop (Green) and the Johnson Moraine Loop (White) on its north side (1.8 mi.) **[6]**.

If you want to lengthen your hike, you can either continue on the 2.5-mi. Steinke Basin Loop, which links with the East Bluff Woods Trail, or turn north to follow the 2.9-mi. Johnson Moraine Loop. To return to your car, head back the way you came in via the Ice Age Trail to enjoy a different perspective of the route you just traversed.

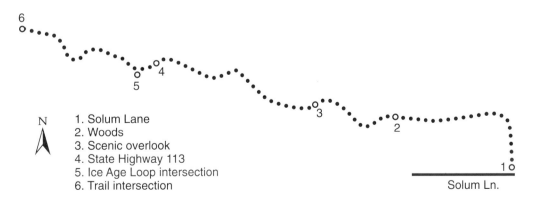

N

1. Solum Lane
2. Woods
3. Scenic overlook
4. State Highway 113
5. Ice Age Loop intersection
6. Trail intersection

Solum Ln.

Parfrey's Glen Trail 👢👢👢

Distance Round-Trip: 1.6 miles

Estimated Hiking Time: 1 hour

Cautions: Slippery rocks near the creek bed, plus jumbles of stones that need to be climbed while ascending the gorge, mean that good hiking shoes are a must. Sometimes the glen is closed because of spring flooding, so be alert for posted warnings and closures. Stay on the marked trail to protect the delicate vegetation that grows in the cool, damp recesses of the glen. Sweaters or jackets are suggested for early-spring and late-summer hiking here because of the noticeable drop in temperatures as you move deeper into the glen.

Trail Directions: Drive 4 mi. east of Devil's Lake on Sauk County Highway DL to the park entrance. A parking lot on Highway DL holds 100 cars. A picnic area and rest rooms are also available there. It is a .25-mi. walk from the lot to the start of the trailhead, along a paved service road that makes for an easy stroll. If folks are tired just reaching the trail, they can sit on the benches at the trailhead to catch their breath before continuing.

Norman Carter Fassett, chairman of the Natural Area Committee for the Department of Natural Resources from 1945 to 1950, selected Parfrey's Glen as Wisconsin's first officially designated natural site. The glen was named after Robert Parfrey, an English man who purchased the gorge in 1865. It had been a prime location for several sawmills and gristmills from at least 1846 on. Look for the foundations of these buildings (.3 mi.) [1] south of the first major stream crossing. An earth and log dam for a millpond plugged the lower end of the gorge where the trail now ascends the base of the west wall, but no traces of it remain. After the mill operations ceased in the 1870s, picnickers and campers flocked to the gorge to enjoy the scenery and coolness in the summer.

There was serious flash flooding in the glen during severe storms in the summer of 1993. The rush of water resulted in the closing of the gorge until trail repairs were completed in 1994. New asphalt walkways were installed and wooden bridges placed over the formerly harder-to-reach spots (.4 mi. and .6 mi.) [2, 3].

There are not any sharp curves or secret side trails within the gorge. It is a straight walk in and out, along the rushing waters of a small streambed. However, since climbing is involved, albeit on stone steps or strategically placed boulders, it is not easy either for people who have physical disabilities or are out-of-

shape. However, the element of adventure that accompanied leapfrogging over water-dashed rocks in the old days has been removed. Darn it.

The trek's conclusion is rewarding. A viewing area (.8 mi.) [4] accommodating 10 to 20 persons fronts a waterfall that tumbles about 100 feet from the ridge top to the creek bed. The glen walls here provide a fascinating look at nature's power. The gorge's sandstone sides are embedded with quartzite pebbles and boulders, as if an interior designer had made an artistic sweep along the cliff face. Thousands of years ago, chunks of rock weighing up to 1,500 pounds were broken off and swept along by the surging water, eventually piling up like building blocks. The largest concentration of these boulders is at the end of the trail. Zoned layers of the wall show where there was once sandy beach. Geologists say that the layers spotlight at least 10 million years of erosion.

Along the way, observe the abundant plant life that has a vibrant existence despite the shade. The most common vegetation is the scouring rush, a relative of the fern. The rush is so tough that pioneers used it to scour their dirty pans, hence the name. The glen's cool encourages plants usually found farther north, such as yellow birch, red elder, mountain club moss, and the hardy clintonia. Their roots make snakelike designs up and down the rock walls throughout the glen. The green tentacles creep into fissures on the wall and are slowly opening them up for more erosion. A keen bird-watcher can spot water thrushes and various species of warblers that make their homes in cliffside condos. Retrace your steps to get back to the parking area.

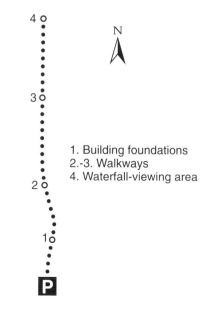

1. Building foundations
2.-3. Walkways
4. Waterfall-viewing area

24. Natural Bridge State Park

- Admire nature's handiwork in creating a bridge from rock.
- Wonder about the people who lived in the cave formations 12,000 years ago.
- Walk along ancient Native American pathways deep into the surrounding forests.

Park Information

For an out-of-the way place to hike, Natural Bridge State Park is one of the best in Wisconsin. The primary feature of this 560-acre park is a sandstone arch with an opening 25 feet high and 35 feet wide. Located in Wisconsin's "driftless," or nonglaciated area, the bridge was created by the effects of wind, water, and frost on the rock. Just below the bridge is a rock shelter where people were living and hunting mastodons between 10,000 and 12,000 years ago. Only 12 miles east, glaciers had blocked Devil's Lake ancient flowage, and the towering ice sheets were in the process of creating today's landscape. State historians point out that non-Indian settlers have been in the vicinity for about six generations (with a generation being about 20 years). If this figure is used, there were Native Americans here more than 500 generations ago.

The bridge and the rock shelter were popular attractions in the late 19th century, with many picnics and parties held on the grassland below the bluff. The park was officially established in 1973 and included a 60-acre state natural area. In addition to the 2 miles of hiking trails within the park, there are 2 miles in the woods across County Highway C to the south.

The park and the surrounding area are rich in wildlife. Hikers can see turkey vultures, bald eagles, finches, Baltimore orioles, deer, raccoons, and other creatures.

Directions: Natural Bridge is 16 miles south of Baraboo on U.S. 12, and 10 miles west on County Highway C.

Hours Open: The park is open during daylight hours from spring to autumn.

Facilities: Picnic area, hiking trails, scenic overlook, rustic toilets.

Permits and Rules: No camping is permitted.

Further Information: Contact Superintendent, Care of Devil's Lake State Park, S5975 Park Road, Baraboo, WI 53913-9299; 608-356-8301.

Other Points of Interest

Take U.S. Highway 12 north from Baraboo to Shady Lane Road and take the exit to the **International Crane Foundation.** Naturalists there work with bird specialists from around the world in saving the 7 species of crane (out of the 15 in existence) that are endangered. Hikers can take guided or self-guided tours daily from May through mid-September. A multimedia presentation on the birds is part of the program. Call 608-356-9462 for more information.

The **Dell Creek Wildlife Area** spreads out over 2,125 acres of state-owned land in Sauk and Juneau Counties. The primary entrance is 7 miles northeast of Reedsburg on County Highway H. Hikers can see ruffed grouse, woodcocks, rabbits, wild turkeys, and deer. There are no marked trails, but strollers can follow meandering deer paths and old logging roads. Call Tower Hill State Park (see park #27), 608-588-2116, for more information.

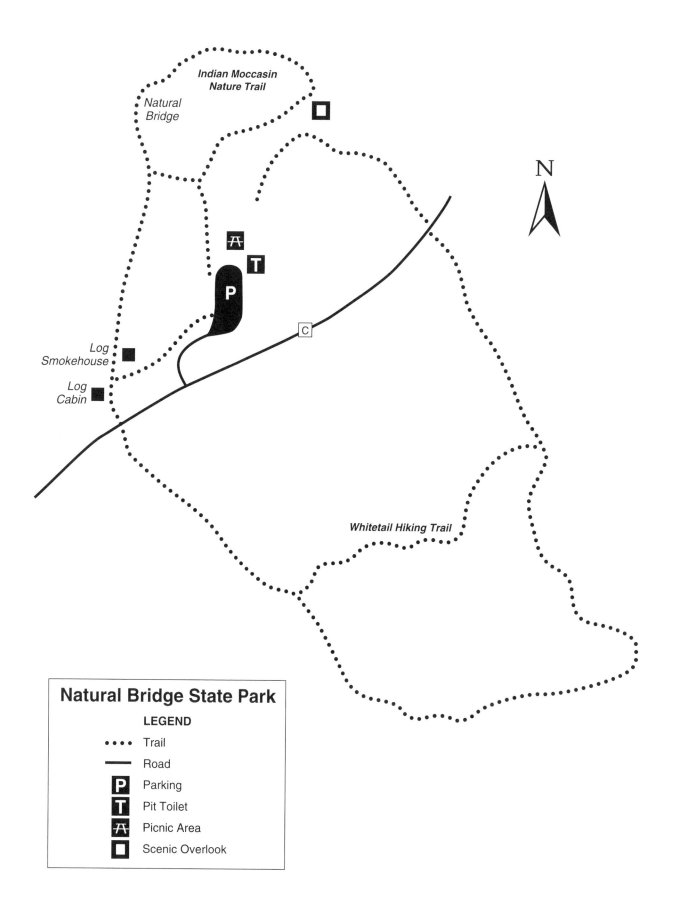

Natural Bridge State Park

LEGEND

- • • • Trail
- —— Road
- **P** Parking
- **T** Pit Toilet
- **⛺** Picnic Area
- ☐ Scenic Overlook

Indian Moccasin Trail 👢👢

Distance Round-Trip: 2 miles

Estimated Hiking Time: 1.5 hours

Cautions: This path entails steep climbs along rocky pathways. There are a few steps with guardrails. Stay on the trail to avoid poison ivy.

Trail Directions: Park in the lot on the north side of County Highway C and walk across the grassy area toward the trailhead at the tree line. There is a sign indicating where to start climbing.

On the way from the parking lot, you will pass rest rooms on the right and a water fountain **[1].** Walk .2 mi. across the mowed parkland past the picnic tables to the oak, ash, beech, and maple forest straight ahead. There is no path—simply walk across the grass. However, the first few hundred feet of the trail is crushed rock. The hill itself makes up a protected state natural area. The path supposedly follows ancient Native American trails leading up to the arch.

Thick underbrush fills the gullies and valleys on each side of the pathway. A heavy canopy of maple and oak overhangs the entire area. At .4 mi., there are six steps **[2]** up the hill leading to an intersection where you can go right to an overlook or go left to get an immediate view of the arch. To prolong the wilderness feeling, take the route to the right and continue climbing. Wild cherry, Virginia creeper, raspberry bushes, and other vegetation flow back from the rocky trail at this point (.5 mi.) **[3].** The sandstone cliff is on the left and a drop-off is to the right. There are no handrails, so watch your step. Every 20 feet for the next .1 mi., there is another built-in step.

Red maple can now be spotted among the other trees. Trappers used to boil their snares in water that contained red maple bark. This removed the scent of the animals last caught in the trap. In addition, a solution made from the tree's inner bark remains an effective homeopathic eyewash.

You now go up and down a series of rolling ledges that front the deep gullies. At .6 mi., another staircase wends its way up around the cliff face **[4].** Many fantastically shaped rock formations are in the vicinity. At the top of the steps is an overlook to the eastern hills. After looking out at the countryside, keep climbing to the left. At .8 mi., there are some

quaking aspen and dwarf juniper along the cliff edge, tenuously hanging on from one generation to the next **[5].** The junipers are the world's most distributed conifer; distant cousins of the trees along this trail are also found in Europe and Asia.

There is now a slight descent in the trail (.9 mi.) **[6]** via some steps with a handrail on the left side. There is a small stump in the middle of the trail—simply walk around it (1 mi.) **[7].** Around the next corner, you encounter the natural bridge.

A wooden fence is across the front of the natural stone shelter under the bridge. Fire pits here have been dated back at least 12,000 years, making this one of the oldest such locales in North America. It was used as a shelter for the Paleo-Indians who preceded the Woodland cultures.

After viewing the bridge, proceed to the right and continue down the wooden stairs leading to a meadow. You can turn to the left and continue along the cliff rim to the point originally ascended. But by proceeding straight ahead, you cross through an upland meadow (1.2 mi.) **[8]** and move down the slope along a grassy path. Scattered oaks dot the scene, which can be viewed from the comfort of a small bench (1.3 mi.) **[9]** on the left of the trail.

From there, stroll .25 mi. back to the county highway where you pass a settler's cabin and a smokehouse **[10]** adjacent to the road. You then have to wander about .12 mi. back east to the parking lot.

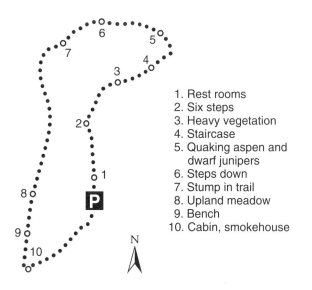

1. Rest rooms
2. Six steps
3. Heavy vegetation
4. Staircase
5. Quaking aspen and dwarf junipers
6. Steps down
7. Stump in trail
8. Upland meadow
9. Bench
10. Cabin, smokehouse

Loop A/Whitetail Hiking Trail

Distance Round-Trip: 2.1 miles

Estimated Hiking Time: 1.7 hours

Cautions: It is a long, hot way across the fields to the trees, so bring water. On the return, the trail is not well marked after it leaves the forest pathway. Hikers need to carefully cut across a cornfield to reach the road in front of the park.

Trail Directions: Cross County Highway C to the south, opposite the settler's cabin where the Natural Bridge Trail concluded. There will be a small hiker logo on a signpost at the entrance to a farm drive that leads to a pasture and cornfield.

Cross the highway and walk down a long farm driveway **[1]** that opens to a cornfield and pasture opposite the state park. Stick to the road and avoid cutting through the corn. Straight ahead is an over-grown trail leading into the trees on the far south side of the field. The trail is not marked here, but follow

the deer path between the trees (.3 mi.) **[2]**. Wild daisies, milkweed, oats, and bluestem can be seen on the climb up from the fields. Silver maple and other upland forest trees conceal the uppermost rim of the hill as you ascend the trail. The path grows more difficult the higher you go (.4 mi.) **[3]**. However, at .6 mi., there is an old trail marker **[4]** affirming that you are heading in the right direction.

You could continue another mile straight ahead before running into posted land. Instead of continuing straight, turn left at what is called the Whitetail Hiking Trail (.8 mi.) **[5]**. This is a narrow footpath that skirts the rim of the valley above the cornfield. There is a bench (.9 mi.) **[6]** in a small glade about 100 feet to the left of the trail. If necessary, rest while enjoying the vista. Then get back on the path and wend your way downhill. Be careful of the slippery leaves and roots underfoot. There is a plank bridge at the bottom, leading over a narrow gully. There are steps with a handrail down to the bridge (1.1 mi.) **[7]**.

The trail disappears at the edge of the cornfield, once you leave the maple and oak forest (1.3 mi.) **[8]**. Turn left. It is a .25-mi. trek (or more) across the open ground to reach another farm service road that leads back to County Highway C. You can see the highway in the distance, but you first need to cross the field. Be careful not to damage any plants.

Another hiking marker **[9]** is visible where the service road hits the highway. Once you reach that roadway, it is a .5-mi. walk back west to the state park entrance. Walk against traffic, well off the pavement whenever a vehicle roars past.

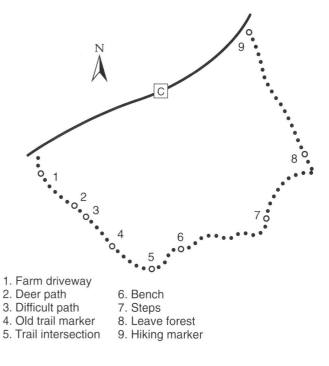

1. Farm driveway
2. Deer path
3. Difficult path
4. Old trail marker
5. Trail intersection
6. Bench
7. Steps
8. Leave forest
9. Hiking marker

25. Black Hawk Unit— Lower Wisconsin State Riverway

- Test your leg muscles on steep hills.
- Get in touch with a tragic period in American history.
- Find prehistoric effigy mounds in the forest.

Park Information

The Black Hawk Unit is one of 26 management regions of the Lower Wisconsin State Riverway, tucked along 92 miles of the river between the Prairie du Sac dam and the Mississippi River. The state riverway covers 79,275 acres and was established in 1989, providing public recreational access to the more scenic aspects of the lower Wisconsin River.

Over the past century, the Black Hawk Unit has been a pioneer homestead, a farm, and a resort. The state purchased the site in 1990, retaining several of the old buildings as warming cabins and for storage. More than 15 miles of trails are available for hikers, cross-country skiers, and horseback riders.

The ridge north of the center's principal parking lot was the scene of a fierce gun battle between Black Hawk's Sauk and Fox nation and American militia and regular army units in 1832. Black Hawk and his starving followers were attempting to return to their ancestral lands in Illinois but were blocked by the soldiers. So he decided to flee north through south central Wisconsin to escape the whites.

The soldiers caught up with him on July 21 but were stalled by warriors firing on them from the high grass and trees on the ridge. This allowed many refugees to flee across the Wisconsin River. In the firefight, one soldier and several dozen Indians were killed. However, the bulk of Black Hawk's people managed eventually to make it to the Mississippi River where they were again attacked by soldiers. Several of Black Hawk's people tried to cross the river but either drowned or were butchered on the Iowa shore by waiting Sioux, longtime enemies of the Sauk and Fox.

Directions: The Black Hawk Unit is 18 miles northwest of Madison. Take State Highway 12 north to County Highway Y and west to State Highway 78. Then go south 1 mile to the parking area along State Highway 78 on the unit's west boundary. The trails lead east into the main property and north to the Wisconsin Heights battleground. Wachter Road, south of the parking lot, allows paved access to the top of the hill and the unit's buildings.

Hours Open: 6 A.M. to 11 P.M. daily, year round.

Facilities: Picnic shelter, open-air pavilion, warming cabin, 19th-century log cabin, fresh water, toilets.

Permits and Rules: Carry out any picnic leftovers. Glass containers of any kind are prohibited. Keep pets on a leash. Camping is not allowed on the state property but is available at nearby Cedar Hills Campground on the unit's south boundary. Horses are restricted to trails marked for their use. Firearms may not be discharged within 100 yards of any building.

Further Information: Contact Lower Wisconsin State Riverway Board, 202 North Wisconsin Avenue, Muscoda, WI 53575; 608-739-3188.

Other Points of Interest

The **American Players Theater** is the only professional repertory theater in the United States devoted exclusively to classic productions, especially Shakespeare. The outdoor amphitheater is on the south side of the Wisconsin River along County Highway C near Spring Green. The American Players Theater season runs from April to the first weekend in October, with performances Tuesday through Sunday. Call 608-588-2361 for more information.

Biking is a favorite recreational activity around Spring Green and Mazomanie. Miles of winding paved and gravel roads offer challenging mixed terrain. The town of Spring Green is the base of most bike tours, with popular loops through Bear Valley and Frank Lloyd Wright country. **Canoeing** along the Wisconsin River is also a major recreational activity for outdoors enthusiasts. Numerous outfitters rent canoes and can provide launch and pickup services along the route.

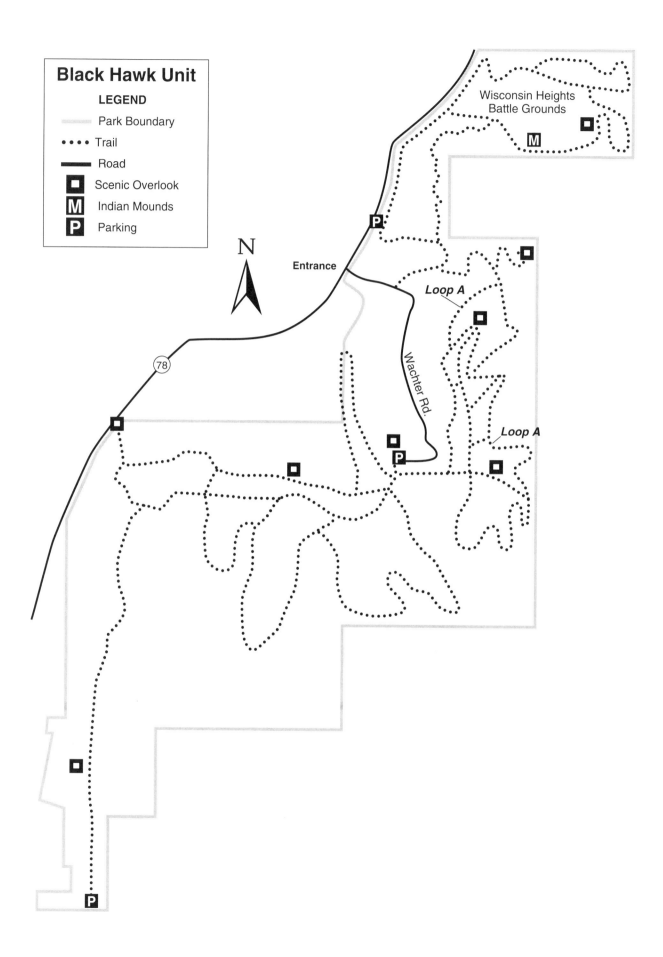

Black Hawk Unit

LEGEND

━━━ Park Boundary

• • • • Trail

━━━ Road

▣ Scenic Overlook

Ⓜ Indian Mounds

Ⓟ Parking

N

Wisconsin Heights
Battle Grounds

Ⓜ

Ⓟ

Entrance

Loop A

Wachter Rd.

Loop A

78

Ⓟ

Ⓟ

Loop A 👢👢👢👢

Distance Round-Trip: 3 miles

Estimated Hiking Time: 3.1 hours

Cautions: The trail is over rugged terrain, with several steep slopes.

Trail Directions: Park in the main lot along State Highway 78. Walk southeast across the lot toward the sign indicating the beginning of the trail.

This is a combination of several loops over hilly terrain, upland prairie, and hardwood forest. From the trailhead, you immediately begin moving up the first steep slope **[1]**. The next .3 mi. seems almost straight up as you start moving to the bluff top. Watch the loose gravel underfoot.

Upon reaching the first plateau, you'll encounter a slight dip in the trail as it goes through an oak grove. Stay right as you pass the trail intersection **[2]** that will carry you north to the Wisconsin Heights Battlefield Trail. Follow the curve to the right (.4 mi.) **[3]**, then turn left at the next trail intersection. All this time, you will again be going uphill. The trail is a mixture of sand, rock, and dirt that is muddy and slippery when wet. When dry, it provides a scrabbly, rough way up.

Yet the vista is worth the climb. The Wisconsin River valley is from 300 to 500 feet below as you walk along the crest of the ridge (.5 mi.) **[4]**. However, summer's heavy undergrowth and thick clumps of silver maples, box elders, and aspens often block the view as you proceed south. Stay on the wide trail as it moves over the rolling terrain at the top of the ridge. The pathway seems wide enough for two trucks to run side-by-side, which is unusual for most hiking trails.

Moving along the trail, pass two paths used as cross-country ski trails. Follow the trail as it swirls to the right, angles left where a ski trail aims to the west, then makes another left. This is followed by another right for a longer straightaway. There is an intersection with a ski trail to the right at .6 mi **[5]**.

Stay on the main trail while walking to the south, passing any intersection with ski trails. Follow the path as it makes its zig-zag route through the maples along the ridge top. After several bends in the trail,

you pass a fence line near a pasture. Follow the trail as it cuts across the pasture to the west. Several buildings are within sight straight ahead.

Beyond the field to the left are a pole pavilion, two cabins, a barn, and equipment storage sheds, with fresh water available from a pump. After resting on one of the picnic tables near the cabin, walk to the north past the trailhead marker. Cross the special events parking lot straight ahead to an overlook of the valley **[6]**. A fresh, cooling breeze slips up the cliffside to rustle the leaves of trees rimming the ridge. In winter, this can be a chilling locale but the view is worth it.

After taking in the view, head back east across the parking lot and turn left on Wachter Road. When the road begins its downhill run, cut across the pavement to the hiking trail that runs back north. Stay on the main trail by following the arrows. The trail intersects with shortcuts and ski trails that you passed on the way south. There is another overlook to the right **[7]** where you can pause briefly for a view of the valley; retrace your steps again to pick up the main trail.

There is again the familiar up-and-down hike along the crest back to the intersection with the trail (2.5 mile) **[2]** leading downhill to the parking lot.

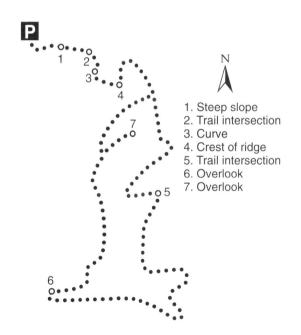

N

1. Steep slope
2. Trail intersection
3. Curve
4. Crest of ridge
5. Trail intersection
6. Overlook
7. Overlook

Wisconsin Heights Battleground 👢👢👢

Distance Round-Trip: 2.5 miles

Estimated Hiking Time: 2.5 hours

Cautions: The sandstone terrain is very hilly and is overgrown with thick brush and stands of birch, hickory, oak, maple, and basswood. However, in 1996 a land-clearing project was begun to develop a history trail featuring the major actions in the 1832 battle between soldiers and Sauk/Fox chief Black Hawk.

Trail Directions: There are three principal ways to enter the battleground site. Take the trail from the north gate off State Highway 78, or hike the north-bound trail from the main parking lot about .25 mi. south of that gate. Hikers can also link up with the trail from Loop A.

By taking Loop A from the south, you move along up-and-down terrain through the upland woods at the top of the bluff **[1].** It is easy to see why Black Hawk chose this site for a rearguard defensive action. His ambush and harrying tactics over this ground made it difficult for the troops to attack in formation.

Move ahead .25 mi. and turn right. Proceed another .2 mi. and see five effigy mounds almost lost in the underbrush **[2].** These date back to between 600 and 1300 A.D. To the left, the state is removing trees and undergrowth in this area to make the land look as it did in the 1830s. Large amounts of cut timber are piled up for shipping away. The trail then makes several curves to the right and left. Walk around the base of a high knob of rock, one of the Indians' defensive positions. Proceed down the next slope and back up the other side of a shallow valley.

Bursting out of the thick forest (1.3 mi.) **[3],** walk north along a fence line with a horse pasture to the right. About .12 mi. beyond, the trail disappears **[4].**

Thick stands of raspberry bushes and other vegetation obscure the pathway. Some of the bushes are higher than a hiker's head, with maple, ironwood and birch crowding in the sides of what a hiker might perceive to be a trail. Logs, branches and other debris litter the ground, making it difficult to plow through the dense undergrowth. It is wise to stop attempting to move forward here. Retrace your steps by following all the broken stalks of plants that you trod on while attempting to move ahead. Stick to this route and you will eventually return to the logged area the same way you entered the scrub brush.

There is an intersection to the right that opens on a clearing. Take that to the west instead of the original route you took into the brushy section. Walk through the clearing, imagining the tragedy that took place here more than 150 years ago. You can walk down the slope to the chained entry to the loggers' service drive and find the trail that runs back to the parking lot. This necessitates an up-and-down climb again. If you're tired, simply walk along the east side of the highway. Be sure to face traffic and stay well to the ditch. It is .25 mi. back to your vehicle.

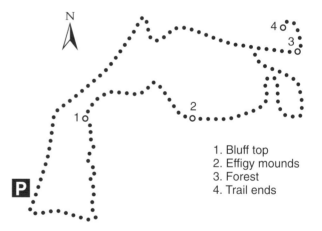

1. Bluff top
2. Effigy mounds
3. Forest
4. Trail ends

26. Blue Mound State Park

- Climb two 40-foot observation towers to look over the Wisconsin countryside.
- Travel along old trails blazed by Native Americans.
- Swim, picnic, and simply relax at a popular park.

Park Information

The park is atop the westernmost of two mounds of limestone that mark the horizon here. The granite "roots" of these Wisconsin-scale mountains are more than two billion years old. The original rock was covered by an ancient sea. Millions of years of subsequent erosion created the ridges, valleys, and knobs of Blue Mound State Park.

Blue Mound was set up as a park in 1959. At 1,716 feet above sea level, it is the highest point in southern Wisconsin. A nature center here was designed by a student of famed architect Frank Lloyd Wright. There are 5 miles of hiking trails and 9 miles of cross-country ski trails.

Directions: The park entrance is on Mounds Park Road, taken from the west side of the village of Blue Mounds in south central Wisconsin. Blue Mounds is 25 miles west of Madison along U.S. Highway 18.

Hours Open: The park is open daily, year round. The campsite closes to visitors at 11 P.M. and opens at 6 A.M. Office hours are 8 A.M. to 4:30 P.M. Monday through Thursday, except for summer when it is open until 8 P.M. Friday and 11. P.M. Saturday. It is closed on Sundays in winter.

Facilities: Camping, hiking, biking, cross-country skiing, off-road biking; swimming pool, picnic areas, interpretive programs, playground equipment, horseshoe court, toilets, water fountains, and two observation towers.

Permits and Rules: Cutting of standing trees for firewood is prohibited, although collecting of dead, downed wood is okay. Year-round camping is permitted at the 78 wooded sites. Reservations are accepted for May 1 through October 31 for campsites #1-56. The remainder of the sites are available on a first-come, first-served basis. There is no group camp. Several sites are accessible to persons with physical disabilities.

Further Information: Contact Park Superintendent, Box 98, Blue Mounds, WI 53517; 608-437-5711.

Other Points of Interest

The **Military Ridge Bike Trail** runs along the southernmost border of the park and links Dodgeville and Verona, along the former Chicago and North Western Railroad line. The grades are gentle, making it an easy bike ride. The highest point on the line is at the village of Blue Mounds, some 1,300 feet above sea level. The lowest is on the Sugar River, between Riley and Verona, at 930 feet. The trail is open from 6 A.M. to 11 P.M. daily. Trail permits are required. For details, contact the state park office, 608-437-5711.

Anyone interested in adventure will find excitement at the **Cave of the Mounds,** 2 miles east of Blue Mounds on County Highway F in Dane County. The cavern has an unusual assortment of stalagmites and stalactites. The cave was discovered in 1939 when the landowner was quarrying limestone. Call 608-437-3038 for more information.

Park Trails

Pleasure Valley Trail 👢👢👢—2 miles—This rolling loop is part of the hiking and off-road biking connection with the John Minix Trail. It takes hikers through open fields ablaze with prairie wildflowers. Remember that cyclists also use the path, and be alert.

John Minix Trail 👢—1 mile—The trail is mostly wooded but is flatter and easy to manage for beginner off-road cyclists and hikers who want a quick study of the park's forestland. The path connects with both the Willow Spring Trail and the Pleasure Valley Trail.

Willow Spring Trail 👢👢—1.7 miles—Willow Spring extends into the northwest part of the park, meandering through forests and fields. The trail hooks up with the John Minix and Flint Rock Nature Trails. Ruffed grouse can sometimes be surprised along the pathway.

Ridgeview Trail 👢👢👢—2 miles—This trail has some of the steepest hills and deepest valleys in the park. There are both forest and prairie areas along the way. Deer and wild turkeys can be seen along here. Occasionally even a reclusive badger is spotted. Ridgeview links up with the scenic .25-mile Walnut Hollow Trail at its east end.

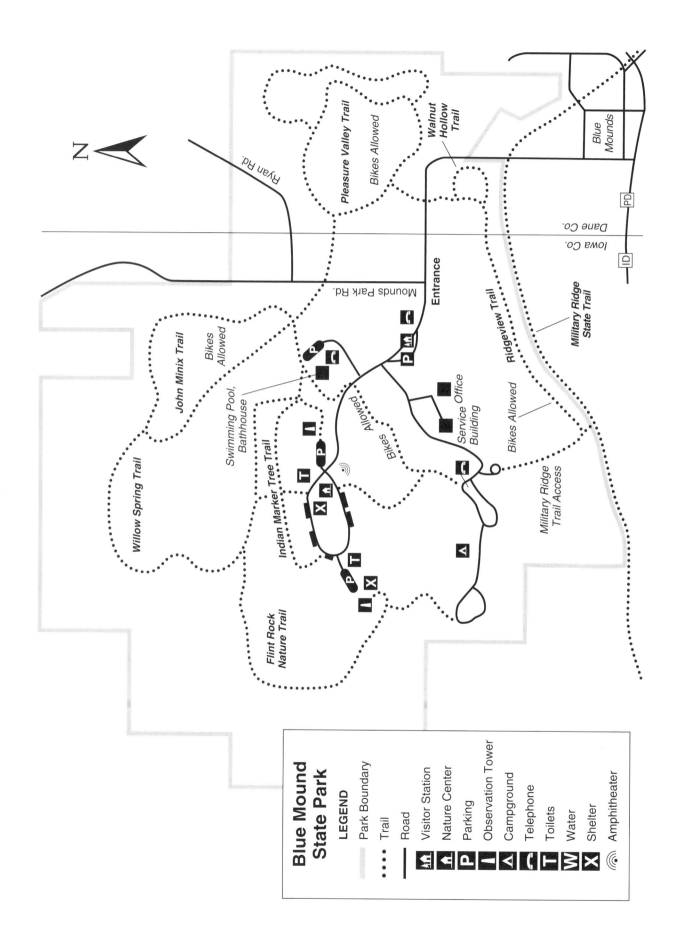

N

Blue Mounds

PD

ID

Iowa Co.

Dane Co.

Ryan Rd.

Pleasure Valley Trail
Bikes Allowed

Walnut Hollow Trail

Mounds Park Rd.

Entrance

Ridgeview Trail

Military Ridge State Trail

John Minix Trail
Bikes Allowed

Willow Spring Trail

Swimming Pool, Bathhouse

Indian Marker Tree Trail

Flint Rock Nature Trail

Bikes Allowed

Service Office Building

Military Ridge Trail Access

Blue Mound State Park

LEGEND

Park Boundary

Trail

Road

Visitor Station

Nature Center

Parking

Observation Tower

Campground

Telephone

Toilets

Water

Shelter

Amphitheater

Flint Rock Nature Trail

Distance Round-Trip: 1.8 miles

Estimated Hiking Time: 1.25 hours

Cautions: The trail is a roller-coaster path over and around rocks, necessitating caution in walking. It can be slippery after a rain. Watch out for roots.

Trail Directions: Depart from the parking area opposite the central picnic shelter to the west of the amphitheater. This is part of the state's Adopt-A-Trail system. A local muzzle loaders' organization is responsible for helping with trail maintenance.

The first 50 feet of the trail is crushed stone as it moves into the forest of oak and maple **[1]**. Hikers immediately bypass huge boulders that are partially buried in the earth, a reminder of tens of thousands of years of erosion. The trail narrows to get around the rocks. At .2 mi., there is the intersection with the Indian Marker Tree Trail **[2]**, which will take hikers to the swimming pool .6 mi. to the east. Continue going straight down the slope, through a dense growth of ferns. Turn left at the intersection and continue straight when the Willow Spring Trail branches off to the right. Cross a plank bridge (.3 mi.) **[3]** over a small stream and continue going forward.

Along the way, beams are buried in the path to slow run-off down the slope (.4 to .9 mi.) **[4]**.

Sometimes it is easier to step around than across them. The water has eaten away at the ground cover, occasionally making it hard to get over. About 50 feet beyond the next plank bridge (.5 mi.) **[5]** is a bench for resting. There are two more bridges (.6 mi.) **[6]**, followed by a culvert and another bridge.

The path now goes uphill again slightly, then descends once more (.9 mi.) **[7]** to a flat boggy area. There is a snow fence to the left. Walk in that direction to a gap in the fence. Just beyond is a bench where you can sit and look out over a meadow. After pausing for the view and your breath, go back to the main trail and continue following the track there. You again bypass a number of large boulders (1 mi.) **[8]** and cross two more bridges.

The path becomes easier now, a trail with a crushed-rock surface, but it begins to rise again. Within a few feet, it ascends sharply. Steps have been placed in the trail, but their ground foundation has mostly been washed away, so it is easier to walk around them. This now makes for a difficult climb, but you soon emerge from the woods near the west observation tower (1.7 mi.) **[9]**. A rest-room building is on the right and a water fountain nearby. You then need to walk across the wide kite-flying field in the middle of the park to get back to your vehicle.

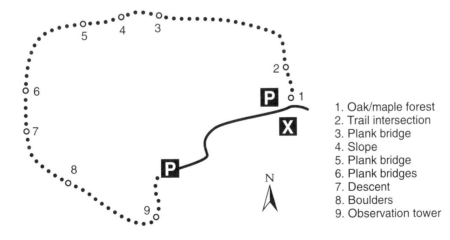

1. Oak/maple forest
2. Trail intersection
3. Plank bridge
4. Slope
5. Plank bridge
6. Plank bridges
7. Descent
8. Boulders
9. Observation tower

N

Indian Marker Tree Trail

Distance Round-Trip: 1.2 miles

Estimated Hiking Time: 1 hour

Cautions: There are steep slopes amid piles of boulders, so strong hiking shoes are necessary.

Trail Directions: The trail begins either at the west end of the park near the picnic areas or at the east end by the swimming pool. Look for the signs indicating the connection. The trail can also be joined midway by descending the initial slope along the Flint Rock Nature Trail.

Leaving the grassy picnic area at the west end **[1]**, hikers immediately encounter thick underbrush consisting of shrubs, wild grapevines, and ground cover such as Virginia creeper. In addition, there are numerous oak, ironwood, bass, and maple trees. The trail rolls along a series of hummocks all the time it is descending the slope (.2 to .3 mi.) **[2]**. At .5 mi. **[3]**, it meets the Flint Rock Nature Trail, but continue going straight ahead amid some interesting stone formations. Tall stands of fern frame each side of the path. Some of the plants are higher than a hiker's head (.6 mi.) **[4]**, a fact that can be disconcerting especially for a youngster not used to the hiking/outdoors scene.

Watch your step here because the trail now starts to descend toward the valley floor. In the distance you can hear shouting and laughter coming from the swimming pool about .5 mi. ahead. You are walking as if through a giant rock garden (.7 mi.) **[5]**, with tumbled landscape and boulders casually tossed about. Waist-high grasses carpet the valley bottom, where you can rest on a bench before continuing (.8 mi.) **[6]**. Go straight ahead if you wish to move toward the swimming pool. Or turn right at the intersection and scramble back up the hill that rises behind you. There are some more stone formations to pass by on the way to the summit.

You emerge from the thicket at the top of the bluff, near the east observation tower **[7]**. If you have had enough climbing for the time being, here are several picnic tables on which to perch while you drink much-needed water. The vista between the maples and oaks is fabulous from this vantage point. Of course, climbing to the top of the tower adds another 40-foot dimension to the view.

Walk back to your car through the center of the park. On the way you will pass more rest rooms, a picnic shelter, and the trailhead to the Flint Rock Nature Trail.

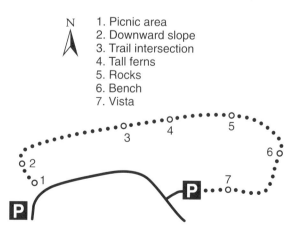

N

1. Picnic area
2. Downward slope
3. Trail intersection
4. Tall ferns
5. Rocks
6. Bench
7. Vista

27. Tower Hill State Park

- View a shot tower dating from the early 1800s.
- Canoe nearby on the Wisconsin River.
- Camp in a secluded grove.

Park Information

At only 77 acres, Tower Hill is one of Wisconsin's smallest state parks. However, it is among the richest in its history. Located along the banks of the Wisconsin River, it is a popular stopover for canoeists who paddle up the Mill Creek tributary to reach the park. In the early 19th century, the site was the village of Helena. The community was one of the first incorporated towns in the state. Its major business was a tower producing millions of pounds of lead shot that was made into ammunition. By 1836, the local economy was so good that Helena was considered a front-runner among choices for the state's capital. Politics prevailed, however, and the village lost its bid for prominence. By 1857, the town was abandoned because it was bypassed by the railroad, and the tower was shuttered shortly afterward. All that remain today of Helena's blacksmith shop, post office, and warehouses are some building foundations in the woods. Emerson Pavilion near the major trailhead is the only building left from the Tower Hill Pleasure Company, a popular resort for Chicago-area Unitarians at the turn of the century. Today, the pavilion can be rented for group functions.

The building of the tower began in 1831 high atop a sandstone cliff overlooking the river. Men using picks and crowbars dug a vertical shaft through 120 feet of sandstone and a 90-foot horizontal tunnel near Mill Creek to connect with the shaft. Lead was secured from mines throughout the region. Shot was produced by pouring molten lead through screens at the top of the shaft. The lead became spherical by the time it hit the bottom, hardening when splashing into a pool of water. The shot was then hauled out via the tunnel, sorted, bagged, and shipped away.

One of the miners who dug the shaft was once challenged to a duel and told to pick his weapons and location for the fight. The savvy miner selected rocks, choosing to stand at the top of the shot-tower shaft. He told his opponent to stand at the bottom. When the other fellow saw those odds, he backed out of the duel.

Directions: Tower Hill State Park is 2 miles south of Spring Green via State Highway 23, then 1 mile east on County Highway C. Look for the signs on 23 and C.

Hours Open: Open daily from May through October. Visitors must leave the campground by 11 P.M.

Facilities: Hiking trails, historic site, children's playground, canoe landing. Picnic grounds include a shelter.

Permits and Rules: There are 15 primitive campsites, with no electrical outlets or showers. Keep fires in the designated fire pits. Pets need to be leashed.

Further Information: Contact Park Superintendent, Tower Hill State Park, Route 3, Spring Green, WI 53588; 608-588-2116.

Other Points of Interest

Canoeing is a popular activity along the Wisconsin River, reached via Mill Creek. The landing is .25 mile from the park. Numerous outfitters are along the river; they will take boaters to launch sites and pick them up downriver. Camping is allowed on sandbars and at the shoreline. But canoeists should be aware of fast currents and high water after localized rainstorms.

The **American Players Theater** in Spring Green is 15 minutes away from Tower Hill Park on Golf Course Road near the park entrance. Classical drama, including Shakespearean plays, is presented throughout the summer in an outdoor amphitheater. Call 608-588-7401 for production details, ticket prices, and performance times.

Park Trails 🥾🥾

Distance Round-Trip: 1.5 miles (main trail); .5 mile (nature trail)

Estimated Hiking Time: 1.5 hours

Cautions: The trail can be slippery when wet. The trail to the top of the slope is steep.

Trail Directions: Leave your vehicle in the parking area near the picnic tables; walk east across the lot toward the sign marking the trail.

The trail moves immediately up the slope via an asphalt track through thick woods **[1]**. At .2 mi. there are benches **[2]** on both sides of the trail to help break the climb. But in wet weather or early summer, hordes of furious mosquitoes prevent much of a pause. At .4 mi., a nature trail that is .5 mi. long branches off to the left **[3]**. To get to the shot tower at the pinnacle, continue to the right and keep going up.

Stone steps and handrails at crown the last 100 feet up the hill, making it easier to climb. Yet even with this help, hikers are always glad that there are benches at the peak (.6 mi.) **[4]**. A replica of the original wooden shot tower can be explored. The drop shaft through the rock is fenced off, but a careful look down shows darkness far below.

Emerging from the tower, take the gravel trail to the left, past some red cedar trees (.7 mi.) **[5]**. You now descend the hill through the woods. The main trail banks off to the right, heading back to the parking lot. To keep walking around the park, continue on a grassy path to the left. The path underfoot becomes a mixture of sand and dirt that is muddy and slippery when it rains. Watch out for partially hidden roots peeking aboveground. Cross a service road (.8 mi.) **[6]** and continue down the hill.

Toward the bottom, the path swings around to the back of the hill. The path hugs the cliffside on the left and a marsh on the right. You can walk carefully around the rocks to the entrance to the tunnel from which the lead was hauled (.9 mi.) **[7]**. The trail ends there at the creek.

Retrace your steps back along the marsh and ascend a flight of steps (1.1 mi.) **[8]**; this is a shortcut to the top of the bluff. Use the handrail, because some of the sidewalk stones are tilted and out of place. As you get near the top, there is a chain-link fence on the cliffside (1.3 mi.) **[9]**. You pop out of the undergrowth just beneath the shot tower to take the trail that continues around to the right. On the west side of the hill, you again pick up the asphalt path (1.7 mi.) **[10]**, after a series of stone steps out of the woods. Although you can see directly far below, trees prevent much of a vista. From here, it is a straight descent down the hill until you emerge about 500 feet (1.9 mi.) **[11]** west of where you originally ascended.

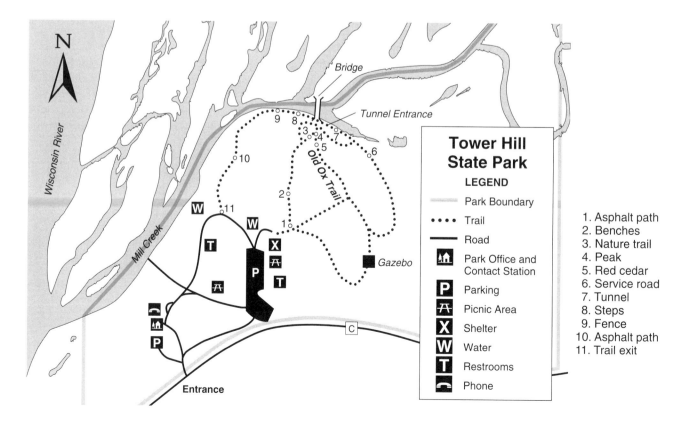

28. Governor Dodge State Park

- Walk through oak stands that date back half a century.
- Enjoy a picnic atop a bluff.
- Count the wildflowers in the spring.

Park Information

Comprising 5,029 acres, Governor Dodge State Park lies in one of the most geographically interesting areas of Wisconsin. In a "driftless" island, the park-lands escaped the crunch of successive waves of glaciers eons ago. Consequently a hiker will encounter steep hills and deep valleys. Sandstone cliffs date back to at least 450 million years ago, when Wisconsin was covered by a warm inland sea. The sand turned to rock as the oceans retreated, and erosion went to work carving exotic land formations. As early as 8,000 years ago, men and women lived here, sheltered by the overhangs and ledges. Discoveries of lead brought an influx of white settlers in the 1820s, with one of the first mines at Jenkins Branch in Cox Hollow just outside the southern border of today's park.

The park was named after General Henry Dodge, one of the region's first settlers. Dodge was instrumental in negotiating peace between the Ho-Chunk (Winnebago) nation and the invading whites. Dodge was later appointed Wisconsin's first territorial governor.

Directions: Governor Dodge State Park is 40 miles west of Madison on U.S. Highway 18. Drive to Dodgeville and turn south on State Highway 23. The park is 10 miles farther south.

Hours Open: The park office is open daily from 8 A.M. to 11 P.M., June through August, plus most spring and fall Friday and Saturday nights. Office hours for the rest of the year are 8 A.M. to 4 P.M.

Facilities: Camping, concessions, picnic shelters and tables, naturalist tours and lectures from June through August, swimming beaches, amphitheater, pay phones.

Permits and Rules: Wisconsin resident park passes are $15 per year or $4 daily. Nonresident fees are $24 annually or $6 daily. A one-hour pass is $2. An annual trail pass (for biking or horseback riding) is $10, and a one-day pass is $3. Camping fees for residents are $10 per night and for nonresidents $12 per night in addition to the entry fee. A $2 discount is offered for Sunday through Thursday nights and off-season.

Further Information: Contact Superintendent, Governor Dodge State Park, 4175 State Road 23, Dodgeville, WI 53433; 608-935-2315.

Other Points of Interest

The **Mount Horeb Mustard Museum** has almost 2,000 varieties of mustards for exhibit and for sale. Aficionados can ogle spreads coming from dozens of countries. For more information, call 800-438-6878 (800-GET-MUST). You will pass Mount Horeb, 10 miles west of Madison, on the freeway while heading to Governor Dodge State Park.

Cave of the Mounds is 20 miles west of Madison on the way to Governor Dodge State Park, just off U.S Highways 18 and 151. The cave is a national landmark, open daily from mid-March through mid-November. One-hour guided tours are given regularly throughout the season. A picnic grounds is also on-site.

Park Trails

Pine Cliff Nature Trail 👢👢—2 miles—This self-guided loop begins and ends at the Enee Point picnic grounds. Signs along the route tell about area wildlife, history, flora, and the environment. Several steep grades will be encountered, along with rocky portions of the trail that may make it difficult for people with physical disabilities.

Lost Canyon Ski/Hiking Trail 👢👢👢—8.1 miles—This trail starts at the Cox Hollow Campground in the center of Governor Dodge State Park. Because of the length and the steep grades, only advanced hikers should attempt this trek. Bring plenty of water or juice and be sure your boots are strong enough to withstand climbing up and down the hills. Most of the path is through thick stands of timber, passing through landmarks such as Lost Canyon, Stephens Falls, and Twin Valley Lakes.

Gold Mine Ski/Hike/Bike Trail 👢👢—2.5 miles—This is an easy walk, accessed .4 miles west of the Twin Valley Campgrounds. The grassy pathway loops through timber and over meadows without the problem of steep grades encountered on many of the park routes.

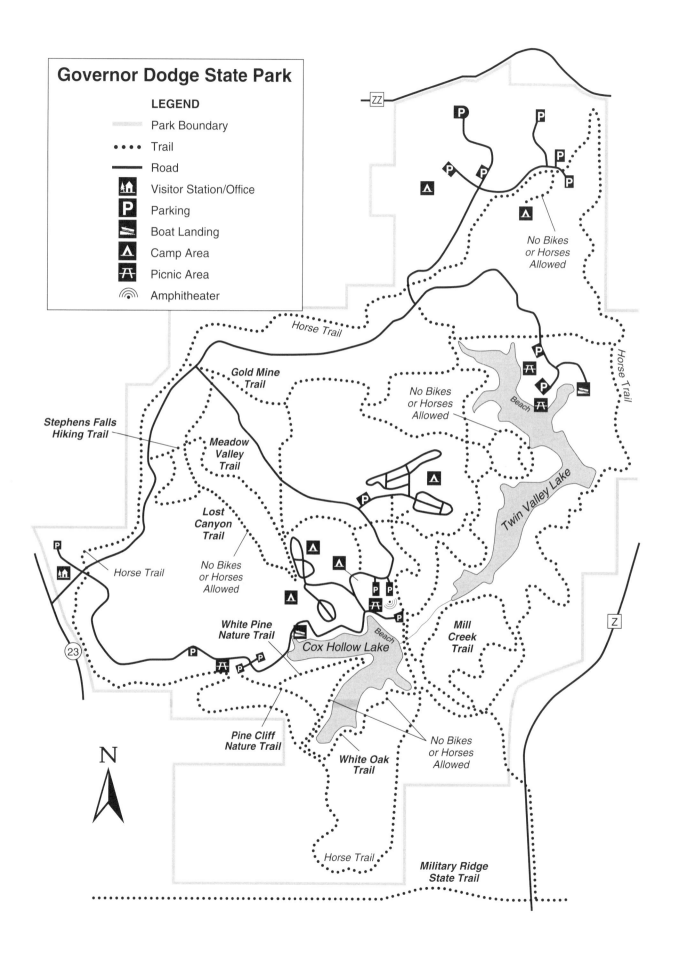

Governor Dodge State Park

LEGEND

▦▦▦ Park Boundary

•••• Trail

—— Road

🏕 Visitor Station/Office

P Parking

🚣 Boat Landing

⛺ Camp Area

🏕 Picnic Area

🔊 Amphitheater

ZZ

No Bikes
or Horses
Allowed

Horse Trail

Gold Mine
Trail

No Bikes
or Horses
Allowed

Horse Trail

Stephens Falls
Hiking Trail

Meadow
Valley
Trail

Twin Valley Lake

Beach

Lost
Canyon
Trail

No Bikes
or Horses
Allowed

Horse Trail

White Pine
Nature Trail

Cox Hollow Lake

Beach

Mill
Creek
Trail

Z

23

Pine Cliff
Nature Trail

No Bikes
or Horses
Allowed

White Oak
Trail

N

Horse Trail

Military Ridge
State Trail

White Oak Trail 👢👢👢

Distance Round-Trip: 4.5 miles

Estimated Hiking Time: 2.5 to 3 hours

Cautions: Be careful of slippery grades and rocks while climbing the uplands. Some poison ivy might be present.

Trail Directions: The trail begins at the Cox Hollow Beach concession stand. Park in the lot and proceed past the picnic area, go down the hill, and cross the dam. At the far south side of the dam (.2 mi.) **[1]**, the White Oak Trail splits immediately to the right. There it joins the Pine Cliff Nature Trail, which originated at Enee Point on the opposite side of Cox Hollow Lake.

Follow the White Oak Trail to the right around the lakeshore. You'll soon move away from the lake to plunge deeper into the forest (.4 mi.) **[2]** for a few hundred feet. But then you cross a culvert and come back out of the trees to the lake again. The trail rises (.7 mi.) **[3]** away from the lake shortly before you enter the Pine Cliff scientific area (1 mi.) **[4]**.

The scientific area spotlights the park's escarpments (steep slopes) and promontories (peaks of high land that jut out over an expanse of water), and you can see thousands of years of erosion at work on the cliffsides. You'll be out of breath by the time you hit the summit (1.1 mi.) **[5]**. There is some white pine up to 16 inches in diameter along this part of the trail, reminding hikers of the forest giants that were here before logging.

At 1.2 mi. **[6]** is a small rock shelter that may have been used by Native Americans; it's tucked into the side of a slope and away from the wind. Continue on past some lightly colored sandstone formations eroded by dripping water from the ridge tops.

At 1.5 mi. **[7]**, you descend into a valley and can see the lake again on the right. The next .5 mi. is a roller-coaster stroll, and you'll intersect with a snowmobile/horse trail (2.7 mi.) **[8]**, part of a 15-mi. loop through the most remote regions of the park. Look both ways for equine traffic. At 2.8 mi. **[9]**, pause at a bench that overlooks the west end of the lake.

You will now move around to the north side of the south branch of the lake, near some long-abandoned lead smelting furnaces (3.1 mi.) **[10]**. At 3.8 mi. **[11]**, you are back along the shore of the 95-acre lake, walking along the White Pine Nature Trail. Several streams course down the ridge and flow into the lake, which was a river before being dammed in 1958. There are no natural lakes in this driftless area.

You will again encounter a steep climb (4.1 mi.) **[12]** into a pine grove, one of the few places in south central Wisconsin where this species grows well. On the descent, a staircase has been built into the ridge. There are at least 21 steps down. Watch out for poison ivy at the foot of the hill.

After traversing several hundred feet from the base of the hill, you will find a footbridge to carry you across a creek toward the Enee Point picnic shelter on the right and the Box Canyon picnic area on the left. At Enee Point, you have to walk back 1 mi. on the Cox Hollow Road to your starting point and parked car at the concession stand. Here's a hint: Bring a bike and drop it off at the opposite end of the trail from the parking area. Riding back to the car is easier on the feet.

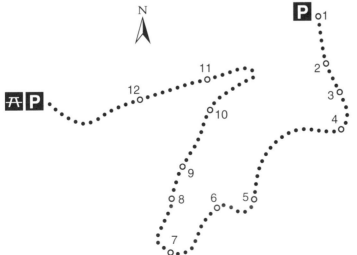

1. Dam
2. Forest
3. Rising trail
4. Pine Cliff scientific area
5. Summit
6. Rock shelter
7. Valley
8. Trail intersection
9. Bench
10. Old lead smelting furnaces
11. Lakeshore
12. Steep climb

Mill Creek Ski/Hiking/ Bike Trail 👢👢👢

Distance Round-Trip: 3.3 miles

Estimated Hiking Time: 1.5 to 2 hours

Cautions: Several steep grades can make walking tiring, although the path is wide and easy.

Trail Directions: The trail begins at the Cox Hollow Beach picnic area. Leave your car in the lot there and proceed past the concession stand, down the hill to the dam where you can cross. You will pick up the trailhead on the south side of the dam, where the White Oak Trail branches off to the right. However, you continue straight ahead on the asphalt road up the hill on the trail.

After you reach the crest (.6 mi.) **[1]**, a large open field (.8 mi.) **[2]** presents a palette of spring wildflowers to delight even the most jaded eye. In the autumn, the breezy heads of goldenrod dapple the ground cover. The road will rise after passing through the field, offering a view to the right of a deep valley (1.1 mi.) **[3]**.

The Military Ridge State Trail runs along the crest of the ridge (1.4 mi.) **[4]**, intersecting with the Mill Creek Trail. You now leave the asphalt, turning left to a sandy track that mountain bikers can also use. Raspberry bushes bear out along the sides of the trail, offering their sweet fruits in the early summer.

One of the better vistas is found at the 2 mi. mark, overlooking a valley crowded with massive oak and maple trees. The trail then makes numerous loops and doglegs as it moves downward through the forest. Deer paths can be spotted packing down the high grasses, the animal highways often bisecting this stretch of trail. There are even places in the brush where you see where they slept.

A steep grade at 2.7 mi. **[5]** offers enough switchbacks and curves to delight avid cross-country

skiers who use this track in the winter. It's no wonder there is a triangular yellow warning sign at the top of the hill. For hikers, the zigzagging makes for an interesting stroll downhill. The hill is steep enough to make most people pick up speed whether they wish to or not. By the time you hit bottom, you could be almost jogging.

The remaining .25 mi. of the trek back to the dam is on level ground, along a part gravel, part grassy path. On the right side is a marshy area crowded with cattails and alive with frogs in season. If you bring kids for a springtime adventure, expect to add another half hour to your trekking. There should be plenty of time to observe tadpoles in the shallow water. Several muskrat houses peek above the mud far out in the marsh.

You will then rejoin the White Oak Trail at the junction just south of the dam. Then simply walk back across the dam to the Cox Hollow Lake concession area and your parked car.

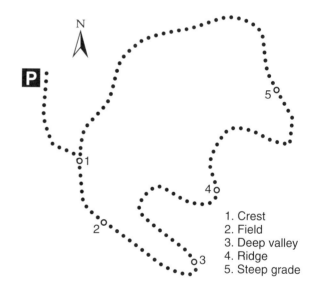

1. Crest
2. Field
3. Deep valley
4. Ridge
5. Steep grade

29. Wildcat Mountain State Park

- Admire scenic views of west central Wisconsin.
- Stretch your legs along hill climbs.
- Discover fields of wildflowers.

Park Information

Wildcat Mountain State Park sits in the Kickapoo River Valley, an unglaciated region of west central Wisconsin. Geologists point out that the hills are made of Precambrian sandstone with limestone covers. Erosion has created many exposed ridges and bluffs that are carpeted with thick stands of birches, pines, poplars, maples, and oaks. The word "kickapoo" is an Algonquin word meaning "he who goes there." Other local Native Americans roughly translated the term as "crooked river." A local farmer donated 40 acres to create the park in 1948. Since then, the park has grown to about 3,500 acres through the purchase of other small farms.

Directions: The park is 1 mile south of the Kickapoo River community of Ontario on State Highway 33.

Hours Open: The park office is open from 8 A.M. to 11 P.M. June through August and from 8 A.M. to 4:30 P.M. during the winter months.

Facilities: Camping, picnicking, canoeing, bicycling, horseback riding, nature trails, and educational lectures are among the recreational opportunities. The family campground has 30 sites atop Wildcat Mountain with stunning views. Flush toilets, showers, dump station, picnic tables, and fire rings are available.

Permits and Rules: Leashed pets are allowed only on the Old Settler's Trail and the Ice Cave Trail. Half the campsites are saved for reservations and half are allocated on a first-come, first-served basis. No electrical sites are available. A primitive canoe campsite is accessed only via the Kickapoo River south of the regular river landing and a picnic shelter in lower Wildcat Mountain State Park. Vehicle admission stickers are required year round. The only exception is on Open House Day on the first Sunday in June, when no admission is charged at any of the state parks. No garbage or recycling bins are in the park so campers must adhere to a carry-in/carry-out policy.

Further Information: Contact Park Manager, Wildcat Mountain State Park, Ontario, WI 54651; 608-337-4775.

Other Points of Interest

The area surrounding the park is an outdoors lover's paradise. Canoe rentals are available on the winding **Kickapoo River**. About 125 miles within the 65-mile-long river valley is navigable from Wilton to Wauzeka, where the river empties into the Wisconsin River. This is generally a slow-moving waterway, but it quickly overflows its banks in heavy rains. Numerous access points are available at bridge crossings on Highway 131. For details on recreational opportunities in the valley, contact the Kickapoo Valley Association, Box 922, LaFarge, WI 54639.

Cycling is another major sport, especially along the 32-mile **Elroy to Sparta Trail,** which traces an old railroad bed to the north of the state park. The grade goes along the watersheds of the Baraboo, Kickapoo, and La Crosse Rivers. The trail even goes through three tunnels that were bored through solid rock in the 1800s. For details on biking, call the Elroy-Sparta National Trail, Inc., 608-463-7109.

The **La Crosse River State Trail** is another major cycling leg that composes 21.5 miles of the state's 117-mile linked recreation trail system in west central Wisconsin. The packed-limestone trail follows the La Crosse River Valley, starting at its headquarters in Sparta and ending in La Crosse. For more information, call the La Crosse River State Trail headquarters, 608-269-4123.

Mill Bluff State Park lies on the border of Monroe and Juneau Counties near Camp Douglas. The park is just off I-94 on County Highway W, offering several excellent hiking trails under 2 miles long. You can climb 125 stone steps to the top of Mill Bluff for a great view over the surrounding flatlands over 1,000 feet below. The steps were built by the Works Progress Administration in the 1930s. For Mill Bluff State Park information, call 608-427-6692.

Park Trails

Ice Cave Trail 👢—.5 mile—This short trail is easy on the feet, leading to a towering rock structure that looks like the mouth of a large cave. A spring runs from the edge of this formation and freezes into a North Pole-sized icicle in the winter. In the summer, picnic at the tables tucked conveniently along the banks of Billings Creek. The trail is reached via County Highway F, south of State Highway 33.

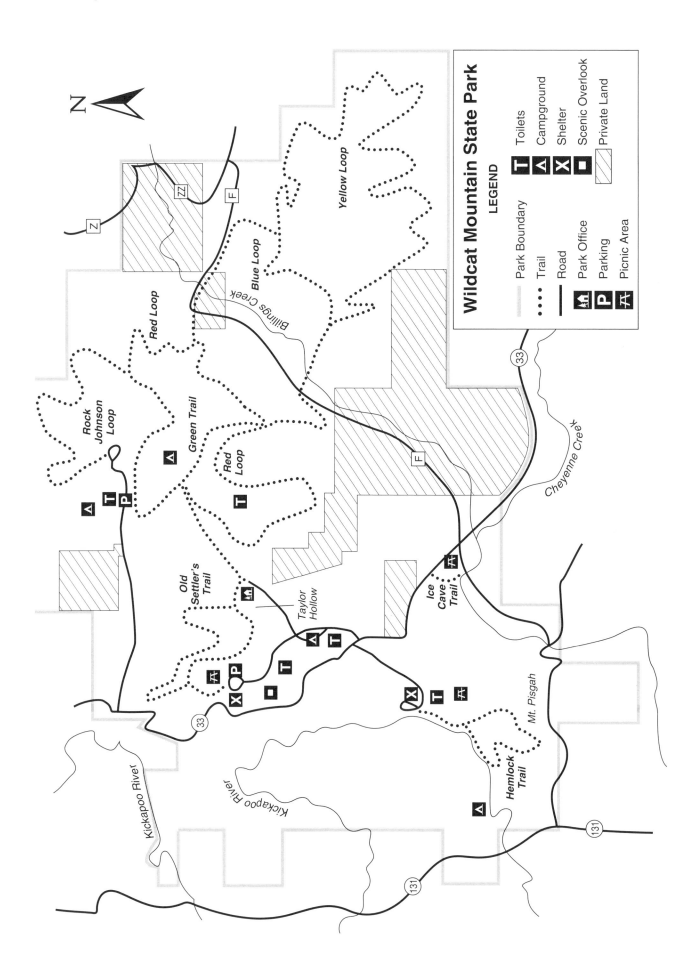

Old Settler's Trail 👢👢

Distance Round-Trip: 2.5 miles

Estimated Hiking Time: 2 hours

Cautions: The trail is slippery when wet. Take notice particularly when descending to the valley floor because there are no handrails.

Trail Directions: Exit on the service road where you see park signs on Highway 33. It is a steep climb to the mountain tip up a narrow lane. Drive past the park office and proceed to the parking area near the northern picnic grounds atop the mountain. Before hiking, pause at the observation point for a stunning view of the Kickapoo River Valley to the west. About 150 feet down from the trail entrance are a location map and signs. By edging to the right, you start the 2.5-mi. walk. By going left, you may exit the trail behind the park office and return to your parked car along a service road. This bypass cuts your trek by two thirds.

A portion of the Old Settler's Trail was once used by early settlers to reach the valley floor. In more recent times, farmers herded cattle along the narrow ridges on their way to pasture. The trailhead is marked with signs at the parking lot **[1]**. Proceed down the steps into the forest; these lead into a switchback trail (.1 mi.) **[2]**. Wild grapevines are entwined around the trees, giving a Tarzan-like look to the forest. Great spreads of purple trillium coat the slopes in spring.

When you reach the intersection, take a left. You next will cross a narrow culvert that carries rain and spring water run-off down the mountainside (.4 mi.)

[3]. Proceed down the trail to a birch grove (.5 mi.) **[4]**. Sturdy legs are now necessary to traverse the next mile plus of up-and-down walking. There is a steep slope to the left, so be careful not to slip over the edge and tumble downhill.

Hikers pass through three pine plantations planted by pupils from the Ontario school district years ago (.7 mi. to 1 mi.) **[5]**. Between the pines at several points, you can see the village of Ontairo about 1.5 mi. to the north. Several large boulders are now on the right side (1.2 mi.) **[6]**. The exposed rock has the appearance of a giant cathedral ceiling that has collapsed inward.

Sandstone ledges draped by ferns provide an excellent seat where you can rest briefly at the 1.3-mi. mark **[7]**. Three log steps help get hikers up and over the next rise (1.5 mi.) **[8]** as the trail continues its up-and-down loop. A bench overlooks a valley vista with a patchwork of farms far below (1.6 mi.) **[9]**. Many are operated by the Amish. Look for the hand-lettered signs announcing what is for sale, nailed on fence posts alongside the road.

A pine grove sighs in the wind whispering up the slopes, the music is soft on the ears, and the thick blanket of needles makes for a cushioned walk (1.7 mi.) **[10]**. An open patch of sandstone rears up along the trail (1.9 mi.) **[11]** overlooking Taylor Hollow on the valley floor. You can sit on a bench there and admire the scenery after taking a short jog to the left. Go straight, however, if you wish to continue on the trail. You will come up behind the park amphitheater and can either walk back to your car via the road or continue through a thick grove of maple. The latter is more eye-catching in the autumn, although the road option is quicker.

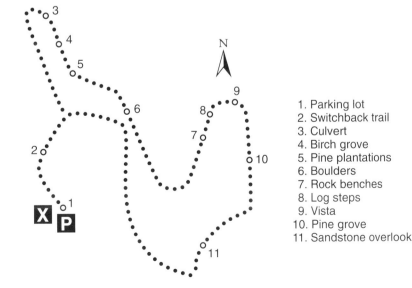

1. Parking lot
2. Switchback trail
3. Culvert
4. Birch grove
5. Pine plantations
6. Boulders
7. Rock benches
8. Log steps
9. Vista
10. Pine grove
11. Sandstone overlook

Hemlock Nature Trail/ Mt. Pisgah 👢👢👢👢

Distance Round-Trip: 1.4 miles

Estimated Hiking Time: 2 hours

Cautions: The loop trail climbs through the Mt. Pisgah Hemlock Hardwoods Natural Area to the summit, which is 1,220 feet above sea level. This is a tough, breath-snatching climb and is not for everyone. Because of its steepness, even an experienced hiker will wonder when (and if) the crest will ever be reached. The trail is narrow and is composed of rock and dirt, making it slippery even in dry weather. However, the first .5 mi. is along the banks of the Kickapoo and is an easy, flat stroll through fields of wildflowers. Watch out for poison ivy, especially when climbing Mt. Pisgah.

Trail Directions: Leave the upper part of Wildcat Mountain State Park and pick up the service road to the lower portion of the area. The entrance is also off Highway 33, but be careful of oncoming cars in making the turn to the left if you are coming from the south. The highway curves here, and the driver of an oncoming fast-moving vehicle may not be paying attention. Park near the shelter along the river. The trail starts immediately to the left. At this point, you are 45 mi. north of the Kickapoo's marriage with the Wisconsin River.

This is a "driftless" area of Wisconsin, untouched by glaciers that crunched much of the state as late as 10,000 years ago. The mountain itself is a survivor of an ancient seabed dating from 600 million years ago.

The rough "kuk-kuk-kuk" of pileated woodpeckers is heard in the basswood groves several hundred feet back from the river (.1 mi.) **[1]**. The woodpeckers are among dozens of species that call the area their home. Larks, nighthawks, swallows, and others can be spotted at various times throughout the year. Keep an eye open for other wildlife. Several rotted silver maples can be seen, their hollow trunks making excellent condos for raccoons, squirrels, and owls (.2 mi.) **[2]**.

The trail now moves away from the river bottom and passes close to a pool near the rock face of Mt. Pisgah (.4 mi.) **[3]**. Take the log steps upward to the first part of the trail (.5 mi.) **[4]**. There is a gradual climb through a stand of red pine, with slippery needles carpeting the pathway.

Follow the trail to the overlook built of logs (.6 mi.) **[5]**. Don't look upward, because the trail continues higher and higher, becoming lost amid the trees. There is still a stiff climb awaiting you. Splash across a gully (.7 mi.) **[6]** where a stream trickles downward as it waters the colorful forest plants. There are hemlocks in the vicinity, with their tiny, flat needles absorbing as much sunlight as possible.

At .8 mi., the climb is getting steeper as it zigzags along the ridge. Don't be embarrassed to grab tree trunks and branches to help you up the next leg of the trail (.9 mi.) **[7]**. Be alert as you climb upward. A wrong turn will take you off into the woods and to a cliff edge. But eventually the crest is reached. The trail skirts an overlook, which is barricaded by a log railing. Perch on a bench there to catch your breath after the struggle up the mountainside. The view is breathtaking. The snakelike Kickapoo River roams in and out of the trees far below the observation point.

There are several log steps leading downward immediately after you leave the overlook. About halfway back down the mountain is a natural bench made of stone, with maidenhair and interrupted ferns creating a stage backdrop of greenery. Watch out for partially hidden roots that can trip the unwary hiker.

White paper birch (hands off!) are along the trailside as you reach the bottom of the cool northern slope (1.3 mi.) **[8]**. Peeling live bark from a tree will kill it. So knowledgeable Native Americans used the dead bark for their canoes and baskets. From here it is a short walk back to the parking lot through fields of purple and white trillium along the Kickapoo banks.

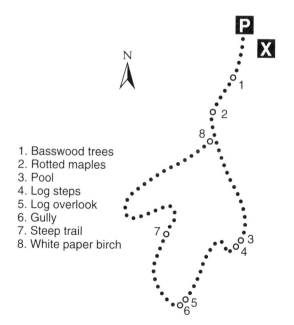

1. Basswood trees
2. Rotted maples
3. Pool
4. Log steps
5. Log overlook
6. Gully
7. Steep trail
8. White paper birch

30. Hixon Forest Nature Center

- Discover an extensive hiking experience in a major Wisconsin city.
- Scramble up a trail to bluffs overlooking the Mississippi River Valley.
- Take part in a nature-study project.

Park Information

Hixon Forest Nature Center provides environmental education for schoolchildren and adults in the La Crosse area. Each year, more than 7,000 youngsters take part in hands-on programs at the center. The center also provides conservation outreach to schools and community groups.

The Nature Center is in the heart of a network of hiking and cross-country ski trails extending from the Mississippi River to the top of La Crosse's bluffs. Hixon Forest itself covers 630 acres of prairie and bluff land where timbering and quarrying took place at the turn of the century. A group of citizens led by Mrs. Ellen J. Hixon, for whom the forest was named, bought the property in 1912 and gave it to the city for park development.

Extensive trail work was done in 1975 as part of the community's bicentennial celebration. In 1988 a River-to-Bluff Trail was completed. An interesting attraction at the place where the Gully and Cellar Trails intersect is a man-made cave that was used as a brick kiln in the late 1800s.

Directions: Hixon Forest Nature Center is located on State Highway 16, just north of the intersection of La Crosse Street and Losey Boulevard in La Crosse.

Hours Open: The Nature Center is open from 11 A.M. to 4 P.M. Monday through Friday, and from 1 to 4 P.M. Saturday and Sunday, year round.

Facilities: Nature center, trails, rest rooms.

Permits and Rules: Stay on the trail. Bikes, horses, motorcycles, and cars are prohibited on the trails. Cars are usually not allowed past a gate on Milson Court; however, visitors with walking difficulties can obtain a key to the gate from the La Crosse Park and Recreation Department so they can drive farther into the forest. Don't carve on the trees or pick flowers. Hunting, trapping, and discharge of firearms are also prohibited. No camping, no fires.

Further Information: Contact Hixon Forest Nature Center, 2702 Quarry Road, La Crosse, WI 54601; 608-784-0303.

Other Points of Interest

La Crosse is an old-time river town with much history. The Riverside USA Museum and the Swarthout Museum have displays tracing the community's past. La Crosse visitors can ride the riverboat *Julia Belle Swain* from its dock at Riverside Park. Rides are also available aboard the stern-wheeler *La Crosse Queen* and the cruiseliner *Island Girl.* There is a swimming beach at Pettibone Park. Follow Main Street east for 2 miles. Call the city's Convention and Visitors Bureau, 800-658-9424.

Park Trails

River-to-Bluff Trail —5.5 miles—Marked by green posts, the trail starts at Riverside Park, crosses the La Crosse River Marsh, cuts over part of Myrick Park, and goes under State Highway 16. The trail then meanders past Hixon Forest Nature Center, crosses the railroad tracks, and proceeds along the center's Sumac and Bicentennial Trails to the top of the bluff.

Sumac Trail —1.5 miles—This is the main trail into the forest from the main parking lot off Milson Court. The trail takes hikers into the center of the forest where the other trails begin. It is probably the most used trail in the forest and is not difficult.

Log Trail —.5 mile—This trail runs through a section with lots of ferns. It is considered a good hiking trail for intermediate and experienced walkers because it is more secluded and less traveled than some of the others.

Upper and Lower Fern Trails —.5 mile each— These east-west trails are easy to stroll, covering only a few low hills through mixed hardwoods. These trails are relatively short, but they link with others in the Hixon system for a full several hours of trekking. Lower Fern is easily accessible for kids and people who use wheelchairs.

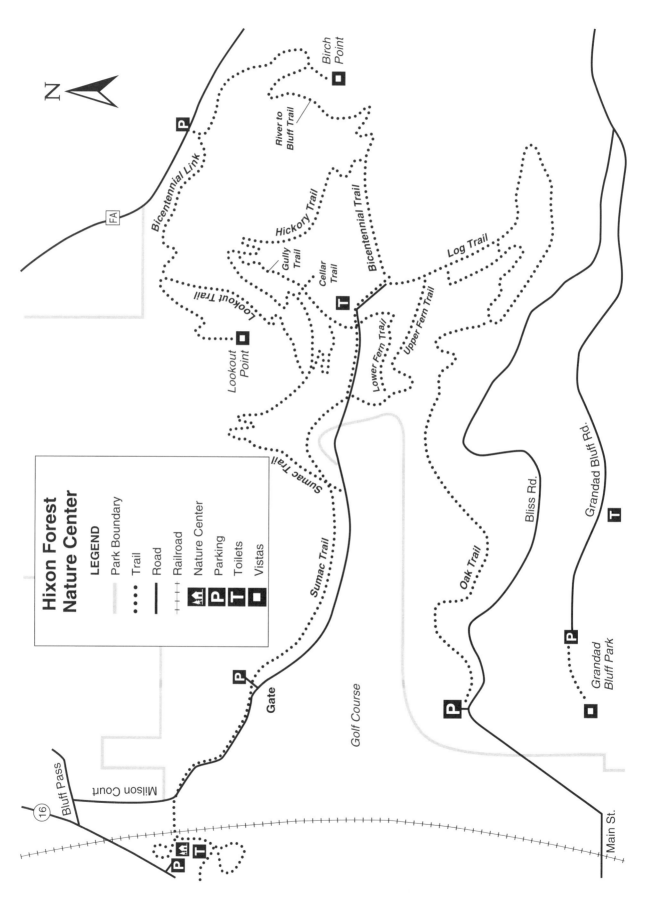

Lookout Trail 👢👢👢👢

Distance Round-Trip: 3 miles

Estimated Hiking Time: 2 hours

Cautions: While the trek starts out easy enough from the Nature Center, the terrain grows very hilly once the Sumac Trail connects with the Lookout Trail. There is a good, leg-stretching climb to the bluff top. Kids can do the trek, but be prepared for sleepy youngsters on the way home.

Trail Directions: This trail hooks up the Hickory Trail with the Bicentennial Trail. Thus hikers can connect at either end. But the best way is to hike south on the Sumac Trail from the Nature Center. It is 1.5 mi. one-way from the parking lot at the Nature Center to the dry prairie atop Lookout Point. The last .5 mi., which is described below, covers the final leg up to the peak. Count on at least 1.5 to 2 hours for the entire round-trip walk.

Lookout Point is reached via a switchback path up the slope **[1]**. This back-and-forth, left-to-right, right-to-left pattern helps ease the climb. While not really steep because of the zigzag route, the trek is strenuous walking because of the elevation. It's not an ear-popping walk, but tired legs certainly let you know when you have completed it. At this section (.1 mi.), the narrow track is a mixture of loose, lightly packed dirt **[2]**.

Lookout Point is on the south face of the bluff, with resulting lush undergrowth taking advantage of the full, rich sunlight. The trail meanders through thick oak and hickory stands with plenty of ground cover; it is difficult to have much of a vista as you ascend because of the density of the woods. However, in early spring and late autumn, your chances of actually seeing the valley floor improve.

Of course, spring brings the added benefits of viewing the new Jack-in-the-pulpits, the violet or white trillium, and other fresh growth peeking from the forest floor. The trail is usually strewn with acorns and leaves, making it a squirrel and chipmunk heaven. There is often the extra plus of seeing turkey vultures, hawks, and—with luck—a bald eagle near the river. Bring binoculars.

Coming out on top (.5 mi.) **[3]**, you find native goat prairie. The open space provides a grand overview of the city of La Crosse and the meandering Mississippi River. A goat prairie means just that, having earned its name because settlers considered such topography too steep to farm and felt it was suitable only for grazing goats. With the full hit of the sun, the ground is dry. However, the shallow soil supports pasque-flowers, asters, goldenrod, butterfly weed, and other prairie plants.

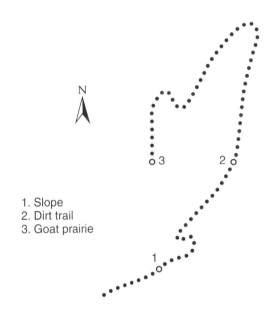

1. Slope
2. Dirt trail
3. Goat prairie

Oak Trail 👢👢👢

Distance One-Way: 1.4 miles

Estimated Hiking Time: 1.5 hours

Cautions: Bring insect repellent during the late spring and early summer.

Trail Directions: Depart from the parking area on Bliss Road 1 mi. south of the Nature Center. Take the first turn to the left as you drive up to the top of the bluff. The trail entrance is right off the lot. The Oak Trail connects with the Log Trail and is not a loop.

This trail ascends the north face of Grandad Bluff through mature areas of a dense forest. The large oaks seen all along the path are more than 100 years old. Their massive trunks and towering canopy show what the entire area might have looked like in pre-settlement days. There are few openings in the trees, making this a generally shaded and cool place on hot summer treks.

The track gradually moves upward, undulating over the rocky landscape in a succession of waves. Keep your eyes open for lady's slippers and orchids, two wildflower species not common in the La Crosse area. Extensive growth of Virginia creeper and grapevines is found along the trail, adding to the ground cover.

At .4 mi., swing to the left as the trail veers over a minor ridge and then angles back to the right (.6 mi.) **[1]**. Listen for the drum of woodpeckers in the distance. There are now several jogs in the trail, which is a well-trodden dirt path with a few loose stones. Watch your step to avoid slipping on an errant pebble, although generally the track is clean and adequately maintained.

As you get midway along the trail (.7 mi.) **[2]**, the hills gradually become steeper. While not difficult for the experienced hiker to traverse, the topography is noticeably different from that at your starting point. Many ferns peek out from the shaded recesses of the bluff as you pass along the system's middle section (.8 mi.) **[3]**. Interrupted ferns seem to be the main variety, but a skilled fern-watcher can probably find maidenhair and other types. Again, the trail continues to move up and down over the landscape. It is generally in a fairly straight line, except for a couple of quick right-then-left-then-right angles at the 1.2-mi. mark **[4]**.

You've reached the conclusion of the Oak Trail when you arrive at a massive rock in the middle of the track (1.4 mi.) **[5]**. The Log Trail begins at this spot. You either proceed deeper into the forest or return the way you came.

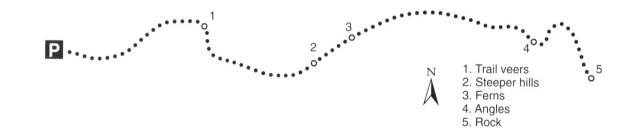

N

1. Trail veers
2. Steeper hills
3. Ferns
4. Angles
5. Rock

South

Topography

South central Wisconsin is primarily gently rolling landscape. The far western rim of the state along the Mississippi River is a "driftless" area, one that escaped glacial action of 10,000 years ago. In the east is a landscape created by those vast ice sheets. There are long ridges called moraines, and drumlins, which are peaks made of glacial debris. During the last ice age, much of this part of lower Wisconsin was flattened and remolded by the crunching ice packs.

Moving water also affected how the landscape was shaped. The glaciers were so large that rivers formed underneath the ice cap, dumping loads of rocky leftovers as they flowed. These are eskers, ridges that can be up to 100 miles long.

Rich, deep soil is the hallmark of southern Wisconsin, making it dear to the hearts of pioneer farmers and contemporary ones too. Prairie land was subsequently plowed under and forests cut, so today's hiker experiences a very different landscape than what the settlers saw. Yet the farm fields, woodlots, and pastures are picturesque and make great backdrops for meandering.

Major Rivers and Lakes

Southern Wisconsin is bordered on the east by Lake Michigan, with its 22,400-square-mile surface of water. On the west are the mighty Mississippi and St. Croix Rivers. The lower third of the Wisconsin River flows westward through the region. Some of the best canoeing streams and rivers make their presence known in southern Wisconsin: the Bark, Fox, Sugar, Platte, and Kickapoo among them.

Lake Geneva in Walworth County has been a major tourist destination since the late 1800s, when wealthy Chicagoans began building summer homes along its shoreline. Lake Koshkonong in Jefferson County and the scattering of small lakes in Waukesha and Washington Counties are rich in bass, perch, and other angling favorites. Lakes Mendota, Monona, Waubesa, and Kegonsa dot the Madison area in Dane County, offering a watery getaway in the urban heart of Wisconsin.

Common Plant Life

This is rich agricultural land, so hikers won't find vast tracts of forestland as in far northern Wisconsin, although there are extensive state forests and heavily wooded county and state parks in the region. Oaks, maples, beech, basswood, and pine are plentiful. The forests are rich in plant life, from ferns to violets. Early spring is one of the best times to hike, when new life appears everywhere. Look for morel mushrooms, Jack-in-the-pulpit, and dainty trillium. In the summer, the prairies explode with goldenrod, asters, and bluestem. Autumn promotes the blazing crimson staghorn sumac.

Since this is farming country, probably the most common "domestic" plants are corn, wheat, beans, and truck crops such as cabbages. Tobacco is also grown in the rich soil here, with drying barns to be spotted along U.S. Highway 18 in Jefferson County. Marshes are ripe with cattails, sedge grasses, and rushes. Beautiful, exotic, but dangerous purple loosestrife is a fast-growing and tenacious plant, causing problems in some wetlands because it crowds out native species.

Common Birds and Mammals

Many wild animals have adapted well to the incursion of human beings on their territory. Some have done too well. The abundance of white-tailed deer can be a problem for motorists, as well as for farmers. Hundreds of deer are killed annually along the roadways when they bound in front of vehicles. The deer often make themselves at home in southern Wisconsin's city parks, as well as in more remote river bottoms and parkland far away from playgrounds and shopping centers. The woods, marshes, and meadows of southern Wisconsin are also home for otters, raccoons, foxes, weasels, and a host of other watchable wildlife. Don't be surprised to see buffalo—on farms, of course.

On the less exotic side, with Wisconsin proudly proclaiming itself as *the* Dairy State, there seem to be cows everywhere. And there are, with thousands of the cud-chewing creatures dreamily grazing across the lush grassy ridges. Holsteins, Guernseys, Jerseys, and their bovine cousins give everything but chocolate milk. Trekkers along the Sugar River Trail detour for good reason toward the Cheesemakers' Ball, Monroe's major fun fest.

There must be several bird feeders for every man, woman, and child in southern Wisconsin. Feeding birds seems to be a state hobby. Among the admired species are robins, chickadees, wrens, hummingbirds, yellow-headed or red-winged blackbirds, pheasants, grouse, and ducks of all kinds. Then there are starlings, crows, hawks, turkey vultures, gray herons, sandhill cranes, and bald eagles for a still wider variety of bird personalities. Don't forget barnyards, where clucking chickens, domestic geese, and cackling guinea hens hold sway.

Currently listed are 392 species of common and rare varieties of birds that make southern Wisconsin their habitat or a migration stopover. The state even offers a rare-bird alert via telephone aimed at serious watchers. For the latest on locales and sighted

species, call the secretary of the Wisconsin State Ornithology Association at 414-352-3857.

Climate

Wisconsin weather has been described as tricky, finicky, fickle, and moody. The climate is generally temperate, but winter temperatures in the south can plunge to –45 degrees or lower. On the other hand, think summer. Well, kind of. In 1995, southern Wisconsin was socked with a midsummer diet of 105 degrees plus. The following summer, the drought turned to floods, as rain never seemed to stop. Over the past 20 years, the rainfall average has been pegged at 20 to 30 inches.

A season's snowfall can pile up to two to three feet in the deeper woodlots. Wisconsin's citizens take all this in stride, using snowshoes and skis to keep active when the weather turns snarly. Snowplows are on the road almost immediately with a storm alert. In summer, fire hydrants are opened and swimming pools and beaches are crowded in the heat.

Best Features

Designated farm trails throughout southwestern Wisconsin open the hiker to discoveries of antiques, cheese, maple syrup, wine, yarn, honey, popcorn, fudge, gourds, and what seems to be an unlimited variety of other products. Look for the Farm Trails signs along the roads and at participating farms and retailers throughout the region for the best buys. For a copy of a brochure listing places to find quality produce, great bargains, and fun, call 608-375-5798. Many of these sites are near state and county parks and campgrounds with their many hiking possibilities. What are knapsacks for but to fill with goodies!

Southern Wisconsin is a treasure trove of historical riches. Every community has its own personality, whether in the Mississippi River's lead-mining region; the Swiss, Scandinavian, and German settlements in the middle of the state; or in Lake Michigan's old-time fishing villages. They present a delightful blend of foods to munch, museums and pioneer homesteads to visit, festivals to enjoy, shopping to savor, and trails to hike. Park your rucksack and go pet a Clydesdale, pick an apple, or dance a polka. Tour Old World Wisconsin or Aztalan and Nelson Dewey State Parks for peeks into how Wisconsinites lived in the past. Then hike through the parklands of southern Wisconsin's cities for a contemporary look at the state.

31. Riveredge Nature Center

- Walk along the gently flowing Wisconsin River.
- Hike through upland meadows and prairie.
- Experience naturalist programs and interpretive sessions.

Park Information

Riveredge Nature Center is a 350-acre stretch of woodland and prairie along the Milwaukee River, with 12 miles of hiking and cross-country ski trails. Numerous naturalist programs, photo shows, and environmental classes are held there throughout the year. They range from in-depth studies of the Milwaukee River to problem-solving activities on the Riveredge Together Trek Challenge course.

The facility opened in the early 1970s with only 73 acres; several refurbished old farm buildings formed the core of an educational center. In 1985 the site was designated as a state natural area. The center is privately funded and served by volunteers. In addition to its local work, Riveredge hosts prairie tours in other states, wilderness explorations in Alaska, and photo workshops in the Rocky Mountains, among other adventure activities.

Directions: The center is 1 mile east of Newburg on County Highway Y.

Hours Open: Trails are open daily. The Visitor Center building is open from 8 A.M. to 5 P.M. Monday through Friday, and from noon to 4 P.M. Sunday. It is closed on Saturday from Memorial Day to Labor Day.

Facilities: Rest rooms, canoe launch site, outdoor classroom, drinking water, visitor center.

Permits and Rules: Trail fees for nonmembers are $1.50 for adults and $1 for children. Visitors are requested to register at the Education Center. Stay on the trails, which are also closed to bicycles. No smoking is allowed on-site. No pets are allowed on the trails.

Further Information: Contact Riveredge Nature Center, 4458 West Hawthorne, Box 26, Newburg, WI 53060-0026; 414-675-6888 (local) or 414-375-3715 (metro).

Other Points of Interest

Lac Lawrann Conservancy is operated by West Bend's Park, Recreation and Forestry Department. Located on the edge of the Kettle Moraine, Lac Lawrann offers many examples of glacial topography. The original 20-acre site was a gift from Lawrence and Ann Maurin, who donated the property to the community as a conservancy in 1979. The city eventually added another 80 acres, with plans to build additional educational facilities there. It has long been known as a bird sanctuary, and more than 224 species have been identified on the property. Regular tours and workshops are held at the site on weekends from May through October. Groups may make reservations by calling the park's office at 414-335-5080. West Bend is 6 miles west of Newburg on State Highway 33.

Park Trails

Maple Trail 👢—.47 mile—This trail edges through an ecologically diverse area close to the Visitor Center. Once a cow pasture behind the barn that has become part of the Riveredge complex, it is now a maple forest.

Big Oak Trail 👢👢—1.4 miles—This trail is accessible only by crossing the Wisconsin River from the Nature Center site. You reach the path via the access easement that goes south from Hickory Road in Newburg. There are numerous towering bur oaks

dating from settlement days generations ago.

Oak Trail 👢—.65 mile—This path snuggles into a bend of the Wisconsin River. The forest floor here provides an excellent opportunity to view an array of wildflowers, including the ostrich fern along the river. The many surrounding stumps show that this was once a spot for prime timber.

Swamp Walk 👢—.3 mile—The trail includes a floating walk over a pond, home of frogs and salamanders. Various species of ducks and Canada geese flock to this watery area.

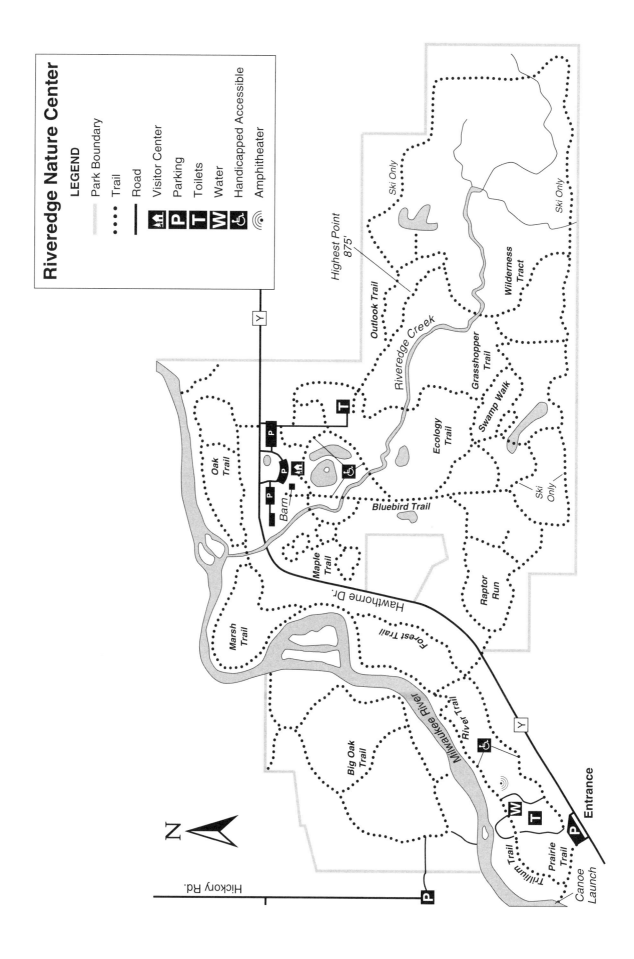

Riveredge Nature Center

LEGEND

- Park Boundary
- Trail
- Road
- Visitor Center
- Parking
- Toilets
- Water
- Handicapped Accessible
- Amphitheater

Loop A 👢👢

Distance Round-Trip: 3.4 miles

Estimated Hiking Time: 3 hours

Cautions: Insect repellent is helpful, especially in the wet spring and summer.

Trail Directions: Park in the lot in front of the Visitor Center and register. Pick up the trail behind the Center, just north of the pond.

This loop is a combination of the Ecology Trail (.9 mi.), Raptor Run (.6 mi.), Bluebird Trail (1.02 mi.), Grasshopper Trail (.55 mi.), and Outlook Trail (.3 mi.). The trail turns to the right as you edge around the pond **[1]** and pick up the .9-mi. Ecology Trail, which offers a variety of settings from fields to swamp. At .1 mi., pick up the grass/dirt track that crosses a prairie with its rainbow of black-eyed Susans and other wildflowers. Go up the hill (.2 mi.) **[2]** to the left and cross the intersections of the Maple Trail. Continue going forward along the Bluebird Trail and enter a state natural area that includes heavy growth of birch on either side of a small bridge (.3 mi.) **[3]**.

Keep walking through the bower to the next field (.7 mi.) **[4]**. One leg of this trail continues to the right toward another pond where it dead-ends at a small pier. Take a look around and return the way you came in. Turn right and walk down a long, straight path between rows of underbrush, oaks, and alders (.8 mi.) **[5]**. Take the first right turn into the mixed hardwood forest. This is the beginning of the wood-chipped Raptor Run, a heavy grove where a sharp bird-watcher can spot numerous hawks. The woods have a contingent of deer, as well. Follow the S-curves through the forestland, where you exit on the far south end of the preserve (1.5 mi.) **[6]**. You cross a small marsh via a boardwalk, at the end of which is a bench.

On the other side of the marsh is a pine grove. The trail leads to a ski-only area that runs along the fence line demarcating the boundary of the center. Go through the pines to the first left intersection and follow it over a bridge across a shallow pond. Pick up the loop to the right on the Bluebird Trail and walk through the hardwood forest (1.9 mi.) **[7]**. Follow the path through the woods and undergrowth, up a rise to connect with the Grasshopper Trail **[8]**, a .5-mi.

link that takes you across Riveredge Creek. There is a bench at the creek crossing (2.1 mi.) **[9]**.

After crossing the bridge and walking through a boggy, low-lying area, proceed up the hill to your right (2.1 mi.) **[10]**. You can continue climbing to the highest point in the park or walk along the base of the hill back to the north. To get to the top of the hill via what is called the Outlook Trail, walk up the gravel-packed dirt path as it ascends in its long, winding crawl to the crest. The path is generally in a northerly direction, yet with the curves in the trail it sometimes swings to the northeast or northwest before straightening out. From atop the hill, you can see for several miles in each direction, and there are benches on which to rest (2.3 mi.) **[11]**.

There are several short trails back and forth along the crest of the hill. However, they either end at a fence line with private property on the north side of the grounds or peter out in the tall grass. Return down the hill the same way you went up and follow the path to the right. You will pass behind a flower-covered hill to the left. Keep walking for about .2 mi. on a straight stretch of path.

Edge through a prairie restoration complete with goldenrod, daisies, milkweed, side oats, and wild grasses. You can either exit at the parking lot there or turn left and walk the meadow. The waist-high vegetation is reminiscent of pre-pioneer prairie land. The center complex is to the right of the path, which loops and swells through the flowers.

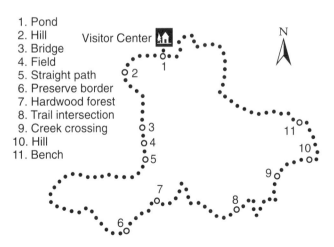

1. Pond
2. Hill
3. Bridge
4. Field
5. Straight path
6. Preserve border
7. Hardwood forest
8. Trail intersection
9. Creek crossing
10. Hill
11. Bench

Loop B 👢👢

Distance Round-Trip: 1.6 miles

Estimated Hiking Time: 1 hour

Cautions: The trail can often be boggy after a rain or in early spring after the river's high water recedes. Use insect repellent liberally.

Trail Directions: Park at the marked lot on the north side of the highway at the edge of Newburg on the way to the main Riveredge driveway. The lot is chained off on Saturdays when the Center is closed.

This loop combines several trails on the north side of County Highway Y, where the Center has property along the Milwaukee River. You can assemble a good package along the Prairie Trail (.25 mi.), the Trillium Trail (.2 mi.), and the River Trail (.5 mi.) with a return along the Forest Trail (.6 mi.).

Cross the parking lot to several wooden steps [1] that lead up to a pine grove. Proceed straight along the bark trail to where it descends the slope. The trail will be spongy underneath, making for a soft, quiet walk. There is a row of posts connected by strong wire along the left of the trail, acting as a protective barrier along the slope. Through the trees are rest rooms (.2 mi.) [2]. Move past an inoperable drinking fountain, past the outdoor classroom, and deeper into the woods. In the spring, the trillium blossoms along this stretch of path. Turn right on the River Trail. This path along the riverbank presents a good opportunity to watch migrating waterfowl. At .5 mi., there is a wooden overlook where you can sit on the railings [3] and watch the passing water.

The dirt path can be muddy from rain or high water along this section, so carefully step around the boggy land [4]. You can usually see fresh deep tracks made by deer along the trail. The trail turns to the right, where you proceed around a bend in the river. Meet the intersection of the Marsh Trail (.7 mi.) [5] to the left or continue to the right through the woods. The latter route is a long, rolling stretch of pathway through the forest. Taking a right, climb up a short slope and walk along the ridge top. Through the trees you can see vehicles passing along County Highway Y. Follow the path back to the parking lot.

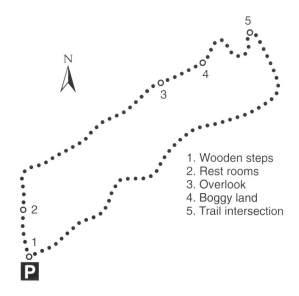

1. Wooden steps
2. Rest rooms
3. Overlook
4. Boggy land
5. Trail intersection

32. Bong State Recreation Area

- Visit one of the state's primary bird-watching areas.
- Enjoy nature programs and guided tours.
- Hiking, biking, and bridle trails offer exploration potential.

Park Information

The Bong State Recreation Area is named after Wisconsin native Richard I. Bong, the number-one ace fighter pilot for the United States during World War II. In the mid-1950s, the federal government purchased 5,540 acres in Racine and Kenosha Counties for an Air Force base. Base construction was due to begin in 1958, but the project was abandoned.

In the 1960s, 1,000 acres of the vacant land was purchased to serve as school forests and a county park. In 1974, 4,515 acres were set aside as the state's first recreation area that would include non-traditional uses of parkland. For instance, space is available for dog training, hang gliding, sky diving, model rocket launching, hot-air ballooning, and falconry among other activities. Only 280 acres have been developed for a picnic and interpretive site. Most of the land has been saved for fish and game research, conservation, and management. Controlled burning is slowly restoring a prairie feel to the region. Bong trails roll over a gentle landscape through the prairies and around East Lake, the result of damming a stream. There are only a few steep hills. All color-coded trails begin and end at the trailhead parking lot northeast of the Molinaro Visitor Center. The recreational area's loops are concentric, enabling the hiker to decide at each junction whether to continue or spin off in another direction.

Directions: From I-94, get off at the Highway 142 exit and drive west about 8 miles. The park is 1 mile west of State Highway 75. Kenosha is the largest nearby city, 17 miles to the east on Lake Michigan.

Hours Open: Park offices are open from 8 A.M. to 8:30 P.M. Memorial Day to Labor Day, and from 8 A.M. to 4 P.M. the remainder of the year. The parkland is open year round from 6 A.M. to 11 P.M.

Facilities: Picnic area, research pond, camping, amphitheater with programs, nature trails with guided tours, wildlife refuge, horse trail, and all-terrain vehicle and dirt-bike trails augment the hiking potential. There is a fishing pier on East Lake accessible to people with physical disabilities. There are also volleyball courts, a ball diamond, and playground equipment.

Permits and Rules: A state park vehicle pass is required for entrance. A Wisconsin fishing license and trout stamp are needed for fishing. All the proper permits and licenses can be purchased at the park office. Pets are prohibited on the nature trails. During hunting season, stay on the Green Loop Trail or the Visitor Center Nature Trail. The resident camping fee is $10 per night; nonresident fee is $12. Electric hookups are $3.

Further Information: Contact Site Manager, Bong State Recreation Area, 26313 Burlington Road, Kansasville, WI 53139; 414-878-5600 or 4145-652-0377.

Park Trails

Visitor Center Trail 👢—.7 mile—This is a five-foot-wide path surfaced with limestone, starting in front of the Visitor Center near the main parking lot. This access makes it convenient for nature lovers who use wheelchairs or those with visual difficulties. The trail edges down a slope to the north shore of East Lake and is well marked with numerous interpretive signs. Rimming the lakeshore is a 100-foot-long boardwalk for bird-watching or checking out the water life.

Vista Trail 👢—1 mile—The trail starts near the Vista picnic area off Kenosha County Highway B, accessed from State Highway 142. The trail slopes to the west though an oak and hard maple forest and concludes at a small pond. This trail is also labeled with nature signs.

Yellow Trail (North Loop) 👢👢—4.4 miles—This is a generally level to moderately rolling trail, but the distance is a challenge for anyone not used to walking far. However, the one steep hill has a stairway that ascends to an overlook. From the top, hikers can look over the entire Bong State Recreation Area. The South Loop includes the 6.4-mile Orange Trail and the 8.3-mile Red Trail, which also take hikers over fairly easy terrain.

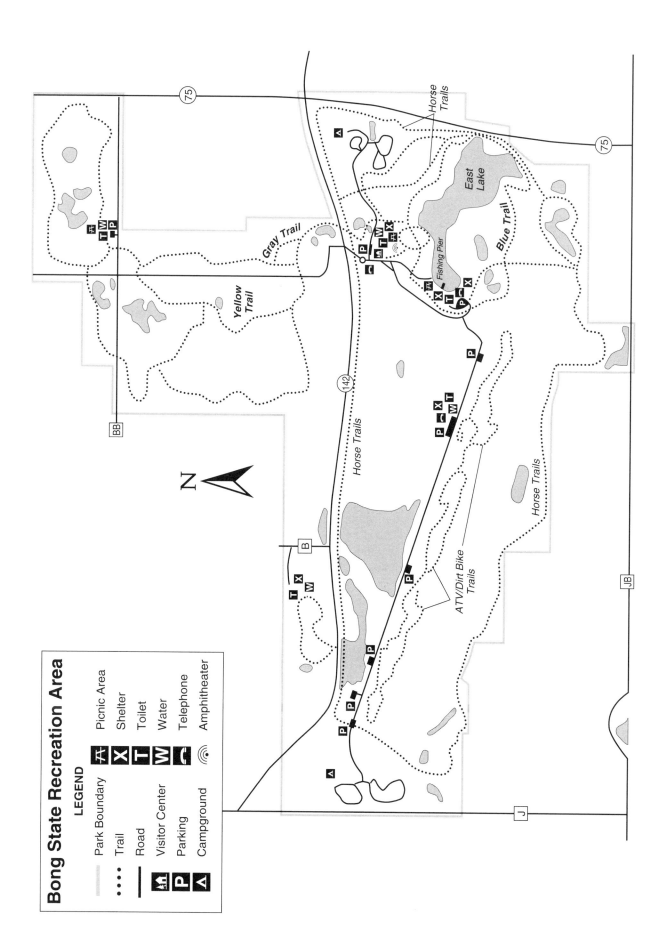

Bong State Recreation Area

LEGEND

Park Boundary
Trail
Road
Visitor Center
Parking
Campground

Picnic Area
Shelter
Toilet
Water
Telephone
Amphitheater

Blue Trail (South Loop) 🥾

Distance Round-Trip: 4.2 miles

Estimated Hiking Time: 2 hours

Cautions: The trail can be slippery after a rain.

Trail Directions: Follow the posts marked with green to the right from the trailhead parking lot.

Hikers move to the south from a small pond **[1]** and cross the playground (.1 mi.) **[2]** on the way to East Lake. Pick up the Nature Trail (.2 mi.) **[3]** for an educational look at the region. You will see a prairie community of plants, with spiderwort, blazing star, and cornflowers in abundance. Bison once roamed here, but the last one was shot in 1832 by early settlers, who also were cleaning out the elk, bears, wolves, and prairie chickens that once called the area their home. Only the rattlesnakes hung on, but hikers will seldom, if ever, see one.

Move along the boardwalk that rims the lake (.4 mi.) **[4].** Depending on the season, look for appropriate underwater critters such as tadpoles, water striders, panfish, and bullheads. You will pass a sign (.6 mi.) **[5]** indicating what an early area settler, Hannah Rhodes, wrote in 1842: "The country is beautiful," she said, noting also that the land was great for cattle raising. "Everything seems to grow plentiful," she wrote. After walking along the Nature Trail you'll connect with the Green Loop, which runs southeast until you meet once again with the Blue Loop by turning right at the intersection.

Picking up the Blue Loop again, hikers can see the first of several blinds (1.2 mi.) **[6]** along the lakeshore that are perfect for bird-watching. You need to wade out several feet to each one, however. The loop runs parallel to State Highway 75 on the east side of East Lake. Rounding the lake, you will encounter an oak grove and a small marshland. There are several hills here (1.4 mi.) **[7]** that are no match for the dedicated hiker but might be tougher for the quickly winded.

Next is more open ground (2.1 mi.) **[8],** regularly burned to keep down the scrub grasses and juvenile trees that would overwhelm a prairie restoration. There are 72 bodies of water scattered around the Bong region. They range from potholes that fill with rainwater in springtime to spring-fed lakes. Many can be spotted in this section of the trail (3 mi.) **[9].** Demonstrating the constant evolution of the area, sedges, rushes, and reeds are reclaiming the more shallow potholes, hastening their demise.

From here it is a quick walk past the ball diamond (3.5 mi.) **[10]** and fishing pier (3.9 mi.) **[11]** back to the Visitor Center.

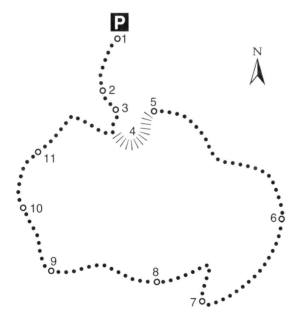

1. Small pond
2. Playground
3. Nature trail
4. Lake boardwalk
5. Hannah Rhodes sign
6. Bird-watching blinds
7. Hills
8. Open ground
9. Potholes
10. Ball diamond
11. Fishing pier

Gray Trail (North Loop) 🥾

Distance Round-Trip: 1.7 miles

Estimated Hiking Time: 1 hour

Trail Directions: From the trailhead parking lot near the Visitor Center, follow the posts marked with gray that lead north. You will cross State Highway 142 after scrambling up an embankment to pick up the trail on the other side of the road.

This is the shortest trail in the Bong system—it makes for a quick, refreshing walk when hikers don't have a lot of time. For the first .3 mi., the trail parallels the Brighton Golf Course **[1]** on the right. At .4 mi. is a grove of second-growth trees and brush **[2]**. To the left about 1,000 feet off the trail is a marshy area filled with waterfowl. Yet look skyward for turkey vultures and hawks.

The trail moves to the north through a stand of oaks (.7 mi.) **[3]** and more scattered brushland. You then loop back to the Visitor Center after bisecting the horseback and bike trail (.8 mi.) **[4]**. It is a straight walk back to Highway 142 where you can cross at the marked site. Watch for onrushing cars.

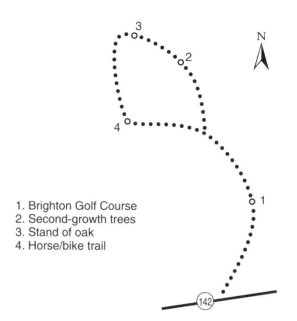

1. Brighton Golf Course
2. Second-growth trees
3. Stand of oak
4. Horse/bike trail

33. Bugline Recreation Trail

- Hike along a former roadbed for a small local railroad.
- Visit county parks and local attractions along the way.
- Watch wildlife that has adapted to encroaching human habitation.

Trail Information

The eight-foot-wide Bugline runs along the former roadbed of the Milwaukee Menomonee Falls and Western Railroad. The railroad was built in the last century by a local quarry owner, Joseph Hatfield, to haul stone. A leftover from those early days is an old stone crusher at the quarry.

The Bugline Trail starts in the 397-acre Menomonee Park located in the villages of Menomonee Falls and Lannon. Hikers can begin their walk in the park with its rich variety of landscapes ranging from marshes to woods.

As evidenced by Hatfield's operations, this was a major stone-producing region. The site of the park was once called Stone City because many quarry workers lived near the southeast end of the quarry. Several pits in the vicinity are still operating. The famed light-colored Lannon stone can be found on numerous building exteriors throughout southeastern Wisconsin.

Directions: Menomonee Park is located between County Highways Y and V about 2 miles west of Menomonee Falls on State Highway 74.

Hours Open: 7 A.M. to 10 P.M. daily, year round.

Facilities: Trailheads have water, rest rooms, park facilities, and connect to other hiking trails. Communities through which the trail passes have restaurants and other amenities for the hiker.

Permits and Rules: A vehicle permit pass ($3.50 weekends, $2 weekdays) is required for Menomonee Park, but no trail pass is necessary.

Further Information: Contact Waukesha County Parks and Land Use Department, 1320 Pewaukee Road, Room 230, Waukesha, WI 53188; 414-548-7801.

Other Points of Interest

The **Old Falls Village** in Menomonee Falls is a re-creation of the original village dating back to the mid-1880s. It features several original buildings of historical significance that have been moved to the site. The community hosts numerous activities in the complex, from ice-cream socials to historical pageants. The buildings are open from 1 to 4 P.M. Sundays, May through September. Call 414-255-8343 for more information.

The **Wild Rice Trail** is a 2.3-mile trek along the rushing Menomonee River from downtown Menomonee Falls. Secluded from the rush of traffic by foliage for part of the walk, the trail meanders past giant willows and stately oaks. Combine this with a downtown walking tour and you gain a good feel for this old Wisconsin community, both in its natural state and with its more urban feel. A flier about the town walk is available from the Chamber of Commerce. For details, call 414-251-2430.

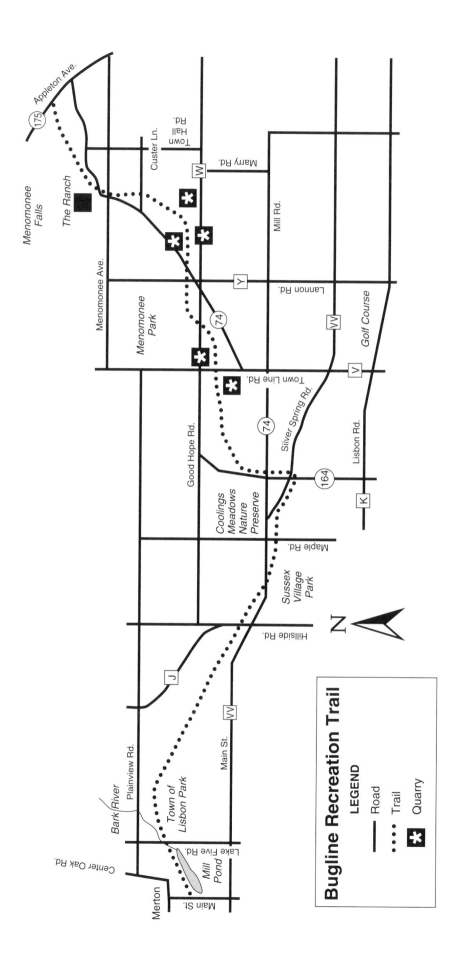

Bugline I—Menomonee Falls to Menomonee Park 🥾

Distance One-Way: 3.6 miles

Estimated Hiking Time: 2 hours

Cautions: Since this is primarily a biking trail, be alert for cyclists. Hikers may wish to bring two cars, leaving one at the beginning of the trek and another at the expected conclusion. Otherwise a back trek is required that in effect doubles the amount of walking. Watch for traffic when crossing streets.

Trail Directions: Pick up the trail at Appleton Avenue (State Highway 175) in Menomonee Falls. Parking is available on side streets in the area.

This is primarily a stroll through town and suburbia **[1]**, although the crushed-rock trail is tree lined. This separates it somewhat from the houses, backyard swimming pools, and garages. At the edge of Menomonee Falls, the trail runs through open country along State Highway 74. This will eventually be built up as well. At 1 mi., hikers pass near The Ranch **[2]**, a camp for persons with physical and developmental disabilities. Custer Lane **[3]** is the next major crossroads at 2 mi.

Pass the deep pits marking the old Lannon quarries at 3.1 mi. **[4].** With the ongoing quarrying, be aware of trucks in the vicinity. A separate four-foot-wide bridle trail is adjacent to the hiking path for the next .5 mi. to Menomonee Park **[5]**, where it links with Menomonee Park's trails.

Bugline II—Menomonee Park to Sussex 🥾

Distance One-Way: 2.6 miles

Estimated Hiking Time: 2 hours

Cautions: Watch for cars.

Trail Directions: The trail is accessible at any road crossing, such as County Highway Y or V or State Highway 164. Parking is permitted wherever legal. However, Menomonee Park is the main trailhead on the northeast.

Park in the lot to the south of the stone crusher, where the park service road begins a curve to the north. The main park trail/bridle path is just south of this parking lot near a picnic area. To the north of the lot is a large quarry lake for swimming and scuba diving, plus a beach and pier. The park has camping, rest rooms, and water as well.

Pick up the trail and walk south through a grove of trees, linking up with the Bugline just outside the park environs. The trail is flat and uneventful; but there are open spaces to study wildflowers and bird-watch. Carefully cross the busy Good Hope Road (1.2 mi.) **[1]** and continue on to the south. There is a slight S-curve **[2]** in the trail just south of Good Hope, but stay on the path.

The Coolings Meadow nature preserve **[3]** is at the 2.1 mi. mark. This 30-acre wetland was donated to Waukesha County by the Nature Conservancy. During spring and autumn, the marshland and ponds make great waterfowl viewing from the trail's vantage point.

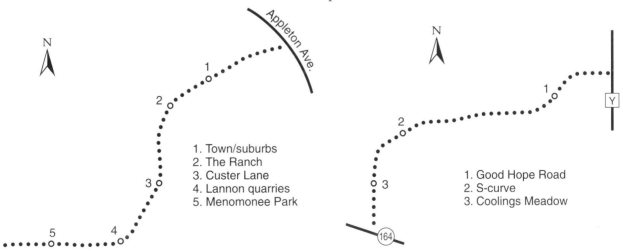

1. Town/suburbs
2. The Ranch
3. Custer Lane
4. Lannon quarries
5. Menomonee Park

1. Good Hope Road
2. S-curve
3. Coolings Meadow

Bugline III—Sussex to Merton 🥾

Distance One-Way: 6 miles

Estimated Hiking Time: 3 to 4 hours

Cautions: Watch for traffic and cyclists.

Trail Directions: One of the better places to depart is from Sussex Village Park **[1],** a 75-acre site south of Main Street (State Highway 74) on Weaver Road in Sussex. There is plenty of parking along nearby side streets. There are shelters, picnic tables, water, rest rooms, and ball diamonds.

Begin your walk west past the ball fields, picnic area, and shelters at the end of town. The trail crosses Hillside Road **[2]** and moves along a straight path to the northwest, parallel to State Highway 74 for about 1 mi. It then cuts through open meadow and scattered oak plots **[3].** This is a good bird-watching stretch, with the usual contingent of blackbirds, sparrows, wrens, and robins flying overhead.

The Town of Lisbon Park **[4]** is at the 5-mi. mark, adjacent to the trail at Oakwood and Lake Five Roads. The park is actually .7 mi. east of the town. Parking, shaded picnic tables, and rest rooms are on-site. The trail goes on for about 1 mi. further. It catches up with the Bark River and concludes at the Town of Merton millpond **[5]** on Main Street. There are restaurants, antique shops, and other stores in Merton as well.

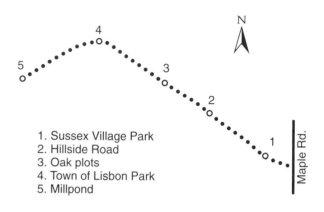

1. Sussex Village Park
2. Hillside Road
3. Oak plots
4. Town of Lisbon Park
5. Millpond

34. Menomonee Park

- Swim and scuba dive in an old quarry.
- Bird-watch on extensive meadowlands.
- Listen to the bullfrogs in the marshes and ponds.

Park Information

The 397-acre Menomonee Park is located in the villages of Menomonee Falls and Lannon. The park has a variety of landscapes, from cattail marshes to maple woods. The area was once a major stone-producing region. In fact, the park was once called Stone City because of the many quarry workers who lived in solidly built homes near the southeast end of the quarry.

The quarry owner, Joseph Hatfield, even built his own railroad to haul stone. His Milwaukee Menomonee Falls and Western Railroad became fondly known as the Bugline. The old railbed is now one of the state's major biking, skiing, and hiking rail-to-trail segments (see park #33). Another leftover from those early days is an old stone crusher at the quarry.

Directions: The park is .5 miles north of State Highway 74 on County Highway V.

Hours Open: Park hours are sunrise to 10 P.M. year round. Beach hours are 11 A.M. to 7 P.M. weekdays, and from 10 A.M. to 7 P.M. weekends.

Facilities: Rest rooms, camping, nature trail, swimming, bridle path, picnic shelters, archery, sledding hill, ball field, volleyball court.

Permits and Rules: A daily entrance fee of $3.50 on weekends and $2 on weekdays is required. Parking is allowed only in designated lots. Dogs must be leashed. Camping is by permit only and in designated areas.

Further Information: Contact Waukesha County Parks and Land Use Department, 1320 Pewaukee Road, Waukesha, WI 53188; 414-548-7801.

Other Points of Interest

The **Bugline Recreation Trail** bike path (see park #33) runs for 12 miles on an old railroad right-of-way. The trail begins at Appleton Avenue in Menomonee Falls and ends at Lake Five Road in the Town of Lisbon, with a good midpoint stop at Sussex Village Park. There is no charge for using the trail; however, a vehicle fee of $3.50 on weekends and $2 on weekdays is charged at Menomonee Park. Among the sights along the way are the deep quarries in the Lannon area. The route skirts the rim of the pits. On the way, bikers and hikers pass many houses made from the famous pale Lannon stone. Call the Waukesha County Parks and Land Use Department, 414-548-7801, for more information.

Park Trails

Entrance Trail —1 mile—The trail, which doubles as a winter cross-country pathway, is accessed at the entrance parking lot and then heads east. It cuts through the center of the park, first crossing a meadow and then through a maple and oak woods. It swings north past the beach and Quarry Lake before it links with another hiking trail at a bridge crossing a marsh stream. From here, the trail becomes part of the longer system of trails in the park, and hikers can go any direction.

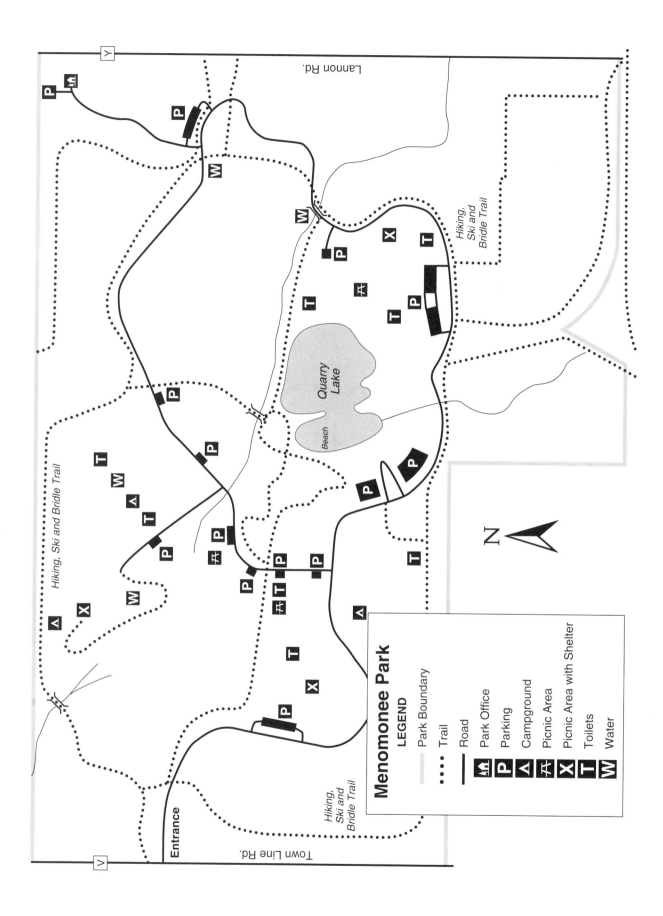

Bridle/Hiking Trail 👢👢

Distance Round-Trip: 2.8 miles

Estimated Hiking Time: 1.5 hours

Cautions: Watch out for horse droppings. Some sections of the trail can be boggy as they cross marshy parts of the park. Bring bug spray in the summer mosquito/mayfly season.

Trail Directions: Since the path rings the park, there are numerous places to begin walking. The horse-trailer parking area is on the south side of the park off the main drive. One of the other major trailheads is from the rear of the main parking lot at the beach. Walk across the lot and enter the path. The bridle trail is open for horses from May 1 to November 1, weather permitting, but hikers can use the path at any time. The trail doubles as a cross-country ski trail in the winter.

Walk toward the southeast, through a thick grove of oak and silver maple **[1]**. The trail skirts the south side of the park and then cuts over a marsh before hitting another clump of trees (.2 mi.) **[2]**. The marsh stretch can be boggy after a rain, so be prepared for mud. You cross the Bugline Recreation Trail bike path at (.3 mi.) **[3]**, which starts in the parking lot across the service road from the bridle path. Just beyond the Bugline Recreation Trail, you can turn right and add another .25 mi. to the trek by walking on a trail that heads south, then swings east. If you take this link, the bridle path here continues on, exiting in the southeast corner of the park. It extends over to The Ranch, a nearby day camp for persons with physical and developmental disabilities. Another segment swings back north from here to reconnect with the original trail.

If you continue on instead of taking the extra loop, you parallel the park road (.4 mi.) **[4]** that swings past two more parking lots near the volleyball courts. The trail traverses an up-and-down landscape past more oak and along a meadow. The trail now angles to the north, past another marsh that will resound with a full bullfrog chorus in mid-July. Cottonwoods and willows mingle with the maple, birch, and poplar (.5 mi.) **[5]**. Next is a mowed area (.6 mi.) **[6]**, with a clump of assorted trees on the right side where you cross the service road. There is another bridle trail access from the east, off Lannon Road (County Highway Y).

After the mowed area is another service road crossing near a parking lot (.8 mi.) **[7]**. For hikers, this is a better place to link up with the trail, rather than the just-passed road access. There is always the strong possibility of getting a ticket if you park outside the park grounds along the highway. Turn left after crossing the park road. The archery area and a great sledding hill are straight ahead. However, continue following the pathway through a meadow and back along a marsh (1.2 mi.) **[8]**. There is a thick woods on the left with oak, silver, maple, basswood, box elder, and other tree species.

Trace the path as it goes north and then swings west into the woods. You pass Camp Pow Wow (1.4 mi.) **[9]** in a small clearing. A short interpretive nature trail can be picked up here that loops around the camp clearing. The camp is operated by the Waukesha County Association of Retarded Citizens for residents with developmental disabilities.

Next, cross a bridge (1.5 mi.) **[10]** that connects marshland on both sides of the path, and then exit the woods onto more meadow. Take the trail south and cross the service road behind the entrance admission booth (1.7 mi.) **[11]**. To the west, there is another bridle trail access off Townline Road. Pass the baseball field to the south (2 mi.) **[12]**. The trail then turns left and concludes either at the horse-trailer parking area or back in the parking lot.

1. Grove	7. Parking lot
2. Grove	8. Marsh
3. Bike path	9. Camp Pow Wow
4. Park road	10. Bridge
5. Marsh	11. Admission booth
6. Mowed area	12. Ball diamond

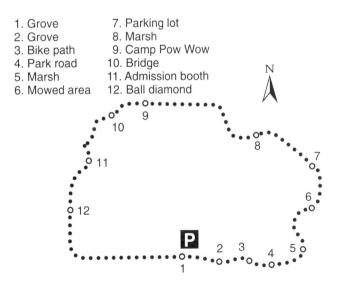

Center Nature Trail 🥾

Distance Round-Trip: .7 mile

Estimated Hiking Time: 30 minutes

Cautions: Bug repellent is necessary in early summer or during the wet season.

Trail Directions: Leave your car in one of the four parking areas along the service road where it bisects the grounds. The parking spots are on the west side of the road, accommodating the family picnic areas.

The trail is accessed from the family picnic area **[1]** in the maple/oak forest making up the center of Menomonee Park. This is a flat dirt and gravel path that cuts through the woods to the east. Pass a marsh (.1 mi.) **[2]** before briefly leaving the woods and move along a fence separating the trees from the beach at Quarry Lake. The trail turns to the north and reenters the woods. Struggling young maple saplings reach toward the tree canopy, trying to seize whatever sun they can (.3 mi.) **[3]**.

Cross a bridge over a small stream. Another trail intersects here on its way to the east (.4 mi.) **[4]**. A hiker wanting to extend the walk can link up with this trail. Otherwise, turn to the immediate left and plunge back into the woods. Follow the muddy route north to where it joins the park service road **[5]**. You can then walk back the short distance to your vehicle on the road. Marsh appears on both sides of the road. Dead trees and brackish water here make the area look like an everglades scene.

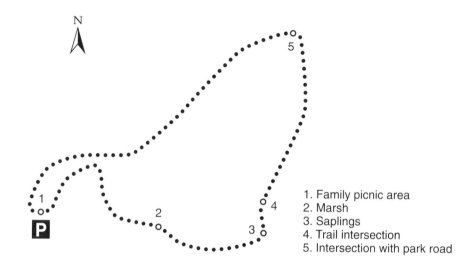

N

1. Family picnic area
2. Marsh
3. Saplings
4. Trail intersection
5. Intersection with park road

35. Muskego Park

- Swim in a cool, refreshing pond.
- Study marsh life.
- Walk through a state hardwoods scientific area.

Park Information

The 160-acre park was the former Arthur Ellarson farm, one of the pioneer farm sites in Waukesha County. The land was purchased in 1958 as the county's first regional park. Sixty acres within the complex were named a state scientific area in 1973. The purpose of the scientific area is to save valuable plant communities, teach conservation practices, and provide a place to study the region's natural history.

Muskego Park has five reserved picnic areas, as well as an acre pond for swimming. Lifeguards are on duty daily, and beginning through advanced swimming lessons are offered in two sessions, two weeks each, in the summer. A beach house has kitchen facilities.

Directions: Muskego Park is .5 miles west of Racine Avenue (County Highway Y) on County Highway L in the southeast corner of Waukesha County.

Hours Open: Sunrise to 10 P.M., year round. Beach hours are 11 A.M. to 7 P.M. weekdays, and 10 A.M. to 7 P.M. weekends.

Facilities: Camping, hiking, bridle paths, marsh walks, picnic shelters, beach, swimming pond, tennis courts, horseshoes, volleyball court.

Permits and Rules: 24 family campsites, available at $8.25 per night with checkout at 3 P.M. Firewood is $2 per bundle. Pets must be leashed. Fires are permitted only in designated areas. Horseback riding is allowed only on the bridle paths. Beer is permissible by picnic permit only.

Further Information: Contact Waukesha County Parks and Land Use Department, 1320 Pewaukee Road, Waukesha, WI 53188; 414-548-7801.

Other Points of Interest

A **farmers' market** is held from 6 A.M. to 1 P.M. each Tuesday, Thursday, and Saturday in Waukesha, the county seat. Look for the stalls at the corner of Barstow and Main Streets. Throughout the area in the summer and fall, farmers sell produce from small stalls near their driveways or along the highways and in the towns of Muskego, Mukwonago, Big Bend, and Genesse.

Vernon Marsh State Wildlife Area is 6 miles west of Muskego Park with several wildlife-viewing areas along the dikes and surface roads. Mallards, canvasback ducks, black terns, great blue herons, sandhill cranes, and blackbirds are abundant during their respective seasons. Spring and autumn are best for watching migratory birds. Bring binoculars and insect repellent. Fishing for bluegills, catfish, and bullheads is also popular. Canoeing is the best way to travel deep into the marsh. For details, call the state's Department of Natural Resources, 668-266-2621.

Park Trails

Pond Trail 🥾—1.5 miles—The loop runs around the busy recreational area of Muskego Park, proceeding through the family campground and past the beach house and picnic areas. It is an easy walk, especially for youngsters. The wide path goes through meadows, over mowed grassy areas, and through a maple woods to show off a variety of topography and flora.

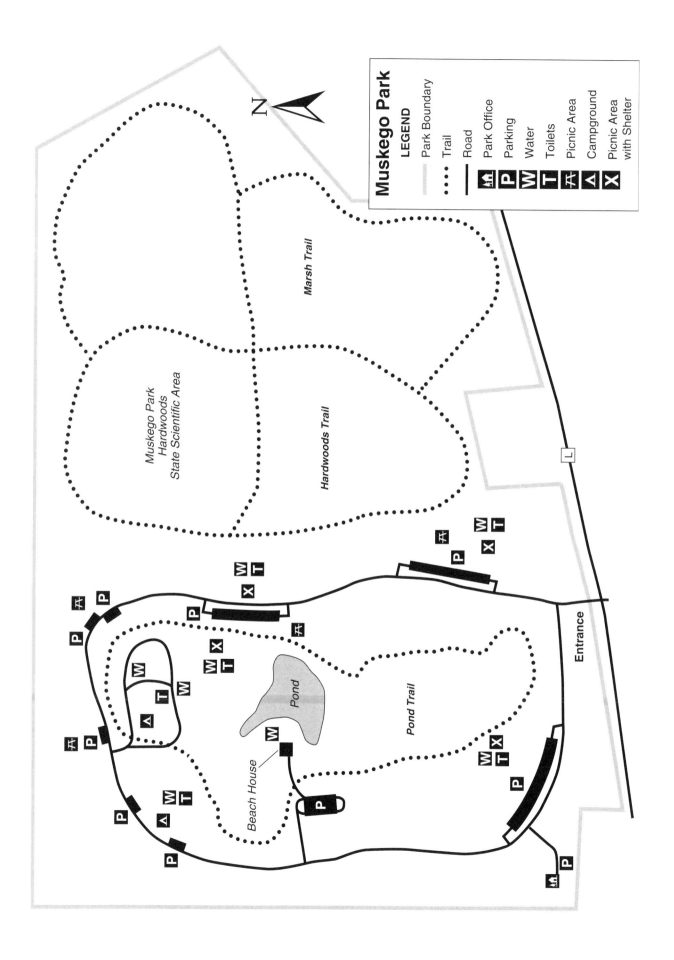

Hardwoods Trail 👢👢

Distance Round-Trip: 1.3 miles

Estimated Hiking Time: 40 minutes

Cautions: Mosquitoes can be a problem in the summer. Sections of the trail get muddy and sloppy after a rain.

Trail Directions: Enter either from the bridle path access or from the path behind picnic shelter #54E on the east side of the main park service road.

The first few hundred feet of the trail are straight and flat **[1]**. Then the path curves right up a slope under high-tension lines (.1 mi.) **[2]**. The woods are made up primarily of such hardwoods as maples and oak, with a number of magnificent specimens of each spotted along both sides of the trail among the second-growth ground cover (.2 mi.) **[3]**. The area used to be primarily field or woodlot. After years of being left alone, it is now proceeding well through rejuvenation, aided by careful forest management.

You can take a shortcut **[4]** to the east across the hardwoods scientific area and head directly to the Marsh Trail. But if woods are your thing, continue ahead up a slight slope and angle to the east along the north side of the park. The trail is wide and flat; it was resurfaced in 1996 to make for a better walk. The path meets the north side of the Marsh Trail at .4 mi. **[5],** then swings south through a heavy stand of maple.

There is a large pond to the right, surrounded by marsh that is a haven for mosquitoes in the early summer. You will cross several culverts (.5 mi.) **[6]** in this stretch, an aid to water run-off during the rainy season. The first has a good dump of gravel across it, lifting the hiker out of what could be a mucky trek through the surrounding mud. The flow is mostly dried up by August, but a good rain pumps it up again. So be aware of this when planning which hiking boots to wear.

Move down the hill and cross the intersection with the shortcut trail mentioned earlier. That leg continues to the east between two large marsh areas hidden beyond the trees. The Hardwoods Trail continues to the south over several small rises and depressions. Chipmunks, squirrels, crows, and the occasional woodpecker do their respective nature things, whether scurrying, cawing, or rapping on a rotted log. There are numerous saplings in this stretch, reaching for the sun in any partially opened area away from the larger trees.

Meet the bottom link (.7 mi.) **[7]** of the Marsh Trail and turn right along the path. The path is only about 50 feet from the park border at this spot, and the back doors of several ranch houses can be glimpsed through the undergrowth. The trail goes north again, meeting the high-tension lines. In a few minutes, you pass the bridle-path entrance, with the trailhead behind the picnic shelter about 100 feet beyond. Exit at either.

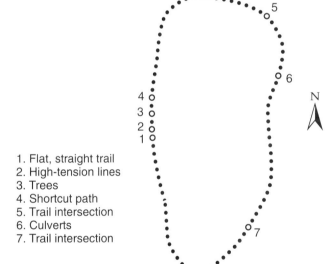

1. Flat, straight trail
2. High-tension lines
3. Trees
4. Shortcut path
5. Trail intersection
6. Culverts
7. Trail intersection

Marsh Trail 🥾🥾

Distance Round-Trip: 1.5 miles

Estimated Hiking Time: 50 minutes

Cautions: Insect repellent is a necessity during the wet season. Wear water-repellent boots, because the pathway can be boggy in the spring and after a rain.

Trail Directions: Enter either from the bridle path access or from the path behind picnic shelter #54E on the east side of the main park service road.

When setting out, you initially trek over the same pathway as on the Hardwoods Trail **[1]**. Walk north under the high-tension lines that run overhead. They disappear into the woods straight ahead when the trail angles to the right. First, however, you meet with the shortcut intersection that can lop off half the trek if you are so inclined. But to get the full advantage of the diversity of vegetation in the state scientific area, continue going straight ahead (.2 mi.) **[2]** along the main path.

Follow the path to the eastward (right) curve, go down the slope, and connect with the top leg of the Marsh Trail (.4 mi.) **[3]**. This continues to the east about another 1,000 feet before sweeping off to the right. There is extensive marshland to the right. It is a bog packed with bullfrogs, lined with enormous cattails, and replete with red-winged blackbirds and dragonflies.

The path keeps going south (.6 mi.) **[4]** and edges around the first large patch of marsh. It then connects with the shortcut trail and moves farther down the line along the east side of the second bog. There must be just as many frogs roaring from the lily pads in this bog as in the first one.

Follow the trail around the bottom (.8 mi.) **[5]** of the marsh, past more cattail stands, as tiny purple butterflies flit in and out of the shade. You join the Hardwoods Trail again, pass the backs of several houses snuggling up to the park border, and turn north on the pathway. It is then a quick stroll back to the trailhead.

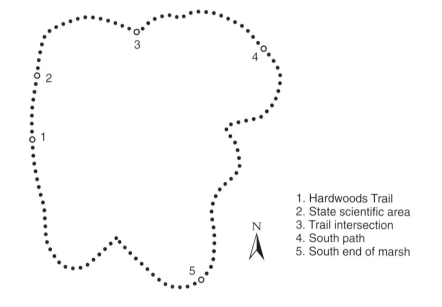

1. Hardwoods Trail
2. State scientific area
3. Trail intersection
4. South path
5. South end of marsh

36. Nashotah Park

- Hike over a variety of terrain.
- Observe the interdependence of two lakes and the vicinity.
- Picnic on wide grassy grounds.

Park Information

Nashotah Park totals 450 acres and is the largest regional park in Waukesha County. It was acquired by the archdiocese of Milwaukee in 1926 and was used as a retreat facility until 1943 when the Gallun family purchased it. The Galluns used the acreage as a farm and game preserve until donating it to the county as a park in 1972. They stipulated in the deed that the property had to be used as a preservation site and public recreation facility. Thus development of picnic areas, ball fields, and other recreational spaces has taken place along the perimeter. This does not disturb the park's core.

About 7 miles of nature and hiking trails lead through eight varying landscapes created by the last glaciers to advance over the state 10,000 years ago. Hikers can travel around a lake system, oak forest, oak savanna, cedar glade, meadow, floating-leaf marsh, shallow marsh, and deep marsh. There has been extensive restoration of prairie vegetation and oak around Grass Lake on the western side of the park.

Directions: The park is located between Oconomowoc and Hartland, .5 mile north of U.S. Highway 16 on the west side of County Highway C.

Hours Open: Sunrise to 10 P.M.

Facilities: Hiking trails, picnic shelters, volleyball court, horseshoe pits.

Permits and Rules: Daily entrance fee or yearly sticker is required for admission. Park entrance is $3.50 for a car on weekends and $2 on weekdays. Fires are permitted only in designated areas. Dogs must be leashed. Hunting, shooting, and littering are prohibited.

Further Information: Contact Waukesha County Parks and Land Use Department, 1320 Pewaukee Road, Waukesha, WI 53188; 414-548-7801.

Other Points of Interest

The **Lake Country Recreation Trail** is located on the old Milwaukee-Watertown Interurban Railway. This had been the main link between Waukesha and the lake district around Oconomowoc. The 8-mile trail now also uses the Wisconsin Electric Power Company right-of-way. The trail reaches between the Landsberg Center trailhead, which is north of I-94 on Golf Road, and Cushing Park in the city of Delafield. The track is surfaced with crushed rock and is open to hikers, bikers, and joggers. For more information, call the Waukesha County Parks and Land Use Department at 414-548-7801.

For golfers and other outdoors lovers, the **Nagawaukee Park and Golf Course** is located north of I-94 between Nagawicka and Pewaukee Lakes on East Glen Cove Road. The 416-acre park offers camping, golf, swimming, and boating. Drinking water is available there, along with concessions during the summer. Call the Waukesha County Parks and Land Use Department, 414-548-7801, for details.

Park Trails

Blue Trail —2 miles—This is the easiest loop in the park. It proceeds around the east side of Forest Lake near the volleyball courts and picnic shelter. The path is relatively flat and straight but takes hikers through some oak groves, through a meadow, and along the lakeshore to demonstrate the variety of topography and flora in Nashotah Park. It skirts a marsh on the north end of Forest Lake. There is a nice vista of the lake through the trees about halfway into the hike. Look for the small path to the left of the trail.

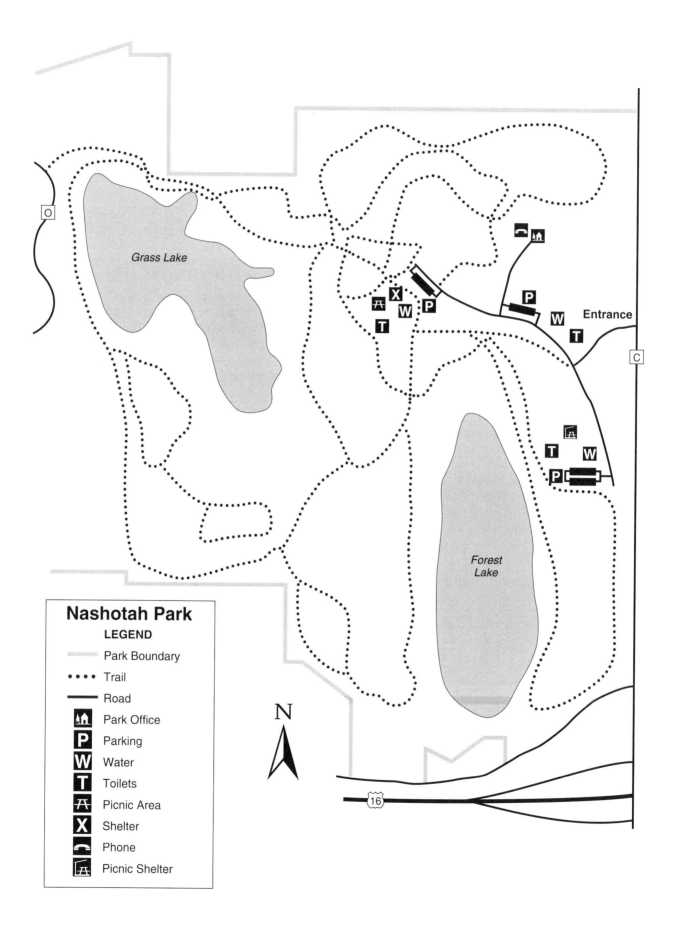

Grass Lake

Forest
Lake

Entrance

N

Nashotah Park

LEGEND

Park Boundary
Trail
Road
Park Office
P Parking
W Water
T Toilets
Picnic Area
X Shelter
Phone
Picnic Shelter

Red Trail 🥾🥾

Distance Round-Trip: 1 mile

Estimated Hiking Time: 45 minutes

Cautions: There are some hilly stretches along this trail.

Trail Directions: Park in the lot in the central recreational area of the park near the volleyball courts and sledding hill. Walk south from the lot, across a wide grassy area and down a slope where there are scattered picnic tables and a shelter. A wooden map board, at the tree line along the bottom of the hill, aids in orientation. The Red, Green, and Blue Trails move out from the same access point.

The trail immediately begins an ascent up a hill **[1],** but the slope is relatively easy, over a wood-chip pathway. The forest cover is primarily old oak and maple, with Virginia creeper, raspberry bushes, and some exotic honeysuckle as ground cover. At .2 mi., the trail descends again **[2],** with a slight angle to the right. It then straightens out. But at .3 mi., the Red Trail goes right while the Green continues straight ahead **[3].** Turn right and continue up the slope, passing a large stand of new saplings.

This is the steepest part of the trail (.4 mi.) **[4],** which continues climbing on its roller-coaster way through the woods. Midway up the hill, you meet a shortcut trail (.5 mi.) **[5]** that will link with the Green Trail at the crest. The shortcut pole marker is tan.

If you do not take the shortcut trail, make a sharp right turn at the red marker (.6 mi.) **[6]** and walk back

north. There is often a flurry of birds here. They explode from the trees and wing their way over a marshland to the left of the trail. The buckthorn and other low-lying shrubs make good cover for the various species.

Continue walking on the straight pathway. As you near the end of the trek, you need to climb one more hill (.8 mi.) **[7]** up from the brush and forest cover, past a break in the overhanging branches and out onto a meadow. This links with the eastern end of the Green Trail. Both return to the picnic shelter (.9 mi.) **[8]** on the hill above the trailhead.

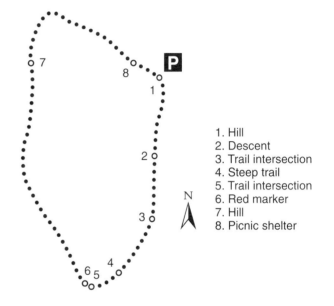

1. Hill
2. Descent
3. Trail intersection
4. Steep trail
5. Trail intersection
6. Red marker
7. Hill
8. Picnic shelter

Green Trail 👢👢

Distance Round-Trip: 3 miles

Estimated Hiking Time: 2 hours

Cautions: This can be a long walk for hikers not used to distances. Hills are encountered.

Trail Directions: Park in the lot in the center of the park, to the right of the admissions booth. Walk down the hill from a picnic area to a wooden map board at the tree line. The same access is shared by the Red, Green, and Blue Trails.

Walk up the same initial slope as for the Red Trail link **[1]**. The path is deeply covered with wood chips, making for a spongy, soft walk. At .3 mi. **[2]**, the Red Trail splits to the right and the Green Trail moves straight ahead. A few shagbark hickories are scattered amid the tall oaks as the trail ascends the slope.

On the left side is Forest Lake (.5 mi.) **[3]**, with a marsh on its south end. You cut by one end of the marsh, with its reedy cover and explosion of red-winged blackbirds, and turn right through the meadow. A tan marker indicates a shortcut to take if you do not want to make a slight angle to the right along the woods. The Green Trail now meets with the other tan cutoff that links with the Red Trail in the woods to the right. There is a bench here.

Continue on the left through an open meadow (.7 mi.) **[4]** with encroaching shrubs around its edges. The remains of the old pasture are slowly losing ground to the rejuvenated forest. Goldenrod here tickles the nose in midsummer, so anyone with allergies should be prepared. Across the meadow are the backs of houses, tight up against the park boundaries. Several bluebird boxes are scattered about the meadow. Follow the path as it turns right and then continues in a straight line. The entrance to the park's nature trail is through a wooden fence to the right (1.2 mi.) **[5]**. Pass into the oak opening where there are a wide variety of plants to study, such as goldenrod. There is a good view of Grass Lake about halfway along the trail (1.3 mi.) **[6]** because the large oaks have prevented much sunlight from reaching ground cover.

You will see numerous deer tracks through the area, especially around the sedge patches at the edge of another oak grove. You can also see a couple of small white ash and mulberry moving into the prairie

setting. In the old days, fires would have kept these plants at bay. After meandering along the nature trail, return to the main path (1.8 mi.) **[7]**. The branches overhanging the trail make a great freeway for squirrels, which jump back and forth with abandon above your head. Pass the rear of a barn located on the private side of a barbed-wire fence running along the park border. There are several spaces between the trees on the right from which to gaze down on Grass Lake (2 mi.) **[8]**. About every 200 feet, there is another wood-chip section of trail over muddy areas.

The trail now runs close to County Road O, with an access point for hikers just before the trail angles right (2.2 mi.) **[9]** around the north end of the lake. The path goes down a series of rolling slopes along the north end of Grass Lake.

Continue along the pathway through the meadow (2.3 mi.) **[10]**. There is a partial barricade of logs on the trail at (2.4 mi.) **[11]**, but step over or around them and continue on. You meet the intersection of the Red Trail where it comes up out of the trees. Turn left and follow the trail through more meadow. The path swings along over the rises in the ground and comes out behind the park office (2.6 mi.) **[12]**. Then simply follow the mowed track to the parking lot by the picnic area from where you started.

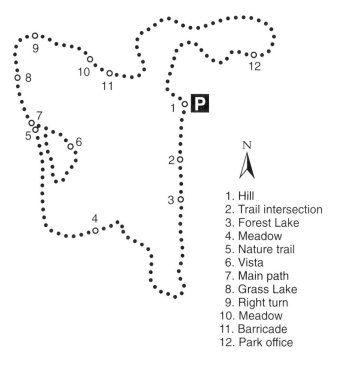

1. Hill
2. Trail intersection
3. Forest Lake
4. Meadow
5. Nature trail
6. Vista
7. Main path
8. Grass Lake
9. Right turn
10. Meadow
11. Barricade
12. Park office

37. Minooka Park

- Swim in a large pond with beach access.
- Trek over various lengths of easily negotiated trails.
- Enjoy large grassy picnic areas.

Park Information

Minooka Park is made up of portions of area farms purchased in 1955 to form a 297-acre outdoor recreational site. The largest parcel had been owned by the Hart family and had been a Waukesha County farm site since 1945. Over the ensuing years, another owner of the property used the grounds as a resort, with guests coming from Chicago and Milwaukee. They were attracted to the region because a spring that flowed from a pool across Racine Avenue supposedly had medicinal properties.

After the site was purchased by the county, it was named Minooka Park by Jane Ann Kusler, an eight-year-old who won a "name the park" contest. The name means "maple forest" or "good earth," depending on which Native American dialect is selected for the translation. Whichever phrase is chosen, it is an appropriate title for the wooded hills and open meadows of the complex.

Directions: The park is 2 miles southeast of Waukesha on Sunset Drive near its intersection with Racine Avenue.

Hours Open: Sunrise to 10 P.M. daily, year round.

Facilities: Swimming beach, bridle trails, hiking paths, picnic shelters.

Permits and Rules: Hunting is not permitted. Dogs must be kept on a six-foot leash. Horseback riding is allowed only on the bridle path, which is open from May 1 to November 1. Parking is permitted only in designated areas.

Further Information: Contact Waukesha County Parks and Land Use Department, 1320 Pewaukee Road, Waukesha, WI 53188; 414-548-7801.

Other Points of Interest

Bits of Britain at the Five Points Corner in downtown Waukesha is the best place this side of the Atlantic to shop for groceries from England and Ireland. Teas, biscuits, pickles, sauces, jams, and candies line the shelves. There is also a tea room. The shop is at 294 W. Main Street (414-896-7772). The staff can take special orders if you don't want to wait until Easter for your Cadbury chocolate eggs. Near the shop is a replica of a **springhouse** dating from the 1870s. At that time, Waukesha was one of the Midwest's leading spas. Water from the city's numerous springs were often bottled and sold for their curative powers.

The **East Troy Electric Railroad Museum** runs trolleys and other electric rail cars on its line from May through October. The volunteer-operated museum also has special events throughout the summer, ranging from a model railroad weekend to Fall Fun Days with reduced fares. The museum is located at 2002 Church Street in East Troy, just one mile west of I-43. Call 414-548-ETER for more information.

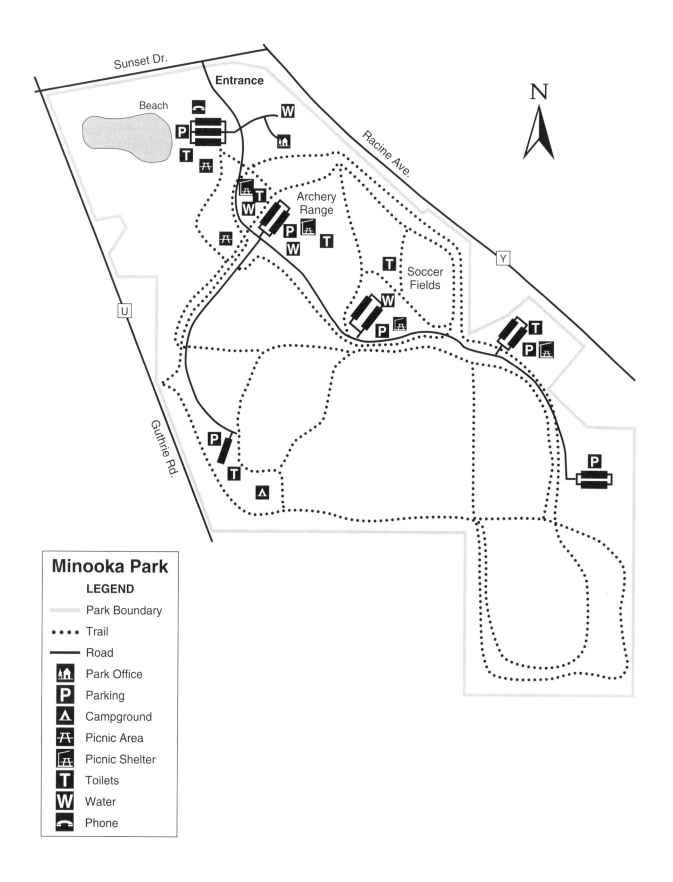

Minooka Park

LEGEND

	Park Boundary
••••	Trail
──	Road
🏕	Park Office
P	Parking
▲	Campground
⛱	Picnic Area
⛱	Picnic Shelter
T	Toilets
W	Water
⌒	Phone

Red Trail 👢

Distance Round-Trip: 1.3 miles

Estimated Hiking Time: 40 minutes

Cautions: Bring bug spray in the wet season.

Trail Directions: Park in the first lot to the left of the admissions booth after entering Minooka. Cross the grassy picnic area to the left and locate the trailhead marker adjacent to the park road. The road, by the way, is open for winter hiking and dog walking.

Take the right-hand trail **[1]**, where the Red and Green Trails move out on the same path. The path here is about 20 feet wide, mowed through a patch of thick grass. Pass through a meadow (.2 mi.) **[2]**, where encroaching shrubs such as buckthorn and honeysuckle, plus some poplar trees, are creeping in around the edges. The trail angles to the left in a 90 degree turn and links up with the bridle path to the southwest.

The Red Trail then crosses the road, plunging into the woods. There are some tall stands of oak here (.5 mi.) **[3]**, with branches reaching over the trail in a leafy canopy. Enter a clearing behind the service road by the parking lots near picnic shelter #3 (.7 mi.) **[4]**. The trail crosses the road and angles between two rows of trees, past the soccer field to the far right. Continue over a mowed area, loop around the archery range, and come back toward the parking lots by picnic shelter #1 (.8 mi.) **[5]**. From here it is a quick walk to the trailhead marker.

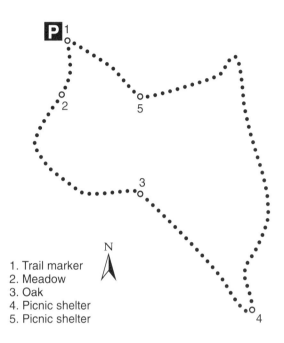

1. Trail marker
2. Meadow
3. Oak
4. Picnic shelter
5. Picnic shelter

Green Trail 👢👢

Distance Round-Trip: 3 miles

Estimated Hiking Time: 2 hours

Cautions: Insect repellent is helpful during the wet season. Watch out for horses on the bridle path.

Trail Directions: Park in the lot to the right of the park admission booth. Cross the grass to the south to the trail marker by the service road. This first post is for both the Green and Red Trails.

Follow the mowed trail through a meadow **[1]** where there is extensive shrubbery creeping in around the perimeter of the field. Follow the wide track up a slight slope (.2 mi.) **[2]** and into the deeper oak and maple grove (.3 mi.) **[3]**. At the east end of the family picnic area, the Red Trail crosses the service road and continues on into a magnificent oak grove. The Green Trail turns right and runs parallel to the service road along the bridle path. The trail crosses the road at .5 mi. **[4]** and continues into the woods.

Some hikers choose to continue along the horse path, which runs to the edge of the park at Guthrie Road and then moves south and east past the group camp. The bridle trail continues around the park perimeter, logging about another 2.5 mi.

The Green Trail, however, continues straight into the oak woods (.7 mi.) **[5],** linking up with a side trail running up from the south parking lot near the group camp. Take this leg for a longer walk through the woods and on to the meadows, about .5 mi. to the east. Several other trails split off from there for walks around the far southeast corner of Minooka.

By taking a compromise route to the right when you first enter the oak woods, you cut along the edge of an open glade (.9 mi.) **[6]**. Pass the group camp and its parking lot (1 mi.) **[7]**. The trail again links with the bridle path (1.1 mi.) **[8]**. Follow it through the mixed hardwoods to another meadow. Turn left (north) when reaching the mowed area and walk straight north (1.6 mi.) **[9]**, keeping the brush and trees on your left.

You again meet the service road (1.9 mi.) **[10]**, but follow the markers back into the trees to the west. You are paralleling the park road, barely seen through the trees. Pass the intersection with the Red Trail (2 mi.) **[11]**, which exits from the woods and crosses the road. The Green Trail continues along the wood line (2.2 mi.) **[12]** and back into the oak and maple grove straight ahead. Continue along the rolling trail until reaching another clearing and the service road again (2.4 mi.) **[13]**. It is an easy amble back to the parking lot from here.

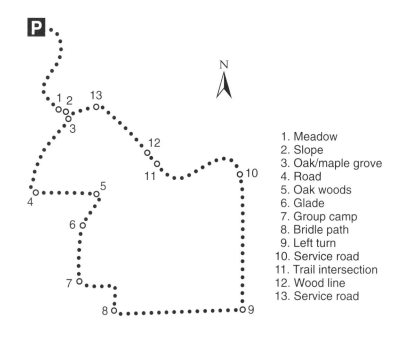

1. Meadow
2. Slope
3. Oak/maple grove
4. Road
5. Oak woods
6. Glade
7. Group camp
8. Bridle path
9. Left turn
10. Service road
11. Trail intersection
12. Wood line
13. Service road

38. Kettle Moraine State Forest, Southern Unit

Forest Information

Ten thousand years ago, the glaciers ground across Wisconsin and left a trail of debris when they finally retreated. As the glaciers moved slowly ahead, they leveled the landscape and filled in low spots. When they retreated, they dumped rubble everywhere in huge piles to form today's hills and ridges in southern Wisconsin. As the weather warmed, human beings moved in. Archaeologists have found artifacts dating back to 6000 B.C. The first white settlers came to the region in the 1830s.

The state forest covers 18,000 acres in sections of Jefferson, Waukesha, and Walworth Counties. It is one of the best places in the state to find rare wild plants, such as pasqueflowers that bloom deep in the forest only in mid-April. There are three major recreational areas within the forest: Whitewater Lake, Ottawa Lake, and Pinewoods, for a total of 265 campsites. The forest has 27 miles of bridle paths, with a horse riders' campground that contains 60 sites. The MacMiller Shooting Range is the only state-owned facility of its kind in Wisconsin. Swimming, boating, fishing, hunting, snowmobiling, skiing, and hiking are among the other recreational opportunities in the area.

Directions: The forest service office is located on the south side of State Highway 59, midway between County Highways Z and S. The state forest extends from the Pine Woods Campground in the north near Wales and to Rice and Whitewater Lakes in the far south. A zig-zag of county highways mark the general east and west boundaries. To determine the exact area, it is advisable to get a map from the forest service office.

Hours: The headquarters is open year round, from 7:45 A.M. to 4:30 P.M. Monday through Friday and 8 A.M. to 4:30 P.M. Saturday and Sunday. Visitors must leave the campgrounds and other forest sites by 11 P.M.; the park reopens at 6 A.M.

Facilities: There is a range of facilities throughout the state park, with toilet facilities at the campgrounds and area gas stations. Some trail entry points have portable toilet units. Within the forest boundaries are ski areas, dirt-bike trails, picnic sites, nature trails, bridle paths, and dog-training grounds.

Permits and Rules: No fires, except in designated campground areas. Appropriate fishing and hunting licenses are necessary. For those 16 or over, a trail pass is needed for biking designated trails (both residents and nonresidents, $3 daily and $10 annually). State park vehicle admission passes are $3 daily or $18 annually for residents. For out-of-state visitors, they are $25 annually and $7.50 daily.

Further Information: Contact Superintendent, Kettle Moraine State Forest, South Unit, S91 W39091 Highway 59, Eagle, WI 53119; 414-594-2135.

Other Points of Interest

The Kettle Moraine State Forest offers more than 34 miles of trails along the Scuppernong and McMiller **hiking/ski** systems. The looped paths are open year round for recreational use. Find interesting geographical features in the forest such as the Stone Elephant, a massive rock dumped there by glaciers thousands of years ago near what is now Blue Spring. The stone is 39 feet in diameter. The spring itself is about 20 feet deep and is one of the largest in the Kettle Moraine.

There are many other **geological attractions** throughout the region as a result of glacial movement eons ago. On State Highway 67, 3 miles north of the intersection with State Highway 59, is an ancient glacial lake bed that was once 40 feet deep. The area remains swampy. A major kettle—a depression in the ground formed when earth-covered ice melted and collapsed inward—can be seen on County Highway H, .7 miles north of the intersection with U.S. Highway 12.

The **East Troy Electric Railroad Museum** brings back memories of the old trolley and electric rail lines that once were a major interurban transportation jewel. The line has a 10-mile ride in coaches dating back to the 1920s and earlier, through woods and along meadows from the museum grounds to a small lake and then back. There are numerous cars and other rolling stock to be toured. The musuem is open from Memorial Day to mid-October. East Troy is about 20 miles south of the Kettle Moraine Forest. For more information, call 414-548-3837.

La Grange Lake is near the Ice Age Trail where it cuts north from U.S. Highway 12. The shallow pool is surrounded by forest and grassland, with bird-watching a major sport in the vicinity. For starters, look for green-backed herons, spotted sandpipers, and the American woodcock. Call 414-594-2135 for more information.

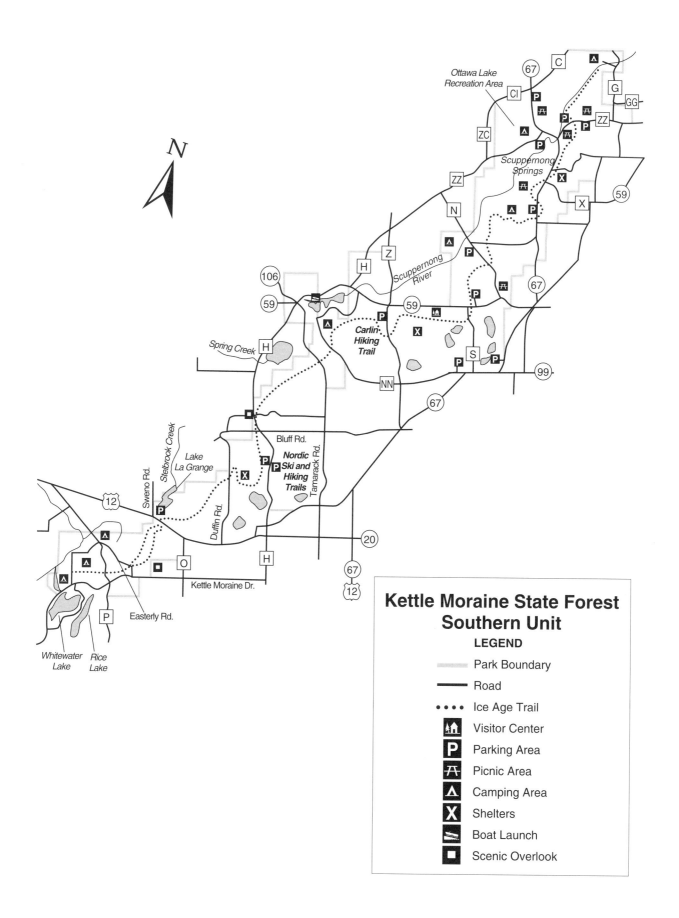

Ottawa Lake
Recreation Area

Scuppernong
Springs

Scuppernong
River

Carlin
Hiking
Trail

Spring Creek

Stelbrook Creek

Lake
La Grange

Bluff Rd.

Nordic
Ski and
Hiking
Trails

Sweno Rd.

Duffin Rd.

Tamarack Rd.

Kettle Moraine Dr.

Easterly Rd.

Whitewater
Lake

Rice
Lake

Kettle Moraine State Forest
Southern Unit
LEGEND

Park Boundary
Road
Ice Age Trail
Visitor Center
Parking Area
Picnic Area
Camping Area
Shelters
Boat Launch
Scenic Overlook

Emma F. Carlin Biking and Hiking Trails

- Stretch your legs while climbing steep hills through rugged moraine country.
- Look for white-tailed deer in the thick undergrowth.
- Experience a landscape created by glaciers.

Trail Information

The Emma Carlin trail system takes hikers and bikers along a steep razorback ridge overlooking a sand plain. Some of the system runs over old logging roads. Bikers are limited only to designated parts of the trails, but hikers are free to walk anywhere on the pathways.

Directions: The trail system is on County Highway Z, 1 mi. south of State Highway 59.

Hours Open: Dawn to dusk daily, year round.

Facilities: Pit toilets.

Permits and Rules: No camping, no fires, no alcohol.

Red Loop 👢👢

Distance Round-Trip: 1.7 miles

Estimated Hiking Time: 1.5 hours

Cautions: There are some steep slopes along the path. This trail is shared with off-road cyclists.

Trail Directions: Park in the lot off County Highway Z and walk toward the trailhead, which is in the center of the lot, marked by a large wooden map.

Stride through a pine plantation [1] and begin ascending a slight slope. At .2 mi., the trail becomes packed dirt and rock. Since cyclists use the Emma F. Carlin, the track is generally firm along the entire route. At the intersection with the Orange and Green Loops (.3 mi.) [2], turn right and proceed along a series of up-and-down ridges through the hardwoods.

Where the trail makes several S-curves, you can spot small ponds on either edge of the pathway (.4 mi.) [3]. This is frog heaven in the spring and mosquito hell in the summer. You continue climbing the sharp razorback ridge that makes up the backbone of the Emma F. Carlin trail system. With the thick foliage in summer, the views are limited.

At .6 mi., there is a sharp left turn near a stand of maple and oak [4]. Make the change in direction and proceed even higher on the ridge. This section, as well as many others along the trail, has mesh matting underneath the dirt to prevent erosion and provide a base for bike tires.

There is a rolling effect to the next leg of path (.7 mi.) [5]. The land falls sharply away on the left as you pass a ravine. There is some poison ivy in the vicinity, but none is close enough to be a bother if you do not stray off the trail. There is also more Virginia creeper running along the forest floor and crawling up the trees and saplings.

Pass several open areas (.8 mi.) [6] among the trees as you turn right and begin moving to the south. Stands of sumac along here can be dazzling in the autumn. Aspen and birch are tossed among the maples as lighter-colored confetti. As you descend the slope, there are several switchback curves (.9 mi.) [7]. Avoid making a shortcut by running downhill through the brush to save a few minutes, rather than using the trail. This causes erosion.

Make a sharp left at the intersection with the Orange Loop (1.1 mi.) [8] and move along a relatively straight pathway back toward the trailhead. The trail proceeds over several smaller hills and down into shallow valleys (1.2-1.5 mi.) [9], with waterways for rain run-off alongside the path. You now reenter the clearing where the Red, Orange, and Green Loops intersect [2]. From here, it is a short walk back to the trailhead.

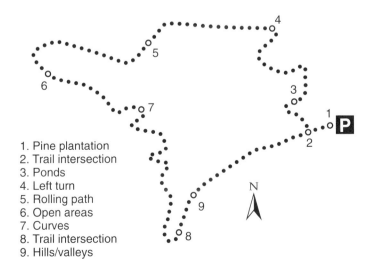

1. Pine plantation
2. Trail intersection
3. Ponds
4. Left turn
5. Rolling path
6. Open areas
7. Curves
8. Trail intersection
9. Hills/valleys

Nordic Ski and Hiking Trails

- Walk ridges and valleys carved by giant glaciers.
- Ski, hike, or bird-watch over a wide variety of topography.
- Check out numerous recreation areas for camping, fishing, and picnicking.

Trail Information

The Nordic Ski and Hiking Trail system offers several options for all levels of hikers, from beginning to advanced. Steep hills, wide meadows, thick underbrush, and heavily forested slopes present a variety of experiences. Several sections are open to off-road cycling as well. Trails vary in difficulty because not all pathways are surfaced.

Directions: The Nordic Ski and Hiking Trail parking lot is on County Highway H about 2 miles south of Bluff Road. It is about 6 miles south of the village of Palmyra.

Hours Open: Trails are open from dawn to dusk.

Facilities: Rest rooms.

Permits and Rules: Pets are allowed on the trails during non-ski season but must be leashed and under control. No fires, no camping, no alcohol.

White Loop 👢👢

Distance Round-Trip: 3.2 miles

Estimated Hiking Time: 1.5 hours

Cautions: The trail is often unmown, overgrown with plantain and tall grass. So do not wear shorts if these conditions persist in midsummer. Mosquito repellent is recommended.

Trail Directions: Start in the Nordic Center parking lot on the east side of County Highway H, about 1.5 mi. north of U.S. Highway 12. Walk over to the trailhead, which is indicated by a marker post in the southeast corner of the lot.

The trail begins beneath a canopy of wild black cherries [1]. Continue on a straight line for about 150 feet to the intersection with your return trail.

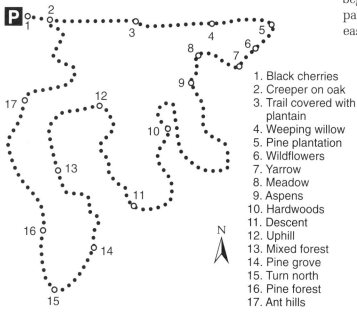

1. Black cherries
2. Creeper on oak
3. Trail covered with plantain
4. Weeping willow
5. Pine plantation
6. Wildflowers
7. Yarrow
8. Meadow
9. Aspens
10. Hardwoods
11. Descent
12. Uphill
13. Mixed forest
14. Pine grove
15. Turn north
16. Pine forest
17. Ant hills

N

Keep following the White Loop markers straight over some easy terrain. A huge Virginia creeper engulfs a patient oak on the left side (.08 mi.) [2]. As you get to .1 mi. [3], plantain covers the trail as it veers right.

At .2 mi., an elegant weeping willow [4] sweeps over the ground on the left of the trail. Enter another pine plantation [5] and veer right along the trail at .4 mi., following the markers. A display of woodland sunflowers and spiderworts [6] is mixed throughout the grass at .5 mi. At .6 mi., yarrow [7] is scattered along the trail, its small white flowers offering a pungent scent.

Ignore the next intersection, with a trail going to the left. Veer right and continue along the White Loop. Enter a meadow at .7 mi. [8]. At .8 mi., enter a thick grove of quaking aspens [9]. About another .1 mi. beyond the aspen, hardwoods [10] begin to dominate the forest cover.

Wild geraniums carpet the forest floor as the trail begins a gradual descent (1.1 mi.) [11]. The trail is patched with loose sand here. The trail next winds easily uphill [12]; the peak is reached at 1.3 mi.

Enter a mixed forest at 1.6 mi. [13]. Black-eyed Susans brighten the trail as you leave the forest and encounter another field. Continue straight ahead and enter a denser pine grove (1.9 mi.) [14].

At 2.5 mi., the path turns north [15] for the return trip back to the trailhead. Highway H appears through the trees for a brief interval on the left. A dense white pine forest shows up at 2.6 mi. [16], where a slow descent takes you along a slope. Alfalfa and sweet clover make their appearance amid the grass of a meadow where two large ant hills stand to the right of the trail (2.9 mi.) [17]. The trail dips briefly, rises, and continues on to a T-intersection. Turn left and head toward the parking lot.

Ice Age Trail—Highway 12 to Easterly Road

- Sample fresh wild raspberries in season as you walk along.
- Look overhead for hawks and turkey vultures soaring above the Kettle Moraine landscape.
- Admire autumn's colors when the leaves change.

Trail Information

The Ice Age Trail cuts through the heart of the Kettle Moraine Forest on its way southward. The forest offers thousands of acres of mixed hardwoods, prairies, meadows, lakes, and marshes that can be explored. There are campgrounds, historical sites, hiking trails, horse paths, and cross-country ski loops—just about anything one needs for outdoor adventure.

Directions: Park in the gravel lot where both the Ice Age Trail and Horse Trail cross U.S. Highway 12. The lot is on the north side of the road near Sweno Road. Look for the orange and yellow markers. The site is 3.4 miles east of Whitewater.

Hours Open: Dawn to dusk.

Facilities: None.

Permits and Rules: No fires, no camping, no firearms, no alcohol.

Ice Age Trail—Highway 12 to Easterly Road 👢👢👢👢

Distance Round-Trip: 2.7 miles

Estimated Hiking Time: 1.7 hours

Cautions: There are steep ascents and descents on this trail, as well as exposed rocks and roots. Special care should be taken on the path to avoid slipping.

Trail Directions: Carefully cross U.S. Highway 12, following the Yellow and Orange Trail markers to the trailhead.

At the trailhead are quaking and bigtooth aspens (.1 mi.) **[1]**, which quickly swallow the trail as it slopes over the first rise. From the top of this moraine, hikers can look out over the Wisconsin horizon and see the city of Whitewater to the east as hawks and turkey vultures circle overhead.

Look for scrapes across the tops of rocks along the next leg of the trail (.3 mi.) **[2]**, a sure sign of glacial activity 10,000 years ago. Take the direction indicated by the yellow marker at the fork where the Orange Trail veers left. Wild apple trees stretch gracefully along the trail (.4 mi.) **[3]**. Now the forest deepens, as white and black oaks dominate their smaller cousins (.5 mi.) **[4]**.

The trail moves into a series of switchbacks where there are numerous shagbark hickories popping out of the forest. There are some aspen scattered about as well. The forest floor is carpeted with violets and buttercups (.6 mi.) **[5]**. The trail is now atop a sharp ridgeline, with both sides falling off into deep ravines, so be very careful walking this natural tightrope (.7 mi.) **[6]**.

Eight steps built into the side of the hill help with the walk as the trail begins to sweep sharply upward (1.1 mi.) **[7]**. On this part of the trail, if you look to the right you can see a beautiful view of a wooded kettle as you near the top of the hill (1.2 mi.)

[8]. From here the scenery changes abruptly to pine trees (1.3 mi.) **[9]** and then moves to an open field in which new pines are pushing upward. A few stalks of mullen stand above them as baby-sitters (1.4 mi.) **[10]**.

The trail now crosses Easterly Road and meets with the Orange Trail again (1.6 mi.) **[11]** where you turn back toward the trailhead. From here, the Orange Trail veers to the edge of a field (1.85 mi.) **[12]**. As you hike for another few minutes, the forest looms ahead again. Pines line the trail, with needles carpeting the pathway. After this brief section of forest, the trail reenters a field (1.9 mi.) **[13]**. From here (2.1 mi.) **[14]** the trail descends on a relatively straight track toward the parking lot across from County Highway 12.

—*Steve Drake*

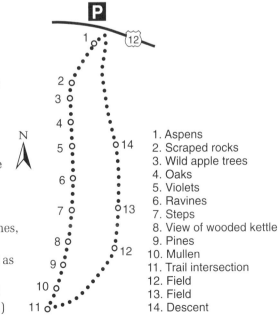

1. Aspens
2. Scraped rocks
3. Wild apple trees
4. Oaks
5. Violets
6. Ravines
7. Steps
8. View of wooded kettle
9. Pines
10. Mullen
11. Trail intersection
12. Field
13. Field
14. Descent

Scuppernong Springs

- See the impact on the landscape made by pioneers.
- Walk through marshes and observe aquatic life.
- Camp nearby and use other hiking trails in the state forest.

Trail Information

This entire area was a prime camping ground for many Native American nations over the centuries before white settlers arrived. There was plentiful food in the surrounding forests, fields, and marshes.

Before the area was developed, the marsh was more than 20 miles long, extending to the west toward Palmyra. Today's marsh is only a few square miles, but it is a prime wildlife habitat.

Directions: The trail is across County Highway ZZ from the Ottawa Lake Recreational Area, about 1 mile west of State Highway 67.

Hours Open: Dawn to dusk, daily.

Facilities: Portable toilets are at the trailhead parking lot.

Permits and Rules: No smoking. Keep pets home. No off-road biking. Don't throw debris into the springs.

Nature Trail 👢👢

Distance Round-Trip: 1.5 miles

Estimated Hiking Time: 1 hour

Cautions: Watch out for poison ivy. The trail can also be muddy in sections after a rain. Mosquitoes can be pesty.

Trail Directions: Park in the lot on the south side of County Highway ZZ, across from the Ottawa Lake Recreational Area. Walk to the trail entrance to the east. A box of maps is at the trailhead.

The path is part of the state's Adopt-A-Trail system, according to a sign at the trailhead **[1]**. Once inside the trees, turn right and follow the flat dirt trail past birch and alder trees. A shallow creek bed is on the left. Walk along what was once a rail bed serving a marl plant at the marshes' edge.

At .3 mi., take a short side path **[2]** into the woods to see the remains of the marl works, a high concrete wall hidden amid the trees. You will see several piles of marl that were dumped in the woods. The marl pit is that large depression to the right, now filled with water.

Walk between the sawed trunk of a decaying oak (.4 mi.) **[3]** that lies over the trail. A boardwalk then crosses the Scuppernong River linking up with the marsh. Take the three log steps up a slight slope (.5 mi.) **[4]** and follow the sandy path to the right. Go past the intersection that takes you over an elevated boardwalk across the marsh and keep going right to a scenic overlook **[5]**.

At .6 mi., the path goes down a hill to a spring. Several more springs are along the trail, marked by narrow paths. The overflow goes into the cattail marsh (.7 mi.) **[6]** spreading out to the left.

A elevated boardwalk is in place now where an earthen dam once blocked the Scuppernong River to create the fish pond in the marsh. At .8 mi., pass the Emerald Spring **[7]**, another of the bubbling pools of water found along the path.

Numerous cottonwoods are along the path near where a trout-hatching house and trout feed mill once stood. The buildings are long since gone. Also departed is the Scuppernong Hotel (.9 mi.) **[8]**. Only the foundation of the building remains, hidden in the undergrowth on the right side of the trail.

A ditch appears along the left side of the trail at 1 mi. **[9]**. Walk over several sections of boardwalk that cross wet areas. In midsummer, the boardwalks can be overhung with reeds. Keep walking along the trail until you exit at the trailhead parking lot.

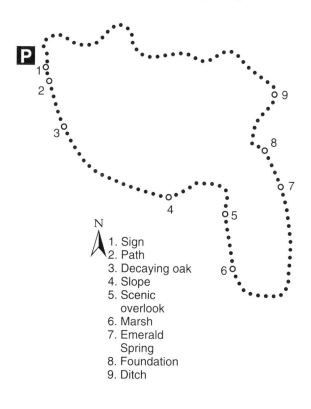

N

1. Sign
2. Path
3. Decaying oak
4. Slope
5. Scenic overlook
6. Marsh
7. Emerald Spring
8. Foundation
9. Ditch

39. Old World Wisconsin

- Travel back into the past to learn about Wisconsin's history.
- Walk through farmsteads dating back 100 years.
- Hike nature trails between today and yesterday.

Site Information

Old World Wisconsin is one of six historic sites owned and operated by the State Historical Society of Wisconsin. The open-air museum began operating in 1976, with more than 50 buildings that had been gathered from around the state and refurbished.

In the late 1840s, Wisconsin had more foreign-born farmers than any other state. More than 50 historic buildings are clustered according to this diverse heritage: German, Polish, Norwegian, Finnish, Danish. There is also a crossroads village typical of an early farm community. Fields and vegetable gardens are planted and tilled in the old-time manner; livestock is taken care of and food cooked to show how the state's pioneer ancestors lived and worked. Special programs are presented throughout the year, including many hands-on learning programs for kids and families.

Guests can walk the 2.5 miles around the 625-acre site or take a tram and get on and off as often as they wish at established stops.

Directions: Old World Wisconsin is about 1.5 miles west of the village of Eagle on State Highway 67 in the rolling Kettle Moraine countryside. Eagle is 32 miles west of Milwaukee, 91 miles north of Chicago, and 58 miles southeast of Madison.

Hours Open: The site is open rain or shine from 10 A.M. to 4 P.M. weekdays and from 10 A.M. to 5 P.M. weekends in May, June, September, and October. In July and August, Old World is open from 10 A.M. to 5 P.M. daily. Several historical farm sites are also open for touring during skiing season.

Facilities: Interpretive tours, historical programs, nature trails, picnicking, rest rooms, restaurant, gift shop, cross-country ski trails.

Permits and Rules: Admission is $7 for adults (13 and over), $3 for children (5 to 12), and $6.30 for seniors (65 and older). Tram rides are $2. Admission to the Caldwell Education Center is $1. Do not use the historically accurate outhouses (there are bathrooms at strategic locations). No smoking. Keep pets at home.

Further Information: Contact Old World Wisconsin, S103 W37890 Highway 67, Eagle, WI 53119; 414-594-6300.

Other Points of Interest

Hiking, off-road cycling, and **cross-country skiing** are popular outdoor recreation activities throughout the entire **Kettle Moraine State Forest, Southern Unit** near Eagle (see park #38). There are dozens of pathways over rough-and-tumble landscapes caused by glacial action. Among the major sites are the Emma F. Carlin Biking and Hiking Trails, the Scuppernong Ski & Hiking Trail, the John Muir Trail, and the Nordic Ski and Hiking Trails . For more information, call forest headquarters, 414-594-2135.

The **Lapham Peak Unit** of the state forest is open year round, with a picnic site, water, rest-room facilities, grills, and an observation tower from which to observe the countryside. During the winter, it has lighted cross-country ski routes. At 1,233 feet above sea level, it is the highest point in Waukesha County. The site is named after Increase A. Lapham, a noted conservationist of the late 1800s who is called the father of the U.S. Weather Service. Call 414-646-3025 for more information.

Visitor's Route 👢👢

Distance Round-Trip: 2.5 miles

Estimated Hiking Time: 3 to 6 hours

Cautions: Walking over the complex's extensive maze of roads is not difficult but can be tiring, although there are benches on which to rest along the way. The farm sites are in remote locations; hiking is over hilly terrain.

Trail Directions: Tram rides can be picked up in the rear of the Ramsey barn, built in 1841. The barn also holds the museum store, rest rooms, and an orientation theater with an audiovisual program. It is possible to bypass the barn by walking south from the parking lot, passing the ticket booth, and heading toward the Finnish complex .5 mi. away to the south.

It is a .25-mi. hike from the Ramsey barn **[1]** to the Ethnic Crossroads Village. On this route, the first building on the right is St. Peter's Church **[2]**, Milwaukee's first church, built in 1839. Set back from the road nearby is the modest home of Irish-born Mary Hafford **[3]**, a house originally located in Hubbelton, Jefferson County.

Other buildings in the village complex **[4]** are typical of the mid-1870s. The Koepsell, Schottler, and Schulz farms are next **[5]**. The German area shows buildings constructed in the *blockbau* (log) style.

Next, you arrive at a Polish farm site **[6]**. An authentic outhouse **[7]** is behind the main house.

Hikers can take the long way around to the Norwegian farms. But for a shortcut, take the nature trail **[8]** near the Schulz farm. Exit on the road just to the north of the 1840s cabin **[9]** built by Norwegian immigrant Knudt Fossebrekke.

Leaving the remote cabin, pass the Raspberry School **[10]** (circa 1906) to the left at the next crossroads. It is then a five-minute walk up the lane to the right to the Kvaale Farm **[11]**. Walk the .25 mi. to the Danish farm **[12]**. The weathered buildings are found up a long lane after you round a bend in the road.

It is .7 mi. to two Finnish homesteads **[13]**. Between 1864 and 1920, more than 300,000 Finns left their homeland and settled throughout northern Wisconsin. In 1890 the Rankinen family emigrated to a desolate section of Bayfield County. Across the gravel road is the Ketola farm, a fine example of log construction dating from 1915. There is a tram stop near the service road leading to the house.

It is now a .25-mi. stroll down the dusty country lane to the village. Pass through town and participate in a temperance rally in a grove near the Sanford house **[14]**. Continue walking along the road to the Caldwell Farmers' Club Hall **[15]**, which served as headquarters for a group of forward-looking farmers in 1874. A stage was added in 1880, making the building a center for many community activities. The restored facility remains a hub for contemporary programs at Old World. From here, the road leads directly to the parking area **[16]**.

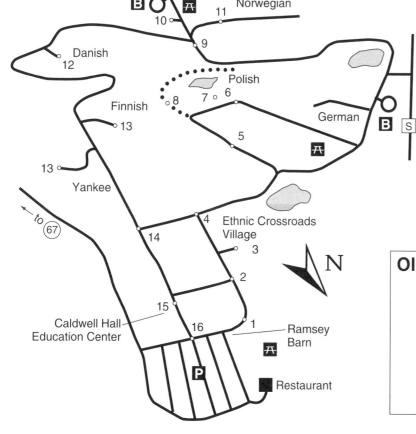

1. Ramsey barn
2. St. Peter's Church
3. Hafford house
4. Village complex
5. German farms
6. Polish farm site
7. Outhouse
8. Nature trail
9. 1840s cabin
10. Raspberry School
11. Kvaale farm
12. Danish farm
13. Finnish homesteads
14. Sanford house
15. Caldwell Hall
16. Parking area

Old World Wisconsin

LEGEND

— Road
•••• Trail
P Parking
⛺ Picnic Area
B Bus Parking

40. Lake Kegonsa State Park

- Explore Indian mounds and learn about the past.
- Study the explosion of colorful wildflowers.
- Bring your bird book and identify dozens of species.

Park Information

Thousands of years before the last ice age, an ancient river meandered through central Wisconsin. It carved a deep valley into the sandstone making up the bottom of a great sea that had covered all of Wisconsin 600 million years ago. During the four great ice ages that ground across the state, huge sheets of ice crunched over the old river valley. They created a long terminal moraine, a glacial deposit of rocks and sand, about 3 miles south and southwest of today's Lake Kegonsa. When the glaciers melted, they dumped gravel and sand into the ancient valley. This debris dammed glacial run-off to create Lake Kegonsa some 12,000 years ago. The marsh north of the lake was once part of the lake. But over centuries, silt and vegetation slowly filled in the shallow water.

Early settlers to Wisconsin originally referred to Lake Kegonsa as "First Lake" because it was the first of four lakes in central Wisconsin they encountered after crossing the winding Yahara River. The other three lakes—Waubesa, Monona, and Mendota—were farther along the river. All four lakes are connected by the Yahara.

"Kegonsa" is a Ho-Chunk (Winnebago) word for "lake of many fishes." The lake is noted for its fishing, especially for walleyes lurking along the underwater rock bars. Northern pike are also plentiful, with live suckers or spoons used as the best bait. Of course, the usual panfish—bluegills, crappies, and perch—as well as rock bass are abundant. Night fishing for bullheads and catfish is also fun. Since this is Wisconsin, use cheese as a fish-tempter. Boat rental firms ring the lake, which covers 3,200 acres and is 31 feet deep at its deepest point.

Directions: Lake Kegonsa State Park is 12 miles south of Madison, the state capital, an easy drive down State Highway 138.

Facilities: Picnic tables, shelters, dump station, and bathrooms are located in the park. There are 80 seasonal camping sites, of which 40 are reservable. The group camp has three sites that can accommodate 20 campers each. Laundry facilities and grocery stores are in nearby Stoughton and McFarland.

Firewood is sold by a private concessionaire. Look for his hours posted at the park office, in the wood yard, and on the campground bulletin board. No electric sites are available.

Hours Open: 6 A.M. to 11 P.M. year round.

Permits and Rules: Pets are welcome but must be leashed and under control at all times. Vehicles are allowed only on paved roads, and no off-road biking is permitted. Register before setting up camp, and only one family or a maximum of six individuals can occupy a site. Double campsites are for two families or up to 12 individuals. Camping fees for state residents are $7 weekdays and $9 Fridays and Saturdays. Out-of-state resident fees are $9 weekdays and $11 Fridays and Saturdays. Daily or year-long state park vehicle admission stickers are also required at $5 (daily) or $18 (annual).

Further Information: Contact Wisconsin Department of Natural Resources, Lake Kegonsa State Park, 2405 Door Creek Road, Stoughton, WI 53589; 608-873-9695.

Other Points of Interest

Wisconsin's bustling capital, **Madison,** is only 12 miles north of the park. Start with a tour of the capitol building, shake hands with a politician, and count the sculpted stone badgers looking down on passersby. The city has 150 parks within its boundaries, with more than 3,600 acres of recreation land. Each park has a special personality. For instance, Law Park on Lake Monona, .5 mile southeast from the Capitol Concourse, features the Capital City Ski Team each summer. The troupe presents a thrill show at 7 P.M. on Thursdays and Sundays from Memorial Day through Labor Day. The Madison Chamber of Commerce can provide details on other events and attractions such as the Henry Vilas Zoo and the University of Wisconsin Arboretum; call 608-256-8348.

The community closest to the park entrance is Stoughton, which annually hosts one of the country's largest Norwegian Independence Day celebrations. **Syttende Mai** is held on May 17 each year, complete with dancing, singing, and loads of delicious Scandinavian foods. For details, call 608-873-7912.

For more hiking, carry your golf clubs along the 36 holes of **Yahara Hills Golf Course** (608-838-3126), .5 mile east of I-90 on U.S. Highway 18. There are also 18 holes at **Coachman's Inn** (608-884-8484), at the intersection of U.S. Highway 51 and I-90, 9 miles east of Stoughton.

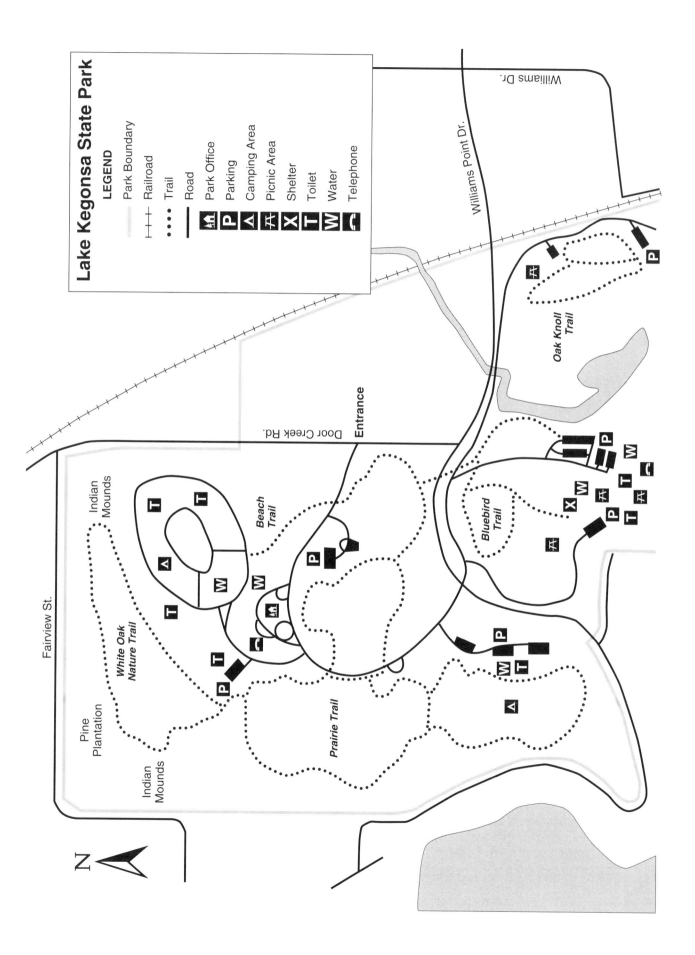

Prairie Trail 🥾

Distance Round-Trip: .7 mile

Estimated Hiking Time: 20 minutes

Trail Directions: From the park entrance, walk past the park office to the marked trail. Parking is on the right.

As the name implies, the Prairie Trail encircles a spectacular restored mesic prairie. Follow the marked trail south from the parking lot. Turn right (west) at you enter the loop. On the left, notice the vibrant grasses **[1]** of the prairie, standing tall in sharp contrast to the European grasses on the right. The predominant prairie grasses are bluestems. Reaching the .3-mi. mark **[2]**, the group camping trail branches off to the right. Continue east. Shortly the two trails will merge again.

The trail then runs parallel to the road, but don't cross. Continue northward. Between .5 and .6 mi. **[3]**, notice the sturdy bur oak on the right. Also to be spotted in late summer along this stretch of trail are black-eyed Susans and blazing stars. Finally, on the right is the connecting segment **[4]** that takes hikers back to the trail parking area.

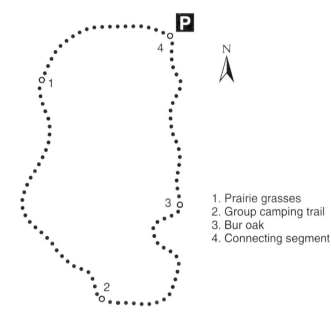

1. Prairie grasses
2. Group camping trail
3. Bur oak
4. Connecting segment

White Oak Nature Trail 👢👢

Distance Round-Trip: 1.2 miles

Estimated Hiking Time: 1 hour

Cautions: Be aware of pesty mosquitoes in the summer; insect repellent can be a hiker's best friend. Trail surfaces are uneven, so be careful when the path is slippery from rain or carpeted with leaves.

Trail Directions: Finding the trail is easy. Simply park in the lot west of the family camp area and look for the trail signpost just to the north.

The trail meanders through a prairie and an 80-acre white oak grove set along gentle hillsides. An abundance of lichens growing on trees can be spotted as you start out **[1]**. The lichens, a combination of fungus and alga, are a good indicator of air quality. They don't survive where there is air pollution. Now enter the white oak grove **[2]** at the .2-mi. mark. The white oak is common in southern Wisconsin, identified by its light gray bark. The trees range from 60 to 80 feet high. There are some dead and dying trees in the grove, victims of a fungus called oak wilt and an insect, the two-lined chestnut borer.

At .5 mi. along the trail are Indian mounds **[3]** built between 300 B.C. and 1300 A.D. They are shaped like a buffalo, a bear, a turtle, birds, and a panther. Supposedly this site was a ceremonial center for the effigy mound builders, a branch of the Woodland Indians. No one is sure, however, because archaeologists have not dug into the mounds. Next are several large white oaks standing individually on open land (.6 mi.) **[4].**

The oaks have short trunks and large canopies, indicating that there used to be an oak savanna in the region instead of today's woodland. The lack of competition from other trees when these giants were saplings shows that they had plenty of room in which to spread out. Several fire-resistant bur oaks can be seen at .8 mi. **[5],** with thick bark able to withstand prairie blazes. The trees here are 150 years old, dating to the time when the first settlers moved into this vicinity and began plowing up the prairie. A 1.4-acre pine plantation (1 mi.) **[6]** has been planted adjacent to the individual oaks, just before you enter an area where the prairie and oak woods meet. This ecosystem is called an "edge." Deer tracks can often be spotted along the trail here, and an occasional grouse will explode into flight as you stroll along. Both the deer and the grouse like this type of habitat.

An oak woodland restoration project is under way in the park (1.1 mi.) **[7]**. Volunteers and park staff have been clearing away non-native species of buckthorn and honeysuckle in order to open up the area. These exotic species are being removed to help promote the growth of the young oaks that can be spotted in the vicinity. In pre-pioneer days, fires did the job of controlling vegetation. You are now back at the parking lot.

—*Steve Drake*

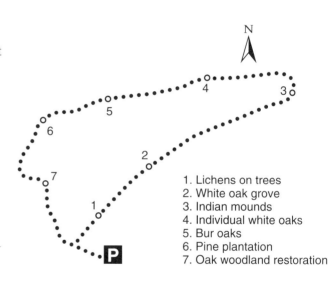

1. Lichens on trees
2. White oak grove
3. Indian mounds
4. Individual white oaks
5. Bur oaks
6. Pine plantation
7. Oak woodland restoration

41. New Glarus Woods State Park

- Enjoy hiking in landscape reminiscent of Switzerland.
- Pause to explore the park while biking on the Sugar River Trail.
- Trek over prairie habitat and through oak/walnut forest.

Park Information

New Glarus Woods consists of 350 acres of woods, prairie, and farmland. This is a favorite picnic site for area residents who use the shelter and many tables scattered around the grounds. New Glarus, 6 miles north of the park, is an historic community in Wisconsin, settled by Swiss immigrants in the mid-1840s. Park guests can get a change of pace in food by visiting the many German- and Swiss-style restaurants in town.

The park is bisected by County Highway NN. As early as 1832, the road was used by ox teams hauling lead from mines at Exeter to Mineral Point and Galena. In 1832, after the battle at the Pecatonica River, Governor Henry Dodge led troops along here to meet the federal army near present-day Madison. The soldiers were chasing the Sauk chieftain Black Hawk and his tribe. The road also brought Niklaus Durst and his fellow Swiss surveyors here in 1845. Another party of Swiss settlers proceeded past this spot on their way to build New Glarus later that year.

Directions: To get to New Glarus from northern Illinois, take I-90 to Beloit, Wisconsin. Exit at I-43 and travel west to State Highway 81. Follow 81 to 11 and on to Monroe. Take the Monroe bypass to the New Glarus Highway 69 exit. Follow 69 south to the park turn-off. If traveling from Milwaukee and northern Wisconsin, take I-90 south at Madison to the junction of I-90 and Highway 18, east of Madison. Follow Highway 18/151 west to Verona. In Verona, turn south on Highway 69 to New Glarus. If you are coming from Iowa, take Highway 11 east from Dubuque to Monroe. Take the Monroe bypass to the New Glarus Highway 69 exit. Drive south from New Glarus to the park. Turn west on County Highway NN off State Highway 69/39. The park is on the north side of the road .5 mile along the county road.

Hours Open: The park office is open from 8 A.M. to 8 P.M. weekdays, and from 8 A.M. to 11 P.M. weekends, April through October.

Facilities: Camping (group camping, plus 31 individual sites, including 14 primitive sites for bicyclists), hiking, biking, rest rooms, picnic area, water, shelter, nature trail.

Permits and Rules: Pets must be leashed. Fires only in designated campsites. No hunting. Campsites closed to outside visitors at 11 P.M. and reopen at 6 A.M.

Further Information: Contact Superintendent, New Glarus Woods State Park, Box 805, New Glarus, WI 53574; 608-527-2335.

Other Points of Interest

The village of **New Glarus** is known as the "Little Switzerland" of the United States because it was settled by the Swiss in 1845. Many locals still speak German Swiss. The town hosts a Swiss Polka Fest, the Heidi Festival, Swiss Independence Day, the Wilhelm Tell Festival, and other activities. Call the Chamber of Commerce, 800-527-6838, for more information.

Park Trails

Basswood Nature Trail —.4 mile—The trail begins at the picnic area near the park office and cuts through the oak and maple grove to the north of County Highway NN. There are 30 interpretive signs along the route that tell about the trees, shrubs, animal life, and landscape. It is a good route to take for youngsters to discover their relationship with the earth.

Chattermark Trail —.4 mile—This short trail is an east park loop from the campgrounds through an oak and maple grove. It links with the Basswood Nature Trail, passing the amphitheater where regular naturalist programs are scheduled during the summer.

Great Oak Trail —.2 mile—This trail can be picked up at the north end of the park, at the end of the primitive camping area. It runs parallel to the Sugar River State Trail, from which it is separated by underbrush and trees. The Great Oak links with the Basswood Nature Trail.

Walnut Trail —.5 mile—The trail starts at the far west end of the main campground, from the trailhead on County Highway NN. It proceeds south through and links with the Havenridge Nature Trail at the far end of the park.

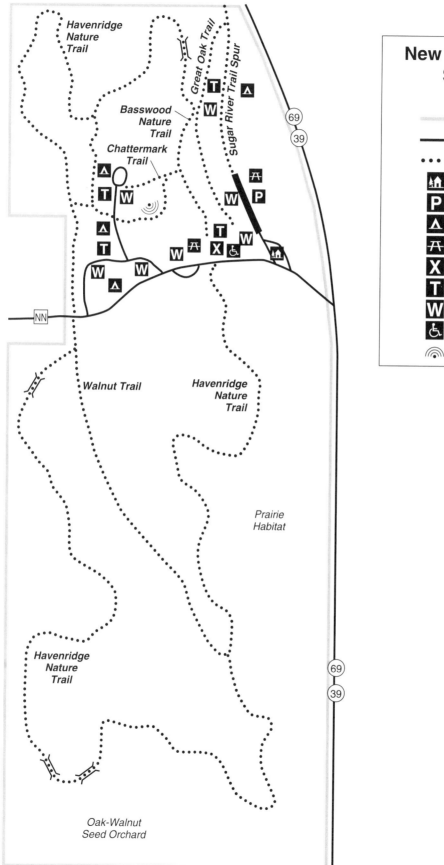

Havenridge Nature Trail— North Loop 👢👢👢

Distance Round-Trip: 1.6 miles

Estimated Hiking Time: 1.5 hours

Cautions: Watch for exposed roots and rocks along the track.

Trail Directions: Start on the Basswood Nature Trail at the picnic shelter in the middle of the park. Basswood links with the Havenridge loop about .2 mi. into the woods.

Walk north across the mowed parkland from the picnic shelter **[1].** Once you hit the woods, walk carefully because of exposed roots. Several black walnut trees (.1 mi.) **[2],** with their heavy brown bark, can be spotted amid the shrubs and towering oaks. The walnut trees are the state's most valuable wood producer, growing naturally only in the southern part of Wisconsin. Early settlers used the crushed nuts as the base for a clothing dye.

Make a left turn and pass the intersection with the Chattermark Trail, which leads to the campground (.2 mi.) **[3],** but go straight ahead, following the major pathway. Some rare nannyberry shrubs peek out from amid the raspberry and blackberry bushes. The crushed nannyberry leaves smell like wet goat, according to those who know about such things. Native Americans ate the berries. Now comes a major downslope through a grove of red oaks (.4 mi.) **[4],** some of which have huge burls. This is bizarre cambium growth that occurs when the tree fights disease or some other damage; the "tangled" wood is prized for turning bowls.

Hikers may wonder at the surrounding ground cover. Seen nearby (.5 mi.) **[5]** is a carpet of black snakeroot, merrybells, bedstraw, woodbine, feverwort, giant hyssop, trefoil, catbrier, enchanter's nightshade, and other foliage plants that live beneath the tree ceiling. These woods are also a bird-watcher's paradise. Keep an eye open for cardinals, scarlet tanagers, white-breasted nuthatches, Baltimore orioles, and even the black-capped chickadees. Some hikers carry their own bird identification books, but even the newcomer to birding can tell the species by their calls. Listen for the "eee-o-lay" of the thrush, a peewee's "peee-weee," the woodpecker's raucous "kwee-oh," and the "keeeeerrrrr" of an overhead hawk.

This section of downhill trail now becomes rutted, with erosion causing gullies and ridges that need to be carefully traversed. There are some well-rotted downed trees on both sides of the trail. The trail then climbs upward again (.5 mi.) **[6].** Turn right, then left, and cross the plank bridge. You continue upward now, making several right and left turns through the woods, brushing spiderwebs from your face. Watch for the exposed rocks on the trail surface. You pass a fork in the road (.6 mi.) **[7],** with the left branch heading south to the campground. So turn right, traverse the gully, and watch out for a thick mat of oak leaves that can be slippery when wet.

Pause at the bench (.7 mi.) **[8]** overlooking the valley, where you can see New Glarus to the north. A pile of logs marks the park boundary with a meadow. A field of goldenrod, giant bluestem, and other prairie plants runs down the slope toward town. After catching your breath, continue left down the hill to the south where you pass a deep gully to the right. The next .25 mi. is an up-and-down walk past ferns, berry bushes, and Virginia creeper. At 1.6 mi. **[9],** cross a wide grassy patch and continue past a trail link to the left (east) that runs to the campground. It is now a short walk up a hill to meet County Highway NN, the conclusion of the Havenridge North Loop. Walk east back to the picnic area where you started or continue on the South Loop.

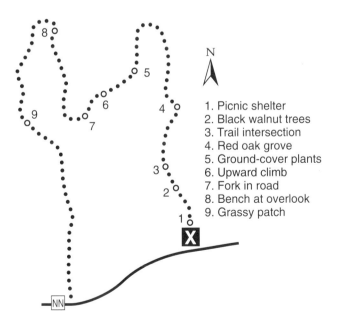

1. Picnic shelter
2. Black walnut trees
3. Trail intersection
4. Red oak grove
5. Ground-cover plants
6. Upward climb
7. Fork in road
8. Bench at overlook
9. Grassy patch

Havenridge Nature Trail— South Loop 👢👢👢

Distance Round-Trip: 2.4 miles

Estimated Hiking Time: 2 hours

Cautions: Mosquitoes can be a problem in the wet spring. The trail has numerous slopes that make for strenuous walking.

Trail Directions: Hikers can start at the trailhead across County Highway NN, opposite from the picnic shelter. Or they can pick up the trail at the west end of the park, after crossing NN where Havenridge's North Loop concludes at the highway.

Pick up the trailhead across from where the North Loop ended at County Highway NN **[1]**. The gravel/dirt path is wide at first, but it soon narrows to about five feet. At .2 mi. **[2]**, turn right and proceed down a grassy section of trail, past raspberry bushes and over a plank boardwalk spanning a stream. On the right beyond the shrubs and brush is a farm field. Some hikers encounter deer here, especially on early-morning or late-afternoon treks. Now cross a gully that can be wet and sloppy after a rain. A large downed log is to the left, marking the start of several S-curves that go up and down the trail slopes (.4 mi.) **[3]**. A beautiful shagbark hickory can be spotted near the path on the right (.5 mi.) **[4]** as you proceed higher on the hill. Again, you may run into more spiderwebs across the path. Just brush them aside and continue.

Leave the woods (.8 mi.) **[5]**, walk down the hill, and cross two bridges (.9 mi.) **[6]**. To the south is a plantation of oaks and maples that rangers use as replantings for damaged trees in the forest. Beyond that is a large oak standing alone in the field, giving plenty of shade for a quick pause and a drink of water from your canteen or bottle. Pass through an old barbed-wire fence line and move through a long-abandoned orchard (1 mi.) **[7]**. Many of the trees have died, but some still have living branches and miniscule apples craved by browsing deer.

Suddenly there is a picnic table in the glen, surrounded by small maple saplings. You can pick up

the .5-mi.-long Walnut Trail to the left if you wish (1.2 mi.) **[8]**. But more scenic views await if you move ahead. High on a hill, you will face a prairie restoration (1.3 mi.) **[9]** that sweeps down to State Highway 69. Waving in the breeze are rough blazing star, five-foot-high compass plants, green milkweed, prairie shrubs called leadplants, gray goldenrod, and spiderwort with its purple juice from beetles favored by box turtles. Prairie smoke and thick clumps of little and big bluestem often grow more than eight feet high in the summer. Imagine buffalo feeding on the side oats that grow thickly on this hillside, a reminder of 150 years ago.

Watch out for the red-winged blackbirds that dive-bomb your head as you proceed back toward the woods. Nests are probably nearby. The trail now goes in and out of the forest and prairie for the next .12 mi. It passes through thick stands of sumac that are higher than one's head (1.9 mi.) **[10]**. Go up the slope and reenter the woods. It is another roller-coaster run, with several wet spots on the way as you come up on County Highway NN and the trailhead there across from the picnic shelter.

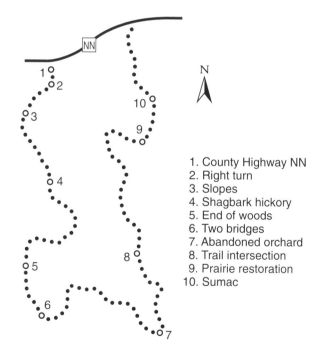

1. County Highway NN
2. Right turn
3. Slopes
4. Shagbark hickory
5. End of woods
6. Two bridges
7. Abandoned orchard
8. Trail intersection
9. Prairie restoration
10. Sumac

42. Browntown-Cadiz Springs State Recreation Area

- Fish from piers alongside trails.
- Watch Canada geese from a dike that divides the lake and marsh.
- See water life up close from the comfort of a land walk.

Park Information

The state recreational area covers 723 acres on man-made Beckman and Zander Lakes, of which 643 acres are state owned and 80 are leased. Zander Lake, the smallest, was used to raise bullfrogs commercially in the 1930s. There are 10 miles of cross-country ski trails that can be hiked and a .75-mile interpretive nature trail, plus a 600-acre wildlife area. Topography ranges from marsh to grassland, with scattered woodlots. Hikers can spot pheasants, grouse, deer, rabbits, squirrels, and an abundance of birdlife.

Be aware that hunting is allowed within the recreational area during game season. Fishing for largemouth bass, panfish, and northern pike is also permitted in the lakes.

Directions: Drive west of Monroe 7 miles on State Highway 11 to the Allen Road exit. Go south a hilly .5 mile to Cadiz Springs Road, turn left (west), and drive 1.5 miles to the recreation area entrance.

Hours Open: 6 A.M. to 11 P.M. year round. The office is just inside the entrance. Look for a small brown building.

Facilities: Picnic tables, canoe and sailboat launch site, swimming beach, fishing piers, nature trail, hunting preserve.

Permits and Rules: Electric motors are allowed on the lakes. No camping is allowed. No food, flotation devices, or pets are allowed on the beach. There is no lifeguard.

Further Information: Contact Department of Natural Resources, Box 7921, Madison, WI 53707; 608-266-2621. Or contact the Department of Natural Resources Pleasant View Annex, N3150 Highway 81, Box 256, Monroe, WI 53566; 608-966-3777 (summer) and 608-325-4844 (winter).

Other Points of Interest

Monroe is the self-proclaimed cheese capital of Wisconsin. In a state noted for its dairy products, this claim is well earned. More than a dozen cheese-manufacturing plants are in the area, and travelers can visit each to sample the wares. The plants open at 5 A.M., with most of the visible work done by midday, so plan accordingly. For descriptions of the plants, contact Monroe Cheese Days, Box 606, Monroe, WI 53566. The city hosts the biennial Cheesemakers' Ball, held in September on even-numbered years. An average of 11 tons of cheese are eaten during the fest. The city is also home to the Foreign Type Cheese-makers Association. And while in Monroe, drop by the Jos. Huber Brewing Company for a tour and more samples.

The 23-mile **Sugar River State Trail** follows the abandoned Chicago, Milwaukee, St. Paul railroad bed in south central Wisconsin. The limestone path provides a hard surface for fast biking. Several trestle bridges along the way carry bikers and hikers over streams and rivers. Several marked trails spin off from the Sugar River and meander around various county roads. The trail can be picked up at Brodhead, about 12 miles east of Monroe, on State Highway 11/81. The community is the easternmost access point to the trail (and is the halfway point between the Mississippi River and Lake Michigan), with additional marked bike trails on area secondary roads. You will find a covered bridge, food, and lodging in the town, and a trailside rest room, water, and parking at West 3rd Avenue and Exchange Street.

The **Brooklyn Wildlife Area** (Green and Dane Counties) consists of 3,938 acres of cropland, wood-lots, marsh, and grassy areas. Partridges, sandhill cranes, and wild turkeys are plentiful. The area is 2 miles east of Belleville on County Highway D. A portion of the Ice Age Trail runs through the property, making for hiking and cross-country skiing opportunities. Trout fishing is also quite good. For details, call the Department of Natural Resources, 608-266-2621.

Nature Trail 🥾

Distance Round-Trip: .8 mile

Estimated Hiking Time: 30 minutes

Cautions: Be careful of multitudinous goose droppings along the dike.

Trail Directions: Enter the recreational area and turn right to the parking area. This trail goes around Zander Lake. A large sign on the north shore of the lake points out the start of the hiking trail. There are 29 interpretive stops along the route.

Depart from the parking area on the asphalt track that runs on a dike between Zander and Beckman Lakes **[1]**. Submerged coontails, cattails, and other marsh vegetation crowd close to shore, providing a good look at underwater life up close. At .1 mi. is a fishing pier **[2]** on the right side, where youngsters can toss out a line. Near the pier is a stand of red mulberries, which turn from green to red to purple as the ripening season advances. Think of fresh jam on hot bread as you continue hiking.

Dragonflies with 1.5- to 4.5-inch wingspans flit along this section of trail. They enjoy the shallow, weedy water habitat. The asphalt trail ends at a second fishing pier (.3 mi.) **[3]** as the path moves into the public hunting grounds. This is now a grassy trail, with fearless Canada geese peeking out of the nearby reeds or floating just offshore. A good bird-watching eye can also spot cedar waxwings, mallards, tree swallows, spotted sandpipers, downy woodpeckers, and finches. This is also frog heaven, so be prepared for a croaking racket.

Out in the wetlands are several muskrat houses almost hidden in the tall water grasses. At .4 mi., pass a small bridge **[4]** that leads to the right over a stream. The trail to the right goes around Beckman Lake, while the nature trail continues straight ahead. Some prickly ash are on both sides of the pathway. At .5 mi., pass through a pine grove **[5]** with its blackberry patches. Seen to the right through the trees are autos driving along Cadiz Springs Road, which passes by the forest entrance.

A plank boardwalk extends over a muddy area as you walk through an oak stand, with a few scattered black cherries in the background. The trail splits at .6 mi. **[6]**; the right portion goes to the parking lot and the nature trail continues ahead for another few hundred feet. Then walk along the recreational area parking lot to get back to your car, past the playground and picnic area.

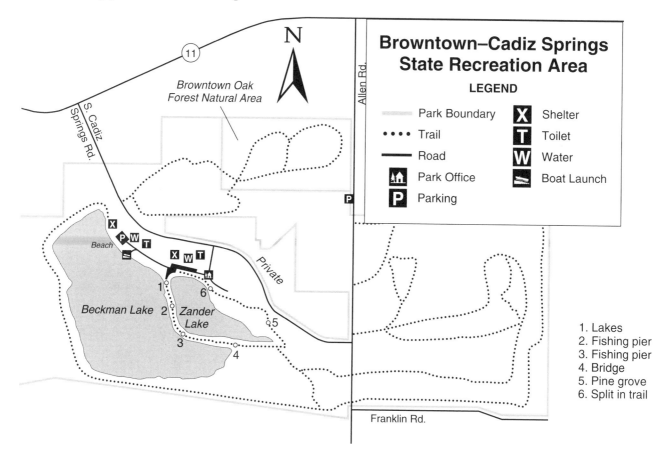

1. Lakes
2. Fishing pier
3. Fishing pier
4. Bridge
5. Pine grove
6. Split in trail

43. Yellowstone Lake State Park

- Fish in one of southern Wisconsin's largest man-made lakes.
- Take part in naturalist programs that run from May through September.
- Sample fresh ice cream in a dairy bar located at the park entrance.

Park Information

Yellowstone Lake is actually a man-made recreation area, created in the 1950s by damming the river that flowed through the Yellowstone Valley. The dam was built in 1954 to create the 8,677th lake in Wisconsin. The body of water is now 2.5 miles long and .25 mile wide, covering 455 acres. The stocked lake is a place for walleye and northern pike. The west end of the lake is a "no motor" waterfowl refuge, with a dike built out into the lake to make fishing easier.

The park covers 5,100 acres of state-owned land. Of these, 875 acres are managed as campgrounds, trails, and recreation tracts, while the remaining are wildlife habitat and cropland. Designated areas are marked, and visitors are encouraged to stay within these boundaries. Lands outside the borders are not maintained.

Directions: The park is bounded on the west and north by County Highway F, along the east by North Lake Road, and on the south by Lake Road and Yellowstone Lake.

Hours Open: The park is open all year from 6 A.M. to 11 P.M. Visitors who are not registered campers must leave the park at 11 P.M. Waterskiing is allowed between 10 A.M. and 8 P.M.

Facilities: Camping, hiking, swimming, fishing, boating, and cross-country skiing in season are available. There are 129 individual family campsites in the east and west areas, with electrical hookups at 36 sites. Pit toilets and drinking water are available year round. A dumping station and showers are open seasonally.

Camping is available from Memorial Day through October. There are eight reservable group campsites for up to 40 persons per site. Extra parking is available near campsite #8 and across from the park office.

Permits and Rules: Campers must register for occupying a site, with registration expiring at 3 P.M. on the last day of the permit. Only two vehicles or five motorcycles are allowed at each campsite. Pets are welcome but must be leashed. Vehicle admission passes are required ($18 annual for residents; $25 annual for nonresidents; $9 annual for seniors). Vehicles are allowed only on paved roads. No one can operate a motorboat at a speed greater than a no-wake speed within 200 feet of shore. Fires are allowed only in fire pits in the campsites and in grills.

Further Information: Contact Superintendent, Yellowstone Lake State Park, 7896 Lake Road, Blanchardville, WI 53516; 608-523-4427.

Other Points of Interest

The **Yellowstone Dairy Stand,** at the park entrance, is an eatery built in 1954 by Lafayette County folks to promote the dairy industry. Proceeds go to the county for college scholarships in the dairy industry. Along with the restaurant are a bait shop and boat rental. Call 608-523-4505 for more information.

The **Cheese Country Recreation Trail** is a 47-mile trail from Mineral Point to Monroe. The track parallels the Pecatonica River along an abandoned railroad corridor. From April 1 to November 15, minibikes, all-terrain vehicles, bicycles, hikers, and horseback riders are allowed. From December 1 to March 30, cross-country skiers, hikers, and snowmobilers can use the trail.

For information, call the Monroe Chamber of Commerce, 608-325-7648.

Park Trails

Windy Ridge Way —2.5 miles—The trail runs along the ridge top at the northern end of Yellowstone Lake. Pick up the trailhead behind the group camp. This is extremely beautiful in the autumn as the leaves change color. The path runs through oak and maple forests and connects on the east with the 1.2-mile Savanna loop.

South Loop —3.0 miles—This is basically a snowmobile route that skirts the park's most extensive wildlife management area. However, hikers can still make their way across the shrub land and forested areas south of Yellowstone Lake. The eastern trailhead is near the Yellowstone Dairy Stand, while the western connection is from the parking lot on Lake Road.

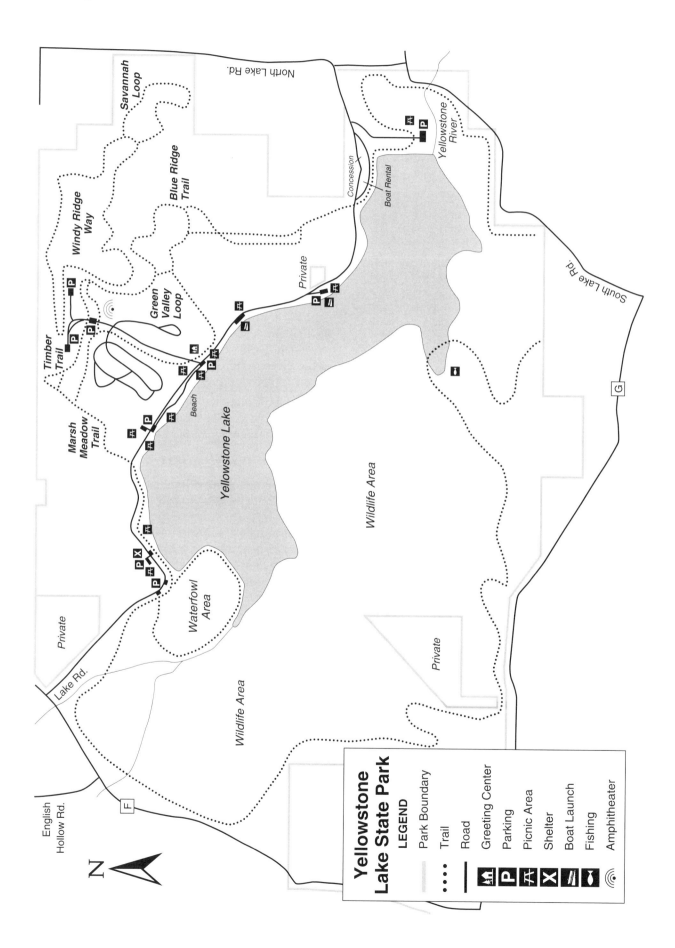

Yellowstone
Lake State Park
LEGEND

Park Boundary
Trail
Road
Greeting Center
Parking
Picnic Area
Shelter
Boat Launch
Fishing
Amphitheater

Timber/Marsh Meadow Trails

👢👢

Distance Round-Trip: 1.7 miles

Estimated Hiking Time: 1 hour

Cautions: There is a steep grade to the trailhead that can be muddy and slippery when wet.

Trail Directions: Enter on Lake Road and park in the lot near the office. Cross the lot to the west and enter the woods where the sign indicates.

For the first .12 mi., hikers ascend the bluff **[1]** that extends past the east side of the family campground. The trail is parallel to the service road that connects the campgrounds at the top of the bluff to Lake Road and the lake. Oak and shagbark hickory are along the way. Just before you reach the top of the hill, there is an open space where the dirt path changes to grass. The group campgrounds are straight ahead once you reach the pinnacle, with a shower building and rest rooms on the right (.3 mi.) **[2].** There is also a parking space here, so if you wish you can simply drive to the top and walk. This beats struggling up the slope, but it lacks the challenge.

Continue to the left, where the trail splits, and take the mowed Timber Trail. This path moves into the shrubland and oak groves (.6 mi.) **[3].** The trail moves downhill from here, along a pathway with a number of loose stones. So watch your step.

At .7 mi., there is a steeper downhill grade, with a gully to the right **[4]** just before you reach the bottom. You now move over open land on the right, with woods to the far right (about 1,000 feet to the west) beyond a row of ash, maple, and shrubs. Now continue ahead on the Marsh Meadow Trail instead of turning to the right when the Timber Trail moves again back to the woods (.8 mi.) **[5].** Stick to the perimeter of the forest and observe the bluestem, gray goldenrod, and other prairie foliage in the field to the

right. Many meadow birds, such as red-winged blackbirds, flit in and out among the foliage.

You now begin to ascend a slope (.9 mi.) **[6]** and cross a low-lying glade that becomes boggy when wet. A truckload of gravel was used to fill in the pathway and make it easier walking. Follow the path left at the trail intersection **(7)** back into the trees and continue up the grade. The Marsh Meadow Trail continues on to the beach. But by returning to the wood line, you pass several large sandstone overhangs. Ferns snuggle in their deep, cool recesses. Large boulders fell from the cliffs years ago and are covered with lichen now. The campground appears through the pines, with tent sites scattered across the hill. You come out again near the shower building where you started the loop. From here it is a short walk south back to your car.

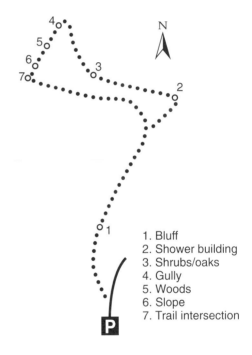

1. Bluff
2. Shower building
3. Shrubs/oaks
4. Gully
5. Woods
6. Slope
7. Trail intersection

Green Valley Loop/ Blue Ridge Trail 👢👢

Distance Round-Trip: 2.1 miles

Estimated Hiking Time: 2 hours

Cautions: The path has loose stones and roots that are obstacles. It can also be slippery when wet. Bring mosquito repellent on sloppy spring and early-summer days.

Trail Directions: Either walk up the slope from the parking lot by the office at the park entrance, or drive to the top of the hill and park near the shower building.

Walk northeast through a pine grove and a sumac patch **[1].** The trail wends its way through the trees in a loop-the-loop fashion, making left and right turns as it descends. There is a large downed tree to the left (.2 mi.) **[2],** victim of some long-ago windstorm. A trickle of water flows down a gully on the left, but it swells during a rain. Next is the intersection with the Blue Ridge Trail (.5 mi.) **[3],** so swing to the left and take that path for more woods walking, continuing straight when you meet a trail intersection to the left **[4].** After .12 mi. or so, the Blue Ridge rejoins the Green Valley Loop, and the sumac patch continues its descent to the lake. However, instead of continuing on the Green Valley Loop, backtrack to that trail intersection mentioned earlier and turn right and proceed down the hill.

There is a marsh (1.7 mi.) **[5]** along the left at the bottom of the hill, so proceed along the rolling pathway skirting the edge of the oaks. The undulating trail meanders between the wetlands and the trees and comes out about 2,000 feet east of the park office. For a quick side trip, and a reward for a trek well taken, stop for an ice-cream cone at the Yellowstone Dairy Stand. The building is across the street from where the trail exits (2.1 mi.) **[6].** After enjoying your treat, head northwest along Lake Road to return to your car.

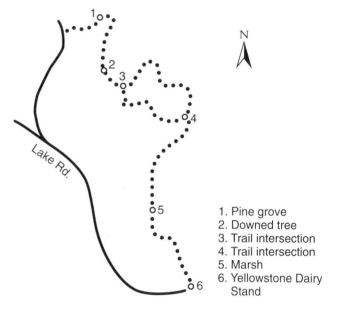

1. Pine grove
2. Downed tree
3. Trail intersection
4. Trail intersection
5. Marsh
6. Yellowstone Dairy Stand

44. Belmont Mound State Park

- Climb to the top of a 40-foot-high observation tower.
- Enjoying hiking, biking, or skiing on a loop trail.
- Visit a nearby state historical site.

Park Information

The park was established in 1967, encompassing 256 acres. Of those, 60 acres on the park's northwest side make up the Belmont Mound Woods State Natural Area. Belmont Mound is part of the vast Niagara dolomite escarpment, a rock formation primarily running from Niagara Falls to eastern Wisconsin. In southwestern Wisconsin, there are a few outcroppings of this rock at Belmont Mound, Platte Mound, Blue Mounds, and Sinsinawa Mound. The name comes from the French *belle monte,* or "beautiful mountain."

The park is operated by the Belmont Lions Club, under contract with the state Department of Natural Resources. The mound is covered with oak, maple, walnut, and basswood. White-tailed deer, raccoons, rabbits, wild turkeys, squirrels, and owls call the woods their home.

Directions: The park is 2 miles north of Belmont on County Highway G and west .25 mile on East Mound Road.

Hours Open: 6 A.M. to 11 P.M. daily.

Facilities: Picnic shelter with electricity, play equipment, rest rooms, water, observation tower.

Permits and Rules: Hiking, off-road biking, and cross-country skiing are allowed on the 2-mile Loop B. Hiking only is allowed on the .75-mile Loop A.

Further Information: Contact Superintendent, Yellowstone Lake State Park, 7896 Lake Road, Blanchardville, WI 53516; 608-523-4427.

Other Points of Interest

First Capitol State Park is 3 miles northwest of Belmont on County Highway G. The park is 1 mile west of Belmont Mound. First Capitol is the site of the Wisconsin Territorial Capitol of 1836. At the time, the territory included Wisconsin, Iowa, Minnesota, and North and South Dakota as far west as the Missouri River. Visitors can tour the rebuilt Council

House (legislature) building and the supreme court building . Both buildings had been moved from their original site and then converted into barns before being renovated. They contain exhibits on lead mining, agriculture, and pioneer history. Call Yellowstone Lake State Park (see park #43) for details, 608-523-4427.

The **Mining Museum** and **Rollo Jamison Museum** in Platteville, 6 miles west on County Highway B, contain more exhibits on mining with tours of the 19th-century Bevans Mine. The museums are open daily from Memorial Day to Labor Day. Call 608-348-3301 for more information.

Loop A 👢👢

Distance Round-Trip: .75 mile

Estimated Hiking Time: 30 minutes

Cautions: Hikers should be aware that turkey hunting is allowed in the spring for holders of a class A disabled permit. There is some poison ivy.

Trail Directions: Park in the lot at the base of hill and walk to the east side of the parking area where there is a trail sign.

The trail is an easy walk up a relatively steep slope [1] to the top of the mound. Thick stands of oak and maple ring the rock, providing cover for wildlife. Ground vegetation ranges from Virginia creeper to raspberry bushes. The path loops around the 40-foot-high observation tower (.3 mi.) [2] atop the hill and extends to the east to dead-end along a mesh fence overlooking the valley below. Return on the same trail, visit the tower, and continue back down the trail, which makes a series of small bends [3] as it descends. In 1995, a small private plane crashed on top of the hill, narrowly missing the tower. Hikers can still see the place where the accident occurred, to the east of the tower. There are several downed trees, and the tops of others were lopped off. Several area teens were on the tower when the accident occurred and quickly summoned help for the injured pilot and passengers.

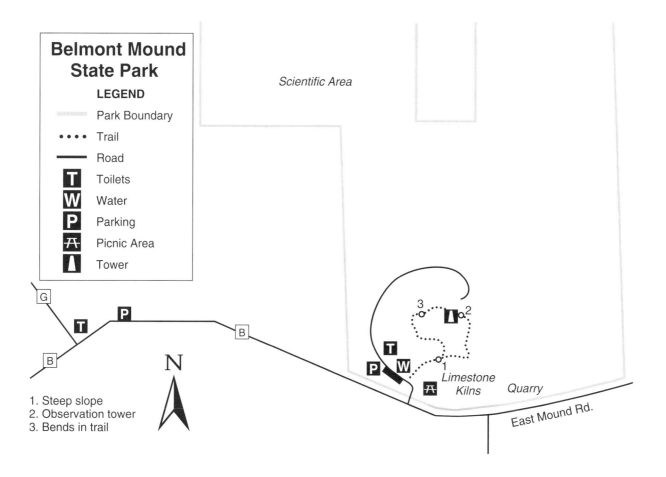

Belmont Mound State Park

LEGEND

▒▒▒	Park Boundary
••••	Trail
▬▬	Road
T	Toilets
W	Water
P	Parking
⛉	Picnic Area
🗼	Tower

N

1. Steep slope
2. Observation tower
3. Bends in trail

Scientific Area

Limestone Kilns   Quarry

East Mound Rd.

45. Nelson Dewey State Park

- Hike along a ridge overlooking the Mississippi River.
- Visit Stonefield, homesite of Wisconsin's first elected governor.
- Play with the full moon in a walk-in campsite.

Park Information

Nelson Dewey State Park is a delightful mix of history and scenery dedicated to Nelson Dewey, Wisconsin's first elected governor. He was only 35 when he was elected. The park's 250 acres were once part of Dewey's 2,000-acre estate along the Mississippi River. After his death in 1889, the complex went through a succession of owners.

Several local governmental bodies purchased Dewey's house and 720 acres in 1936. In the 1950s, the partially furnished home was opened for tours. Two years later, the State Historical Society of Wisconsin agreed to operate the site, which includes several of Dewey's original farm buildings. It now includes a reconstructed village of the late 1800s and the state agricultural museum as well as Dewey's home.

Today the main park area, with its campgrounds, overlooks, and hiking trails, is across County Highway VV atop the bluff overlooking the Mississippi and Dewey's Stonefield.

Directions: The park is on County Highway VV, 20 miles south of Prairie du Chien. Take State Highway 133 to Cassville and drive north on VV about 2 miles to the park entrance.

Hours Open: 6 A.M. to 11 P.M., daily, year round.

Facilities: The park contains one family campground with 40 sites, and one group site for 20 campers. Electrical outlets are at 16 of the individual sites and four sites in the group campground.

Permits and Rules: Register and pay camping fees before setting up. Self-registration is available if no one is at the park office. Picking of plants and flowers is prohibited.

Further Information: Contact Park Superintendent, Nelson Dewey State Park, Cassville, WI 53806; 608-725-5374.

Other Points of Interest

The **Upper Mississippi River National Wildlife and Fish Refuge** consists of 200,000 acres and 260 miles of riverway from Minnesota's Lake Pepin to the Illinois border. There are numerous locales along the route from which to watch migratory waterfowl and bald eagles. The refuge's main Visitor Center is across the river from Prairie du Chien on U.S. Highway 18 in McGregor, Iowa. For more information, call 319-873-3423.

The **Dickeyville Grotto** is a fantastic mix of concrete, petrified wood, marbles, glass, and metal built between 1925 and 1931 by the Reverend Mathius Wernerus and his parish in Dickeyville. The site is at the intersection of U.S. Highways 151 and 61 in the village, 10 miles south of Nelson Dewey State Park. The complex is open daily throughout the year, with extended hours in the summer. Call 608-568-3119 for more information.

All-Inclusive Hike 👢👢

Distance Round-Trip: 3 miles

Estimated Hiking Time: 2.5 hours

Cautions: Some portions of the trail skirt the bluff ledge. Hikers should stick to the path. Remember that scenic rocky overlooks can be slippery when wet.

Trail Directions: Drive to the far south end of the park atop the bluff [1] and cross the grass to the marker indicating the Dewey Heights Prairie Trail. Another option is to start at the campground area and walk back south to the far end of the bluffs overlooking Stonefield. Since this all-inclusive hike traverses all of the trails in the park, only main trail highlights (rather than mileage points) are given.

The Dewey Heights Prairie portion of a park walk is along a gravelly .3-mi. path on the open ridge overlooking the Mississippi River Valley. This vantage point is one of the best for seeing Stonefield [2] with its farm buildings and craft operations. The smokestacks of the Dairyland Power Plant can also be seen 2 mi. south in Cassville. The trail dead-ends at the ledge lip, so hikers need to return the same way they came.

The Cedar Trail is a .3-mi. loop along the rim of the ridge, where there are many loose rocks but excellent overviews. This trail is farther to the south than the Dewey Heights Prairie Trail, which can be seen from this position. Hikers can get to the Cedar Trail by walking from the Prairie Trail across the parking lot near the overlook at this end of the park. Walk around the left side of the stone wall. The Cedar Trail runs down the hill in front of the stone wall and dead-ends at the cliff edge. You'll see the remains of an old stone fence [3] to the left as you proceed around the bluff.

From the Cedar Trail, walk back around the stone wall at the overlook. Cross the parking lot and either walk along the roadway or take the Prairie Trail to the road. Stroll along the road or the parkland on its south side, past two parking lots on the north and another overlook on the south. At the next parking lot, cut south across the grass toward the cliff, turn right and walk toward the next parking area just on the other side of several mounds. Pick up the trail here next to the picnic site overlooking the river valley. This is called North Point, and the trail now runs along the top of what is called North Ridge. This trail becomes Mound Point Trail, a .4-mi. walk along the bluff edge from the effigy mounds near the south end of the upper park [4]. On this route, you pass an impressive array of 20 round and long mounds [5] dating back to between 600 and 1300 A.D.

At the end of the Mount Point Trail, you'll intersect with the Wildlife Trail [6], which takes hikers through a thick oak woods connecting with the campgrounds [7]. You cross several gullies running down the slope. You exit at the parking lot opposite the campground restrooms. From here, walk back to your car through the woods on the opposite side of the drive from the Mound Point Trail, passing several more mounds on your way.

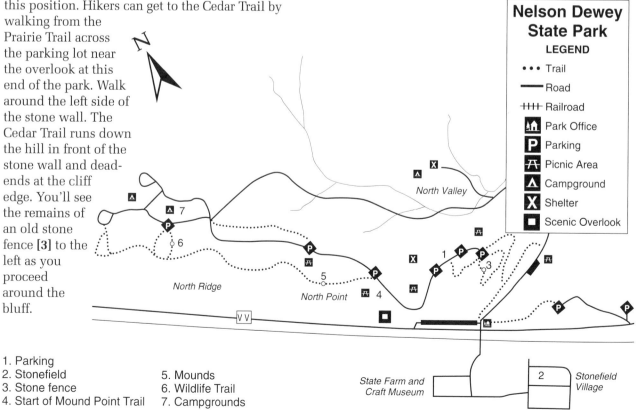

Nelson Dewey State Park

LEGEND

- • • • Trail
- —— Road
- ╫╫╫ Railroad
- 🏠 Park Office
- P Parking
- 🛉 Picnic Area
- 🔺 Campground
- X Shelter
- ◼ Scenic Overlook

North Valley

North Ridge

North Point

State Farm and Craft Museum

Stonefield Village

1. Parking
2. Stonefield
3. Stone fence
4. Start of Mound Point Trail
5. Mounds
6. Wildlife Trail
7. Campgrounds

46. Wyalusing State Park

- See numerous historic Indian mounds.
- Enjoy views of the Mississippi River from high bluffs.
- Take narrow trails along cliff edges for an exciting hike.

Park Information

Native Americans arrived in the Mississippi River Valley at least 11,000 years ago. The people of the Red Ochre, Hopewell, and effigy mound cultures were among the most ancient residents of the picturesque valley. An extensive array of earthworks is seen throughout the state park.

The first Europeans in the area were Father Jacques Marquette and Louis Joliet. Lead was eventually discovered in nearby hills, resulting in an economic boom during the early 1800s. Before more permanent structures were built, the miners burrowed into the ground for warmth and shelter. Their dugouts looked like badger holes. Thus Wisconsin earned the nickname "Badger State."

As early as the turn of the century, the idea for a park at the junction of the Mississippi and Wisconsin Rivers was advanced by area residents. The park was established in 1917. It was first named Nelson Dewey State Park, but the name was soon changed to Wyalusing. The term is a Munsee-Delaware word meaning "home of the warrior." Today's park consists of 2,674 acres.

Directions: The park is 2 miles south of Prairie du Chien via U.S. Highway 18. Turn east on either County Highway C or County Highway P to County Highway X. Follow the park signs on Highway X to the park entrance.

Hours Open: Park offices are open from 8 A.M. to 11 P.M. daily from June through August, and from 8 A.M. to 4:30 P.M. Saturdays, Sundays, and most weekdays the remainder of the year.

Facilities: Camping, biking, cross-country skiing, fishing, picnicking, and education programs are available. Overlooks provide magnificent views. There are two group camps. The outdoor site can accommodate five tents with a total capacity of 108. Reservations must be made a year in advance. The indoor camp has four dorm buildings with a capacity of 27 each, plus a main lodge with kitchen and dining facilities. Groups need to furnish their own food and linens.

Permits and Rules: Reservations are accepted for 67 of the 132 family campsites only between May 1 and October 31. There is a $4 reservation fee plus the camp fee of $8 for state residents from Sunday through Thursday. Camping is $10 on Fridays, Saturdays, and holidays. Fees for out-of-state residents are $10 and $12. Downed wood can be collected or purchased at the park concession stand. Keep pets leashed.

Further Information: Contact Park Manager, Wyalusing State Park, 13342 County Highway C, Bagley, WI 53801-1055; 608-966-2261.

Other Points of Interest

In Prairie du Chien, the second-oldest settlement in Wisconsin, drop by the **Villa Louis.** The mansion was built in 1870 by French trader Hercules Dousman. The grounds surrounding the Villa are the site of an annual fur traders' rendezvous each Father's Day.

The **Fort Crawford Medical Museum,** is also a fun tour. Fort Crawford was one of the main military garrisons during the Black Hawk Indian wars. At **La Riviere Park,** hikers can enjoy several loops of a nature trail, picnicking, and primitive camping. For details on other attractions and activities in Prairie du Chien, call the tourism office at 800-733-1673.

Park Trails

Walnut Springs Trail 🥾🥾—2.6 miles—This is a wide, grass pathway crossing some rocky areas. But the two-hour trek is mostly over gently rolling countryside.

Mississippi Ridge Trail 🥾—3.5 miles—Hikers will not have any difficulty with this stretch of path, which rolls along the ridge tops overlooking the Mississippi River. This also doubles as a cross-country ski trail, and mountain biking is allowed.

Sentinel Ridge Trail 🥾🥾—1.6 miles—The trail runs south from the park's main campground along the high ridge tops overlooking the Mississippi. Many Indian mounds can be found along the route. You will also get some of the best views of the river along this stretch of pathway. This trail takes hikers from Point Lookout to a boat landing on marshy ground that is part of the Upper Mississippi Wildlife and Fish Refuge.

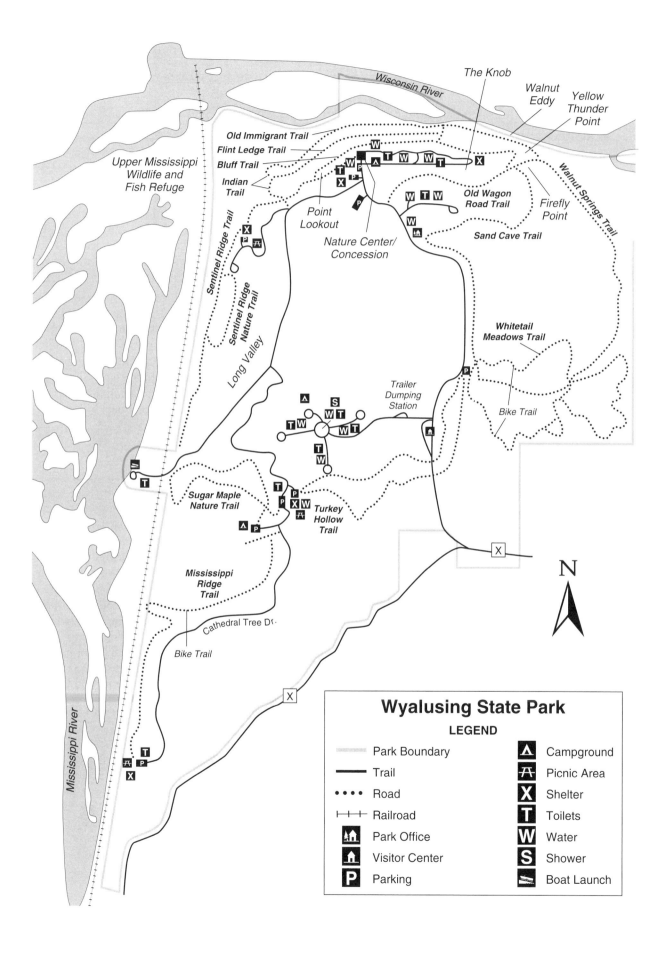

Wisconsin River

The Knob

Walnut Eddy

Yellow Thunder Point

Upper Mississippi Wildlife and Fish Refuge

Old Immigrant Trail

Flint Ledge Trail

Bluff Trail

Indian Trail

Point Lookout

Nature Center/ Concession

Old Wagon Road Trail

Walnut Springs Trail

Firefly Point

Sand Cave Trail

Sentinel Ridge Trail

Sentinel Ridge Nature Trail

Long Valley

Whitetail Meadows Trail

Bike Trail

Trailer Dumping Station

Sugar Maple Nature Trail

Turkey Hollow Trail

Mississippi Ridge Trail

Cathedral Tree Dr.

Bike Trail

Mississippi River

N

Wyalusing State Park

LEGEND

Park Boundary

Trail

Road

Railroad

Park Office

Visitor Center

P Parking

Campground

Picnic Area

X Shelter

T Toilets

W Water

S Shower

Boat Launch

Bluff/Indian/Flint Ledge Trails

Distance: Bluff Trail, .9 mile; Indian Trail, .5 mile; Flint Ledge Trail, .8 mile

Estimated Hiking Time: 2 to 3 hours

Cautions: These interlocking trails edge down the steep cliffside under Point Lookout, so use extreme caution. None are surfaced, and this means they can be slippery when wet or when covered with leaves. Be alert for loose stones. Walk slowly, especially when descending, and use the few handrails available. Stay as far away as possible from the cliffsides, which are not protected by barricades. This is not trivial if one considers that the trails are no more than two feet wide in some places. There are man-made steps in only a few places.

Trail Directions: Start at Point Lookout at the west end of the Wisconsin Ridge Campground, just beyond the park office buildings. Follow the paved pathway toward the river, past the outhouses and picnic shelters. You then take several steps to the trailhead.

From Point Lookout (.1 mi.) [1], gaze out over the Mississippi River Valley. From Point Lookout you can see numerous landmarks, such as the radio towers on the Iowa side of the river, several Wisconsin and Iowa towns, and the U.S. Highway 18 bridge over the Mississippi. Leaving the lookout, scramble down the trail to the junction of the Bluff, Indian, and Flint Ledge Trails (.2 mi.) [2]. The same sights of the river can be seen on each section, but from different levels. By taking the Bluff Trail to the immediate right, the hiker needs to carefully edge along the cliff to encounter steps leading to Treasure Cave (.3 mi.) [3]. Climbing up the stairs from the trail is not for the faint of heart. The steps rise almost straight up to the large hole in the sandstone.

Hikers can see fallen trees along the route as their few remaining roots hang on tenuously to the loose soil and rock (.5 mi.) [4]. Be alert for falling stones from above your head. The rocky ledge of Signal Point sticks out above the valley floor, giving an excellent, unobstructed view (.6 mi.) [5]. Don't get too close to the lip of the cliff. Hidden in the foliage below is the Flint Ledge Trail zigzagging farther down the cliff and the Old Immigrant Trail along the river

bottom. As you go along the Bluff Trail, look at the impressive rock facings of the cliffside. Let your imagination put faces on promontories (.7 mi.) [6]. The junction with the Sand Cave Trail is at the .8-mi. mark [7]. At .9 mi., turn left and descend cautiously to the Flint Ledge Trail [8] for a loop back to the west underneath the Bluff Trail.

The trail will also skirt the cliffs, and you will end up again at the junction of Flint Ledge, Bluff, and Indian Trials. Now take the Indian Trail downward. This is one of the most difficult stretches of the 22-mi. trail system. The trail connects with the Old Immigrant Trail. If you wish to return to the crest, simply turn around at the junction of the Indian Trail and walk back to the initial intersection. Then walk up the rocky slope to Point Lookout, the site where the hike started. Or you can take another trail on the bluffside, such as the Old Immigrant Trail (lower level). Each trail connects with the other at both ends, so it is easy to return to the trailhead intersection.

If you wish to continue walking, you can take the ascent up the cliff face to The Knob. There you will find a small, round shelter house. Seven openings in the hut look out over the valley, presenting a different perspective from that at Point Lookout. From here is an easy walk up a gravel path to the Wisconsin Ridge Campground. You can then walk through the campground to the parking lot. Tired hikers can reach The Knob without all the cliff-hugging crawling along the Old Immigrant, Flint Edge or Bluff trails. Simply drive to the east end of the Wisconsin Ridge Campground, park, and walk along the paved path for about 100 feet or so to the overlook.

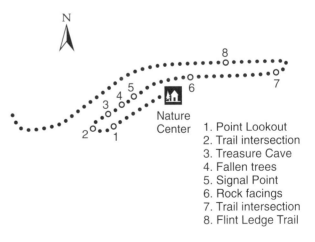

N

Nature Center

1. Point Lookout
2. Trail intersection
3. Treasure Cave
4. Fallen trees
5. Signal Point
6. Rock facings
7. Trail intersection
8. Flint Ledge Trail

Old Immigrant/Old Wagon Road/Sand Cave Trails

Distance: Old Immigrant Trail, 1.3 miles; Old Wagon Road Trail, .8 mile; Sand Cave Trail, 1.3 miles

Estimated Hiking Time: 2 to 3.5 hours

Cautions: The Old Immigrant Trail moves along the river bottom and can be wet and muddy after rains, especially in spring with the snowmelt from the cliffs. The Sand Cave Trail involves steep slopes, with only some helpful steps. So be prepared to move slowly and carefully along the narrow ledges.

Trail Directions: Start on the west at Point Lookout and descend to the Old Immigrant Trail via the .5-mi. Indian Trail.

These trails were used by pioneers in their struggle toward the western frontier. This means that the Immigrant and Old Wagon Road paths are relatively easy; they had to be in order to allow oxen and mules to move carefully down from the hill country to the promised land of Iowa's rich prairies.

The Old Immigrant Trail is a sloping path downward from the bluff (.1 mi.) **[1]** through heavy woods (.3 to 1.2 mi.) **[2]**. Walk along the narrow path as it heads east to the junction with the Walnut Springs Trail (1.2 mi.) **[3]**, which is directly under one of the major highlights of the park, Yellow Thunder Point, **[4]**, near Firefly Point **[5]** at the east end of the trail near the junction with Old Wagon Road. Fine views of the Mississippi can be had at both locales, through the maples and oaks overshadowing the trail. This is a great trek for autumn, with its blaze of crimson, gold, and orange leaves. Turn right at the intersection with the Walnut Springs Trail and head toward the intersection with the Old Wagon Road Trail **[6]**,

which will take you back to the service road next to the park's ballfield.

The Old Wagon Road was one of the major routes from inland Wisconsin to the river landing. The .8-mi. road remains a wide, gentle run downhill. It follows a streambed active only in the spring and autumn or after a heavy summer rain. It ends up in the abandoned settlement of Walnut Eddy, where only memories of this once-thriving community remain.

To take the Sand Cave Trail for another hiking experience, pick up the pathway behind the park office on the north side of the service drive. There are some steps to help today's hikers descend the steepest slopes. The trail cuts through a maple forest clinging to the ledges. A small creek is encountered about midway through the walk, with a waterfall that pours in the spring and drips in the summer. Regardless of the season, its special music is a delight to the ear. The trail connects with the the Old Wagon Road Trail at Firefly Point. You can continue along the Old Wagon Road Trail, the Bluff Trail, the Old Immigrant Trail, or the Walnut Springs Trail from the intersection here.

1. Bluff
2. Heavy woods
3. Walnut Springs Trail
4. Yellow Thunder Point
5. Firefly Point
6. Old Wagon Road Trail

Urban

Topography

Milwaukee, Madison, Kenosha, Racine, Green Bay, La Crosse, Janesville, Eau Claire, the Fox Cities (Neenah, Menasha, and Appleton), Fond du Lac, Stevens Point, Wausau, and Beloit are Wisconsin's largest urban centers. Containing most of the state's population, these communities are in the lower half of Wisconsin. Superior, the largest city in the far north, is on the border with Minnesota. With about one million residents, the Greater Milwaukee area is the state's most densely populated region.

Despite Wisconsin's ever-growing urban crunch, each city has hiking opportunities within or near its limits. Green space and trails are where you find them. State residents have excellent trekking in city and county parks, through school forests, along parkways, and even along downtown streets. State parks, riverways, and other locales with hiking opportunities are never more than a few minutes' drive from a dedicated hiker's front door.

Major Rivers and Lakes

Wisconsin was a pioneer state, with its cities and towns springing up along waterways. Settlers followed the lead of Native Americans who located their lodges in prime crossroads sites. It was for good reason that Milwaukee means "gathering place by the waters," located as it is at the confluence of the Milwaukee and Menomonee Rivers and Lake Michigan. As such, it became one of the nation's prime entry points for new blood, ideas, and dreams.

Almost every city in the state was founded because of its proximity to water. Great Lake harbors allowed the delivery of goods and arrival of immigrants. Rushing rivers and waterfalls were a power source for mills and factories, as well as a transportation resource. Green Bay was a French fur-trading post from the late 1600s on. Located on the rolling waters of Green Bay, with its open passage to Lake Michigan and the world, the city could not help but grow. Lumber-mill towns such as Stevens Point sprang up along the Wisconsin River, accepting the millions of board feet of timber floating downstream. The vast acreage of Lake Winnebago is rimmed by Fond du Lac, Appleton, and other communities. The list goes on.

Common Plant Life

In pre-European settlement days, vast stands of white pine covered much of the northern reaches of the state, with prairie and mixed hardwoods jostling for predominance in the south. Villages were literally chopped out of the forests. Where urban centers sprang up, the native vegetation mostly disappeared.

Except for a few escapees from the woodsman's axe, the farmer's plow, and the developer's bulldozer, what is seen today in Wisconsin's cities are second-growth preserves. There are also carefully nurtured woodlands, arboretums, parks, and restored habitat. The cities reflect the vegetation that grows in the more open space around them.

Most cities have forestry and parks departments in charge of maintaining their "wild" spaces. Yet suburban growth continues to gobble ever wider swaths of land around the cities. Consequently, preserving green space and outdoor-recreation opportunities remains a constant civic fight. And on the micro level, many homeowners are now planting their yards with prairie flowers. Hike and bike paths are more and more common, such as Stevens Point's 24-mile Green Circle Tour and Madison's well-used pathway system around its lakes.

Common Birds and Mammals

Many of the state's animals have readily adapted to the encroaching urban environment. Raccoons and white-tailed deer consider wooded parks favored residences. Coyotes roam suburban lawns. Skunks and woodchucks discover safe havens under garages.

Occasionally, however, the critters become nuisances as their wilderness territory diminishes. For instance, deer management is a constant battle, with cities trying to balance concerns of animal-rights activists with environmental needs. Too large a deer population can quickly destroy a fragile forest community that is already restricted by surrounding streets and houses. In addition, several thousand deer are killed or injured annually in vehicle accidents.

Birds have also adapted to the city scene. Songbirds make full use of feeders, parks, gardens, flower beds, and tree-lined streets for food and lodging. Game birds such as pheasant and grouse hide in gullies and along roads. Canada geese and ducks find food in man-made lagoons outside trendy offices. Again, some of the birds become trouble. To control its pigeon population, Milwaukee introduced falcons to its downtown. The raptors have nests on the tops of some of the city's tallest buildings.

Climate

Wisconsin has a "continental" climate with hot summers and cold winters. However, the proximity to the Great Lakes gives shoreline cities milder winters and cooler summers than communities inland. The mean annual temperature of the state is about 44 degrees Fahrenheit. The extreme range is from 110 Fahrenheit and above to –50 degrees Fahrenheit and below. Wisconsin is the type of state where seasoned residents know that the weather changes often and quickly. Average rainfall is from 29 to 32 inches, most of it falling in the spring and autumn.

There are several rules concerning Wisconsin weather, especially for an urban resident. If you want rain, plan a family camping adventure over an extended holiday weekend. There will be a deluge. If you wish to cross-country ski and it hasn't snowed for weeks, volunteer to work overtime. The season's best powder will descend on the days you can't get away. Want dry, sunny weather? Don't water your garden, and hope for rain.

Best Features

Each Wisconsin community has its own personality, from the multiethnic charm of the big cities to small town hospitality. Many communities are geared to the needs of outdoors enthusiasts, with restaurants, accommodations, service firms, and guides. Hikers along the state's trails are generally assured of a friendly welcome when they visit towns along the route.

When hiking, take in the local flavor. Visit the festivals, art shows, and fairs; take the museum tours and drop by the stores. Often a city trek carries you past a public event or near an exciting attraction. Don't stroll past. Check out everything: the logging museum on the Wolf River in Keshena; the American Outdoor Learning Center in Crivitz; Peshtigo's fire museum; Milwaukee's lakefront Irish Fest; Prairie du Chien's fur traders' rendezvous.

The Wisconsin Division of Tourism and area convention and visitor bureaus can offer suggestions. Call 800-432-8747 for free recreation guides, event calendars, campground directories, historic sites, and information about auto and bike tours.

47. Boerner Botanical Gardens

- Pick up hints on plantings for your own landscaping.
- Admire hundreds of varieties of plants and flowers.
- Walk on the wild side through bogs and rock gardens.

Park Information

The 120-acre Boerner Botanical Gardens and 1,000-acre arboretum were built between 1932 and 1941. Landscape architect Alfred L. Boerner capitalized on the glacially created kettle moraine land in Milwaukee County's Whitnall Park to create wetlands, ponds, and woodlots around 50 acres of formal gardens. The design is reminiscent of an English formal garden, with plantings of perennials leading to the Rose Garden. That garden alone has more than 50,000 blooms of 500 varieties of roses.

Grassy malls link the gardens to the surrounding forests and meadows. There are smaller gardens scattered around the site featuring shrubs, wildflowers, spring bulbs, peonies, annuals, herbs, and daylilies. Research on plants is conducted in the trial garden. Walls and colonnades made of glacial fieldstone provide accents. More than 250,000 persons annually visit the botanical gardens. But guests are free to walk anywhere they want throughout the gardens.

Construction of the park was undertaken by the Civilian Conservation Corps, the Work Progress Administration, the National Youth Administration, and Milwaukee County relief labor.

Directions: The gardens are 15 minutes from downtown Milwaukee on South 92nd Street, with access from either the east or the west from I-94 or U.S. 45 to I-894 on exits 5A and 5AB.

Hours Open: 8 A.M. to sunset, daily, April through October. The formal gardens are closed from November through March.

Facilities: Rest rooms, gift shop, paths, walkways, trails.

Permits and Rules: No alcohol, pets, bikes, or kites. Take only photos, not flowers. Wedding parties need special permits for photography. No fishing in the carp pond. Admission is free, but parking is $3 per car; season passes are $15.

Further Information: Contact Boerner Botanical Gardens, 5879 South 92nd Street, Milwaukee, WI 53130; 414-529-1870 or 414-425-1130.

Other Points of Interest

Whitnall Park surrounds the Boerner Gardens with picnic areas, sport fields, walkways, and river and pond vistas. Also within the park is the **Wehr Nature Center** (see park #49), only .9 mi. southeast of the botanical gardens. The Wehr Nature Center has trails, educational programs, and an amphitheater for interpretive programs. The **Root River Parkway** runs near the Boerner Gardens, with miles of hiking opportunities through woodlots and along the river.

Lake Michigan is on the east side of Milwaukee, only a 30-minute drive from the gardens. In addition to the typical lake activities such as charter fishing and swimming there are extensive paths for hiking, biking, and jogging, plus playing fields for soccer and rugby, golf courses, and open areas for festivals and other outdoor recreation.

Park Trails

Evergreen Trail 🥾—.4 mile—This path wends its way through a thick stand of conifers on the south side of the park drive near the 92nd Street entrance. There are numerous picnic tables and benches along the way. Spruce and pine are the predominant species. You pass an old Civilian Conservation Corps building that was used during the construction of the park in the 1930s. The building was restored in 1986 as a reminder of this aspect of the park's history. The building is now a horticulture classroom for schoolchildren.

Bog Garden Walk 🥾—.2 mile—Walk along a wooden boardwalk over a marshy area of the gardens for an elevated view of cattails, swamp milkweed, and numerous other varieties of plants. This is in a wild setting, unlike the formal gardens in the main part of the complex. The Bog Garden Walk is on the east side of the Rock Garden complex at the south end of the Boerner Gardens.

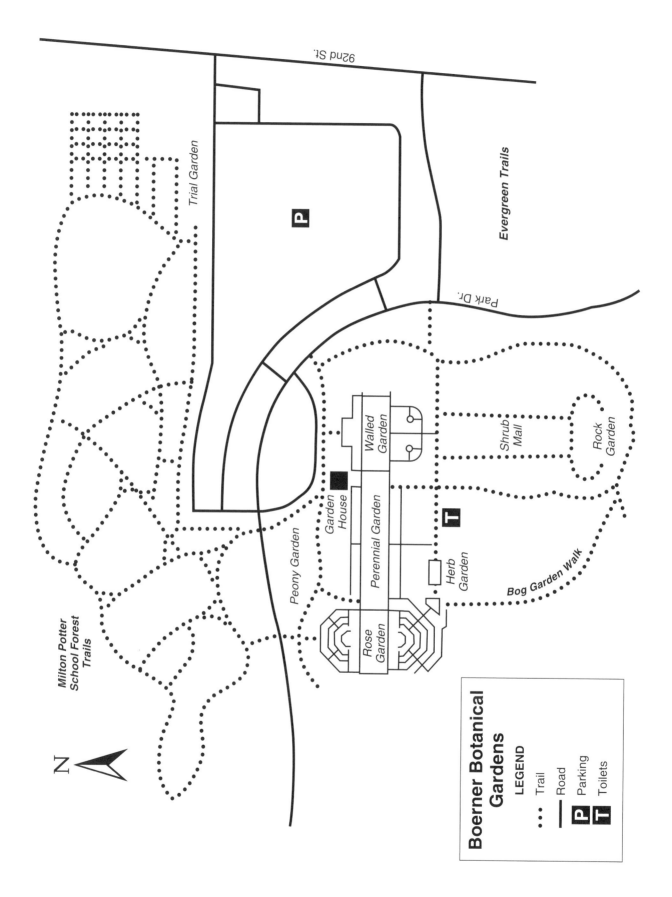

Boerner Botanical Gardens

LEGEND

· · · Trail

—— Road

P Parking

T Toilets

North Park Stroll

Distance Round-Trip: 1.3 miles

Estimated Hiking Time: 1 hour

Cautions: Watch for "Closed for Pesticide Application" notices.

Trail Directions: Enter the gardens from the 92nd Street entrance and park in the northernmost lot near the viburnum plantings.

Numerous meandering sidewalks branch off from the parking lot here **[1].** Take one of the closest and simply meander along the paths to see the various plantings, separated by wide, mowed grassy spaces. By going east, the hiker will see many species of dwarf shrubs scattered throughout the area (.1-.9 mi.) **[2].** An extensive planting of tulips can be seen from the parking lot. This is a colorful place to visit in early spring when the explosion of flowers occurs. Aim for mid-May and you won't go wrong. By going this way, you head toward the trial garden (.3 mi.) **[3],** which was established in 1950. The best time to see this area is between June and August. A stand of yews is on the far north side of this planting.

Walk back to the west along the wood line at the northern perimeter of the gardens. A sidewalk here rolls gently along the topography, making it easy for those who have physical disabilities. At .4 mi. **[4]** and .5 mi. **[5],** look over lilac bushes and more tulips. Keep going along the sidewalk, brushing branches out of the way—the trees and shrubs crowd close to the walk. At .6 mi. **[6]** is an entrance, amid the silver maple, to the Milton Potter School Forest nature trail (see park #48). The hardwood acreage and its outdoor environmental study area are administered by the Milwaukee public school system.

You can either turn right and go into the woods along the trail or continue along the sidewalk to see more tulip plantings (.7 mi.) **[7].** Around a curve in the sidewalk is another entrance to the Potter Forest trail. Continue along the walk past the perfumed lilac; then turn west on the pathway. A large field is to the right (.8 mi.) **[8],** with a stand of magnolia (.9 mi.) **[9]** down a small slope in that direction. Feel free to walk across the grass to take a closer look. Back on the sidewalk, you will pass a clump of crab apple trees (1.2 mi.) **[10].** Their springtime scents add a special dimension to a Boerner tour. Return to your vehicle in the parking lot or continue walking to the south to see the formal gardens.

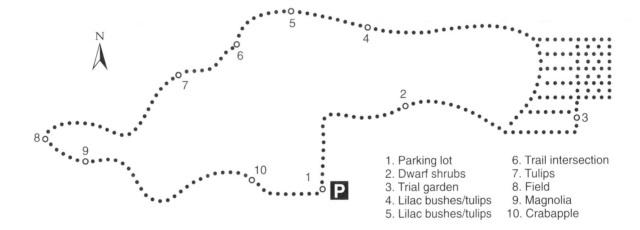

1. Parking lot
2. Dwarf shrubs
3. Trial garden
4. Lilac bushes/tulips
5. Lilac bushes/tulips
6. Trail intersection
7. Tulips
8. Field
9. Magnolia
10. Crabapple

South Park Stroll 👢👢

Distance Round-Trip: 1.5 miles

Estimated Hiking Time: 1 hour

Cautions: Don't go into areas marked with pesticide warnings. Look both ways when you cross the service road in front of the central park building. Numerous limos with their wedding parties pull up here on sunny summer weekends.

Trail Directions: From the parking lot, go to the main entrance to the formal gardens. Either walk around the building or go through, visiting the gift shop, meeting room, or the rest rooms.

The Garden House [1] is open for exhibits, meetings, and plant sales as well as housing the park office and the offices of the Friends of the Boerner Botanical Gardens. The stone building was constructed in 1936 and is designed like a Wisconsin farmhouse. The hand-hewn oak furniture in the Garden House was designed by Richard Wilken; several wooden animals were carved by Karl Kahlich. An inscription over the fireplace in the main meeting room is a quote from Alexander Pope, selected by park designer Whitnall: "Nature . . . where order in variety we see, and where, though all things differ, we agree."

Walk out the back door. To the left are plantings of Japanese bayberry and Oriental bittersweet. In other beds are iris and hibiscus. The walled garden straight ahead has a gazebo available for a romantic tryst or as a place to rest your feet. Continue walking along the shrub mall (.3 mi.) [2], where there are daylilies, junipers, and peony plantings, as well as many varieties of bushes.

Take the steps around to the bottom of the Rock Garden (.4 mi.) [3] for a look at the waterfall and spring. Looking to the north, you'll see an expansive meadow and arborvitae. Go to the west, toward the Bog Garden Walk (.5 mi.) [4], and use the boardwalk to cross the marsh. You can either take the surfaced path to the top of the next hill beyond the marsh or turn to your immediate left after crossing the walk.

This takes you through a thick stand of underbrush and out onto a meadow. Hike on the grass along the tree line to the right and come up on the base of the hill where the Rose Garden is located. In the summertime this hill is a favorite of kids for rolling down the lush grass.

Climb the hill and stroll through the Rose Garden (.7 mi.) [5], an official All-American Rose Selections display plot. The roses bloom their best in May and August. Their names are as dazzling as their tints. Prima Donna, Spring Hill Freedom, Pride-n-Joy, and All That Jazz are just a few of the 500 selections. Take a look into the shallow carp pond, where fat lazy fish roll their orange bodies to the surface. The sculptures in the area were made from stone that was quarried in the county's Curry Park years ago. George Adams Dietrich designed the statue of the boy and girl in the Perennial Garden (.8 mi.) [6], as well as much other Work Progress Administration artwork of the period. For a quick side jaunt, turn to your right on any of the walks and wander through the Herb Garden with its sage, parsley, and thyme plantings.

From here, turn right and continue strolling toward the Garden House and the parking area. Remember that garden concerts are held on the lawn here throughout the summer, in classical, jazz, and other musical styles. Picnicking is allowed on these evenings. Bring your own blanket or lawn chair.

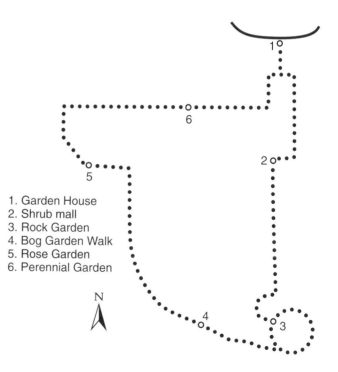

1. Garden House
2. Shrub mall
3. Rock Garden
4. Bog Garden Walk
5. Rose Garden
6. Perennial Garden

N

48. Milton Potter School Forest

- Walk through a diverse hardwood forest.
- Enjoy flowers and plantings in adjacent botanical gardens.
- Count the squirrels and chipmunks rambling through the leaves.

Forest Information

The area of Potter's Forest was farmed beginning in the mid-1800s. Potawatomi who lived in the area prior to white settlement had kept the area cleared by fire. When the fires were stopped, stands of trees were allowed to take root and grow, and these form the core of today's forest.

In the 1940s, local conservation groups and the Milwaukee public schools sought to acquire land for a school forest to be used for educational projects. Fifty acres of what was to become Potter's Forest were acquired in 1947 and dedicated on June 5, 1949. The site was named after Milton C. Potter, a former Milwaukee public schools superintendent and an advocate of environmental studies. Hardwood and conifer trees that pupils planted back then on barren flat farmland are now mature. Today, the school system has the Ropes and Challenge Course laid out around those trees.

Directions: The school forest is on the north side of the Boerner Botanical Gardens; access is from the parking lot in front of the Garden House by walking along the sidewalk edging the woods. The forest and gardens are in Hales Corners, a south-side Milwaukee suburb.

Hours Open: 8 A.M. to dusk.

Facilities: Trails, educational compound.

Permits and Rules: No camping. No fires. No motorized vehicles.

Further Information: Contact Outdoor Education, Division of Community Recreation, Milwaukee Public Schools, 2414 West Mitchell Street, Milwaukee, WI 53204-3015; 414-647-6050.

Other Points of Interest

The **Boerner Botanical Gardens** (see park #47) consists of 120 acres of rolling hills, plantings, and woodlots. The gardens are similar to those of English country manors, with roses, yews, spring bulbs, peonies, and wildflowers. The gardens have been among 23 official All-American Rose Selections test gardens since 1957. The gardens are included in the Whitnall Park complex in Franklin, a Milwaukee suburb. For more information, call 414-425-1130.

The **Wehr Nature Center** (see park #49) is an education and research center operated by the Milwaukee County Park system and the University of Wisconsin Extension. More than 5 miles of trails meander through woods, prairies, meadows, and marshes. You can admire a wetland boardwalk and a waterfall on Mallard Lake. Call 414-425-8550 for more information.

Woodland Trail 🥾

Distance Round-Trip: 2 miles

Estimated Hiking Time: 1.5 hours

Cautions: A maze of trails within the forest makes it easy to lose track of direction because there are no named or marked loops. However, all eventually lead to the forest edge.

Trail Directions: From the Boerner Botanical Gardens on the south, park in the northernmost lot and walk straight ahead across the grass. Meet the sidewalk running along the forest edge and turn left (west). The opening to the forest trails is hard to find in the summer, but look for the large sign between the brush, just inside the tree line.

Leaving the Boerner Botanical Gardens side **[1]**, enter the forest and walk up the first slope. Angle to the left and walk along the dirt pathway that rolls and swings amid the silver maple and oak. Occasionally, mayapples can be spotted where there are deeper piles of leaf mold on the ground. The mayapples flower in the spring and recede by midsummer.

Continuing on this trail will link the hiker with another entrance at .3 mi. **[2]** that also connects the school forest with the Boerner grounds. This second entrance (or exit) is not as easy to find as the first.

There are numerous downed trees scattered throughout the forest, well on their way to decay.

They demonstrate the birth-death-rebirth process of natural life. Animals hide in the hollowed logs, so look closely. Early morning and late afternoon are the best times to spot forest creatures.

There are many ways to wander throughout the school forest, so let yourself roam. At .5 mi. is a circular clearing **[3]** with logs on which to sit. This quiet site is used as an outdoor classroom for Milwaukee public schools environmental classes. There are three distinct paths leading out of the clearing.

Take the one on the far right (.5 mi.) **[4]** and keep walking along toward another clearing past the Solomon's seal and yellow fawn lilies. Here, you find six tables set up as workstations for hands-on study programs for the pupils. An old cabin is tucked in the woods on part of the trail that spins off from the education clearing.

An elevated stand, about five feet off the ground, is at the edge of the clearing. Part of the Ropes and Challenge Education Program, this structure has a removable ramp that allows youngsters who use wheelchairs to participate.

Leaving the clearing, walk to the left, where a conifer plantation is behind a row of hardwoods (.7 mi.) **[5]**. Beyond the conifers is a prairie. Then walk along the well-trod path down a slope past towering oak and maple growths (.8 mi.) **[6]**. Mixed in among them are a few black cherry and hickory. The ground cover includes Virginia creeper, raspberry bushes, and ferns. The spring flowers are particularly lovely. Look for blue violets, skunk cabbage, and trillium.

There are several piles of cut logs on each side of the pathway, attesting to the management program that goes on within the school forest. By taking this trail past some limestone outcroppings (1.2 mi.) **[7]**, you return to the entrance on the Boerner Botanical Gardens side.

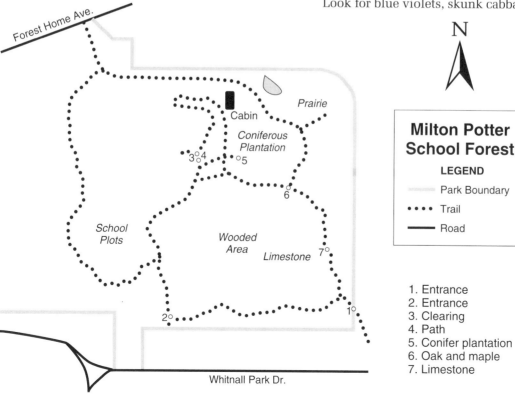

N

Milton Potter School Forest

LEGEND

⬜ Park Boundary

•••• Trail

— Road

1. Entrance
2. Entrance
3. Clearing
4. Path
5. Conifer plantation
6. Oak and maple
7. Limestone

49. Wehr Nature Center

- Experience hiking woods, prairie, and marsh environments.
- Take a nature tour in a peaceful urban setting.
- Watch for wildlife and birds that have adapted to human encroachment.

Park Information

The Wehr Nature Center is a 200-acre preserve within Milwaukee County's Whitnall Park. The park has wetland, oak savanna, prairie, and glacial landscape over which to wander on 6 miles of trails. Since 1974 the Nature Center, in cooperation with the University of Wisconsin Extension, has been the county park service's main source of environmental education. The center annually serves 90,000 persons, more than half of them schoolchildren participating in organized programs. The center's outreach project, Nature in the Parks, organizes field trips through other county parks.

Many activities are offered to the public throughout the year at the Wehr Nature Center. The center's Prairie Days Celebration in midsummer includes Civil War-era music, a buffalo hunter's encampment, prairie walks, Native American storytelling, and pioneer cooking. There are also lectures, workshops, and scheduled hikes.

Directions: The Nature Center is located within the 660-acre Whitnall Park, adjacent to the Root River Parkway in the Milwaukee suburban community of Franklin. The center entrance is on College Avenue between 92nd and 108th Streets.

Hours Open: 8 A.M. to 4:30 P.M. daily. The center and parking lot are open daily year round except for Thanksgiving and Christmas Day. The nature store is open from 8:30 A.M. to 4 P.M. The trails are open to hikers from sunrise to sunset.

Facilities: Auditorium, gift shop, displays, rest rooms.

Permits and Rules: Parking is $2 with a trail donation of $1 for adults and 50 cents for children. Fees vary for special events. No bikes allowed on trails. No camping, pets, or picnicking. No collecting of plant material.

Further Information: Contact Wehr Nature Center, Whitnall Park, 9701 West College Avenue, Franklin, WI 53132; 414-425-8550.

Other Points of Interest

The **Root River Parkway** meanders through south central Milwaukee County, with many walking opportunities through mixed hardwood forests and meadows, along the roadways and trails, and over mowed parkland. Along the way are picnic grounds, soccer fields, historical sites, and floral gardens. Call the Milwaukee County Parks Department, 414-257-6100, for more information.

Park Trails

Mallard Lake —1.5 miles—There is no single loop for this walk, but hikers can trek around the lake by following a series of marked trails. The 20-acre lake was created in the 1930s after the Civilian Conservation Corps built a dam at an outlet to a marsh. Bird Blind Point juts into the lake, allowing hikers to watch waterfowl up close without disturbing them. Surrounding the lake are numerous black walnut trees.

Woodland Trail Loop —.5 mile—The trail edges along a glacial moraine, a line of debris deposited by a retreating sheet of ice from the last ice age. The forest consists of wildflowers, shrubs, and trees such as oak and hickory. This is one of the better walks in the autumn when the maples change colors.

Oak Savanna Loop —.5 mile—The path goes through a restored prairie, with several bur oak making their presence known. The center burns the ground cover every three years to replicate nature's environmental control.

Wetland Loop —.6 mile—Moving along a path past a lowland forest, shrub land, and a sedge meadow, the hiker can see how moisture affects different types of plant life. Black walnut, black willow, and gray dogwood are the predominant trees, with joe-pye weed and swamp milkweed the most extensive among the sedges and wildflowers.

Glacial Trail Loop —1 mile—The loop starts at the Wehr Nature Center and moves on into the surrounding Whitnall Park. The land was formed by glaciers that covered the state from 10,000 to 20,000 years ago. There are numerous "erratic" stones along the path, dumped there by the glaciers or moved to one side by farmers who tried to till the soil.

Natural History Trail 👢👢

Distance Round-Trip: 1.7 miles

Estimated Hiking Time: 1.5 hours

Cautions: This trail involves a lot of walking up and down hills. Bring insect repellent in the spring and early summer.

Trail Directions: Pick up the trail at the rear of the outdoor amphitheater behind the center building. Follow the markers with the imprint of a foot and toes.

Start at Bird Blind Point **[1]**, which juts out into Mallard Lake, just to the east of the Nature Center's major building. A bird blind is on the point to allow a closer look at the waterfowl. Move north along the edge of Mallard Lake (.2 mi.) **[2]**, built in the 1930s by the Civilian Conservation Corps. Swimming was allowed in the lake until the 1940s when bacteria counts increased because of ground run-off. Around the edges of the water is a meadow with goldenrod, red and blue lobelia, and gentian. This is a good place to see goldfinches, tree swallows, and sparrows.

At .4 mi. are the dam and waterfall **[3]** that formed Mallard Lake. This is the largest of four dams in Whitnall Park. Next is a 15-acre prairie habitat that was originally cleared for farming and pastureland. The farming halted when the land became a park in 1930. But there are still exotic species like timothy amid the big bluestem, Indian grass, and switchgrass.

Cross an old railroad bed—it was built in the 1860s, but the tracks were never laid. The ground is now overgrown, providing cover for pheasants, rabbits, and the occasional red fox. An expanse of bur and black oak making up a new oak savanna is next (.6 mi.) **[4]**. The savanna loop angles to the left, amid a spread of prairie dock, bluestem, and a few outsiders such as wild apple. Walk along the forest edge (.7 mi.) **[5]** and move into the woods.

The timber species include hawthorn, oak, cherry, and ash.

A windstorm in the 1950s damaged part of the forest, causing openings in the tree cover. Ash, maple, and oak saplings are filling in the spaces. You pass a large patch of sumac (.8 mi.) **[6]** when leaving the forest cover and angling back to the south. Cross the savanna again and enter the Nature Center Woods (1.2 mi.) **[7]**, to the west of the center building. The trees here are thick, mature, and tall. There is a large stand of shagbark hickory to the left (1.3 mi.) **[8]**. Several midforest openings appear, with gooseberry and raspberry bushes. The Natural History Trail continues to the left. Cross a small bridge (1.5 mi.) **[9]**; under it is a boulder-choked gully. Pass the intersection with the Woodland Trail, which goes up a hill to the left.

Walk down the steep slope behind the amphitheater, which was formed by earth taken from the lagoons and Mallard Lake below this site. There are widely spaced dirt steps to help. Tall arches of sumac act as canopies over the trail. You come out behind the amphitheater near the rear of the center building.

1. Bird Blind Point
2. Mallard Lake
3. Dam/waterfall
4. Oak savanna
5. Forest edge
6. Sumac
7. Nature Center Woods
8. Shagbark hickory
9. Small bridge

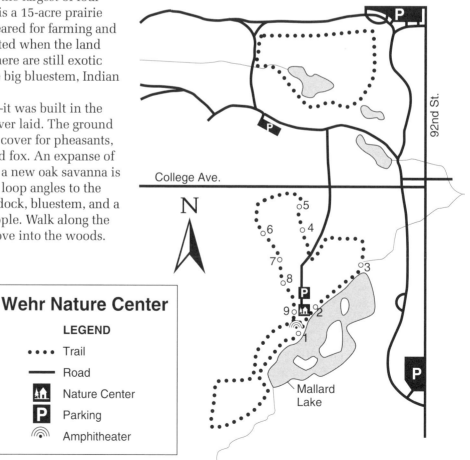

Wehr Nature Center

LEGEND

•••• Trail

── Road

🏠 Nature Center

🅿 Parking

📡 Amphitheater

50. Havenwoods State Forest

- Stroll over a compact section of prairie and woodland in the heart of Milwaukee.
- Take part in a nature program, focusing on everything from snakes and butterflies to flowers and trees.
- Visit the gardens and yard-care area to get ideas for your own green space at home.

Forest Information

Havenwoods State Forest is a 237-acre site featuring open grasslands, young woods, and seasonal wetlands. In the mid-1800s, settlers cleared the original forests for farming. From 1917 to 1945, the land was the site of the Milwaukee County House of Corrections. The inmates lived and worked on-site, tending a prison farm and constructing furniture in a factory. Between 1945 and 1970, the land was used for an army disciplinary barracks, a Nike missile site, an army reserve center, and a municipal landfill.

In the mid-1970s, the land that was to become Havenwoods was a large vacant lot. No longer needed by the army, its future was wide open. Citizens, community leaders, and public officials cooperated to prevent the site from becoming another industrial park or residential area. The Friends of Havenwoods and neighbors worked together—with nature, of course—to begin the healing process on the land. In 1979, the Department of Natural Resources became caretaker of the property. In 1986, the Havenwoods Environmental Awareness Center complex was completed.

Havenwoods is bounded on the north by the Chicago and North Western Railroad and Schoenecker County Park. On the western perimeter are the Wisconsin and Southern Railroad and a U.S. Army Reserve Center.

Directions: Havenwoods State Forest is on Milwaukee's north side. From the intersection of Sherman Boulevard (North 43rd Street) and Silver Spring Drive, head north. At the second stoplight, turn left (west) onto Douglas Avenue. Cross Hopkins Street and continue up the entrance road to the parking lot on your left (south). Havenwoods is also easily reached by bus on the Milwaukee County Transit System.

Hours Open: The grounds are open from 6 A.M. to 8 P.M. daily, with the Environmental Awareness Center open from 7:45 A.M. to 4:30 P.M., Monday through Friday.

Facilities: Indoor rest rooms, water, public pay phone, auditorium, classrooms, small exhibit area, garden and yard-care demonstration area, a small picnic site, and more than 6 miles of trails. In the winter, there are 2.5 miles of cross-country ski trails.

Permits and Rules: Pets are prohibited in areas designated by posted notice. All animals and plants are protected. No motorized vehicles, alcohol, fires, firearms, or camping.

Further Information: Contact Superintendent, Havenwoods State Forest, 6141 North Hopkins Street, Milwaukee, WI 53209; 414-527-0232, TDD 414-527-0761.

Other Points of Interest

McGovern Park is across West Silver Spring Drive, south of the state forest. The park has extensive picnic areas, ball fields, basketball courts, and open space for lazing about. A senior center is also located within the park environs. The park hosts numerous public activities throughout the year, such as July 4 fireworks. For more information, call 414-527-4507.

To the north of Havenwoods are the ball diamonds and open spaces of **Schoenecker County Park.** The park, tucked between the railroad tracks and the state forest, is also accessed from Douglas Avenue. Call 414-527-9023 for details.

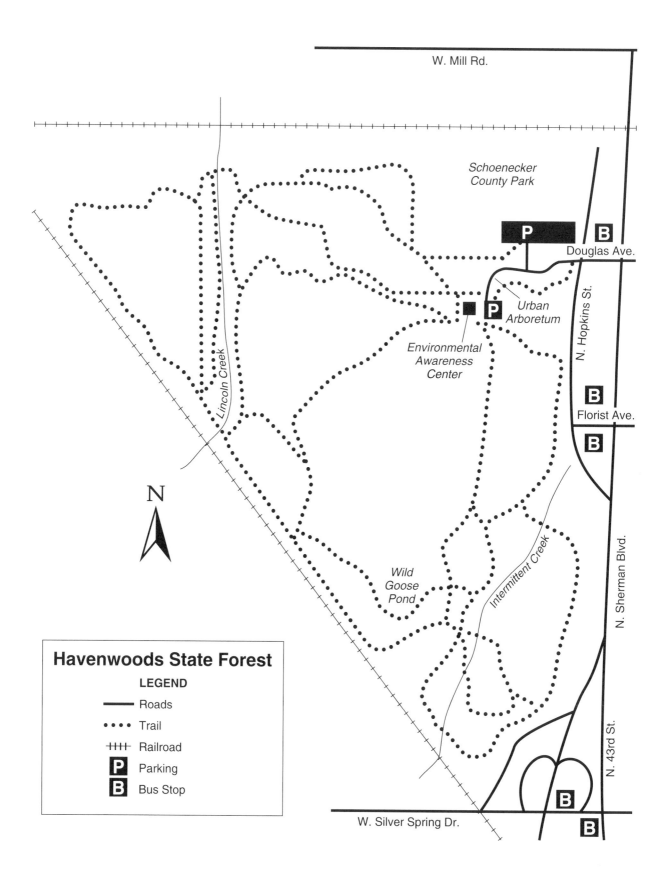

W. Mill Rd.

Schoenecker
County Park

P **B**

Douglas Ave.

*Urban
Arboretum*

N. Hopkins St.

B

Florist Ave.

B

P

*Environmental
Awareness
Center*

Lincoln Creek

N

Intermittent Creek

N. Sherman Blvd.

*Wild
Goose
Pond*

N. 43rd St.

B

Havenwoods State Forest

LEGEND

—— Roads

•••• Trail

+H+ Railroad

P Parking

B Bus Stop

B

W. Silver Spring Dr.

B

Nature Trail—Orange Loop 🥾

Distance Round-Trip: 1.4 miles

Estimated Hiking Time: 1 hour

Cautions: Bikers are permitted on the limestone roads within the state forest, so be alert when crossing from one part of the property to another. Pets are not permitted on the Nature Trail.

Trail Directions: When the Nature Center is open, stop by and request a trail guide titled "People and the Land." From the kiosk in the southwest corner of the parking lot, walk southeast and look for the orange marker in the grove of Norway maples. The House of Corrections buildings once stood here **[1].**

Follow the curved grass path south and east toward Hopkins Street. Watch for plants that seem out of place in this area. Many, such as the spruces and peonies, are landscape plants left over from the prison era. Others, such as Queen Anne's lace and dandelions, are alien invaders from Europe and Asia.

The path curves to the right (.1 mi.) and parallels North Hopkins Street for about 1,000 feet **[2].** This area is in transition. Once a landscaped lawn, it is becoming a young woods. Look among the grasses for thousands of trees and shrubs planted by school children. Continue walking along the gently rolling path, following the orange markers. You enter a meadow, to be greeted by a riot of colors in spring and summer **[3].** The yellow goldenrod, blue chicory, purple new england aster, and soft pink bindweed make a summer extravaganza here.

At marker #5 (.4 mi.), turn left and follow the wood-chip trail through a wooded area **[4].** You can follow the arrow to marker #7 on the Nature Trail or turn right. The marker is on the site of two old silo foundations (.5 mi.) **[5].** These were built by settlers in the late 1800s. Retrace your steps and continue to marker #8.

The wood-chip trail crosses a limestone road **[6]** and becomes a grass path. The path leads past Wild Goose Pond (.7 mi.) **[7],** which was dug in 1983. It is a seasonal wetland that is home to red-winged blackbirds, leopard frogs, green darner dragonflies, and many other wetland animals.

After the wetlands, angle to the right along the path. Proceed through the high grass toward the woods. In summer, American goldfinches and gray-headed coneflowers bring splashes of color to these fields. But watch out for the other yellow flower: meadow parsnip. Some people are very allergic to this plant's sap.

Enter the wooded area **[8]** and proceed on the wood-chip trail. In a short distance it reverts to a grass path. Turn right at the orange marker (.8 mi.) and continue on to a great place for wildlife observation **[9].** In winter, you can follow the tracks of white-tailed deer, red fox, raccoons, and cottontail rabbits along and across the trails.

Angle to the right (.9 mi.) and pass through an area that was burned in 1982 **[10].** Some very hardy pioneer trees such as box elder, elm, ash, and hawthorn have invaded and are slowly reclaiming the space. As you leave the woods, you will see the Education Center **[11]** to the east. About halfway to the center, the field is planted in prairie flowers and grasses. In late and early summer, there are wild quinine, rosinweed, big bluestem, Indian grass, and blazing star dotting the landscape with color.

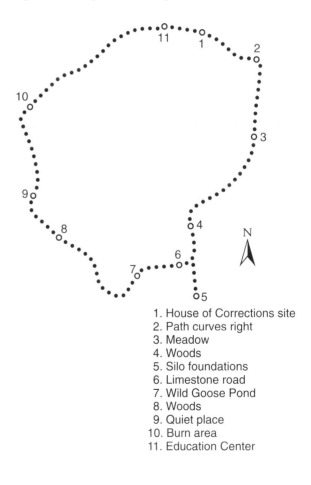

1. House of Corrections site
2. Path curves right
3. Meadow
4. Woods
5. Silo foundations
6. Limestone road
7. Wild Goose Pond
8. Woods
9. Quiet place
10. Burn area
11. Education Center

Loop A

Distance Round-Trip: 2.1 miles

Estimated Hiking Time: 1.7 hours

Cautions: While this is over mostly gentle terrain, the distance may cause youngsters to tire if they aren't used to hiking.

Trail Directions: Start on the crushed-limestone road that departs to the south from the Education Center parking lot. The first .25 mile is a quick stretch along the road **[1]**, which is also used for bicycling. Early in the morning and in the evening, watch for deer feeding in the fields to the right. Turn left off the road at the mowed-grass path **[2]**. When the path forks, go left. This is a good place to watch for birds. During various times of the year, chickadees, cedar waxwings, cardinals, and brown creepers call this area home. Take the first right off this path and head downhill to cross over Intermittent Creek (.4 mi.) **[3]**. As the name implies, sometimes this creek has water and sometimes not.

The meadow skirts the edge of Havenwoods, parallel to North Sherman Boulevard. Look up while walking. Red-tailed hawks and kestrels may be seen hunting the fields. There are young trees scattered in the grassland. Someday this trail will lead through a forest. Follow the trail through the grass and flowers, cross over a trail leading down to Sherman, and continue on your trail as it turns west. Recross the creek bed. On hot summer days, look for butterflies among the purple bergamot.

When you come to the limestone road, turn left **[4]** and then left again **[5]** at the forks. As the road curves right, you are walking parallel to the Wisconsin and Southern Railroad. The roadbed was built in the 1850s, and since then the right-of-way has remained relatively undisturbed. Over the years, a wide diversity of trees, shrubs, and wildflowers have crowded into this forgotten space.

In the open area to your right is Wild Goose Pond (1.2 mi.) **[6]**. If lucky, you might see and hear bobolinks calling in the springtime. Next, enter a cool "tunnel" made of trees. This comes as a welcome break on a hot summer day. A single tree can produce the cooling effect of 10 room-sized air conditioners operating 20 hours a day.

Just before crossing the bridge over Lincoln Creek (1.6 mi.) **[7]**, turn to the right down the slope to the grass path. At the first fork, take a left. This is a good place to get away from it all. As you walk down the path parallel to the creek, the city sounds are filtered out. It's easy to forget that you are in the heart of a large metropolitan area. In fall and winter, take a close look at the trees. Long-eared owls are often seen here by careful observers. The owls blend in perfectly, so take your time looking.

Take a right at the fork and follow the trail up the slope (1.9 mi.) **[8]**. The trail curves right and continues to twist through this area. When you emerge, you see the Education Center to the east. Approaching the building, notice the gardens on the left (2 mi.) **[9]**. The unfenced gardens on the eastern edge are demonstration plots maintained by the University of Wisconsin Extension master gardeners. Visit the yard area just behind the gardens for helpful hints on maintaining yards in earth-friendly ways.

—*Beth Mittermaier*

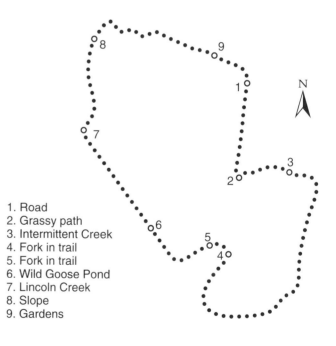

1. Road
2. Grassy path
3. Intermittent Creek
4. Fork in trail
5. Fork in trail
6. Wild Goose Pond
7. Lincoln Creek
8. Slope
9. Gardens

51. Cofrin Memorial Arboretum

- See limestone outcroppings of the Niagara Escarpment.
- Stroll along the cold waters of Lake Michigan.
- Follow the winding trails through forest and meadows.

Arboretum Information

The arboretum has 290 acres encircling the University of Wisconsin-Green Bay campus. Preserving natural communities and developing others are the main goal of the facility. More than 50 bird species permanently live within the park boundaries, along with a wide variety of other animals from rabbits to white-tailed deer. Flowering plant species include bloodroot, marsh marigold, wood anemone, and trillium.

The eastern boundary of the arboretum is the Niagara Escarpment—part of the outcropping of ancient limestone that extends across Wisconsin for 200 miles. West of the arboretum are the waters of Green Bay, with more than .5 miles of shoreline. Mahon Creek forms the southern boundary as it winds its way through the mixed hardwood forest. The system has two main trails: a bike trail of 4.1 miles and the 4.6-mile footpath.

Directions: Take I-43 south to exit 185, or take Highway 172 east and then I-43 north to exit 185. Drive in the Sturgeon Bay/Algoma exit lane and follow Highways 54/57 a short distance to the first exit (University Avenue/Nicolet Road). Take Nicolet Road to the campus. The Nicolet entrance is the first gateway to the right. Just inside the entrance is a small gravel area with a station featuring an oversized map station of the campus and its walkways. Park here to hike the trails, or take the second entrance to the right (the main entrance) and pay $1 to use the campus parking lot.

Hours Open: Dawn to dusk, daily, year round.

Facilities: On campus, there are public telephones, rest rooms, and food-vending machines. Souvenirs of the University of Wisconsin-Green Bay are available at the Phoenix Bookstore, and a nearby golf course is open to the public. Maps of the arboretum trails are at the information desk on the ground floor of the Cofrin Library through its circle entrance.

Permits and Rules: Hunting, trapping, and harassment of wildlife are not allowed. Collecting of plants, use of motorized vehicles on or off the trails, and pets are prohibited.

Further Information: Contact Director, Cofrin Arboretum, University of Wisconsin-Green Bay, Green Bay, WI 54301-7001; 414-465-2277.

Other Points of Interest

Pamperin Park, within metropolitan Green Bay, is the largest developed park in the county's system. Duck Creek flows through the center of the site, crossed by a picturesque suspension bridge. There are picnic areas, baseball diamonds, walking paths, and other amenities. Call the Brown County Park Department, 414-448-4466, for more information.

At 83 miles, the **Mountain Bay Trail** is the longest hiking/biking trail in Wisconsin. The pathway runs through Brown, Shawano, and Marathon Counties. It starts in Green Bay's Memorial Park and travels east of Wausau through farm country, subdivisions, factory districts, and woodland. There are access points in Anston, Pulaski, Shawano, Hatley, Ringle, Kelly, and other towns. A section of the trail near Bonduel is used by Amish farmers and their wagons, thus avoiding the busy State Highway 29. Call the Marathon County Park Department, 715-847-5235, for further information.

Park Trails

Scottwood Entrance Trail 🥾—1.6 miles—This trail moves through meadow and woods along the north side of the campus off Scottwood Drive (County Highway I). The link is not a loop, but is a continuation of the White Cedar Trail and paved section connecting to Upper Ledge and Ledge Creek Ponds on the southeast and the Green Bay area trail system on the west. Its conclusion is adjacent to the golf course at the Shorewood parking lot.

Arboretum Center Trails 🥾—1.7 miles—The trailhead is at the center buildings, where there is a parking lot. The trail passes Bay Shore Pond. At the east end of the system, hikers can link up with the grassy path to the Bay Beach Wildlife Sanctuary (see park #52) to the west. Be aware that the gate there is open only until 4:30 P.M., when the sanctuary trails are closed. To get to the Wildflower Trail on South Circle Drive, either walk under the bridge or cross the street.

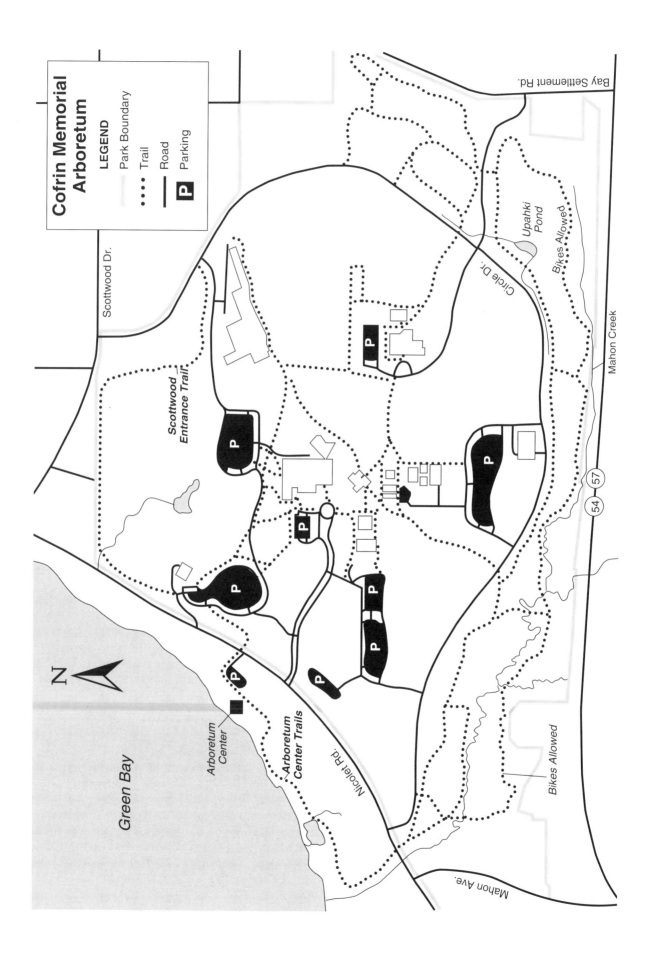

Cofrin Memorial Arboretum

LEGEND

- Park Boundary
- ⋯⋯ Trail
- ▬ Road
- P Parking

Scottwood Dr.

Scottwood Entrance Trail

Green Bay

N

Arboretum Center

Arboretum Center Trails

Nicolet Rd.

Mahon Ave.

Circle Dr.

Upahki Pond

Bikes Allowed

Mahon Creek

Bay Settlement Rd.

54 57

Bikes Allowed

Wildflower Trail 👢👢

Distance Round-Trip: 1.5 miles

Estimated Hiking Time: 1.5 hours

Cautions: The trails are supposed to be covered with wood chips, but rains can take away some of the ground cover.

Trail Directions: Park in the lot on South Circle Drive, at the Nicolet entrance to the university campus. The trail starts there immediately.

Leave the lot and walk south through an open area **[1]** toward the Mahon Woods. Cross the bridge over shallow Mahon Creek (.2 mi.) **[2]** and continue south through the mixed hardwood forest consisting primarily of oak trees. There are several low hills, but they are easily traversed. Follow the path when it turns east (.3 mi.) and walk through a section of the woods thick with red maple and basswood among the oak **[3].** The young trees are scattered in this area, with subsequent open spaces that will eventually be shaded as the trees grow.

Enter what is call the Old Fields section of the trail, which goes along on a fairly straight line with only a few curves. The next major attraction is Tadpole Pond on the right (.9 mi.) **[4],** with an observation dome at 1 mi. **[5].** From this point, you look out over Upahki Pond. Continue on to the road leading to the campus from the Bay Settlement entrance. Don't cross the road, but meet the paved path there and continue around the top of Upahki Pond. The trail runs parallel to South Circle Drive adjacent to the campus.

Walk along the paved road to Prairie Pond (2.1 mi.), where there is a link trail **[6]** through the woods to the left to connect with the wood-chip trail taken previously. There is also a paved path to the right, crossing South Circle Drive to the campus.

Keep walking along the pathway and meet another wood-chip trail intersection (2.3 mi.) **[7]** to the left. You can take that along the banks of Mahon Creek or stay on the paved trail. Both go back to the trailhead parking lot.

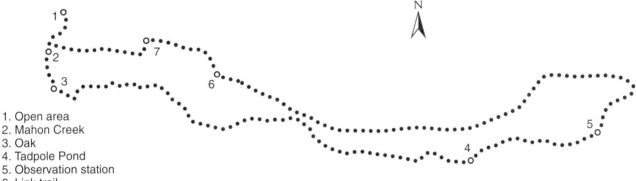

1. Open area
2. Mahon Creek
3. Oak
4. Tadpole Pond
5. Observation station
6. Link trail
7. Wood-chip trail

White Cedar Trail 🥾

Distance Round-Trip: 2 miles

Estimated Hiking Time: 1.3 hours

Cautions: Bring insect repellent in damp weather.

Trail Directions: Park in the main lot at the Bay Settlement entrance drive off Bay Settlement Road on the east side of the campus. The trailhead is in the southeast corner of the lot.

Depart the parking lot **[1]** and pick up the wood-chip trail where it links to the paved trail (.1 mi.) **[2]**. The wood-chip trail moves across an open meadow on the Niagara Escarpment before progressing into an oak and maple grove with a number of birches nearby (.2 mi.) **[3]**. The trail moves along parallel to Bay Settlement Road. Pass through a clearing (.5 mi.) **[4]** and go around an arboretum parking lot and map just before reaching the observation tower (.6 mi.) **[5]**.

Ascend the tower and look out over the campus to the west; you can get a bird's-eye view of the surrounding woods and the waters of Green Bay in the distance. Coming down from the tower, take a short loop walk (.7 mi.) **[6]** straight ahead through more woods. Return to the intersection, turn right, and pick up the paved trail. Going straight ahead leads to the campus, but turn right and walk along the path to the Upper Ledge Creek Pond (1 mi.) **[7]**. You cross between two sections of the pond and walk through more oak and maple woods at the top of Ledge Creek Pond, which is connected to the other pond by a shallow stream.

After studying the waterfowl and turtles in the pond, turn around and retrace your steps to the junction of the paved and asphalt trails. This time, continue back to the parking lot via the paved trail. To the right, across a field, is the University's weather station.

—Linda Gray

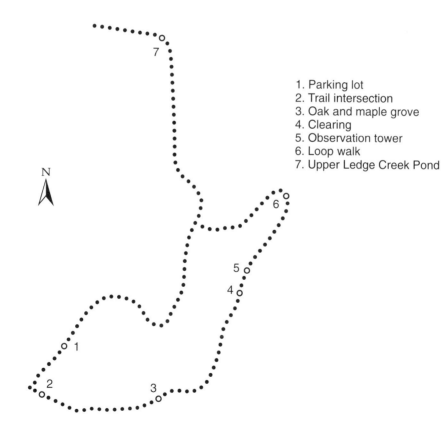

1. Parking lot
2. Trail intersection
3. Oak and maple grove
4. Clearing
5. Observation tower
6. Loop walk
7. Upper Ledge Creek Pond

52. Bay Beach Wildlife Sanctuary

- Learn about wildlife rehabilitation.
- Try hands-on exhibits in the nationally recognized Nature Center.
- Wander through the Whistling Wings art gallery.

Park Information

In 1929, the city of Green Bay bought 250 acres for the purpose of building a golf course. But in 1935, area residents came up with the idea of using the site as a wildlife refuge. Famed conservationist Aldo Leopold assisted in the project's planning. The Green Bay city board gave five acres as an initial step in the project in 1936. The first pond was dug by hand to serve as a resting place for injured waterfowl.

Today, the sanctuary is the city's largest park, spreading over 700 acres. Each year the facility receives more than 2,000 injured and orphaned animals. After rehabilitation, they are set free in the wild, or if unable to survive in the wild, kept in the sanctuary or some other nature center or zoo. The sanctuary is also home to some 3,000 geese that stay year round.

The sanctuary has 11 hiking trails, with an approximate total of 5.8 miles along Green Bay and through the reserve. The terrain ranges from lowland forest to grassland and marsh. At the Woodland Building, see an indoor and outdoor wildlife-viewing area that includes wolves, an otter, flying squirrels, and amphibians. The Observation Building has an animal rehab unit, with a live Birds of Prey exhibit and a feeding station.

Directions: The sanctuary can be reached via I-43 South. Get off the freeway at exit 187. At the bottom of the ramp, turn to the north on East Shore Drive; after stopping, proceed through the four-way stop sign. The park is on the right.

Hours Open: The sanctuary is open from 8 A.M. to 8 P.M., April 15 to September 14; and from 8 A.M. to 5 P.M., September 15 to April 14. There are varying hours in the summer for the wildlife sanctuary, wildlife habitat, Observation Building, Woodland Building, and office. Trails are open from 8 A.M. to 4:30 P.M. in the summer.

Facilities: Art gallery, rehabilitation facilities, picnic areas, gift shop, lecture rooms, hiking trails.

Permits and Rules: Do not chase the geese or other animals. Feed only the geese and ducks. No pets allowed. Walk bikes on paths and trails. Do not pick the flowers or plants. Keep off the lagoons; no swimming is permitted. No alcohol. Dispose of trash properly and recycle when possible. Admission is free but donations are accepted.

Further Information: Contact Bay Beach Wildlife Sanctuary, 1660 East Shore Drive, Green Bay, WI 54302; 414-391-3671.

Other Points of Interest

Bay Beach Amusement Park is two blocks north of the sanctuary. The sanctuary offers horse-drawn wagon rides to the amusement park with its 13 rides, fast-food concessions, picnic shelters, rest rooms, volleyball courts, and other amenities. There is no admission fee, but rides cost 10 cents. Call 414-391-3671 for more information.

Bayshore County Park (see park #6) is 15 miles north of Green Bay, off State Highway 57. The park, which is open from May 1 to October 15, has 100 campsites and a boat launch. For more information, call 414-448-4466.

In Kaukauna, the **1000 Islands Environmental Center** has 240 acres of hiking paths, ski trails, and woodlands tucked along the Fox River. The center offers interpretive programs and events throughout the year. The facility is open from 8 A.M. to 4 P.M. daily, year round. For more information, call the center at 414-766-4733. Kaukauna is 20 miles south of Green Bay.

Acres for Recreation is a popular picnic and swimming area on Shawano Lake in Shawano. A nature preserve, hiking, snowmobiling, and cross-country ski trails, and trapshooting are on-site. The site is open year round. Call 715-526-6055 for more information. The nearby **Wolf River** has numerous county and local parks from which to launch a canoe. Shawano is 40 miles northwest of Green Bay.

Sanctuary Trails

Distance Round-Trip: 5.8 miles

Estimated Hiking Time: 4.5 hours

Cautions: Stay on the trails because the ground can be wet.

Trail Directions: All trails branch out from or connect to other trails, linking the parking lot to the Nature Center. Since most of the trails are short, any combination is possible for a longer trek. Thus, no mileage figures are given below. Most of the paths are surfaced, so they are generally accessible to people with physical disabilities.

Start with the .2-mi. Chipmunk Trail [1] near the entrance to the Nature Center. It runs toward another parking lot across East Shore Drive. At the end of the Chipmunk Trail, cross the parking lot and turn right to reach the .2-mi. Habitrek Trail [2]. This trail leads to the Woodland Building [3], where you can pick up the main hiking trail to the left or continue to the Habitrek to the right. The trail is paved up to the deer habitat [4]. It leads to the Grassland Habitat and the observation tower.

You can go straight on the Habitrek Trail or turn right onto the .2-mi. Fawn Trail [5]. The Fawn Trail leads back to the Woodland Building. However, if you continue straight ahead, you come out on a paved road at the end of the trail. To go to the Nature Center and parking lot, turn right. To continue on more trails, turn left and proceed past the steel gates. Keep going until you come to a post with a yellow marker pointing to a narrow grassy path on the right side of the road.

This is the .7-mi. Hussong Trail [6]. A wooden bridge [7] passes through head-high cattails. At the end of the bridge, bear right to continue. This brings you back to the paved road via a loop. Or you can turn left for a more direct route back to the road. Then go straight across the road to the marked path ahead [8]. This leads you onto a wooden walkway and across another bridge with a seating board. At the end of the bridge turn left and return to the road.

The .4 mi. Red Fox Trail [9] forks to the left of the Woodland Building as it leaves the Habitrek Trail. Where the footpath divides, turn left to continue on the trail. Turn right to head for the paved road or the Hussong Trail. The Red Fox pathway continues until it reaches Danz Avenue [10]. Then enter through another gate to hike along the .3-mi. Squirrel Trail [11]. The rest of the trails here overlap, making about another 3.7-mi. trek. After the Squirrel are the Rabbit [12], Deer [13], Raccoon [14], and Badger [15] Trails. On the left side of the trails is East Shore Drive, with the rolling waters of Green Bay just beyond.

If you return to the Nature Center after exploring the western end of the sanctuary, you can also catch the paved .2-mi. Web of Life Trail [16] that begins at the back of the Nature Center. Pass the Duck Shack [17]. When the road forks, turn to the left. Just past the Duck Shack is an enclosed prairie habitat. A bridge [18] crosses the lagoon, with the trail continuing to the Rehabilitation/Observation Building. Retrace your steps to the Nature Center, then take the Chipmunk Trail to return to your car.

—Linda Gray

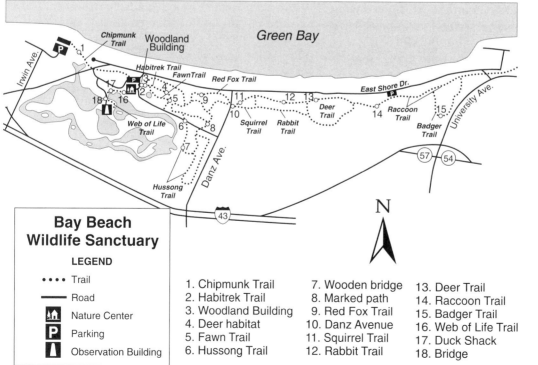

Bay Beach Wildlife Sanctuary

LEGEND

- •••• Trail
- —— Road
- Nature Center
- P Parking
- Observation Building

1. Chipmunk Trail
2. Habitrek Trail
3. Woodland Building
4. Deer habitat
5. Fawn Trail
6. Hussong Trail
7. Wooden bridge
8. Marked path
9. Red Fox Trail
10. Danz Avenue
11. Squirrel Trail
12. Rabbit Trail
13. Deer Trail
14. Raccoon Trail
15. Badger Trail
16. Web of Life Trail
17. Duck Shack
18. Bridge

53. Lake Geneva

- Travel through yards of stately mansions and admire the gardens and architecture.
- Feel the fresh lake breeze while hiking a paved 8-mile route.
- Stop for ice cream, take in an art show, and walk through woods all on the same trek.

City Information

Lake Geneva has been a resort community since the early 1870s. Wealthy Chicagoans came to the area, attracted by the fishing, hunting, and other recreational opportunities. The 1871 opening of the Chicago and North Western rail line to the village made it more accessible. Almost immediately, summer mansions were constructed throughout the vicinity.

The community is sometimes called "the Newport of the Midwest" because of its recreational opportunities. Like many resort areas, it has campgrounds, golf courses, shops, restaurants, and galleries catering to the tourist. In the winter, cross-country skiers, snowmobilers, and ice-fishing fans enjoy the lake area.

Lake Geneva is the second deepest in Wisconsin at 142 feet and covers 5,263 acres. It is 7.5 miles long from east to west and 2 miles wide from Williams Bay on the north to the south shore. The Potawatomi nation migrated here in the 1600s from northern Wisconsin to get away from encroaching Sauk, Fox, and Menominees. The Native Americans called it Kishwauketoe, which means "clear water" or "lake of the sparkling water." The first recorded white sighting of the lake was in 1831. In 1834, surveyor John Brink named the lake after his hometown of Geneva, New York.

Directions: The city of Lake Geneva is 1 mile south of U.S. Highway 12 in southern Wisconsin, about a 45-minute drive from Milwaukee and one hour from Chicago's northern suburbs.

Hours Open: Dawn to dusk year round.

Facilities: Restaurants, shops, accommodations, parks, and campgrounds.

Permits and Rules: No alcohol, firearms, fires.

Further Information: Contact Lake Geneva Convention and Visitors Bureau, 201 Wrigley Drive, Lake Geneva, WI 53147; 800-345-1020 or 414-248-4416.

Other Points of Interest

From early May to late summer, take an 8-mile shoreline walk and then enjoy a **Sunday brunch cruise** on Lake Geneva. The Geneva Lake Cruise Line offers a narrated tour of the shoreline sights while presenting a champagne brunch. Hikers depart by 8:45 A.M. from the cruise line's Riviera Docks in Lake Geneva and then take the footpath to Williams Bay. There they are picked up by the *Belle of the Lake* for the cruise. Reservations are necessary. Passengers who don't want to walk can join the cruise at 11 A.M.

The hiking/cruising package is also available from Monday through Saturday, but without the brunch. The brunch cruise costs $25.95 and hikers get a $3 discount. Call 800-558-5911.

Big Foot Beach State Park, on the shore of Lake Geneva, is open from mid-May to November. The 272-acre park is within the Lake Geneva city limits and has wooded campsites, 2,200 feet of sand beach, and picnic sites. Call 414-248-2528 for more information.

Yerkes Observatory in Williams Bay, on the west shore of Lake Geneva, is open for tours. The facility has the world's largest refracting telescope. For details, call 414-245-5555.

City Trails

Chapin Road to Williams Bay 👢👢—3.5 miles—This trek takes about 1 to 1.5 hours along Lake Geneva's north shore. Hikers pass a house called Glen Fern, built in 1911. It is easily identifiable with its huge stone arches in front. Another house on the route was built by the Elwood family, who were among the earliest developers of barbed wire. At Cedar Point, hikers can see the Yerkes Observatory dome. Cedar Point itself is a subdivision built in 1923, thus one of the oldest in the country. Look for the statue of a Potawatomi woman made by artist Doug Henderson.

Williams Bay to Fontana 👢—3.5 miles—Park at Edgewater Beach in Williams Bay and walk south along the northwest shore of Lake Geneva. One of the first sights is a cluster of small cabins and a large main building typical of early resorts in the area. A good fishing locale is off Conference Point. This link of the trail system goes through the 150-acre campus of George Williams College educational center.

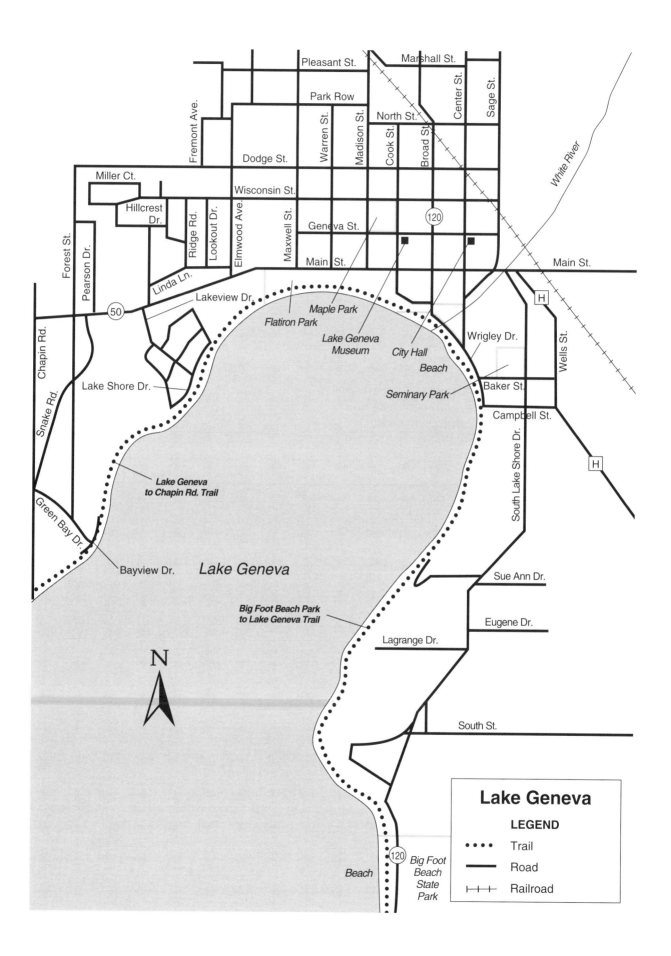

Trek I—Lake Geneva to Chapin Road 👢👢

Distance One-Way: 3.5 miles

Estimated Hiking Time: 1.5 hours

Cautions: Stay on the path and don't trespass on private property. Since this is a one-way trek, it is wise to park a second vehicle at the far end of the route. Parking is available in the lot of Foley's Bar & Grill, at the corner of Chapin Road and Highway 50. This is .6 mi. from the path but out of the way of traffic. Without this return ride, hikers must continue walking around the lake or retrace their steps to the original trailhead in town. There is also parking along side streets.

Trail Directions: Start at the corner of Wrigley Drive and the Lake Geneva beach downtown. Walk south on the sidewalk. There are free parking lots near some of the shops, with nonmetered areas west of Madison Street. To save a few steps, however, drop some change in the five-hour meters along Wrigley Drive to Main Street. Parking along this stretch is a problem on summer weekends because of the tourist traffic.

The Wrigley Drive neighborhood **[1]** offers a beach, boat rentals, cruise line docks, swank and casual restaurants, bars, and shops. Walk toward the maple-shaded Lake Geneva public library (.2 mi.) **[2]**, a low stone prairie-style building designed by a student of famed architect Frank Lloyd Wright in 1954. Throughout the summer the lawn of the library is the scene of arts and crafts fairs and various local festivals. In the winter a skating rink is erected to the south of the building. Across the street are bed and breakfasts, craft shops, and galleries (.3 mi.) **[3]**. The first major historical house you will pass is Maple Lawn (.4 mi.) **[4]**, identifiable by its blue shutters. The home was built in 1870, making it the oldest estate on the lake according to local historians. The Lake Geneva Manor subdivision is next (.7 mi.) **[5]**. The houses sit on the site of an old mansion built in 1879. The property was originally owned by Levi Zeiter, who cofounded the firm that became Marshall Field and Company.

Look for the Victorian boathouse to the left (.9 mi.) **[6]**. It is one of the few structures remaining from an estate called Snug Harbor. The property was owned by John Borden, an arctic explorer and member of the wealthy Borden dairy-products family. The Covenant Harbor Bible Camp is now on the site. At the conclu-

sion of a brick path is Blacktoft (1.1 mi.) **[7]**, a home with three chimneys. Next comes Northwoodside (1.4 mi.) **[8]**. This house is identifiable by its fancy porch railings. The home was eventually owned by Olaf Teavander, the inventor of tab caps for milk bottles.

At 1.9 mi. is a brick house (1.9 mi.) **[9]** that was part of the old Wrigley estate, where the chewing-gum magnate and his family lived. Along the lake is the Wrigleys' original boathouse **[10]**. Look for the crane painted on the side of the building. The family kept their speedboats inside, one of which was powered by a 600-horsepower Curtiss-Wright aircraft engine.

You continue passing homes of other prominent business leaders such as E.F. Swift, son of the well-known meat-packer (2.3 mi.) **[11]**. Look for the white stucco house with the red tile roof. One of the prettiest houses on this hike is Wadsworth Hall (2.5 mi.) **[12]**, built in 1905 for Norman W. Harris of Harris Trust. The next house (2.9 mi.) **[13]** has a huge pipe organ inside, according to those lucky enough to be invited in. The House in the Woods stands at the 3-mi. mark **[14]**. This was built under a circus tent during the winter of 1905.

Just before the end of this trail link is a green house with a red roof (3.1 mi.) **[15]**. It was owned by Martin Ryerson, whose fortune stemmed from the fact he had one of the few surviving lumber yards in Chicago after the city's great fire. The last house on the route was originally a boathouse (3.5 mi.) **[16]**. At this point you'll end the walk on Chapin Road.

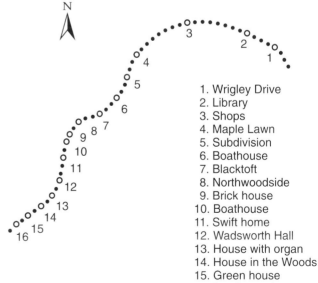

1. Wrigley Drive
2. Library
3. Shops
4. Maple Lawn
5. Subdivision
6. Boathouse
7. Blacktoft
8. Northwoodside
9. Brick house
10. Boathouse
11. Swift home
12. Wadsworth Hall
13. House with organ
14. House in the Woods
15. Green house
16. Boathouse home

Trek II—Big Foot Beach State Park to Lake Geneva

Distance One-Way: 2.1 miles

Estimated Hiking Time: 45 minutes

Cautions: Stay on the trail and avoid walking across private lawns. A park vehicle admission sticker is required. This trail can became rough and hilly, skirting the edge of the lake on a narrow track. There are several deep gullies to cross. The path can be very slippery when wet. There are no guardrails even where the path cuts close to the water's edge.

Trail Directions: The park is 1.5 miles south of Lake Geneva's downtown on State Highway 120. Park in any of the park's lots.

Walk along the path leading from the entrance to the park **[1],** which was named after a Potawatomi chief. His people were the last Native Americans to inhabit the area around the lake. In the Treaty of 1833, the nation gave up all its land east of the Mississippi and was told to move to a Kansas reservation. In 1836, the Potawatomi near Lake Geneva still had not left their ancestral homes and were forced out at gunpoint. The land was then sold by the government for $1.25 an acre. The park site eventually came into the hands of the Maytags of washing machine fame. Their home was razed in 1957, and the state park was developed as the only one in the state within city limits.

Look for the long sand beach **[2]** and the eight-acre Ceylon Lagoon **[3],** built by Maytag's son as a miniature of Lake Geneva. North of the beach, pass through a black iron gate (.3 mi.) **[4]** and continue walking along wooded Maytag Point. Throughout the area, woodchucks and foxes can sometimes be seen, as well as white-tailed deer.

Walking past the Vista del Lago condominiums (.4 mi.) **[5],** you can look across the lake and see the community of Fontana. On this hilly up-and-down path, pass Fair Oaks, a gray house built in 1889 (.9 mi.) **[6].**

Stone Manor (1.4 mi.) **[7]** is the largest mansion on Lake Geneva and once housed a girls' private school and a restaurant. In the 1960s, the massive gray stone building was sold for back taxes. The place has subsequently been divided into condominiums. The lawn has a tennis court, and there is a swimming pool on the roof. You can get a good look at the front of the building on an alternative walk along Lake Drive instead of on the path along the lake edge. On that route, you need to peer over a high stone fence and look down a wide grassy grade to the building.

Watch out for several deep ravines (1.5-1.8 mi.) **[8]** with extremely steep sides as you continue walking north. This is a wooded area along the shoreline, with hillsides sloping up to the back lawns of the houses. On this link, the trail often degenerates into a dirt track and the foliage obscures the view of homes. The walk ends as a flat gravel path at Wrigley Drive (2.1 mi.) **[9].** Hikers pass through an opening in a low brick wall, about two blocks from the Lake Geneva Beach.

—Ellen Burling, Harold Freistad of Geneva Lake Cruise Line

—Laura Lima, Chris Hawver, and Pat Groh of Walk, Talk and Gawk

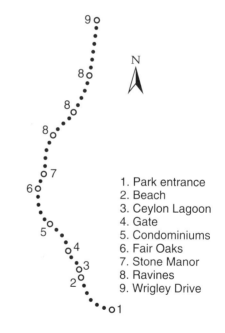

1. Park entrance
2. Beach
3. Ceylon Lagoon
4. Gate
5. Condominiums
6. Fair Oaks
7. Stone Manor
8. Ravines
9. Wrigley Drive

54. Schmeeckle Reserve

- Visit the Wisconsin Conservation Hall of Fame.
- Reflect on the environment while strolling along the "reflections path."
- Link with the Green Circle Tour, a 24-mile hiking/biking loop around the city of Stevens Point.

Park Information

The site's 200 acres are used by the University of Wisconsin-Stevens Point as a research and teaching resource. Environmental study plots are tucked into its far northwest corner and are not accessed by any of the public trails. The preserve's main building has extensive displays on environmental subjects, including several large dioramas. One of the exhibits depicts a game warden raiding an illegal deer-hunting camp in the 1930s.

Schmeeckle Reserve is also home to Wisconsin's Conservation Hall of Fame, honoring numerous state residents who have contributed to environmentalism over the years. A wall lined with plaques overlooks the nature area in back of the main building.

Directions: Stevens Point is located on U.S. Highway 51, in the center of Wisconsin. It is 107 miles north of Madison. The entrance to Schmeeckle Reserve is on Northpoint Drive on the north side of Stevens Point. From the city's downtown, drive north on Business Highway 51 and turn right to the reserve grounds.

Hours Open: The Visitor Center is open from 8 A.M. to 5 P.M. Monday through Friday, from 10 A.M. to 5 P.M. Saturday, and from noon to 5 P.M. Sunday.

Facilities: Visitors can enjoy boating, walking/running trails, 19-station fitness trail, wildlife observation, biking, and fishing.

Permits and Rules: A valid Wisconsin fishing license is required for angling. No fires.

Further Information: Contact Schmeeckle Reserve, University of Wisconsin-Stevens Point, Stevens Point, WI 54481; 715-346-4992.

Other Points of Interest

The **Green Circle Tour** skirts Stevens Point's environs, covering 24 miles of pathway for hiking, biking, jogging, and cross-country skiing. The trail starts downtown, along the rolling Wisconsin River. Along the way are natural and historic sites, restaurants, and other amenities. The project was funded by the community and dedicated in 1996.

There are numerous attractions in the Stevens Point area, including the **Stevens Point Brewery** and **Sentry Insurance.** The University of Wisconsin-Stevens Point hosts the **Spud Bowl** football championship each autumn. The name is a tongue-in-cheek nod toward the humble potato, a major crop on the surrounding farms. There are also many rural back roads outside the city for **biking** adventures. **Canoeing** is a popular sport on the Wisconsin River.

Schmeeckle Reserve Nature Trail 🥾

Distance Round-Trip: 1.5 miles (There are actually four to six small loops within the reserve, including the fitness trail, depending on how a hiker counts intersecting links.)

Estimated Hiking Time: 1 hour

Cautions: Watch for traffic along Michigan Avenue, which bisects the reserve. The trails are also used by joggers and bikers.

Trail Directions: A parking lot is on the east side of the reserve, accessed from Northpoint Drive across the street from the Sentry Golf Course. The lot is about .5 miles east of Business Highway 51, which runs along part of the preserve's western perimeter.

Access to the trail is also possible at Maria Drive, on the reserve's south side near Lake Joanis. In addition, hikers can enter the trail from Michigan Avenue, which cuts through the center of Schmeeckle, and from the Green Circle, entered either from Northpoint Drive west of Michigan Avenue or from Maria Drive near a shelter house adjacent to the fitness trail.

An information kiosk **[1]** is at the parking lot, with a carved wooden relief map detailing the trails. Walk along the path west to the Visitor Center **[2]**, where you can pick up the trail from the facility's back door or walk around behind the building. Hikers can also enter the trail from the parking lot, crossing a small prairie site and entering a grove.

Begin a hike by touring the reserve's Visitor Center with its numerous exhibits about the wildlife and flora of Portage County.

From the building, walk to the south along the bark trail through pine groves and stands of maples (.2 mi.) **[3]**. The main path is a gently rolling .25-mi. Reflections Trail that has benches along the way near markers with quotes from famous environmentalists and outdoors enthusiasts (.3-.6 mi.).

Wetlands are between the trail and Michigan Avenue to the west. At .4 mi., hikers pass a frog pond **[4]** where the bullfrogs sing a loud spring chorus. The path now loops back to the building (.5 mi.) **[5]**. Another trail **[6]** leaves the reflections path and moves to the east through woodlands, with other branches looping around Lake Joanis. Before taking this trail to the east, continue north to the visitor's center **[2]** to complete the Reflections Trail loop. Then backtrack to the trail intersection **[6]** and continue your hike through the rest of the park. This path passes by the northern edge of Lake Joanis **[7]**, traverses more wetlands via a boardwalk **[8]**, crosses Michigan Avenue **[9]**, and meanders through the pine, oak, and maple woods before coming back across the street and to the center building **[2]**.

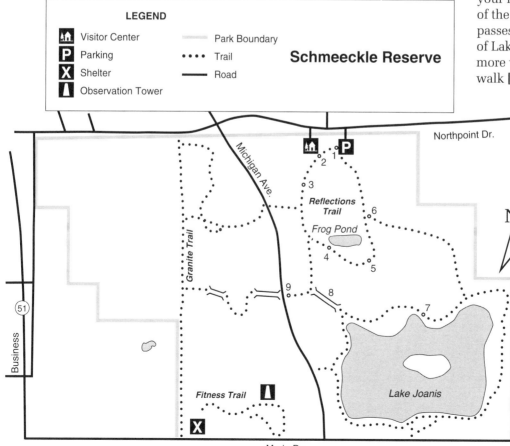

LEGEND

🏠	Visitor Center	░░░	Park Boundary
P	Parking	••••	Trail
X	Shelter	———	Road
⛰	Observation Tower		

Schmeeckle Reserve

Northpoint Dr.

Michigan Ave.

Granite Trail

Reflections Trail

Frog Pond

N

51

Business

Fitness Trail

Lake Joanis

Maria Dr.

1. Information kiosk
2. Visitor Center
3. Pine/maples
4. Frog pond
5. Path loops north
6. Trail intersection
7. Lake Joanis
8. Boardwalk
9. Michigan Avenue

55. Green Circle Tour

- Sample nature's wildlife in a small-city setting.
- Take a quick hike without traveling miles to reach a trailhead.
- Meet interesting people from all walks of life who also enjoy hiking.

City Information

Stevens Point was founded after a strip of land along the Wisconsin River was ceded to the federal government by the Menominee nation in 1836. The town was founded by lumbermen and was named for one of them, George Stevens. He built a shanty on the riverbank to store materials for shipment upstream, but he never actually lived in Stevens Point.

Eventually the city became a hub of the lumber industry, with mills and complementary businesses serving the needs of loggers. As the woods disappeared, the economy diversified.

Potatoes and other vegetables grow well in the area's sandy soil, so Polish, German, and Scandinavian émigrés found the area to their liking. Numerous farms are still under the same families after four generations. Amish farmers also live in the vicinity. University students and staff represent many ethnic groups. Hmong and Laotian immigrants are the community's latest arrivals, providing an exciting new look to the city.

The city is home to the University of Wisconsin-Stevens Point, one of the state's major university campuses offering degree programs in natural resources, business, and paper science. Sentry Insurance, Consolidated Papers, vegetable-processing plants, food distribution centers, and publishing companies are now the community's backbone industries. The city is also a popular tourist destination, hosting the National Wellness Conference, the American Suzuki Institute, Badger State Winter Games, Wisconsin Special Olympics, triathlons, the world's largest trivia contest, and other special events.

Stevens Point has a well-used 24-mile nature trail, the Green Circle, one of the few such trails in the United States that encircle a city. Nearly 90 percent of it is a pathway in wooded areas and along shaded riverbanks. There is a sense of history as one walks the trail, recalling the pine forests, Native American camps, pioneer settlements, and lore of the river men on the Wisconsin and Plover Rivers. The trail cost $600,000 and was dedicated in early June of 1996.

The Green Circle includes the university's popular Schmeeckle Preserve, which features its own nature trail; the Wisconsin Conservation Hall of Fame; Lake Joanis; a nature center; and leisure areas.

Directions: Stevens Point is located in central Wisconsin, 110 miles north of Madison on U.S. Highway 51. Minneapolis/St. Paul is 195 miles to the west, and Green Bay 90 miles to the east.

Facilities: The city has numerous restaurants, plus hotels and bed and breakfasts, parks, athletic stadiums, camping, parks, shopping, and arts facilities.

Further Information: Contact Stevens Point Convention and Visitors Bureau, 23 Park Ridge Drive, Stevens Point, WI 54481; 715-344-2556.

Other Points of Interest

The **Stevens Point Brewery,** 2617 Water Street, is one of the oldest independent breweries remaining in Wisconsin. It offers regular tours at 11 A.M. and 1:30 P.M. Monday through Saturday during the summer, and 11 A.M. Monday through Friday during the off-season. Product samples are part of the fun. Every September during the Spud Bowl football classic at the University of Wisconsin-Stevens Point, the brewery issues a collector's can containing a smooth potato beer. A dollar from the sale of each of these cans goes to the university for scholarships.

Boating and canoeing are available on the **Wisconsin, Tomorrow, Plover,** and **Little Eau Pleine Rivers,** all of which flow through the Stevens Point area. Sailing and sailboat races are regular features on **Lake DuBay,** 13 miles north of Stevens Point. There are more than 36 miles of groomed cross-country ski trails in or near the city, including the **Wisconsin River Country Club, Schmeeckle Reserve** (see park #54), **Iverson Park, Plover River Trail, Lake Emily Trail, Jordan Park, Wolf Lake Trail,** and **Standing Rocks.**

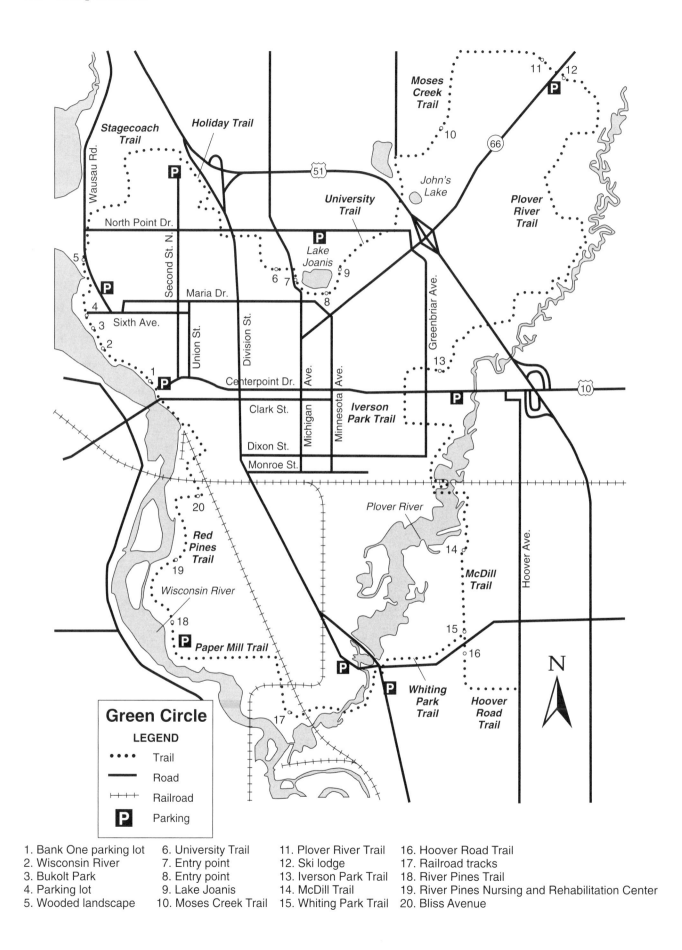

Green Circle

LEGEND

•••• Trail

——— Road

╫╫╫ Railroad

P Parking

1. Bank One parking lot
2. Wisconsin River
3. Bukolt Park
4. Parking lot
5. Wooded landscape
6. University Trail
7. Entry point
8. Entry point
9. Lake Joanis
10. Moses Creek Trail
11. Plover River Trail
12. Ski lodge
13. Iverson Park Trail
14. McDill Trail
15. Whiting Park Trail
16. Hoover Road Trail
17. Railroad tracks
18. River Pines Trail
19. River Pines Nursing and Rehabilitation Center
20. Bliss Avenue

The Green Circle 👢👢

Distance One-Way: 24 miles

Estimated Hiking Time: Open

Cautions: All but three trail segments are open to both hiking and biking. Alternate bike routes are indicated by signs so that hikers may complete the circle. Two segments are asphalt, three are wood chip, and seven are crushed granite. The speed limit for bikers is 10 miles per hour, and bell or horn warnings are required. But, as always, stay alert for those few who stretch the rules.

Trail Directions: The trail brings together Stevens Point and its neighboring municipalities in Portage County. From the north or south on U.S. Highway 51, turn west on U.S. Highway 10. This highway becomes CenterPoint Drive as it nears the downtown.

Since there are almost a limitless number of entry points on the trail, no mileage figures from any single point are given for the Green Circle. There are 12 major segments, running from .9 mile to more than 4 miles. Each is marked with appropriate signs.

The chip trail meanders around Stevens Point through woodlands, along the Wisconsin and Plover Rivers, and around Lake Joanis. The trek is an easy bike loop, with many cyclists making the run in three to six hours. Hikers can make it in six to eight hours but probably want to divide their walk because of time. The trail crosses the Plover River and wetlands via bridges and boardwalks.

One of the best places to begin a trek along the Green Circle is at the western edge of downtown, just east of the CenterPoint Mall. The mall is part of the city's refurbished downtown, with many historic buildings and an open-air farmers' market during the growing season. Park at the Bank One lot at CenterPoint Drive and Crosby Avenue [1] just before State Highway 10 crosses the Wisconsin River.

The Chamber of Commerce is tucked into a small building along the picturesque river. A small duck pond outside the structure is to the north. Proceed north along the river [2] through Bukolt Park [3], where college students toss frisbees, parents picnic with kids, and elders stroll. Concerts are held throughout the summer and autumn in the park's open band shell.

From the park, proceed along the river, once a major route for log flotillas coming downstream to the area's giant mills. Millions of board feet of prime timber were harvested in the late 1800s through the 1920s in north and north central Wisconsin. At that time, the region's sawmills and paper mills employed thousands of workers. Today, the river here is mainly a power and recreation resource. There is another parking lot where Sixth Street dead-ends at the river [4].

The Stagecoach Trail now takes a series of dogleg jaunts north and east through forests and meadows inland [5] from the river. There is a .9-mi. section of crushed red granite (the Holiday Trail) from the southeast corner of the Zenoff Softball Park to near the Holiday Inn. The path then goes east on North Point Drive past Sentry Insurance to the University Trail [6].

In the university area, the trail moves through the heavily wooded Schmeeckle Reserve, named for the founder of the environmental studies program at the University of Wisconsin-Stevens Point. The University Trail section can be accessed in three locales: hikers can take the south side of North Point Drive [7] across from Sentry Insurance, enter at the northeast corner of Michigan Avenue and Maria Drive [8], or enter at the Schmeeckle Reserve Visitor Center on North Point Drive about a block east of Michigan Ave.

The trail loops around the natural-looking, but man-made, Lake Joanis [9], created in the 1970s. The lake can be fished and is sometimes a caravansary for migrating Canada geese and mallards.

Leaving the preserve, the route heads northeast along Moses Creek Trail [10]. Hikers can continue their walk on the attractive Plover River segment [11]. Some hikers may wish to start the circle at the east end of Barbara's Lane. Take Highway 10 to Green Avenue in the Park Ridge suburb.

Turn north to Jordan Lane, then east again on Janick Circle, which becomes Barbara's Lane. Another way to link up with the Plover River Trail is by going east on State Highway 66 past the Stevens Point Airport and Torun Road to a ski lodge [12]. The building, actually an old home used in the winter as a warming hut, is in a wooded area along the south side of Highway 66. This leg of the trail is about 4 mi. and is open to hikers, bikers, and cross-country skiers in season.

The 1.3-mi. Iverson Park Trail [13] is a pleasant nature hike along the Plover River, where there is a bird and wildlife sanctuary. You can start here from the parking lot at Iverson Park at the foot of Hillcrest Drive. If you aren't following the Green Circle south from the Plover River Trail, you can go to Park Ridge on Highway 10 East and turn south on Sunrise Avenue to Hillcrest Drive. Turn east through the gate and edge downhill to the parking lot where skiers, bikers, and hikers share the trail space.

Leading to the McDill Trail [14], hikers can spot McDill Pond on the west, a wide section of the turgid Plover River. This woodsy leg of the Green Circle extends 2 mi. from Patch Street to County Highway

HH where it joins the Whiting Park Trail **[15]**. Here you proceed another mile along the banks of the Plover. This stretch is also limited to hikers, a relief from the rush of other recreational traffic. The rustic Plover seems to be almost a wilderness stream thrown into the heart of a city. Only the occasional sounds of nearby traffic interfere with this feeling.

You can also take the Hoover Road Trail **[16]**, a spur that is not part of the major Green Circle system. The pathway runs south for more than 3 mi. from the Budgetel Motel on Highway 10 East to Lake Pacawa in the village of Plover. The path meanders through dense foliage that separates it from the urban rush. However, be careful if you walk down from the Budgetel Motel on Highway 10. The road is narrow there and has a lot of traffic, and there's no trail alongside it. You could take the asphalt-surfaced Hoover Road Trail from where it starts below County Highway HH (McDill Avenue) and walk down to County Highway B and then to Lake Pacawa. About midpoint, you cross the Little Plover River, a trout stream.

But if you don't take this south leg, go west along County Highway HH to Whiting Park Trail as already described. Follow the Paper Mill Trail to the railroad tracks **[17]** near Jacobson Street and proceed along Sherman Avenue to River Pines. You are now on one of the most picturesque legs of the Green Circle, called the River Pines Trail **[18]**.

Starting from the River Pines Nursing and Rehabilitation Center **[19]**, the trail goes north along the Wisconsin River to Bliss Avenue **[20]**. Thick stands of pine line the riverbanks. Hikers are often lucky enough to spot great blue herons and soaring eagles. Since the river in the Stevens Point area was cleaned up in the 1970s and 1980s, the reclaimed flowage here has become a great site for serious angling. At dusk, there are curious white-tailed deer in the vicinity.

From here, walk north through the pine groves, then along Water Street and back to the bank parking lot.

—George Rogers